SUPERMAN BATMAN
WORSHIP

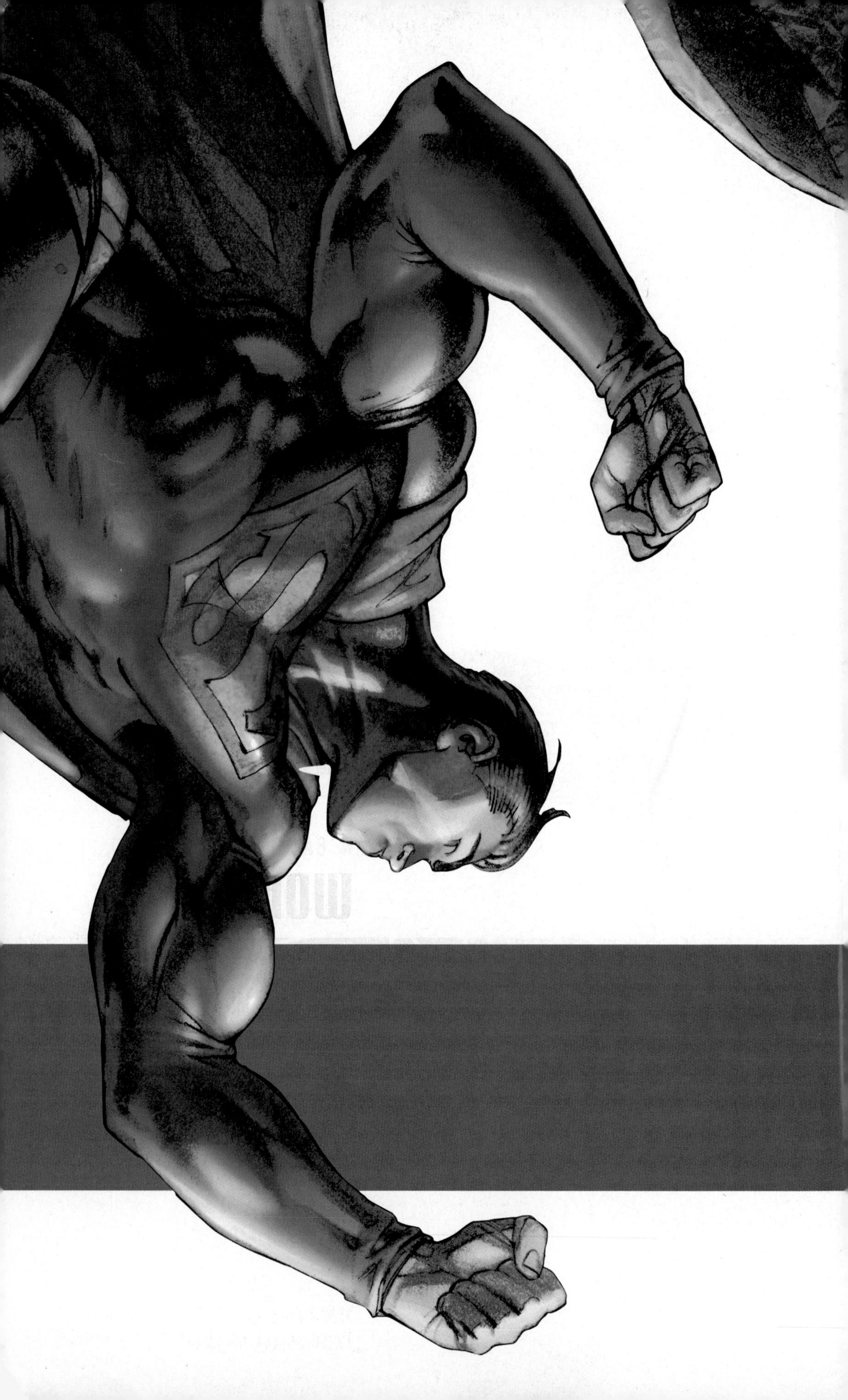

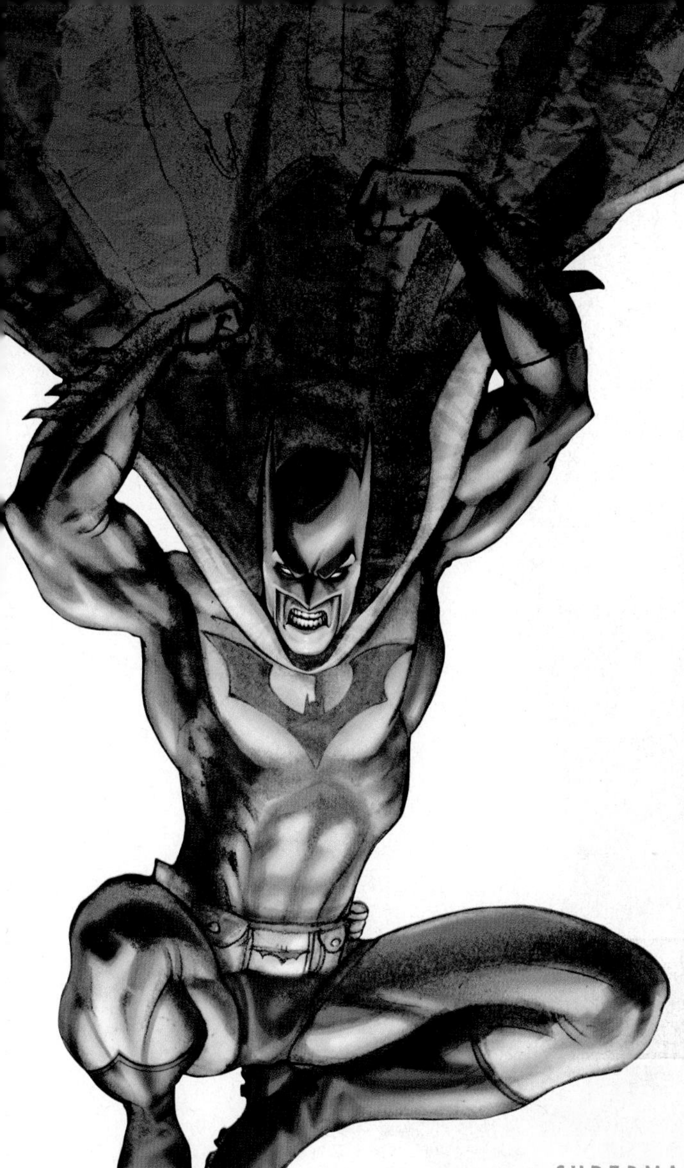

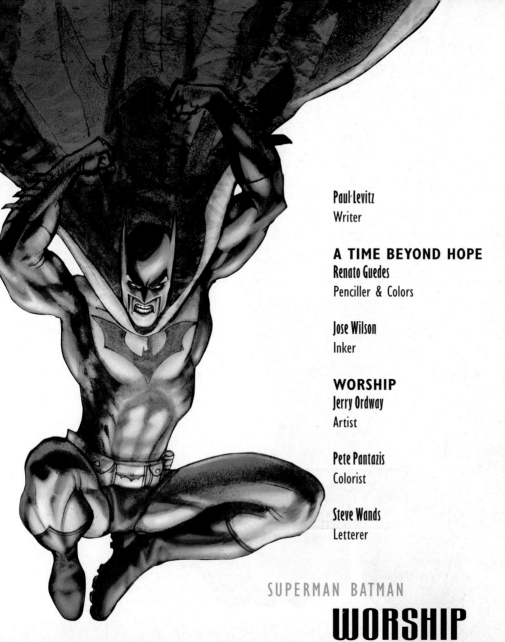

Paul Levitz
Writer

A TIME BEYOND HOPE
Renato Guedes
Penciller & Colors

Jose Wilson
Inker

WORSHIP
Jerry Ordway
Artist

Pete Pantazis
Colorist

Steve Wands
Letterer

SUPERMAN BATMAN

WORSHIP

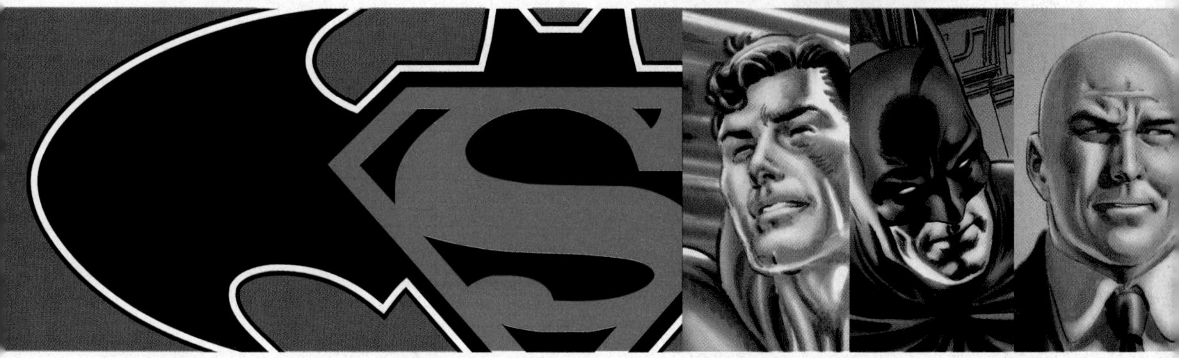

Frank Quitely & Val Staples
Collection cover

Superman created by Jerry Siegel and Joe Shuster
Batman created by Bob Kane

EDDIE BERGANZA Editor-Original Series   REX OGLE Assistant Editor-Original Series
BOB HARRAS Group Editor-Collected Editions   ROBBIN BROSTERMAN Design Director-Books

DC COMICS
DIANE NELSON President   DAN DIDIO and JIM LEE Co-Publishers   GEOFF JOHNS Chief Creative Officer   PATRICK CALDON EVP-Finance and Administration
JOHN ROOD EVP-Sales, Marketing and Business Development   AMY GENKINS SVP-Business and Legal Affairs   STEVE ROTTERDAM SVP-Sales and Marketing
JOHN CUNNINGHAM VP-Marketing   TERRI CUNNINGHAM VP-Managing Editor   ALISON GILL VP-Manufacturing   DAVID HYDE VP-Publicity
SUE POHJA VP-Book Trade Sales   ALYSSE SOLL VP-Advertising and Custom Publishing   BOB WAYNE VP-Sales   MARK CHIARELLO Art Director

SUPERMAN/BATMAN: WORSHIP
Published by DC Comics. Cover and compilation Copyright © 2011 DC Comics. All Rights Reserved.

Originally published in single magazine form in SUPERMAN/BATMAN 72-75, SUPERMAN/BATMAN ANNUAL 4. Copyright © 2010
DC Comics. All Rights Reserved. All characters, their distinctive likenesses and related elements featured in this publication are
trademarks of DC Comics. The stories, characters and incidents featured in this publication are entirely fictional. DC Comics does
not read or accept unsolicited submissions of ideas, stories or artwork.

DC Comics, 1700 Broadway, New York, NY 10019
A Warner Bros. Entertainment Company
Printed by Quad/Graphics, Dubuque, IA, USA. 3/18/11. First Printing.
ISBN: 978-1-4012-3032-6

Fiber used in this product line meets the
sourcing requirements of the SFI program.
www.sfiprogram.org SGS-SFICOC-0130

Library of Congress Cataloging-in-Publication Data

Levitz, Paul.
   Superman/Batman. Worship / writer, Paul Levitz ; pencils, Jerry
Ordway.
      p. cm.
   "Originally published in single magazine form in Superman/Batman
72-75, Superman/Batman Annual 4."
   ISBN 978-1-4012-3032-6 (pbk.)
   1. Superman (Fictitious character)--Comic books, strips, etc. 2.
Batman (Fictitious character)--Comic books, strips, etc. 3. Graphic
novels. I. Ordway, Jerry. II. Title. III. Title: Worship.
   PN6728.S9L48 2011
   741.5'973--dc22
                                                    2011007264

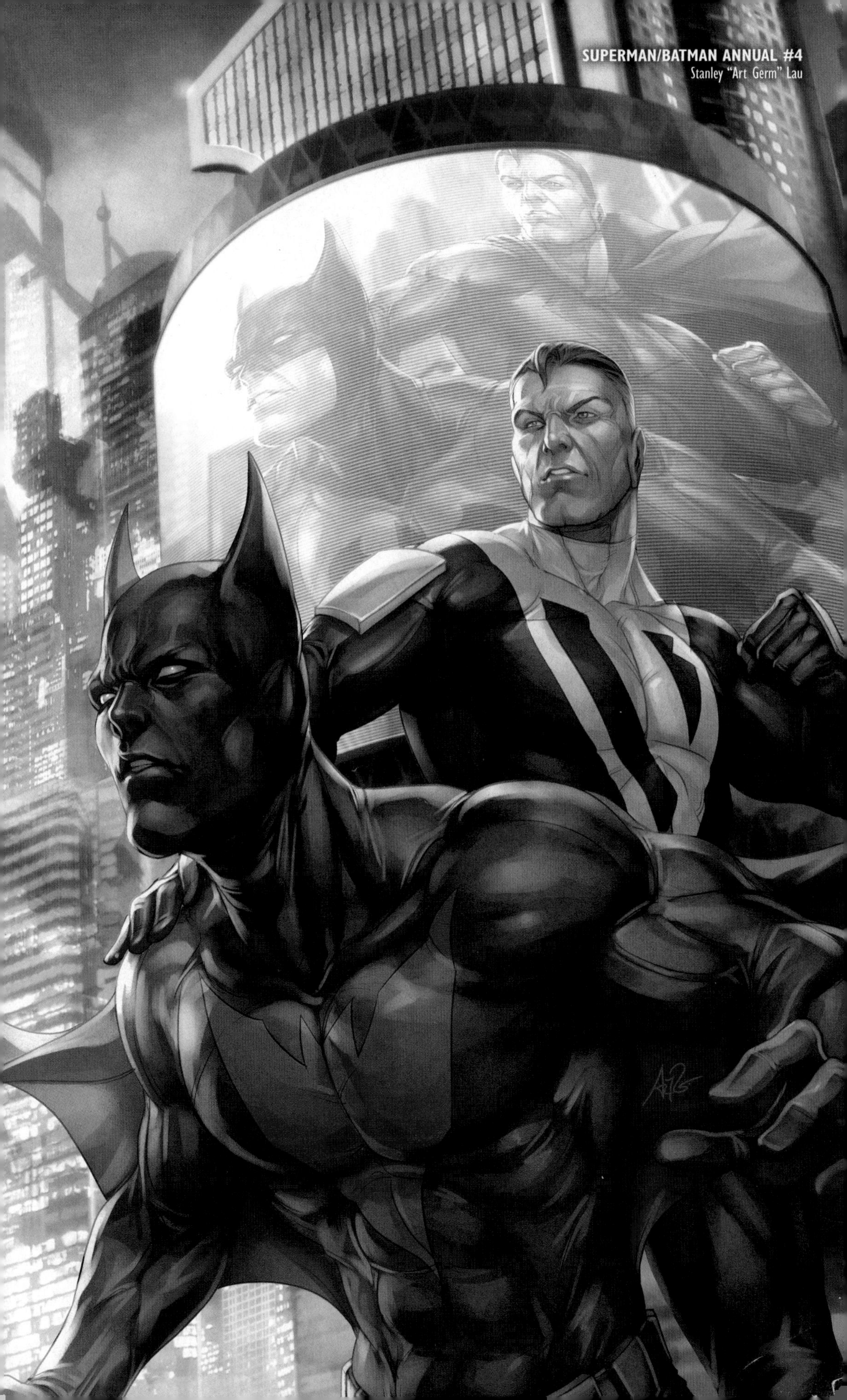

SUPERMAN/BATMAN ANNUAL #4
Stanley "Art Germ" Lau

A TIME BEYOND HOPE

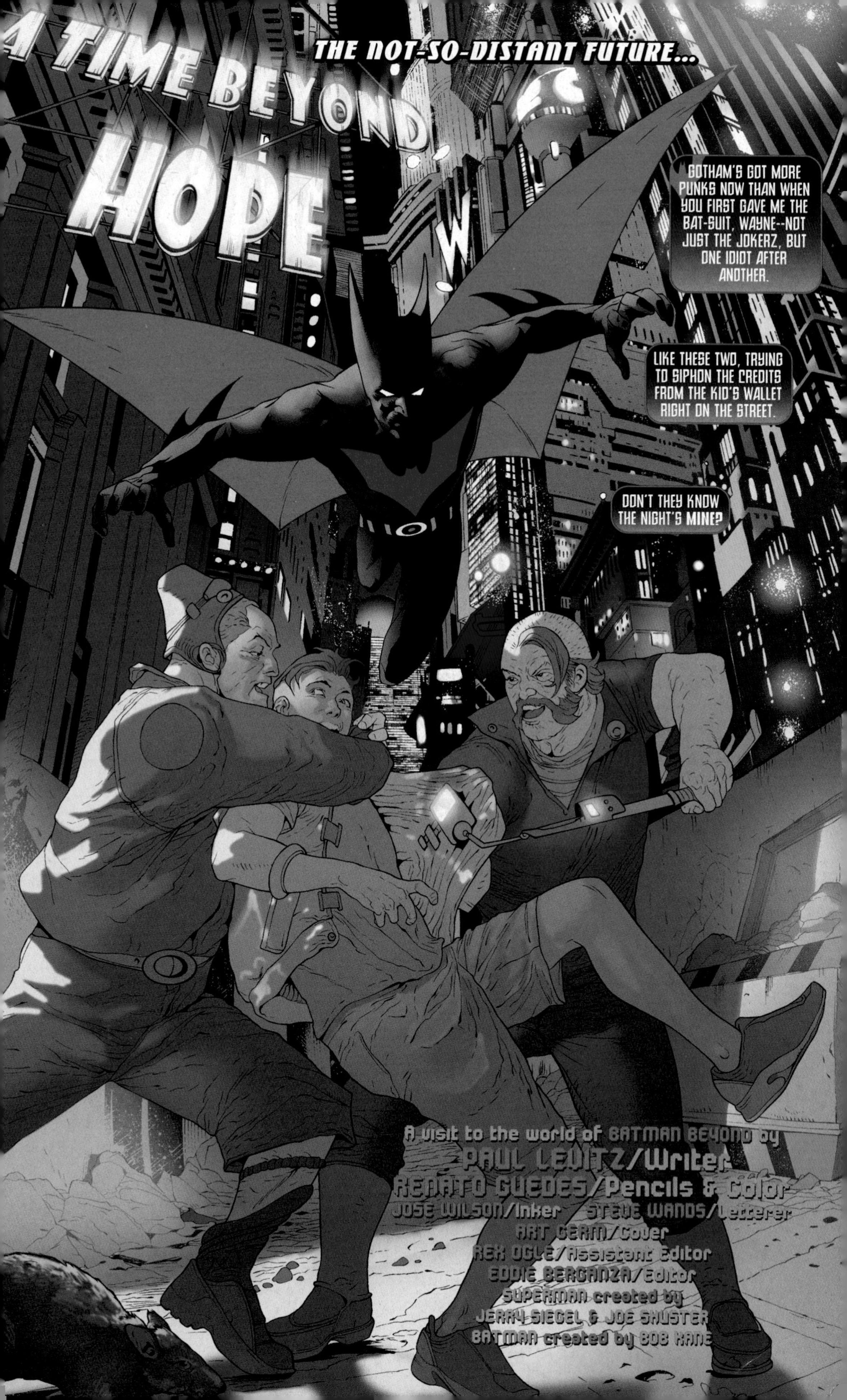
A TIME BEYOND HOPE
THE NOT-SO-DISTANT FUTURE...
GOTHAM'S GOT MORE PUNKS NOW THAN WHEN YOU FIRST GAVE ME THE BAT-SUIT, WAYNE--NOT JUST THE JOKERZ, BUT ONE IDIOT AFTER ANOTHER.
LIKE THESE TWO, TRYING TO SIPHON THE CREDITS FROM THE KID'S WALLET RIGHT ON THE STREET.
DON'T THEY KNOW THE NIGHT'S MINE?
A visit to the world of BATMAN BEYOND by
PAUL LEVITZ/Writer
RENATO GUEDES/Pencils & Color
JOSE WILSON/Inker STEVE WANDS/Letterer
ART GERM/Cover
REX OGLE/Assistant Editor
EDDIE BERGANZA/Editor
SUPERMAN created by
JERRY SIEGEL & JOE SHUSTER
BATMAN created by BOB KANE

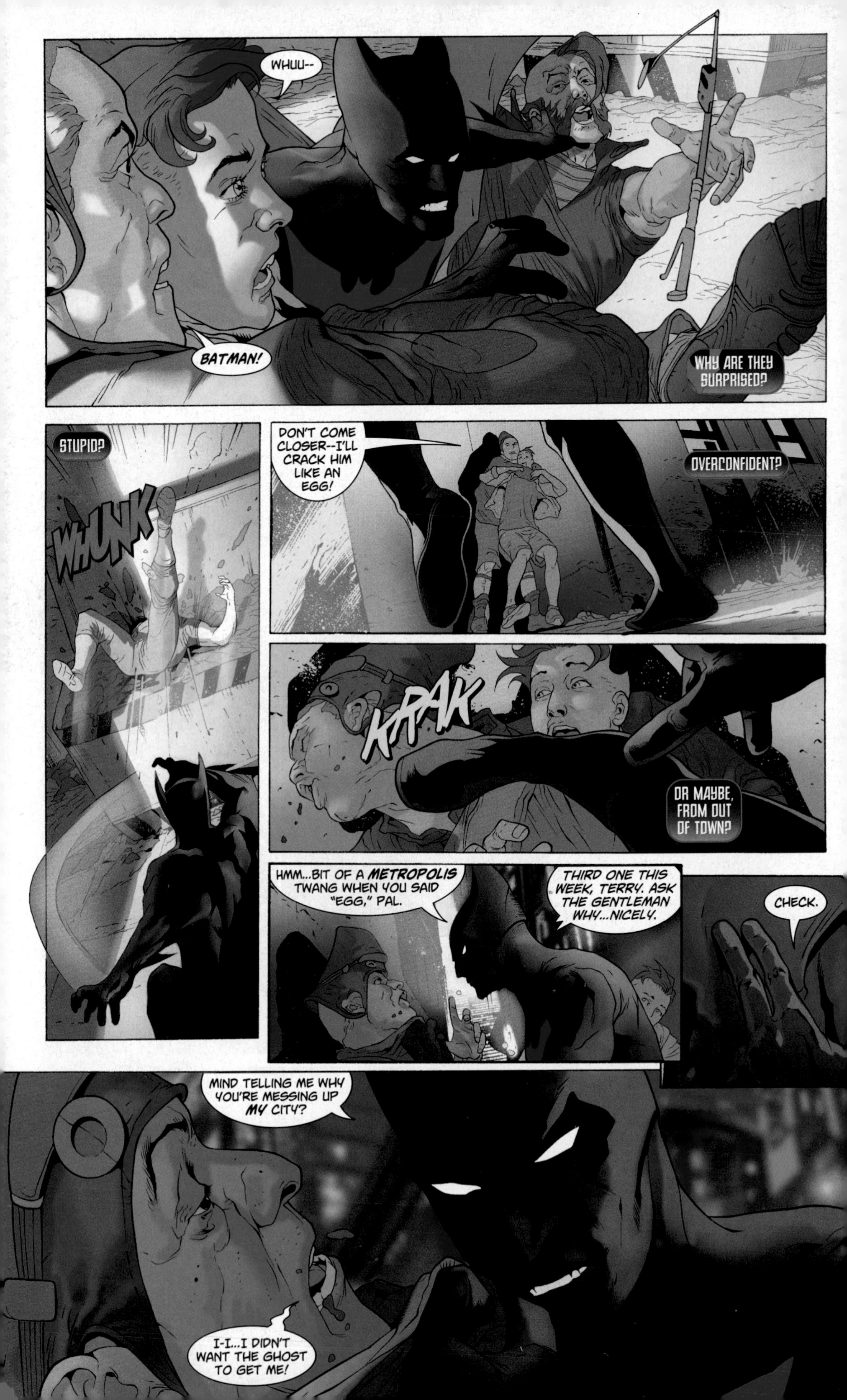
WHUU--
BATMAN!
WHY ARE THEY SURPRISED?
STUPID?
WHUNK
DON'T COME CLOSER--I'LL CRACK HIM LIKE AN EGG!
OVERCONFIDENT?
KRAK
OR MAYBE, FROM OUT OF TOWN?
HMM...BIT OF A METROPOLIS TWANG WHEN YOU SAID "EGG," PAL.
THIRD ONE THIS WEEK, TERRY. ASK THE GENTLEMAN WHY...NICELY.
CHECK.
MIND TELLING ME WHY YOU'RE MESSING UP MY CITY?
I-I...I DIDN'T WANT THE GHOST TO GET ME!

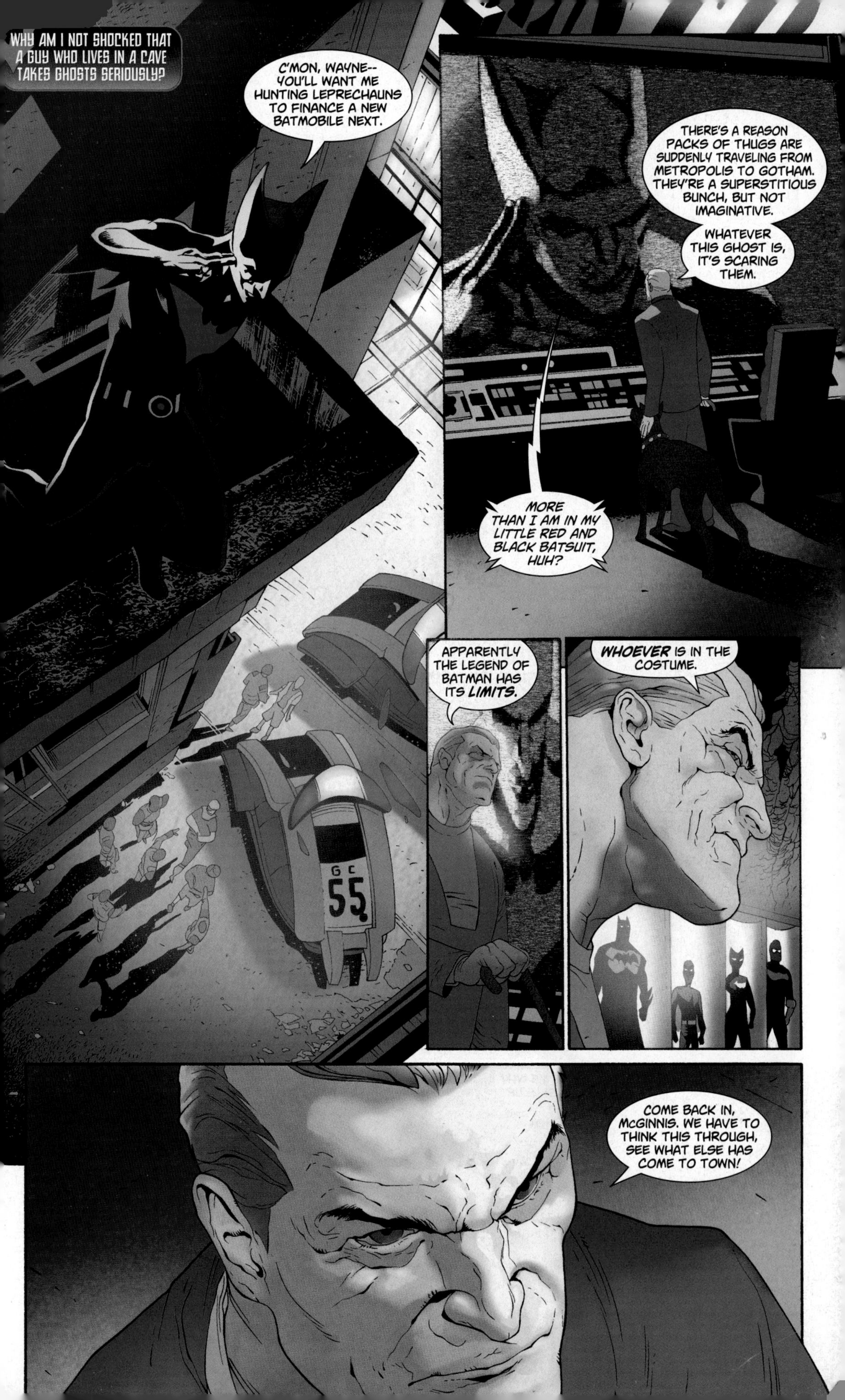
WHY AM I NOT SHOCKED THAT A GUY WHO LIVES IN A CAVE TAKES GHOSTS SERIOUSLY?
C'MON, WAYNE-- YOU'LL WANT ME HUNTING LEPRECHAUNS TO FINANCE A NEW BATMOBILE NEXT.
THERE'S A REASON PACKS OF THUGS ARE SUDDENLY TRAVELING FROM METROPOLIS TO GOTHAM. THEY'RE A SUPERSTITIOUS BUNCH, BUT NOT IMAGINATIVE.
WHATEVER THIS GHOST IS, IT'S SCARING THEM.
MORE THAN I AM IN MY LITTLE RED AND BLACK BATSUIT, HUH?
GC 55
APPARENTLY THE LEGEND OF BATMAN HAS ITS LIMITS.
WHOEVER IS IN THE COSTUME.
COME BACK IN, McGINNIS. WE HAVE TO THINK THIS THROUGH, SEE WHAT ELSE HAS COME TO TOWN!

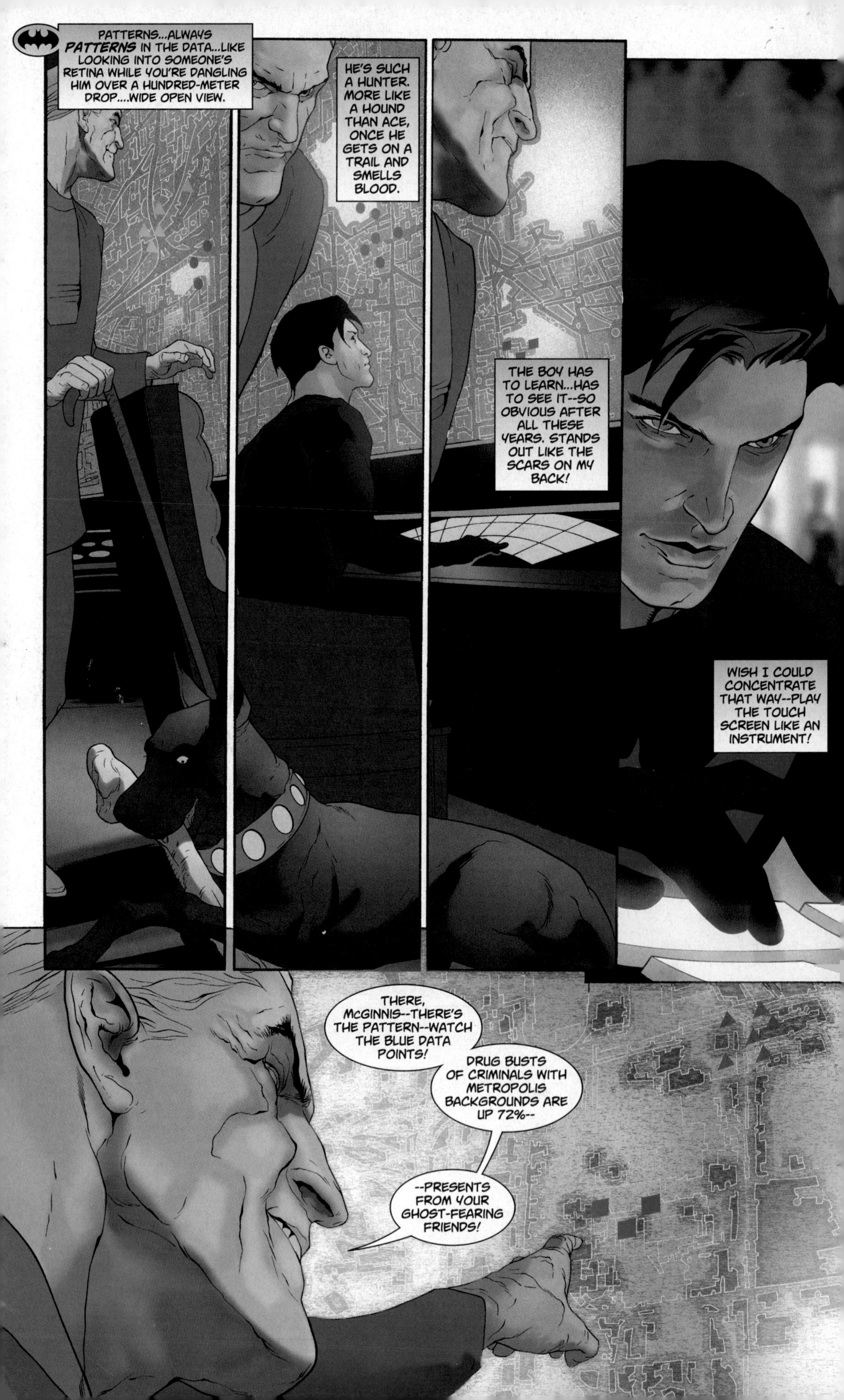
PATTERNS...ALWAYS PATTERNS IN THE DATA...LIKE LOOKING INTO SOMEONE'S RETINA WHILE YOU'RE DANGLING HIM OVER A HUNDRED-METER DROP....WIDE OPEN VIEW.
HE'S SUCH A HUNTER. MORE LIKE A HOUND THAN ACE, ONCE HE GETS ON A TRAIL AND SMELLS BLOOD.
THE BOY HAS TO LEARN...HAS TO SEE IT--SO OBVIOUS AFTER ALL THESE YEARS. STANDS OUT LIKE THE SCARS ON MY BACK!
WISH I COULD CONCENTRATE THAT WAY--PLAY THE TOUCH SCREEN LIKE AN INSTRUMENT!
THERE, McGINNIS--THERE'S THE PATTERN--WATCH THE BLUE DATA POINTS!
DRUG BUSTS OF CRIMINALS WITH METROPOLIS BACKGROUNDS ARE UP 72%--
--PRESENTS FROM YOUR GHOST-FEARING FRIENDS!

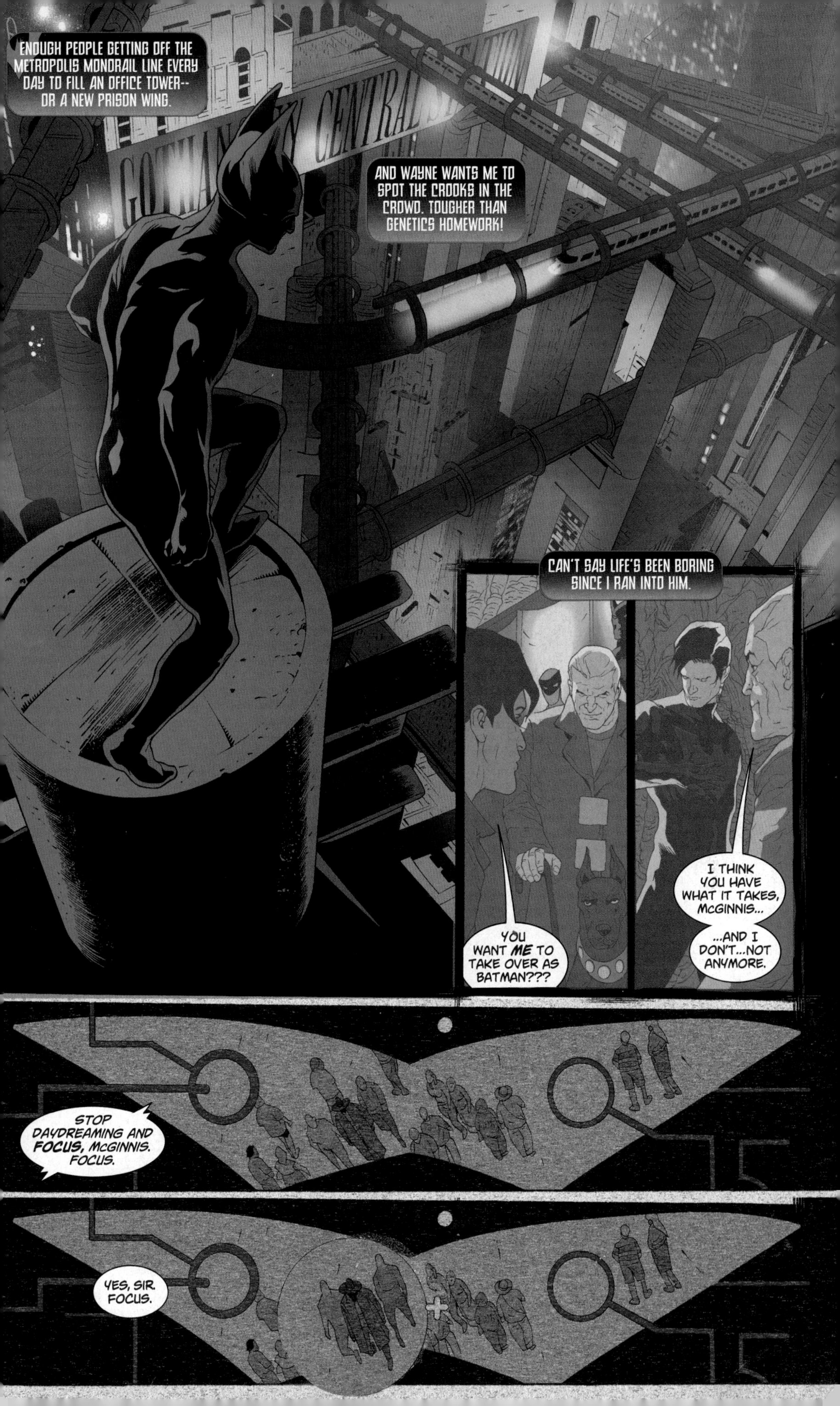
ENOUGH PEOPLE GETTING OFF THE METROPOLIS MONORAIL LINE EVERY DAY TO FILL AN OFFICE TOWER--OR A NEW PRISON WING.
GOTHAM CITY CENTRAL STATION
AND WAYNE WANTS ME TO SPOT THE CROOKS IN THE CROWD. TOUGHER THAN GENETICS HOMEWORK!
CAN'T SAY LIFE'S BEEN BORING SINCE I RAN INTO HIM.
YOU WANT ME TO TAKE OVER AS BATMAN???
I THINK YOU HAVE WHAT IT TAKES, McGINNIS...
...AND I DON'T...NOT ANYMORE.
STOP DAYDREAMING AND FOCUS, McGINNIS. FOCUS.
YES, SIR. FOCUS.

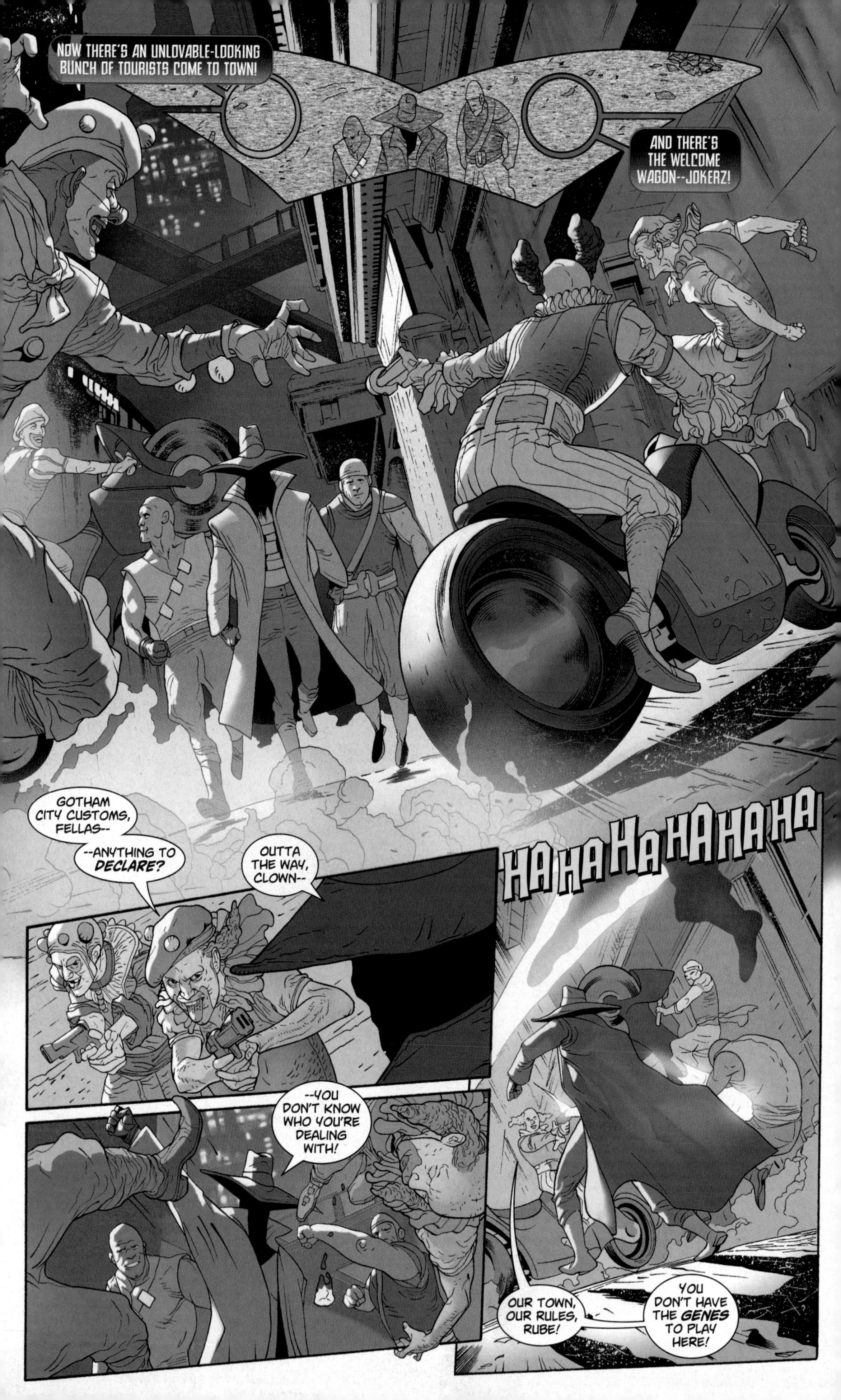
NOW THERE'S AN UNLOVABLE-LOOKING BUNCH OF TOURISTS COME TO TOWN!
AND THERE'S THE WELCOME WAGON--JOKERZ!
GOTHAM CITY CUSTOMS, FELLAS--
--ANYTHING TO DECLARE?
OUTTA THE WAY, CLOWN--
HA HA HA HA HA HA HA
--YOU DON'T KNOW WHO YOU'RE DEALING WITH!
OUR TOWN, OUR RULES, RUBE!
YOU DON'T HAVE THE GENES TO PLAY HERE!

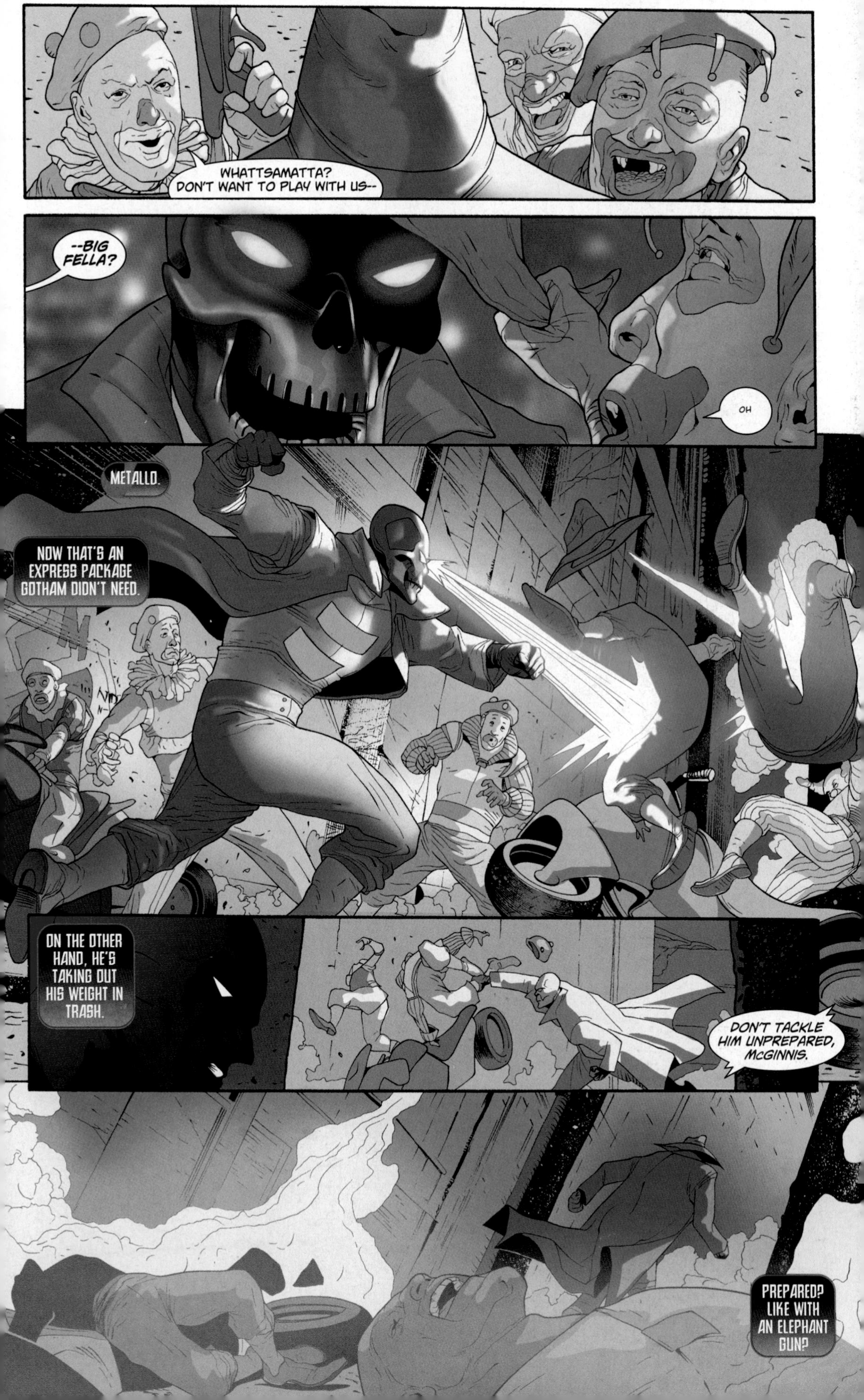
WHATTSAMATTA? DON'T WANT TO PLAY WITH US--
--BIG FELLA?
OH
METALLO.
NOW THAT'S AN EXPRESS PACKAGE GOTHAM DIDN'T NEED.
ON THE OTHER HAND, HE'S TAKING OUT HIS WEIGHT IN TRASH.
DON'T TACKLE HIM UNPREPARED, McGINNIS.
PREPARED? LIKE WITH AN ELEPHANT GUN?

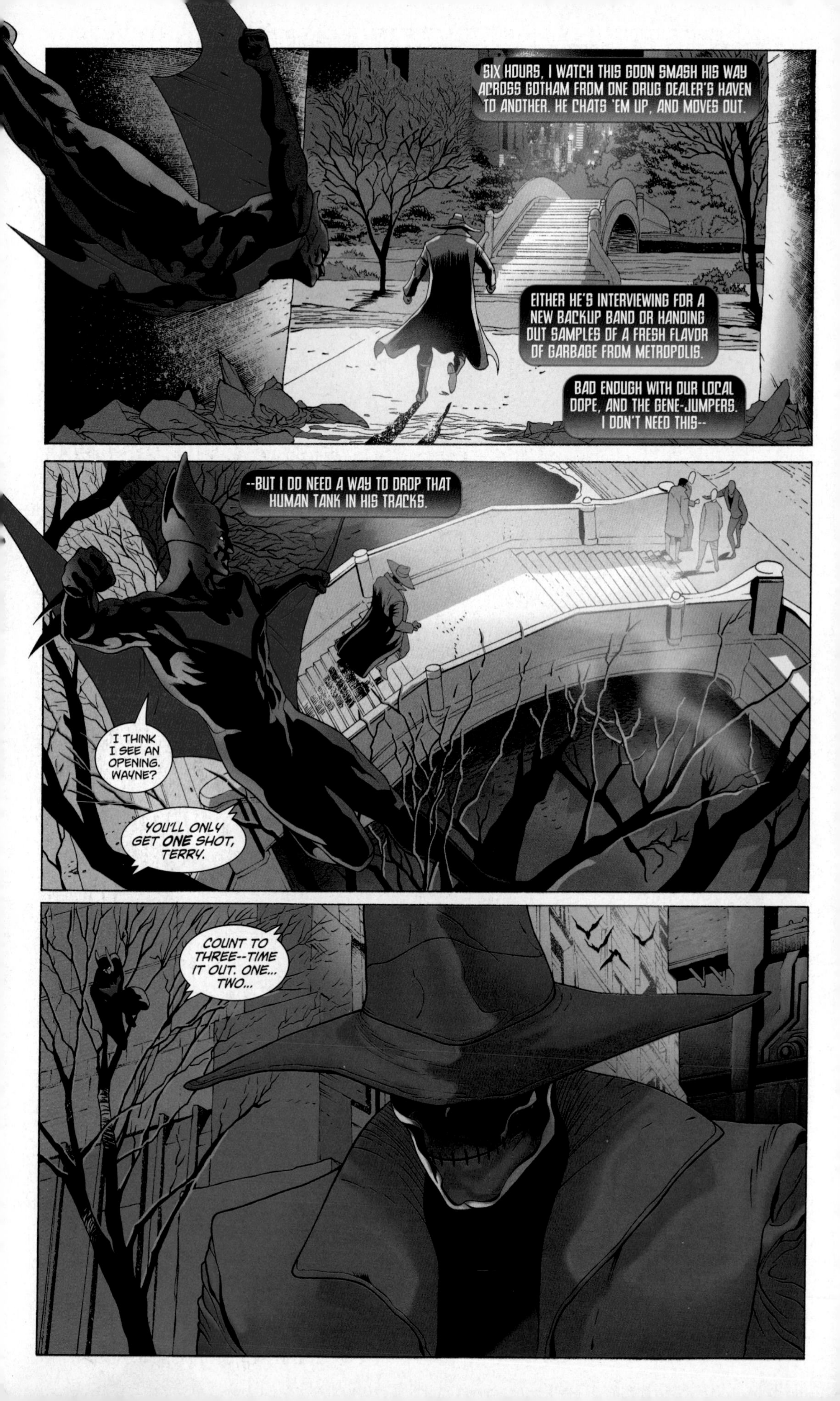
SIX HOURS, I WATCH THIS GOON SMASH HIS WAY ACROSS GOTHAM FROM ONE DRUG DEALER'S HAVEN TO ANOTHER. HE CHATS 'EM UP, AND MOVES OUT.
EITHER HE'S INTERVIEWING FOR A NEW BACKUP BAND OR HANDING OUT SAMPLES OF A FRESH FLAVOR OF GARBAGE FROM METROPOLIS.
BAD ENOUGH WITH OUR LOCAL DOPE, AND THE GENE-JUMPERS. I DON'T NEED THIS--
--BUT I DO NEED A WAY TO DROP THAT HUMAN TANK IN HIS TRACKS.
I THINK I SEE AN OPENING. WAYNE?
YOU'LL ONLY GET ONE SHOT, TERRY.
COUNT TO THREE--TIME IT OUT. ONE... TWO...

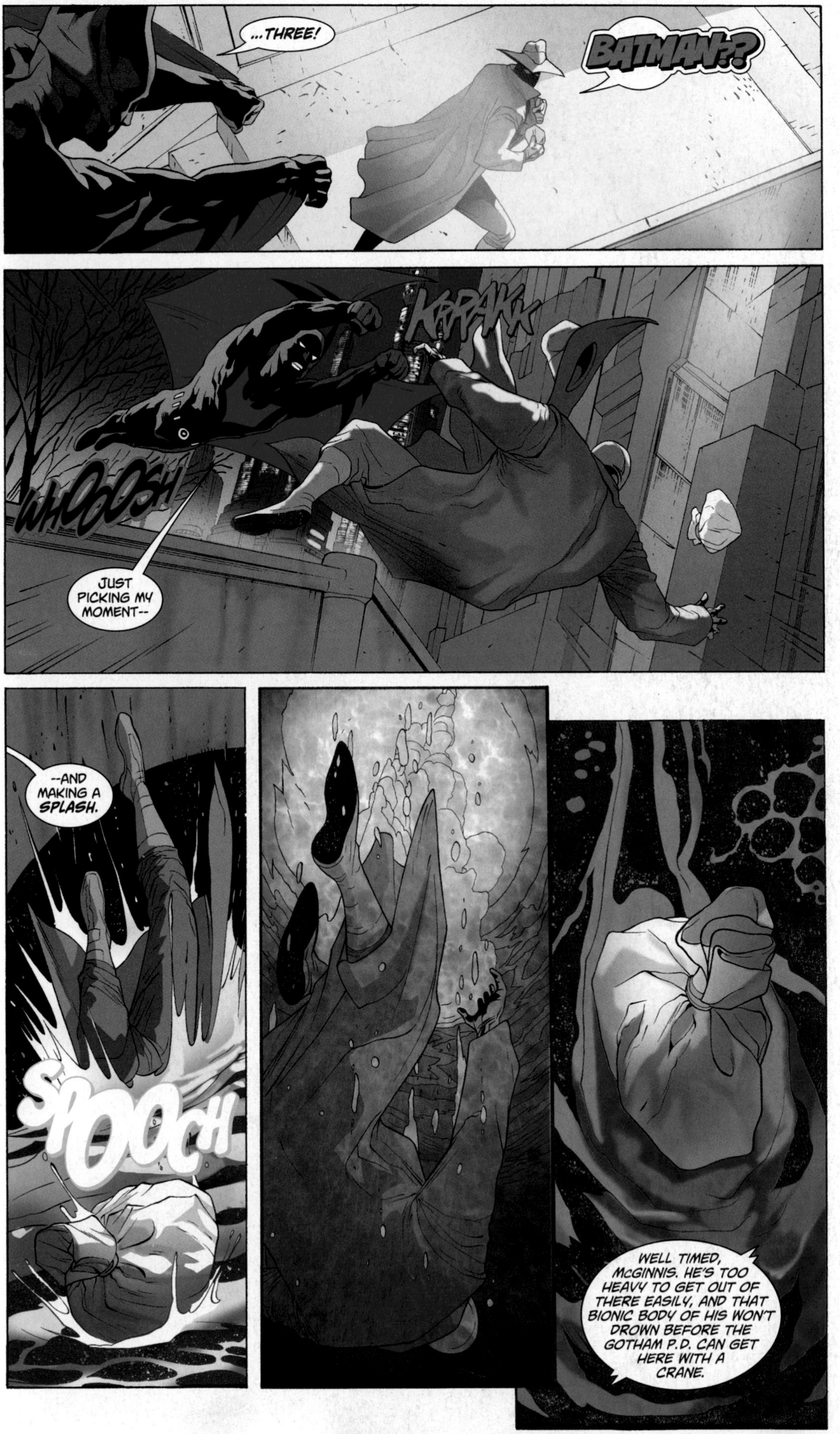
...THREE!
BATMAN??
KRAKK
WHOOOOSH
JUST PICKING MY MOMENT--
--AND MAKING A SPLASH.
SPOOOCH
WELL TIMED, McGINNIS. HE'S TOO HEAVY TO GET OUT OF THERE EASILY, AND THAT BIONIC BODY OF HIS WON'T DROWN BEFORE THE GOTHAM P.D. CAN GET HERE WITH A CRANE.

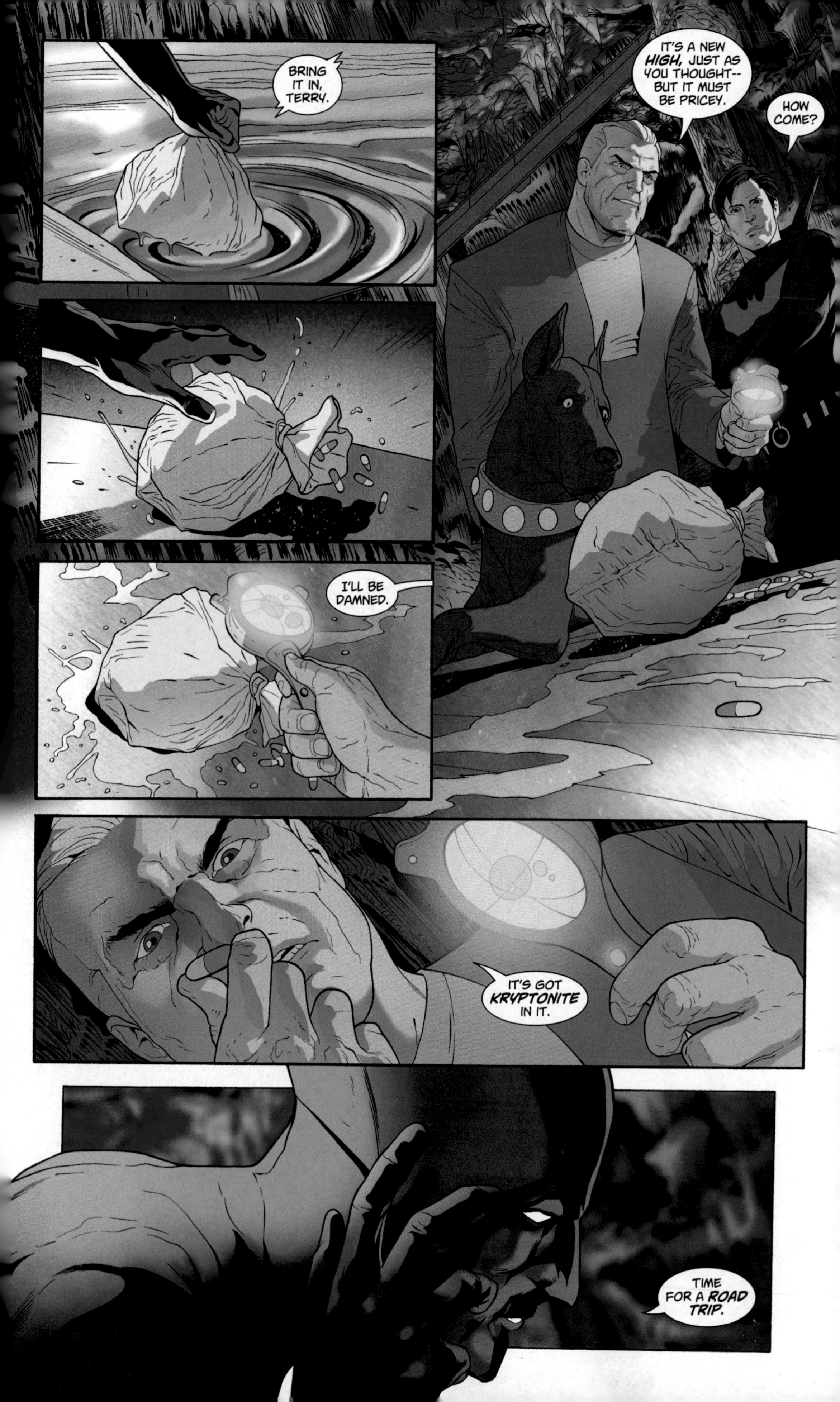
BRING IT IN, TERRY.
IT'S A NEW HIGH, JUST AS YOU THOUGHT-- BUT IT MUST BE PRICEY.
HOW COME?
I'LL BE DAMNED.
IT'S GOT KRYPTONITE IN IT.
TIME FOR A ROAD TRIP.

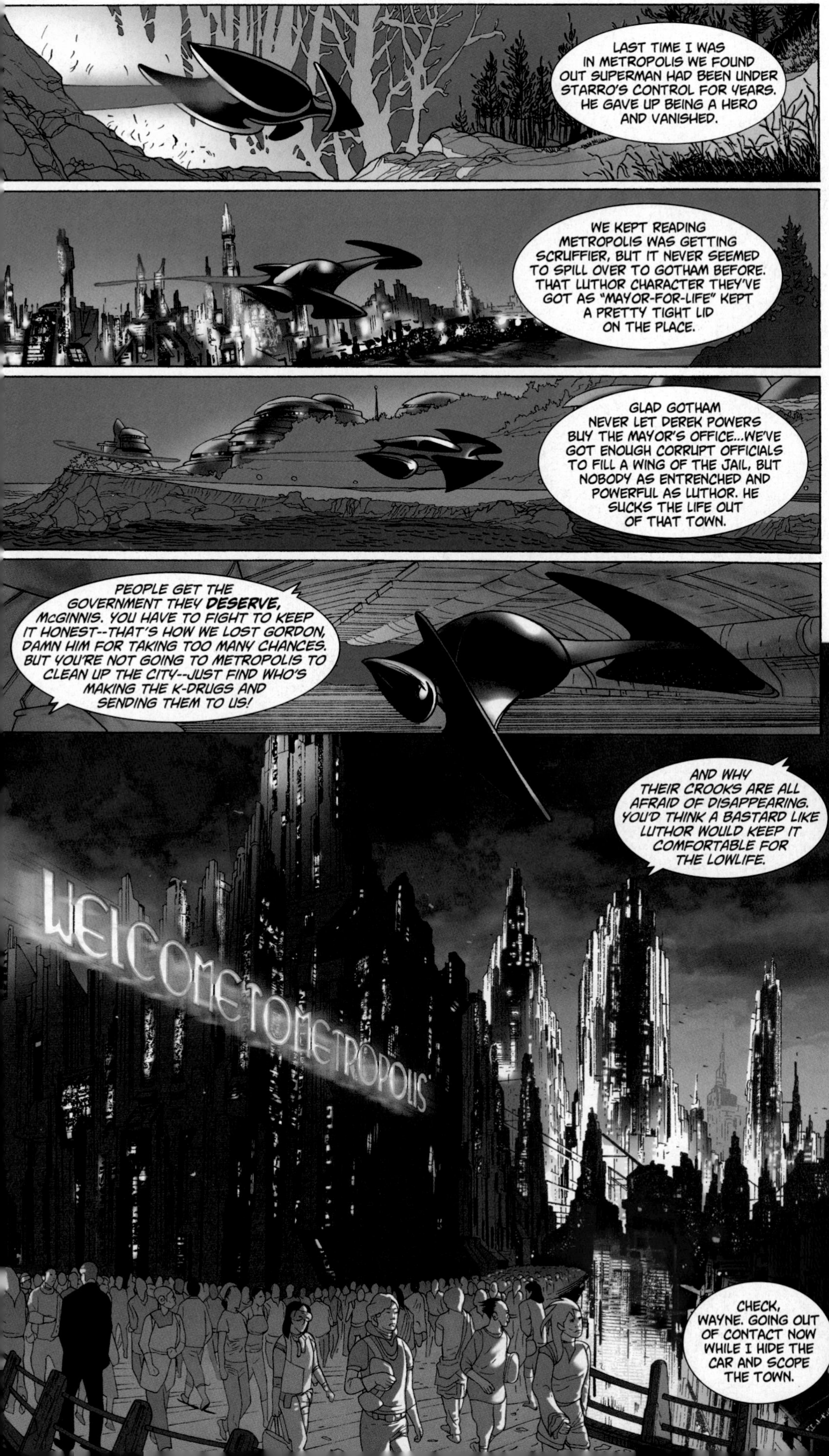
LAST TIME I WAS IN METROPOLIS WE FOUND OUT SUPERMAN HAD BEEN UNDER STARRO'S CONTROL FOR YEARS. HE GAVE UP BEING A HERO AND VANISHED.
WE KEPT READING METROPOLIS WAS GETTING SCRUFFIER, BUT IT NEVER SEEMED TO SPILL OVER TO GOTHAM BEFORE. THAT LUTHOR CHARACTER THEY'VE GOT AS "MAYOR-FOR-LIFE" KEPT A PRETTY TIGHT LID ON THE PLACE.
GLAD GOTHAM NEVER LET DEREK POWERS BUY THE MAYOR'S OFFICE...WE'VE GOT ENOUGH CORRUPT OFFICIALS TO FILL A WING OF THE JAIL, BUT NOBODY AS ENTRENCHED AND POWERFUL AS LUTHOR. HE SUCKS THE LIFE OUT OF THAT TOWN.
PEOPLE GET THE GOVERNMENT THEY DESERVE, McGINNIS. YOU HAVE TO FIGHT TO KEEP IT HONEST--THAT'S HOW WE LOST GORDON, DAMN HIM FOR TAKING TOO MANY CHANCES. BUT YOU'RE NOT GOING TO METROPOLIS TO CLEAN UP THE CITY--JUST FIND WHO'S MAKING THE K-DRUGS AND SENDING THEM TO US!
AND WHY THEIR CROOKS ARE ALL AFRAID OF DISAPPEARING. YOU'D THINK A BASTARD LIKE LUTHOR WOULD KEEP IT COMFORTABLE FOR THE LOWLIFE.
WELCOMETOMETROPOLIS
CHECK, WAYNE. GOING OUT OF CONTACT NOW WHILE I HIDE THE CAR AND SCOPE THE TOWN.

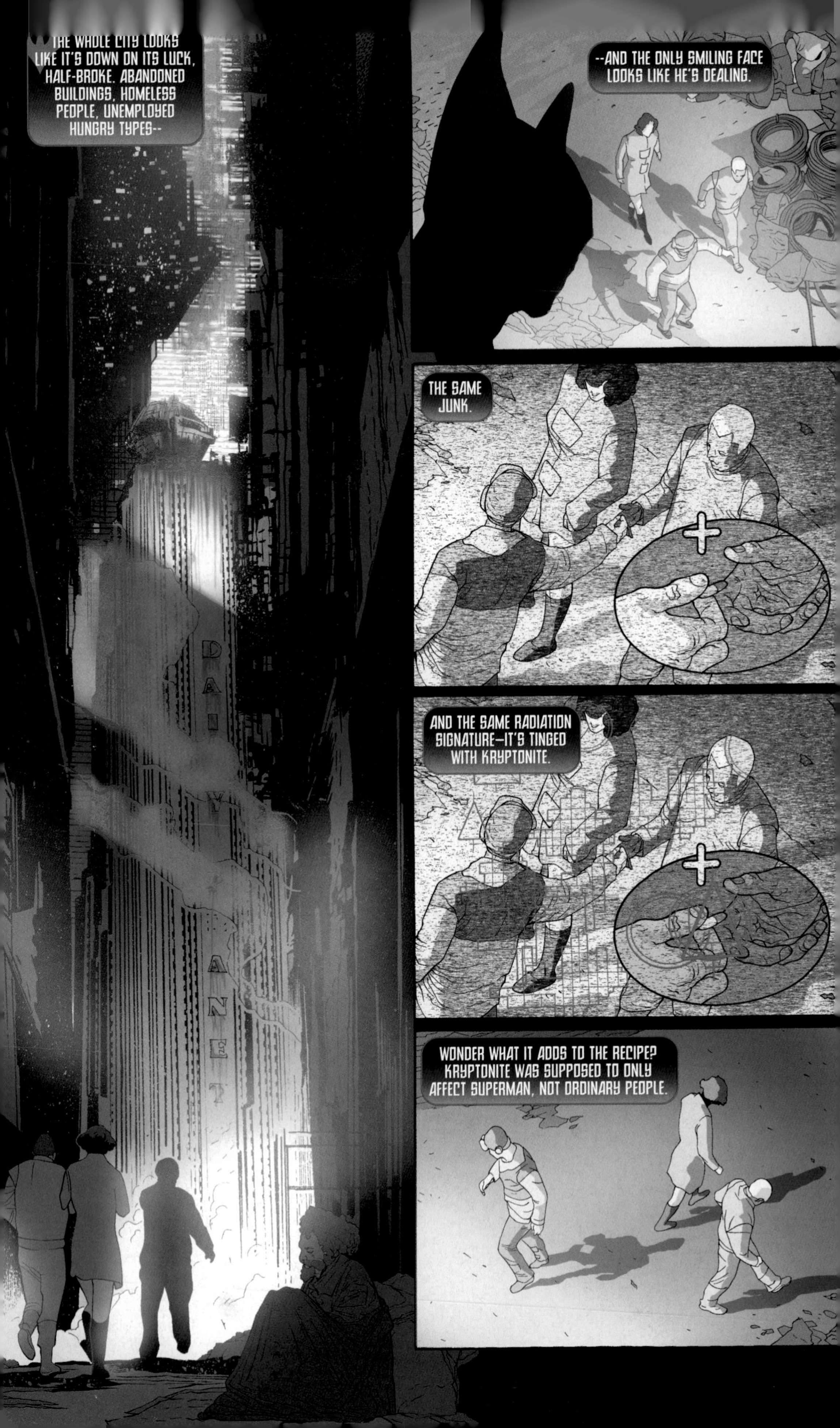
THE WHOLE CITY LOOKS LIKE IT'S DOWN ON ITS LUCK, HALF-BROKE. ABANDONED BUILDINGS, HOMELESS PEOPLE, UNEMPLOYED HUNGRY TYPES--
--AND THE ONLY SMILING FACE LOOKS LIKE HE'S DEALING.
THE SAME JUNK.
AND THE SAME RADIATION SIGNATURE--IT'S TINGED WITH KRYPTONITE.
WONDER WHAT IT ADDS TO THE RECIPE? KRYPTONITE WAS SUPPOSED TO ONLY AFFECT SUPERMAN, NOT ORDINARY PEOPLE.

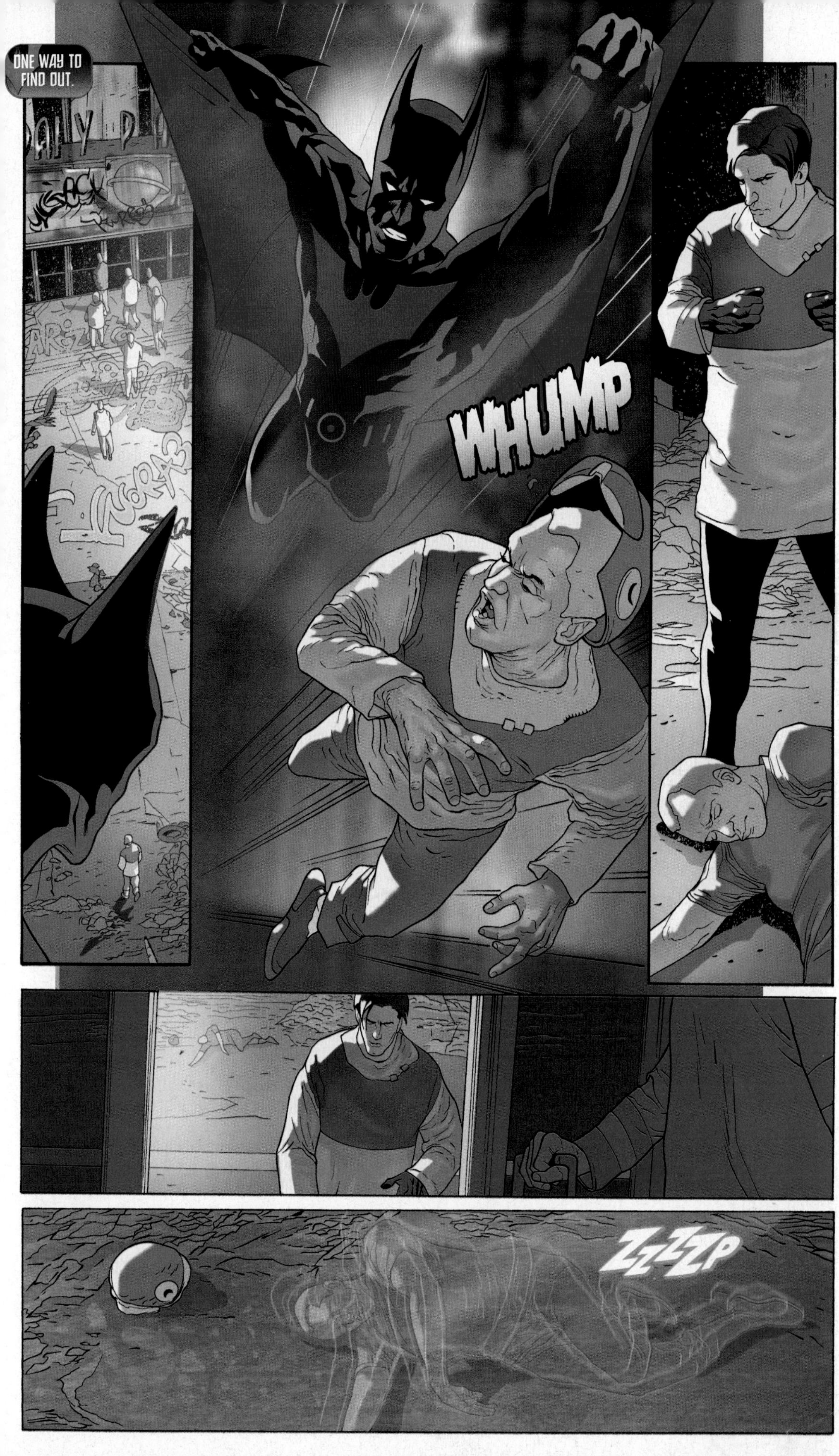

ONE WAY TO FIND OUT.
WHUMP
ZZZZP

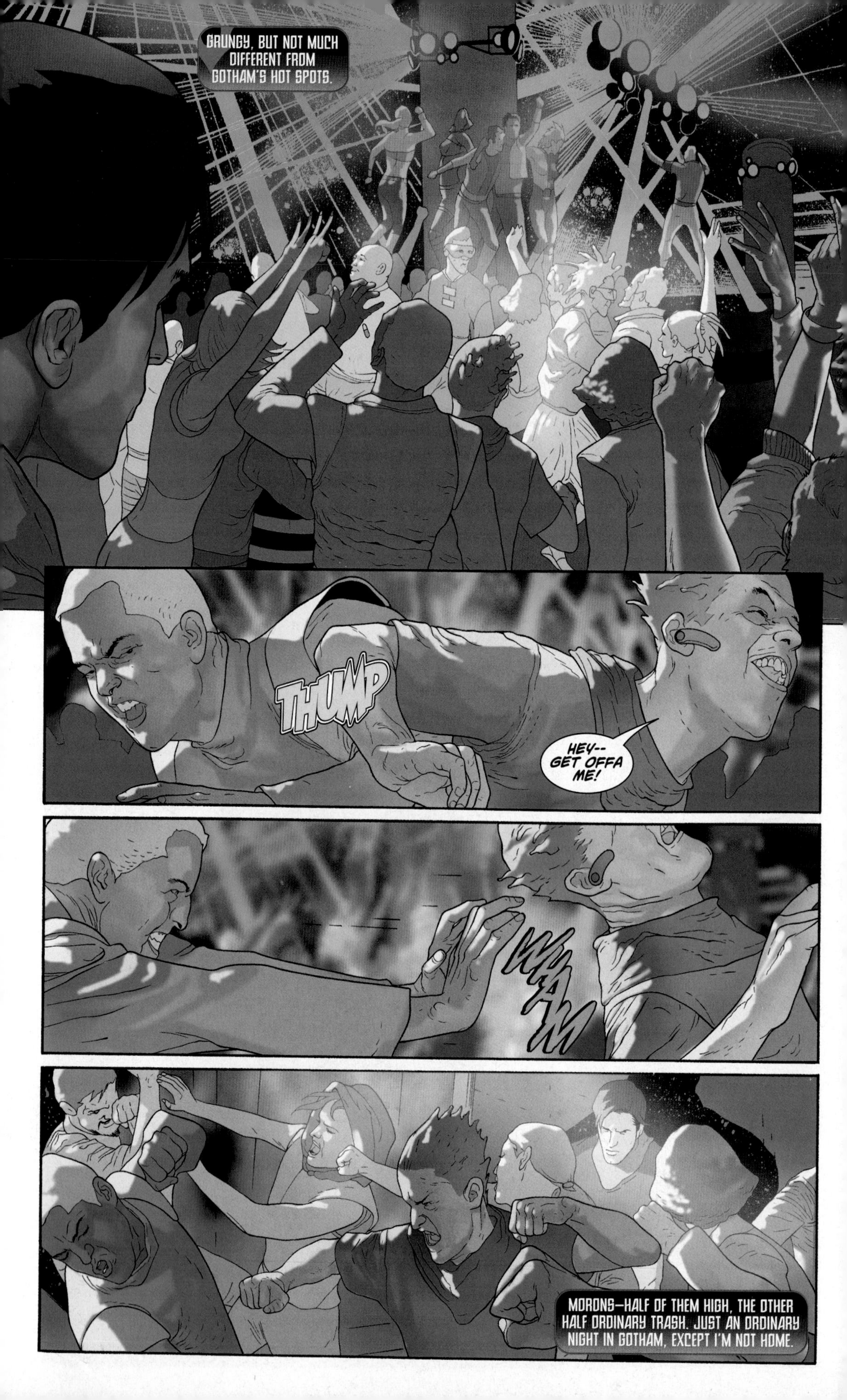
GRUNGY, BUT NOT MUCH DIFFERENT FROM GOTHAM'S HOT SPOTS.
THUMP
HEY-- GET OFFA ME!
WHAM
MORONS—HALF OF THEM HIGH, THE OTHER HALF ORDINARY TRASH. JUST AN ORDINARY NIGHT IN GOTHAM, EXCEPT I'M NOT HOME.

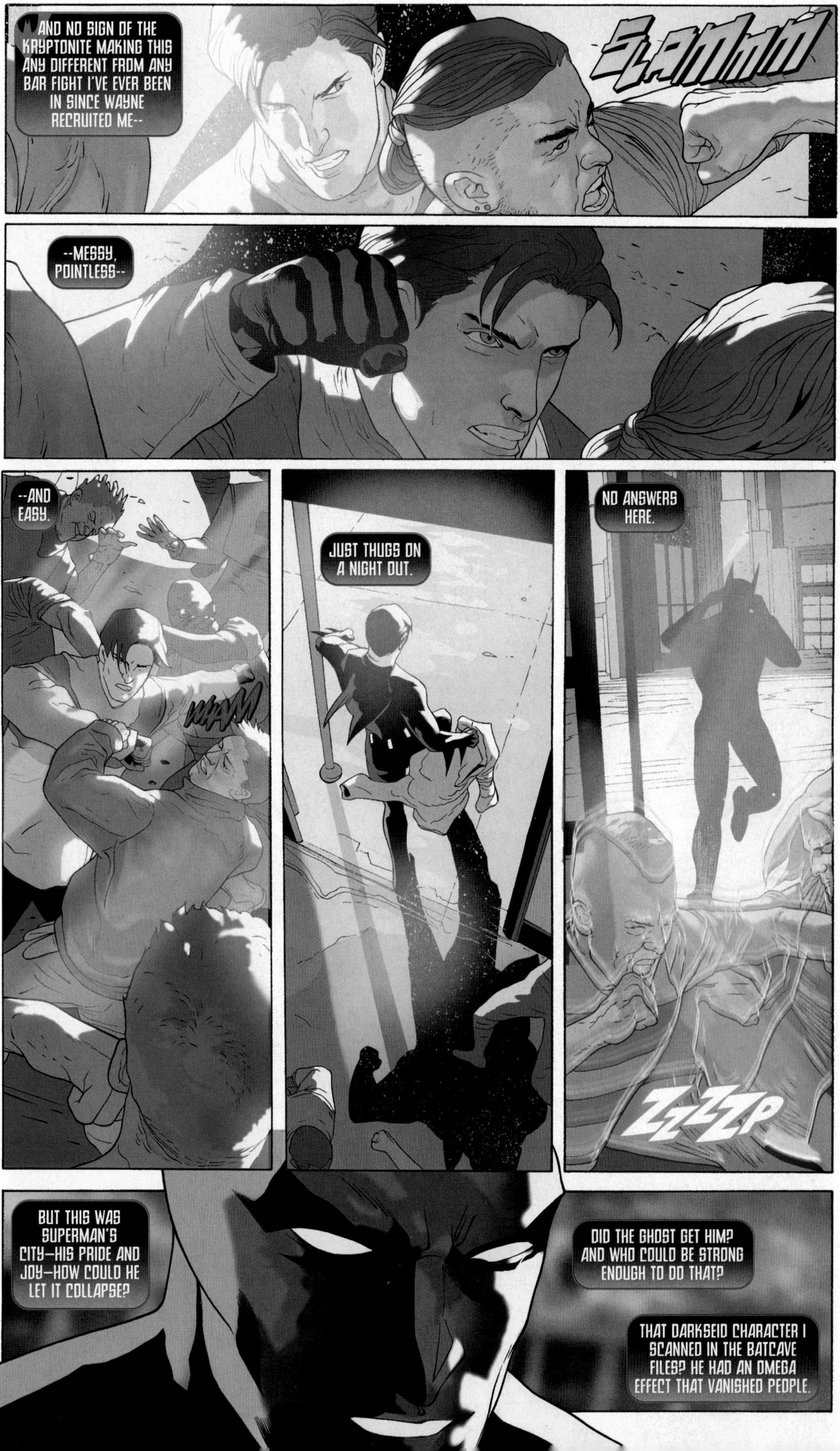
AND NO SIGN OF THE KRYPTONITE MAKING THIS ANY DIFFERENT FROM ANY BAR FIGHT I'VE EVER BEEN IN SINCE WAYNE RECRUITED ME--
SLAMM
--MESSY, POINTLESS--
--AND EASY.
WHAM
JUST THUGS ON A NIGHT OUT.
NO ANSWERS HERE.
ZZZZP
BUT THIS WAS SUPERMAN'S CITY--HIS PRIDE AND JOY--HOW COULD HE LET IT COLLAPSE?
DID THE GHOST GET HIM? AND WHO COULD BE STRONG ENOUGH TO DO THAT?
THAT DARKSEID CHARACTER I SCANNED IN THE BATCAVE FILES? HE HAD AN OMEGA EFFECT THAT VANISHED PEOPLE.

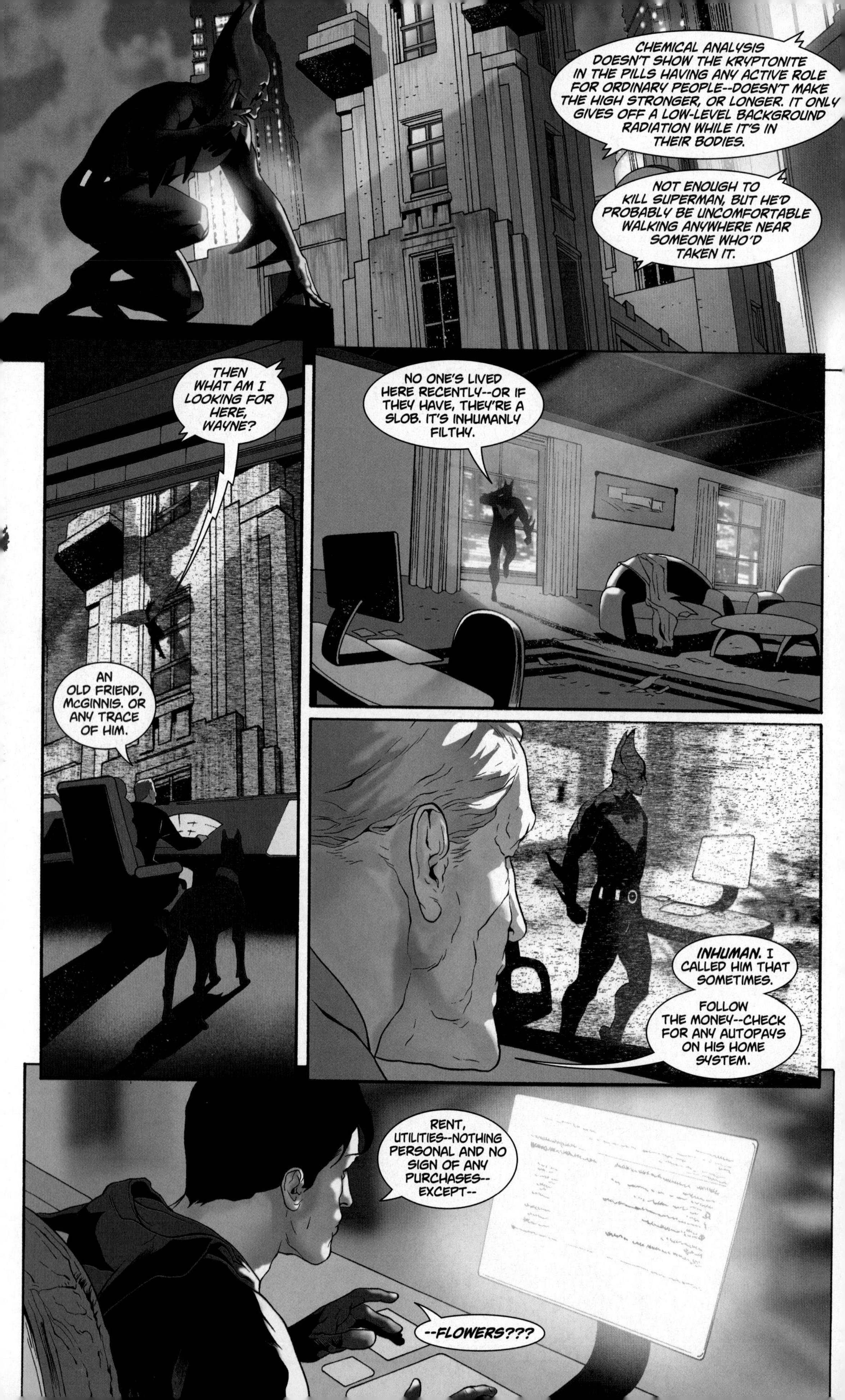
CHEMICAL ANALYSIS DOESN'T SHOW THE KRYPTONITE IN THE PILLS HAVING ANY ACTIVE ROLE FOR ORDINARY PEOPLE--DOESN'T MAKE THE HIGH STRONGER, OR LONGER. IT ONLY GIVES OFF A LOW-LEVEL BACKGROUND RADIATION WHILE IT'S IN THEIR BODIES.
NOT ENOUGH TO KILL SUPERMAN, BUT HE'D PROBABLY BE UNCOMFORTABLE WALKING ANYWHERE NEAR SOMEONE WHO'D TAKEN IT.
THEN WHAT AM I LOOKING FOR HERE, WAYNE?
AN OLD FRIEND, McGINNIS. OR ANY TRACE OF HIM.
NO ONE'S LIVED HERE RECENTLY--OR IF THEY HAVE, THEY'RE A SLOB. IT'S INHUMANLY FILTHY.
INHUMAN. I CALLED HIM THAT SOMETIMES.
FOLLOW THE MONEY--CHECK FOR ANY AUTOPAYS ON HIS HOME SYSTEM.
RENT, UTILITIES--NOTHING PERSONAL AND NO SIGN OF ANY PURCHASES--EXCEPT--
--FLOWERS???

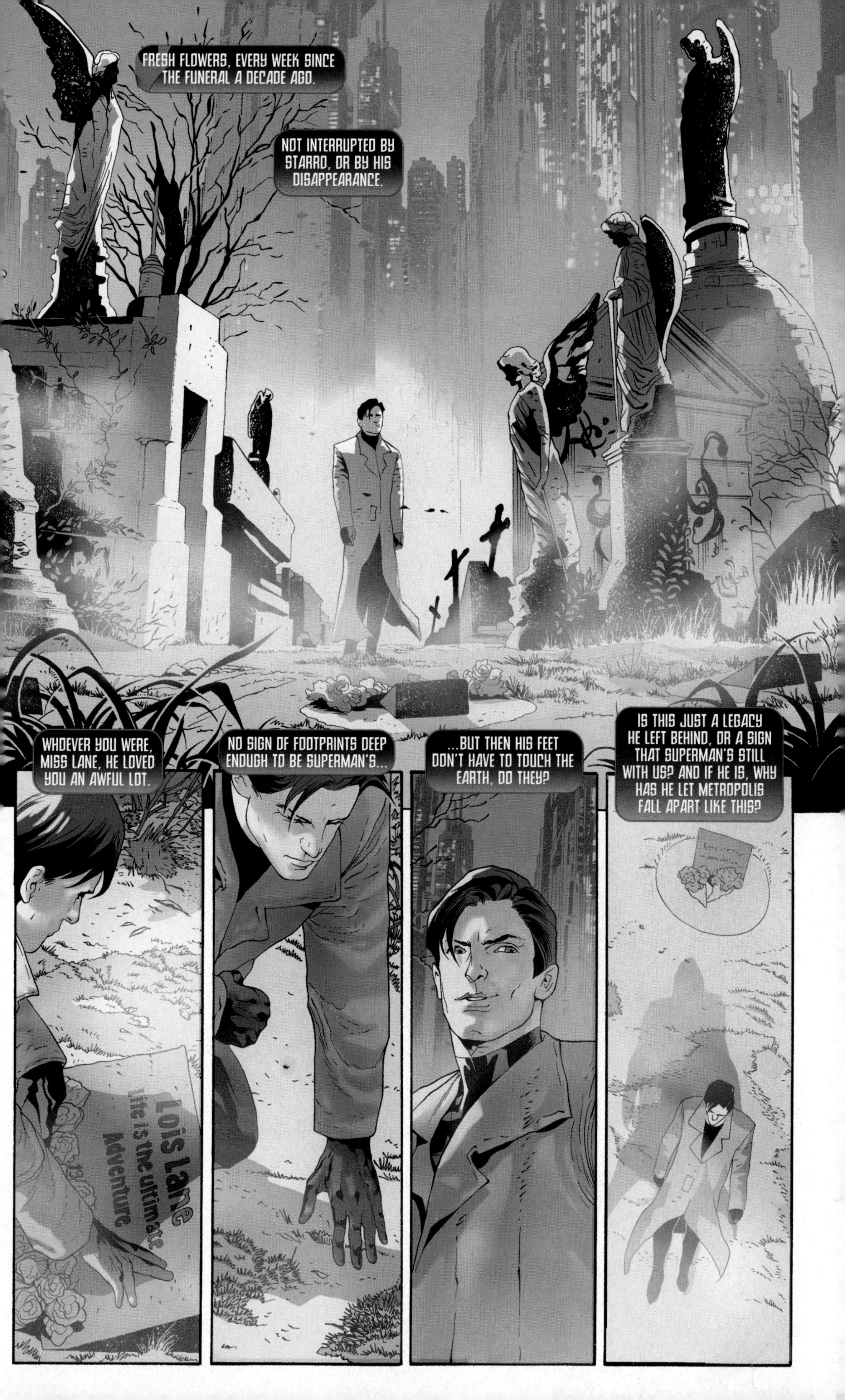
FRESH FLOWERS, EVERY WEEK SINCE THE FUNERAL A DECADE AGO.
NOT INTERRUPTED BY STARRO, OR BY HIS DISAPPEARANCE.
WHOEVER YOU WERE, MISS LANE, HE LOVED YOU AN AWFUL LOT.
Lois Lane
life is the ultimate Adventure
NO SIGN OF FOOTPRINTS DEEP ENOUGH TO BE SUPERMAN'S...
...BUT THEN HIS FEET DON'T HAVE TO TOUCH THE EARTH, DO THEY?
IS THIS JUST A LEGACY HE LEFT BEHIND, OR A SIGN THAT SUPERMAN'S STILL WITH US? AND IF HE IS, WHY HAS HE LET METROPOLIS FALL APART LIKE THIS?

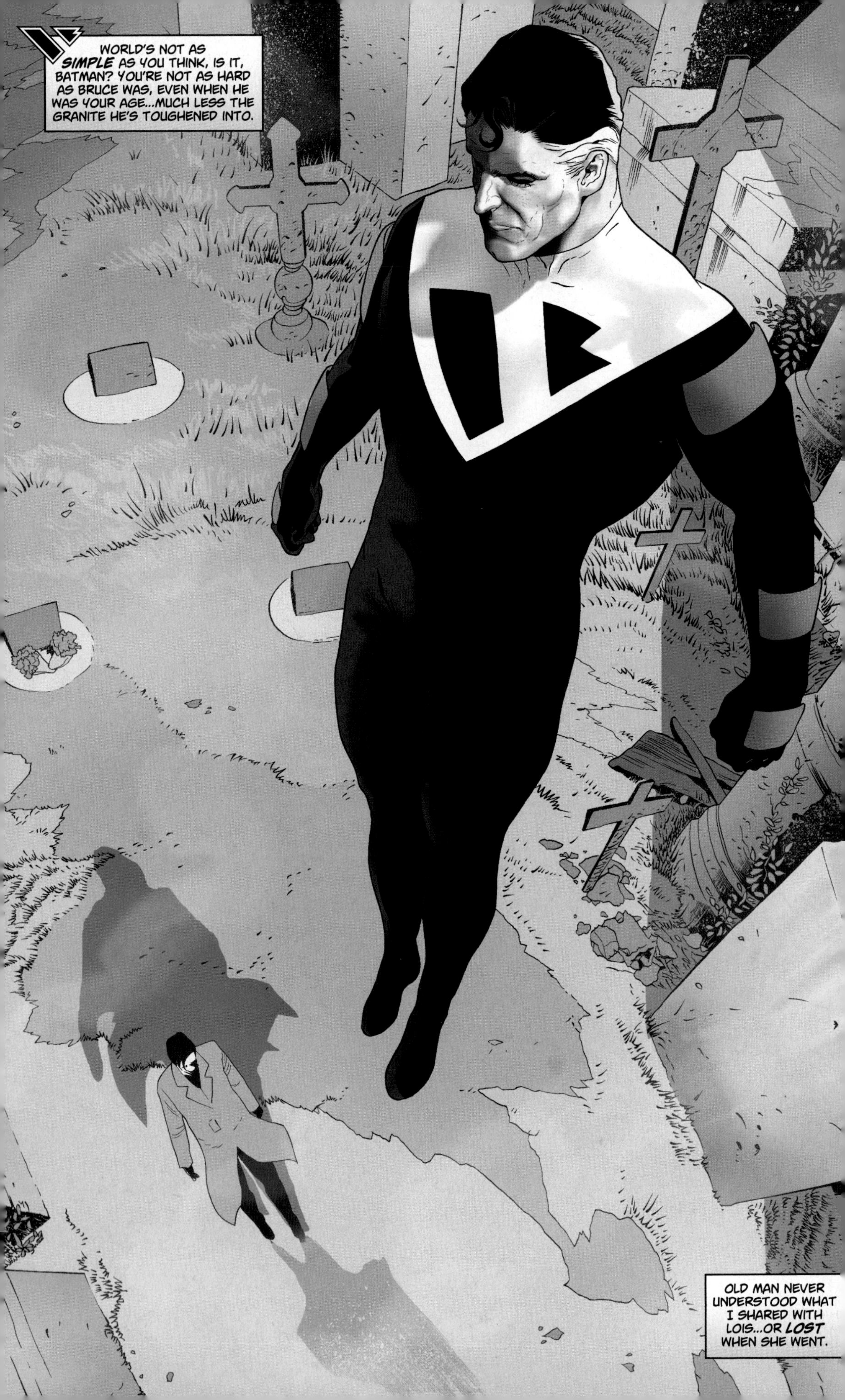
WORLD'S NOT AS SIMPLE AS YOU THINK, IS IT, BATMAN? YOU'RE NOT AS HARD AS BRUCE WAS, EVEN WHEN HE WAS YOUR AGE...MUCH LESS THE GRANITE HE'S TOUGHENED INTO.
OLD MAN NEVER UNDERSTOOD WHAT I SHARED WITH LOIS...OR LOST WHEN SHE WENT.

HE *FORGOT* HOW TO LET A WOMAN INTO HIS HEART...

HOW *GOOD* IT FEELS TO LET YOURSELF BE THAT *VULNERABLE.*

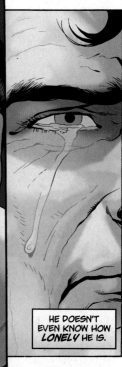

HE DOESN'T EVEN KNOW HOW *LONELY* HE IS.

I KNOW.

Lois Lane
Life is the ultimate Adventure

I GOT RID OF THAT DAMN PARASITE AND WOKE UP, BUT I'D LOST YOU...

...LOST MY *WHOLE* CITY.

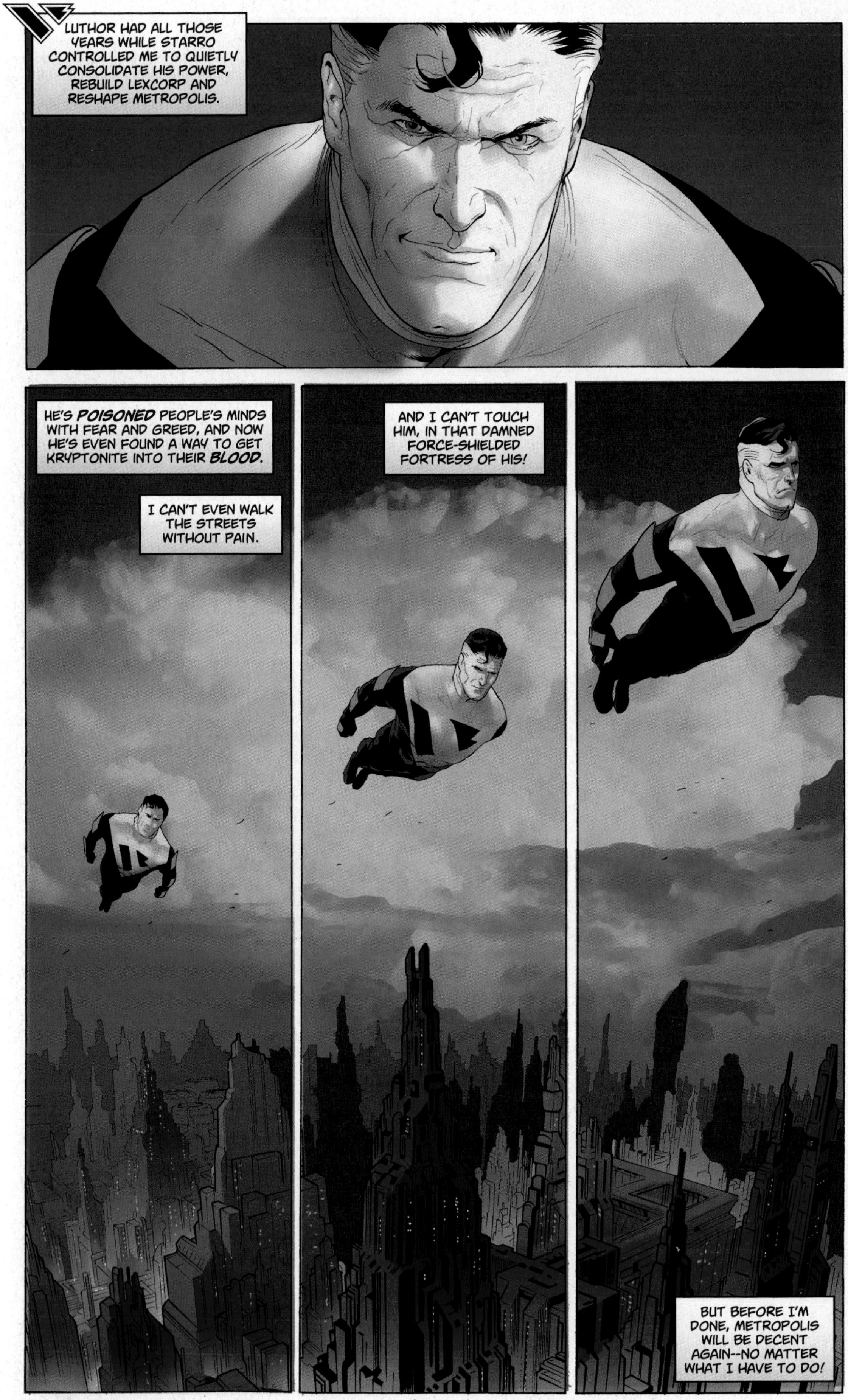
LUTHOR HAD ALL THOSE YEARS WHILE STARRO CONTROLLED ME TO QUIETLY CONSOLIDATE HIS POWER, REBUILD LEXCORP AND RESHAPE METROPOLIS.
HE'S POISONED PEOPLE'S MINDS WITH FEAR AND GREED, AND NOW HE'S EVEN FOUND A WAY TO GET KRYPTONITE INTO THEIR BLOOD.
I CAN'T EVEN WALK THE STREETS WITHOUT PAIN.
AND I CAN'T TOUCH HIM, IN THAT DAMNED FORCE-SHIELDED FORTRESS OF HIS!
BUT BEFORE I'M DONE, METROPOLIS WILL BE DECENT AGAIN--NO MATTER WHAT I HAVE TO DO!

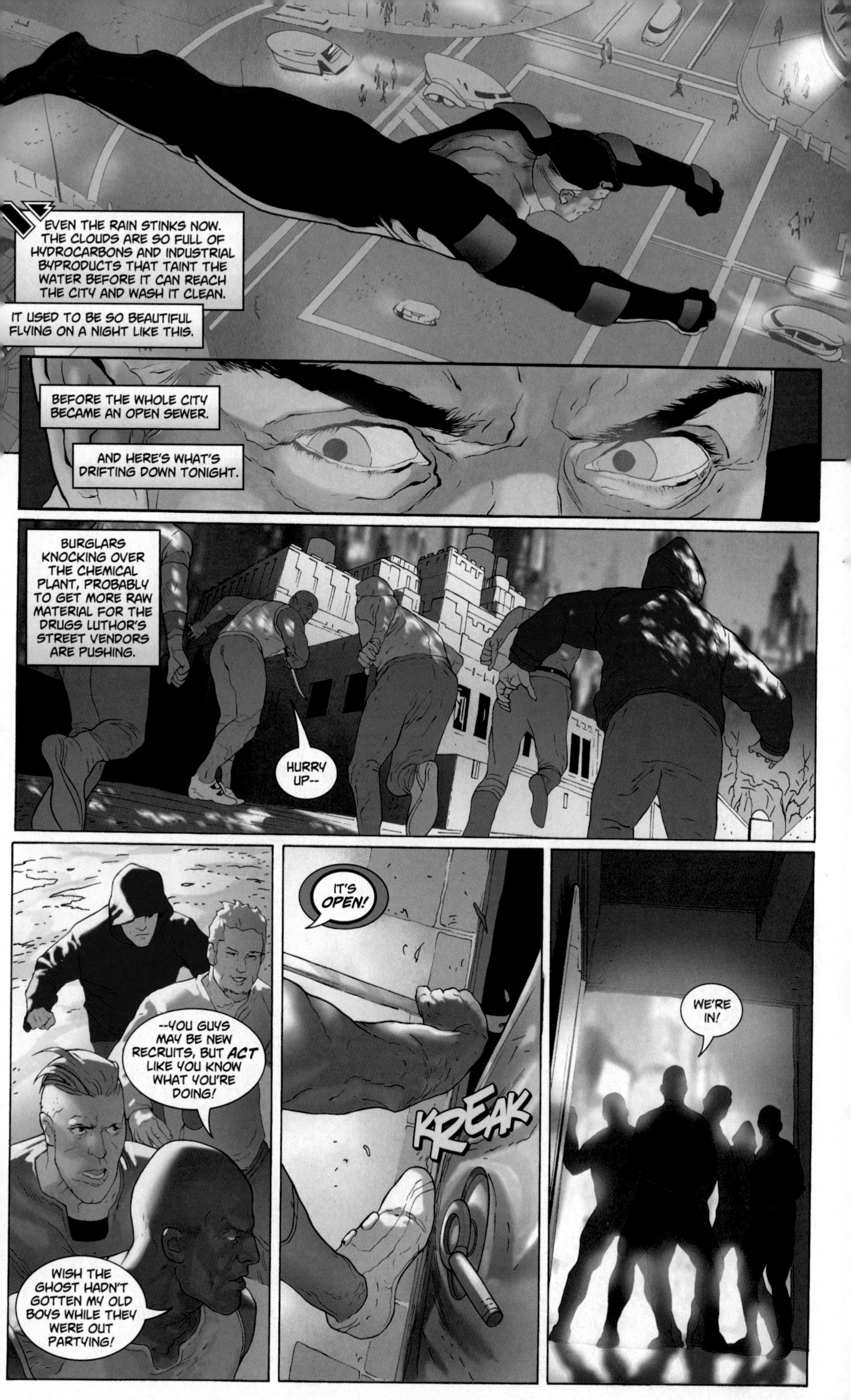
EVEN THE RAIN STINKS NOW. THE CLOUDS ARE SO FULL OF HYDROCARBONS AND INDUSTRIAL BYPRODUCTS THAT TAINT THE WATER BEFORE IT CAN REACH THE CITY AND WASH IT CLEAN.
IT USED TO BE SO BEAUTIFUL FLYING ON A NIGHT LIKE THIS.
BEFORE THE WHOLE CITY BECAME AN OPEN SEWER.
AND HERE'S WHAT'S DRIFTING DOWN TONIGHT.
BURGLARS KNOCKING OVER THE CHEMICAL PLANT, PROBABLY TO GET MORE RAW MATERIAL FOR THE DRUGS LUTHOR'S STREET VENDORS ARE PUSHING.
HURRY UP--
--YOU GUYS MAY BE NEW RECRUITS, BUT ACT LIKE YOU KNOW WHAT YOU'RE DOING!
WISH THE GHOST HADN'T GOTTEN MY OLD BOYS WHILE THEY WERE OUT PARTYING!
IT'S OPEN!
KREAK
WE'RE IN!

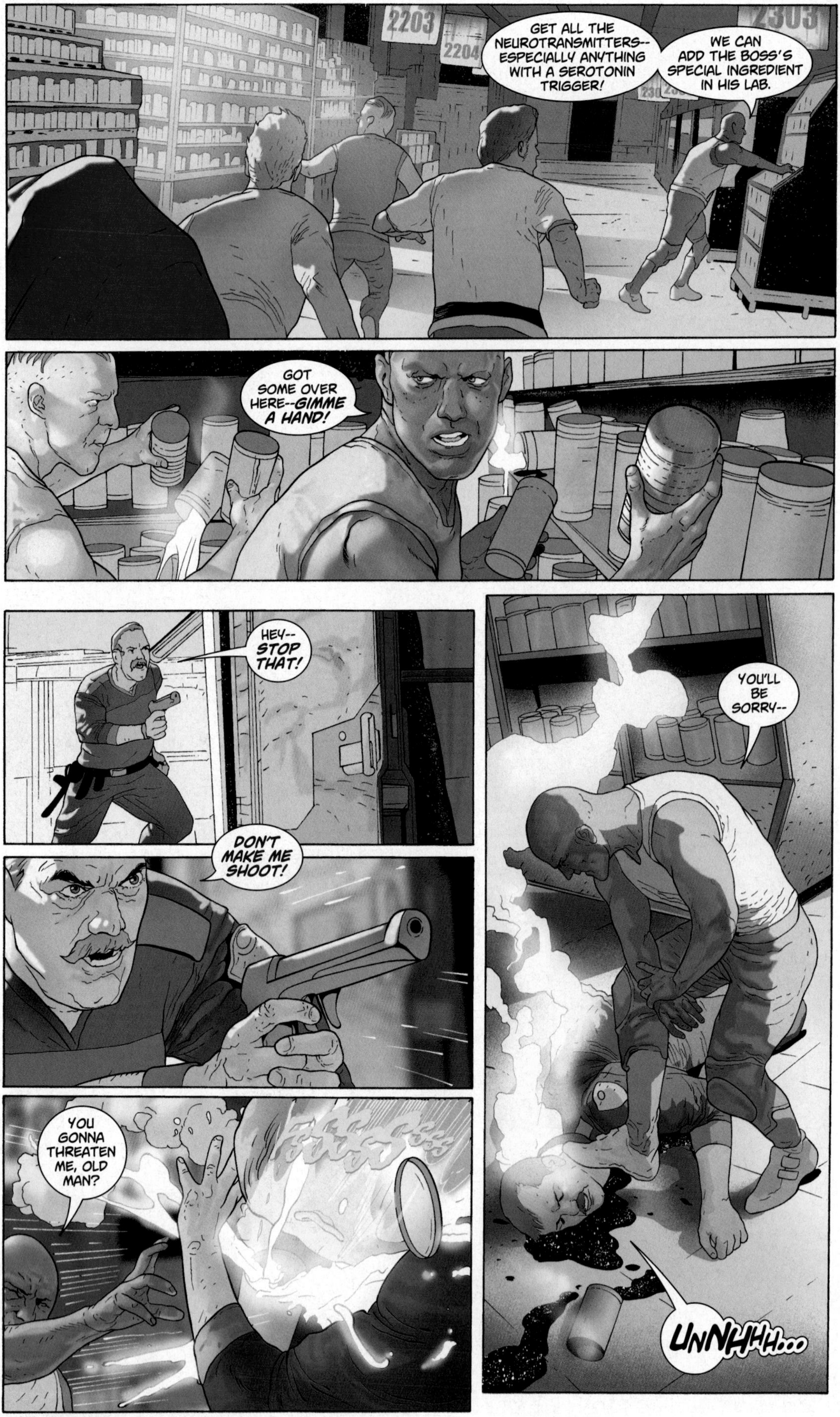
2203
2204
2303
GET ALL THE NEUROTRANSMITTERS--ESPECIALLY ANYTHING WITH A SEROTONIN TRIGGER!
WE CAN ADD THE BOSS'S SPECIAL INGREDIENT IN HIS LAB.
GOT SOME OVER HERE--GIMME A HAND!
HEY-- STOP THAT!
DON'T MAKE ME SHOOT!
YOU GONNA THREATEN ME, OLD MAN?
YOU'LL BE SORRY--
UNNHHH...

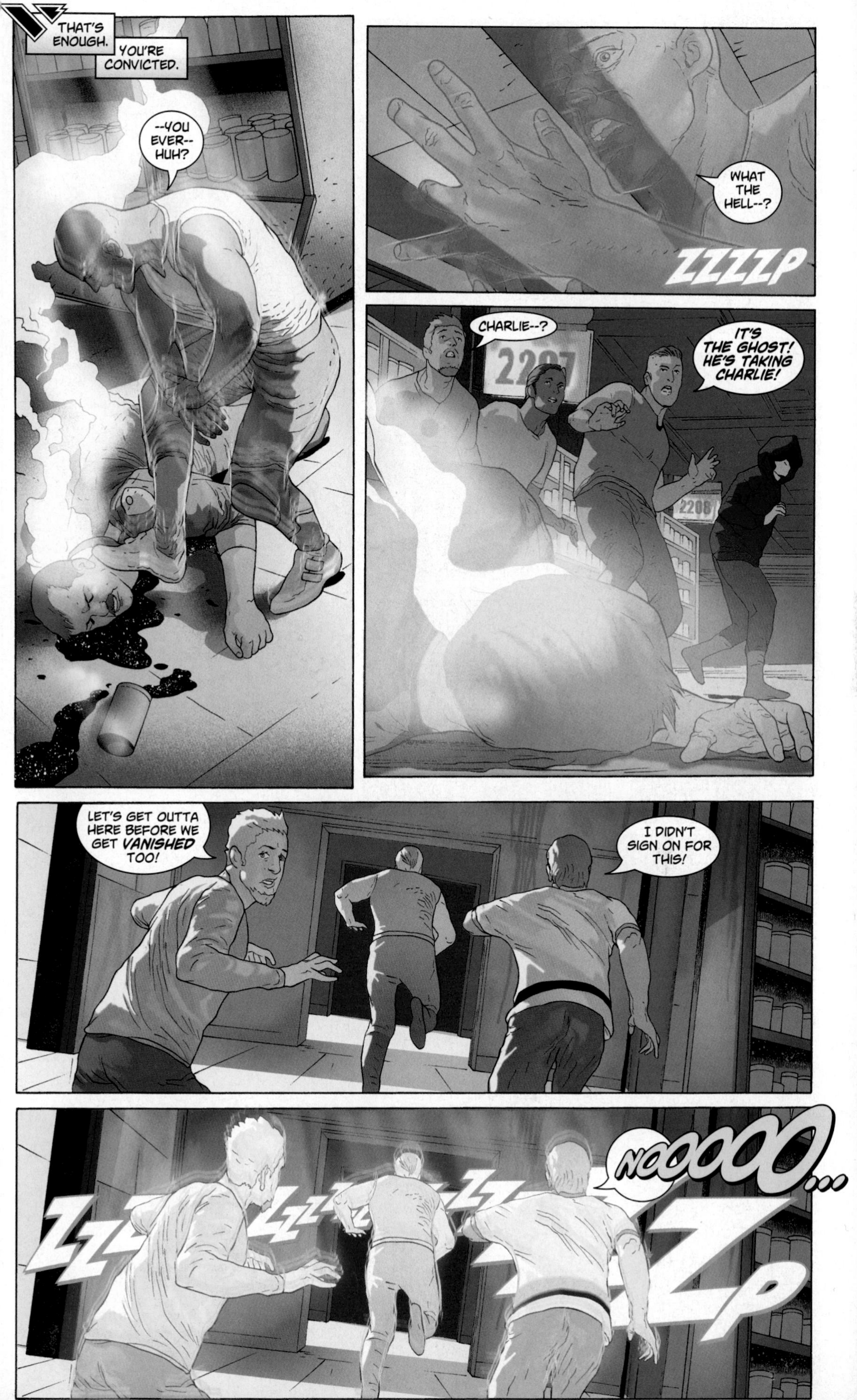
THAT'S ENOUGH.
YOU'RE CONVICTED.
--YOU EVER--HUH?
WHAT THE HELL--?
ZZZZP
CHARLIE--?
IT'S THE GHOST! HE'S TAKING CHARLIE!
2208
LET'S GET OUTTA HERE BEFORE WE GET VANISHED TOO!
I DIDN'T SIGN ON FOR THIS!
NOOOOO...
ZZZZZZZZZZP

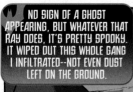

NO SIGN OF A GHOST APPEARING, BUT WHATEVER THAT RAY DOES, IT'S PRETTY SPOOKY. IT WIPED OUT THIS WHOLE GANG I INFILTRATED--NOT EVEN DUST LEFT ON THE GROUND.

A DISINTEGRATOR WOULD LEAVE MORE OF A TRACE. HOW DO I EVEN BRING BACK PROOF TO THE GUY WHO HIRED US FOR THIS BREAK-IN?

IF I WANT TO TRACE THE DRUG RING BACK TO ITS SOURCE, I HAVE TO EARN THEIR TRUST.

CAN'T TELL IF THE GHOST IS STILL AROUND, BUT I'LL HAVE TO TAKE MY CHANCES...

...AND TAKE SOME EVIDENCE THAT THE RAID WENT BAD.

PLUS A LITTLE OF THE CHEMICAL WE CAME FOR--HATE TO GIVE HIM ANYTHING TO COOK UP MORE JUNK, BUT IT'LL LET ME SHOW I'M ON THE DARK SIDE.

0705-1/2

UNTIL HE FINDS OUT I'M NOT.

THAT'S FOUR LESS ANIMALS OUT OF METROPOLIS WHERE THEY BELONG...

...BUT WHAT WERE *YOU* DOING PRETENDING TO BE ONE OF THEM, BATMAN?

AND WILL YOU HELP ME GET TO LUTHOR?

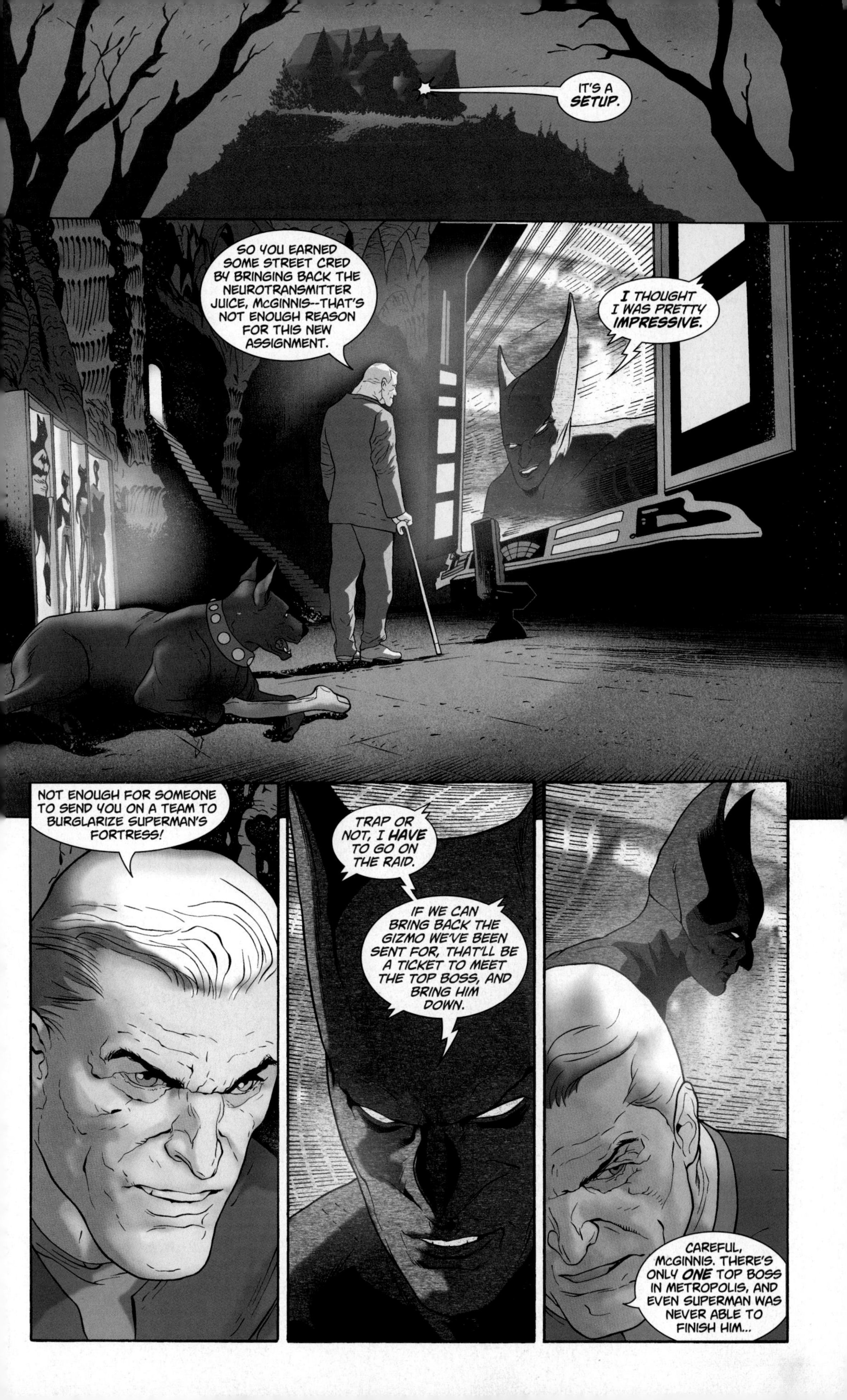
IT'S A SETUP.
SO YOU EARNED SOME STREET CRED BY BRINGING BACK THE NEUROTRANSMITTER JUICE, McGINNIS--THAT'S NOT ENOUGH REASON FOR THIS NEW ASSIGNMENT.
I THOUGHT I WAS PRETTY IMPRESSIVE.
NOT ENOUGH FOR SOMEONE TO SEND YOU ON A TEAM TO BURGLARIZE SUPERMAN'S FORTRESS!
TRAP OR NOT, I HAVE TO GO ON THE RAID.
IF WE CAN BRING BACK THE GIZMO WE'VE BEEN SENT FOR, THAT'LL BE A TICKET TO MEET THE TOP BOSS, AND BRING HIM DOWN.
CAREFUL, McGINNIS. THERE'S ONLY ONE TOP BOSS IN METROPOLIS, AND EVEN SUPERMAN WAS NEVER ABLE TO FINISH HIM...

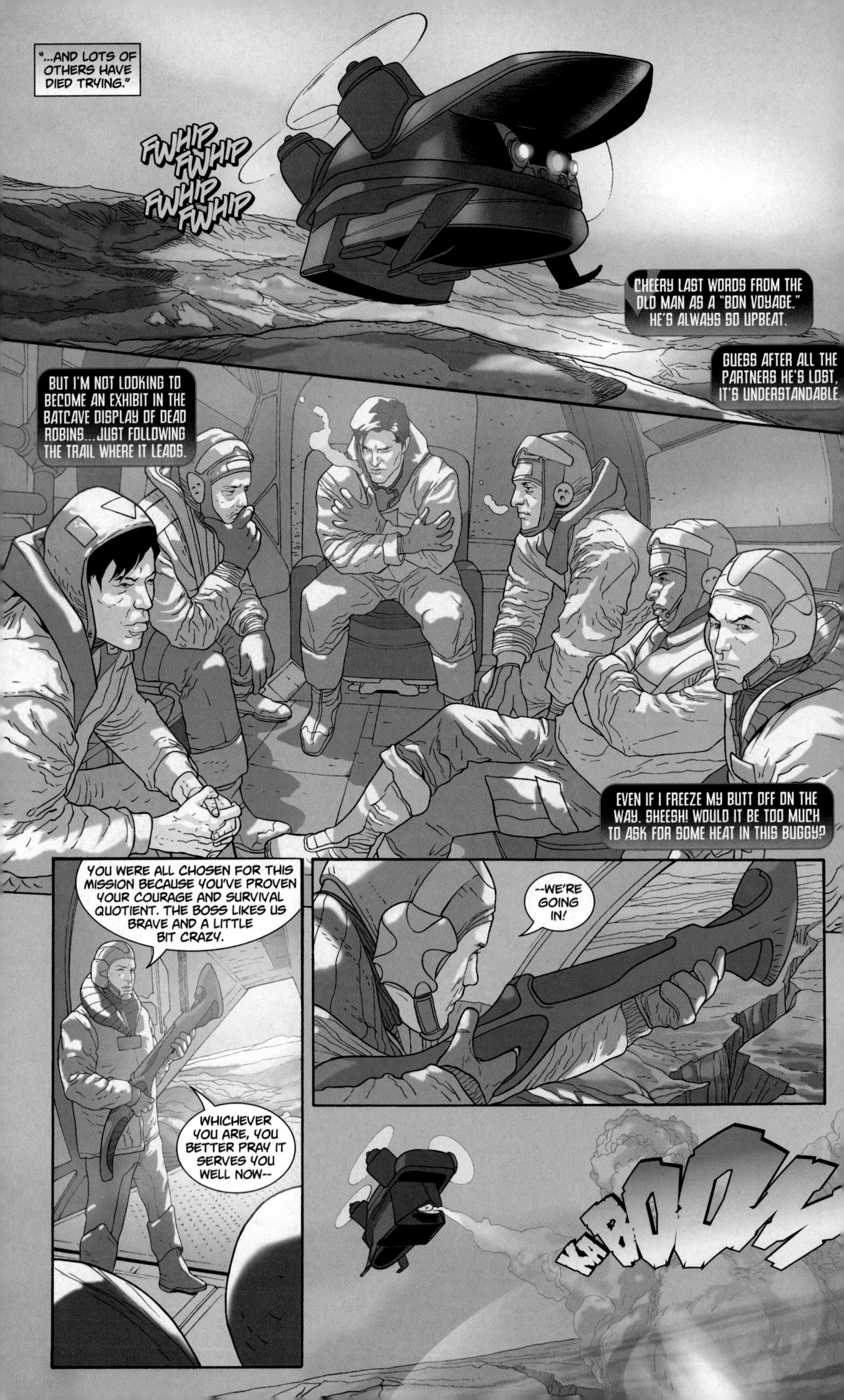
"...AND LOTS OF OTHERS HAVE DIED TRYING."
FWHIP FWHIP FWHIP FWHIP
CHEERY LAST WORDS FROM THE OLD MAN AS A "BON VOYAGE." HE'S ALWAYS SO UPBEAT.
GUESS AFTER ALL THE PARTNERS HE'S LOST, IT'S UNDERSTANDABLE.
BUT I'M NOT LOOKING TO BECOME AN EXHIBIT IN THE BATCAVE DISPLAY OF DEAD ROBINS... JUST FOLLOWING THE TRAIL WHERE IT LEADS.
EVEN IF I FREEZE MY BUTT OFF ON THE WAY. SHEESH! WOULD IT BE TOO MUCH TO ASK FOR SOME HEAT IN THIS BUGGY?
YOU WERE ALL CHOSEN FOR THIS MISSION BECAUSE YOU'VE PROVEN YOUR COURAGE AND SURVIVAL QUOTIENT. THE BOSS LIKES US BRAVE AND A LITTLE BIT CRAZY.
WHICHEVER YOU ARE, YOU BETTER PRAY IT SERVES YOU WELL NOW--
--WE'RE GOING IN!
KA-BOOM

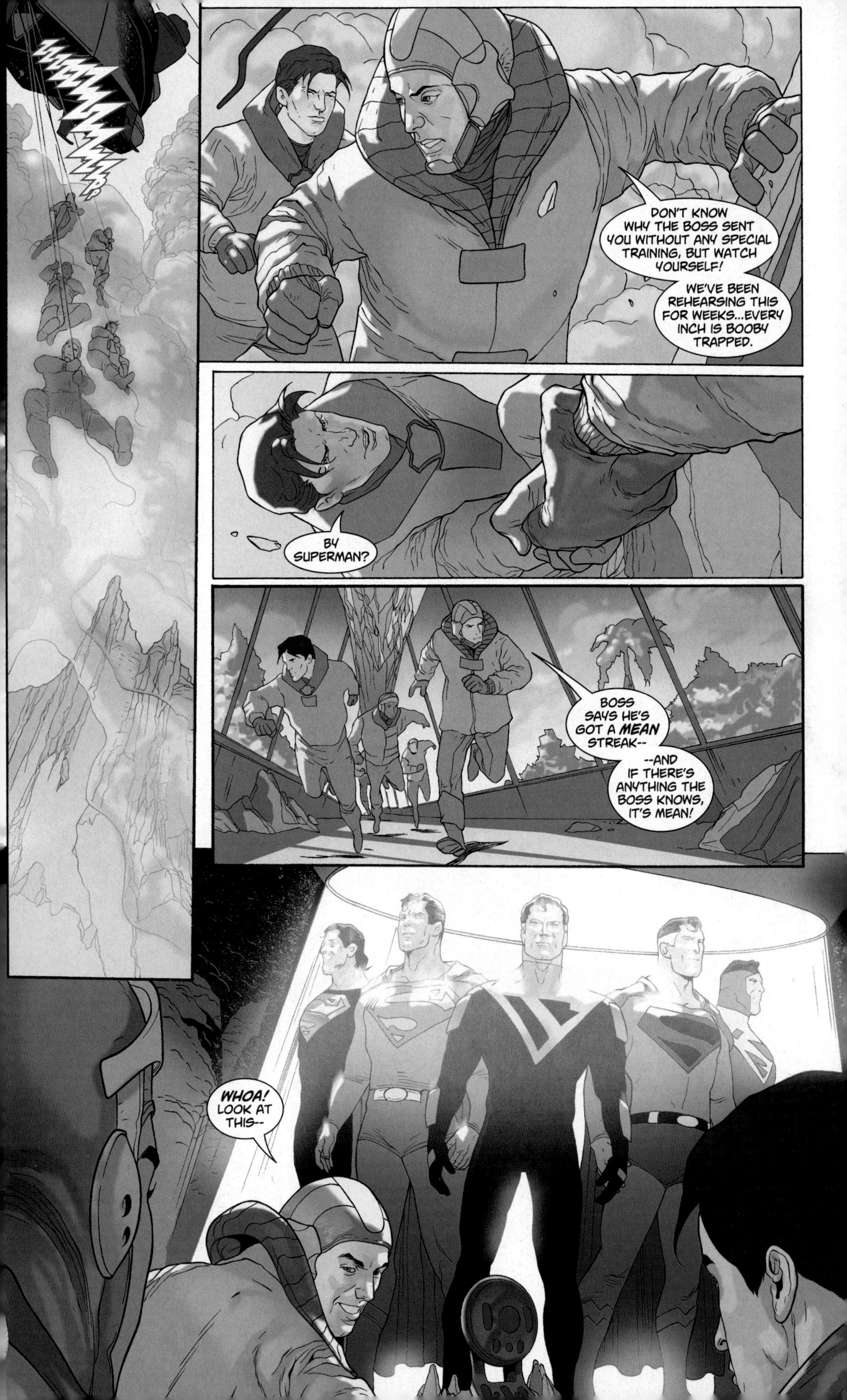

DON'T KNOW WHY THE BOSS SENT YOU WITHOUT ANY SPECIAL TRAINING, BUT WATCH YOURSELF!
WE'VE BEEN REHEARSING THIS FOR WEEKS...EVERY INCH IS BOOBY TRAPPED.
BY SUPERMAN?
BOSS SAYS HE'S GOT A ***MEAN*** STREAK--
--AND IF THERE'S ANYTHING THE BOSS KNOWS, IT'S MEAN!
WHOA! LOOK AT THIS--

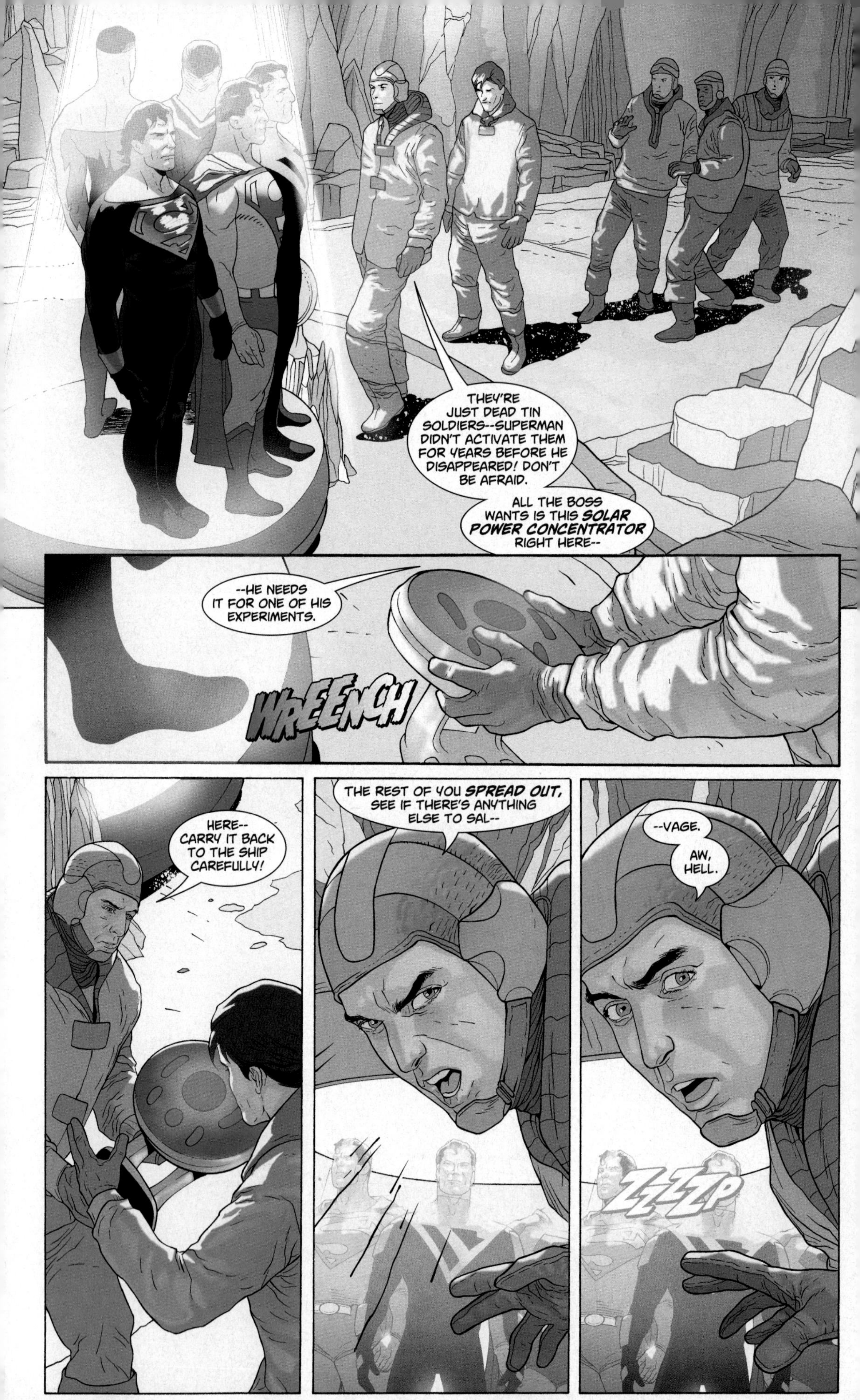
THEY'RE JUST DEAD TIN SOLDIERS--SUPERMAN DIDN'T ACTIVATE THEM FOR YEARS BEFORE HE DISAPPEARED! DON'T BE AFRAID.
ALL THE BOSS WANTS IS THIS SOLAR POWER CONCENTRATOR RIGHT HERE--
--HE NEEDS IT FOR ONE OF HIS EXPERIMENTS.
WREENCH
HERE-- CARRY IT BACK TO THE SHIP CAREFULLY!
THE REST OF YOU SPREAD OUT, SEE IF THERE'S ANYTHING ELSE TO SAL--
--VAGE.
AW, HELL.
ZZZZP

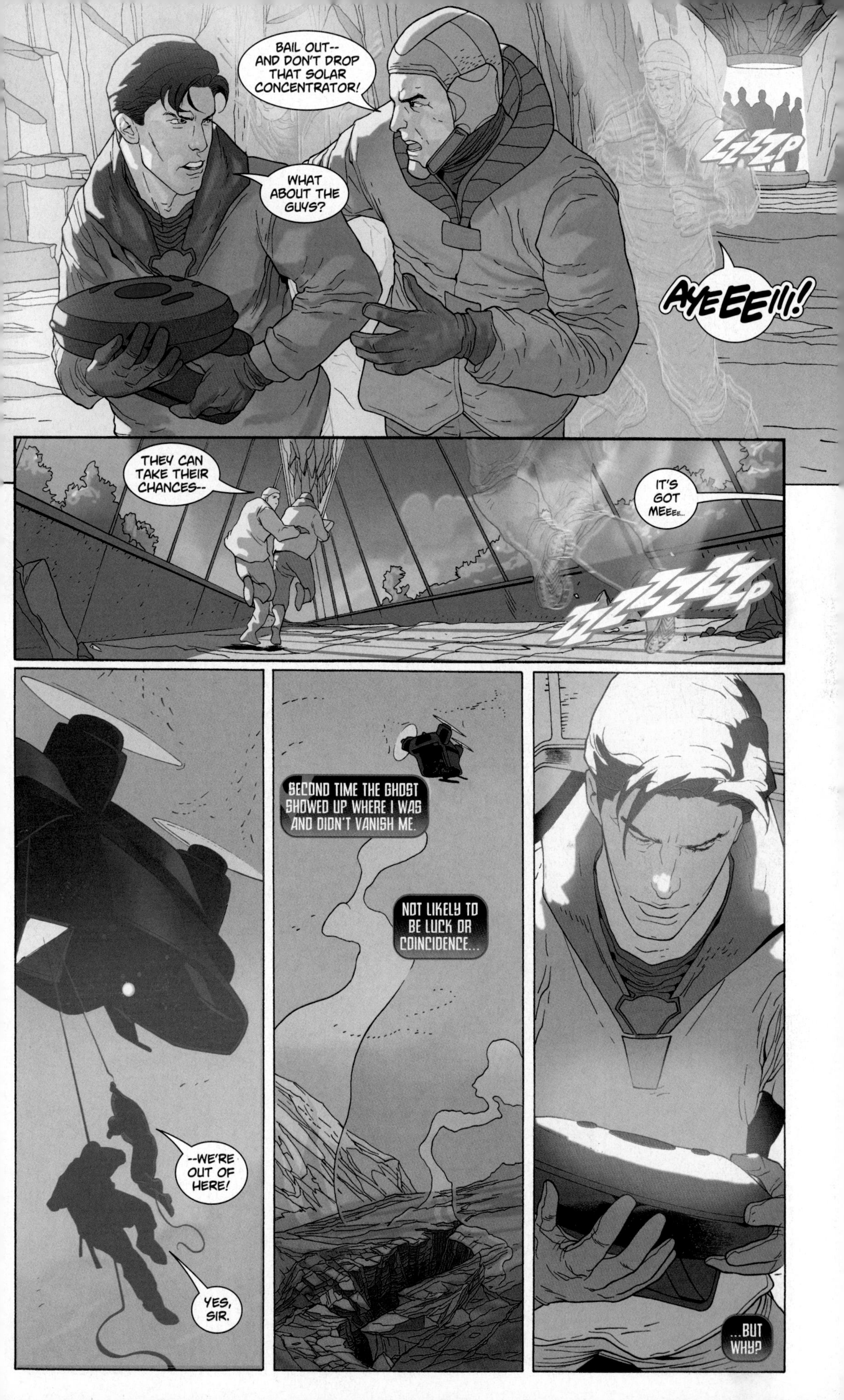

BAIL OUT-- AND DON'T DROP THAT SOLAR CONCENTRATOR!
WHAT ABOUT THE GUYS?
ZZZZP
AYEEE!!!!
THEY CAN TAKE THEIR CHANCES--
IT'S GOT MEEee...
ZZZZZZZZP
--WE'RE OUT OF HERE!
YES, SIR.
SECOND TIME THE GHOST SHOWED UP WHERE I WAS AND DIDN'T VANISH ME.
NOT LIKELY TO BE LUCK OR COINCIDENCE...
...BUT WHY?

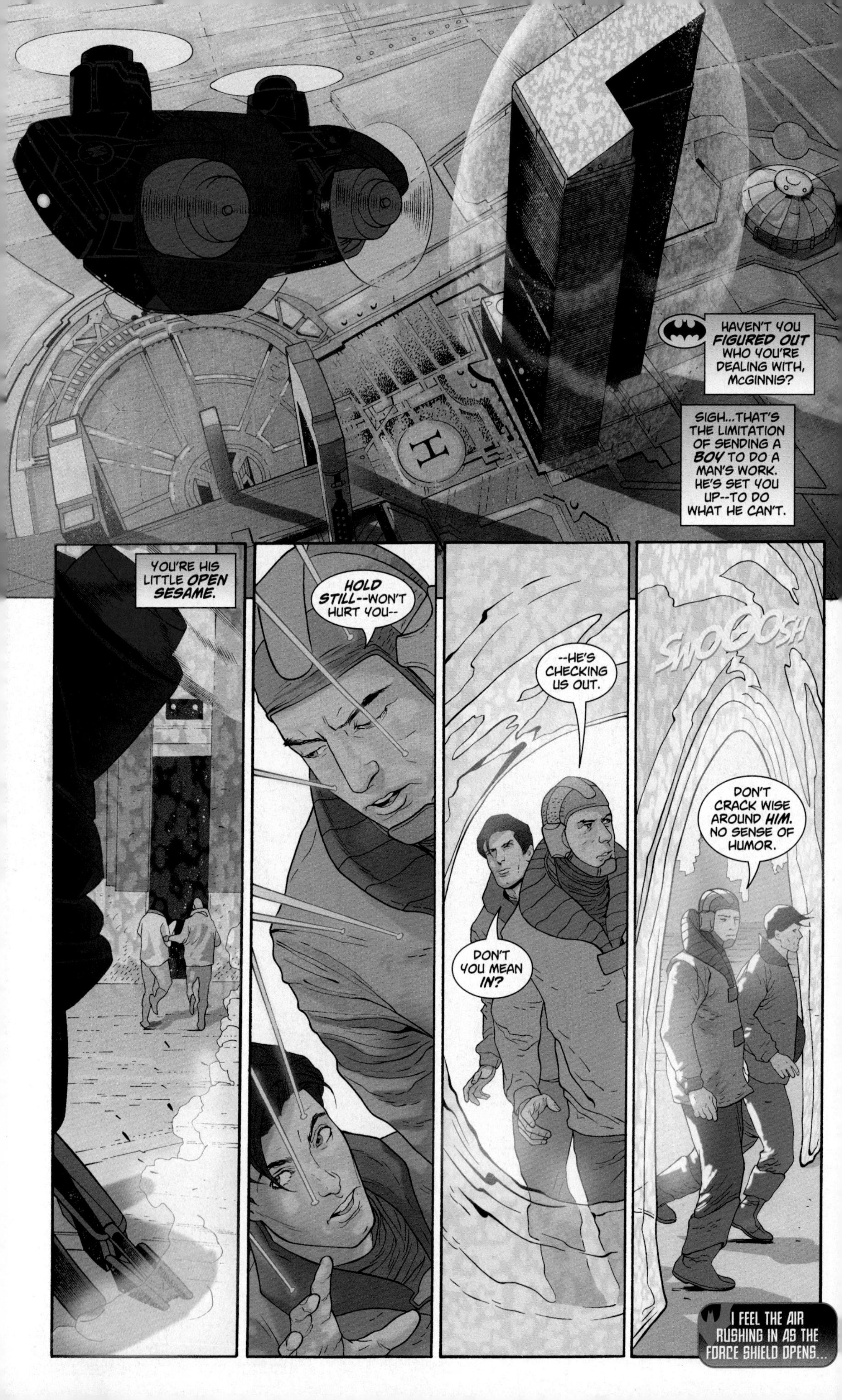

HAVEN'T YOU FIGURED OUT WHO YOU'RE DEALING WITH, McGINNIS?
SIGH...THAT'S THE LIMITATION OF SENDING A BOY TO DO A MAN'S WORK. HE'S SET YOU UP--TO DO WHAT HE CAN'T.
YOU'RE HIS LITTLE OPEN SESAME.
HOLD STILL--WON'T HURT YOU--
--HE'S CHECKING US OUT.
DON'T YOU MEAN IN?
SWOOOSH
DON'T CRACK WISE AROUND HIM. NO SENSE OF HUMOR.
I FEEL THE AIR RUSHING IN AS THE FORCE SHIELD OPENS...

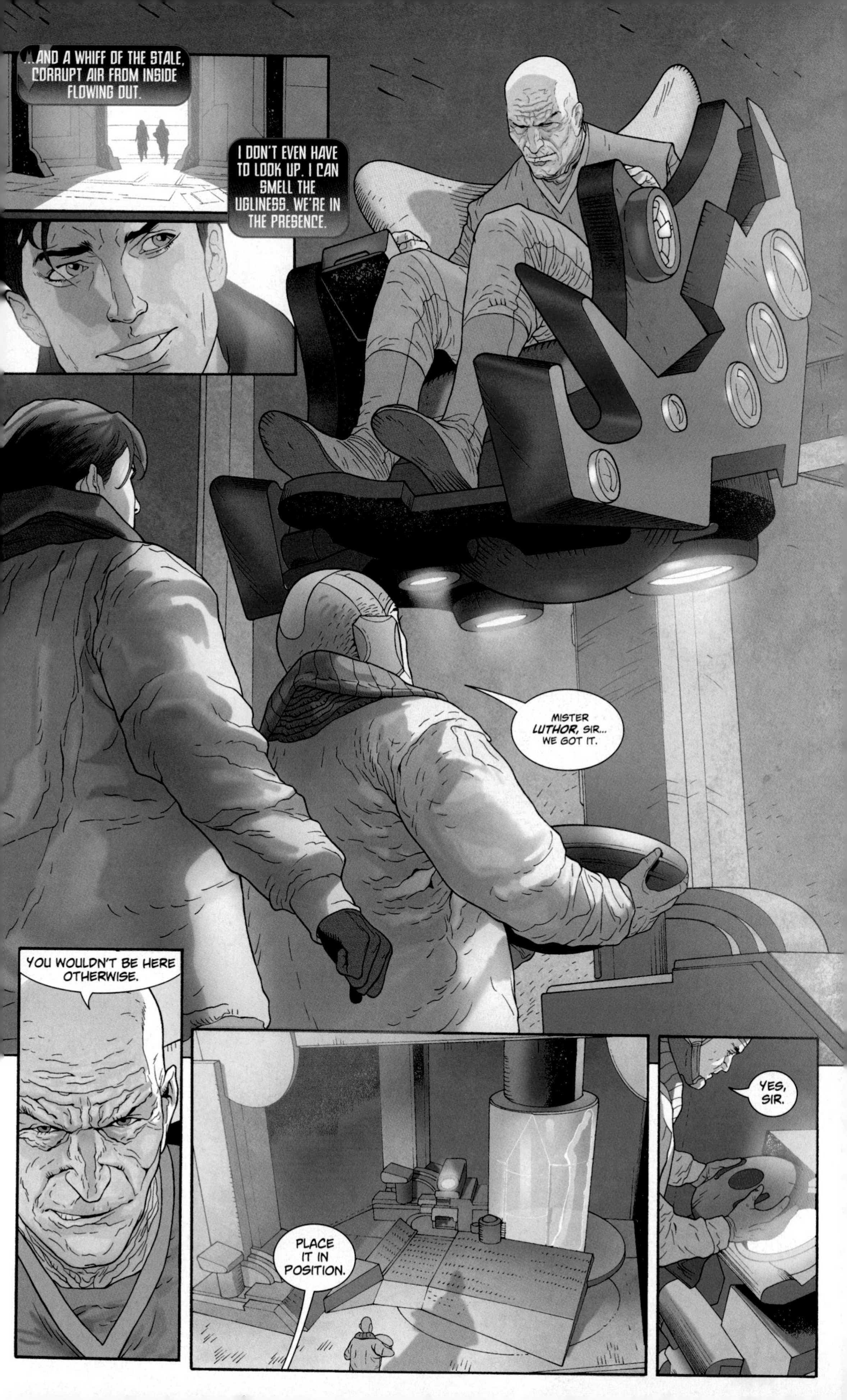
...AND A WHIFF OF THE STALE, CORRUPT AIR FROM INSIDE FLOWING OUT.
I DON'T EVEN HAVE TO LOOK UP. I CAN SMELL THE UGLINESS. WE'RE IN THE PRESENCE.
MISTER LUTHOR, SIR... WE GOT IT.
YOU WOULDN'T BE HERE OTHERWISE.
PLACE IT IN POSITION.
YES, SIR.

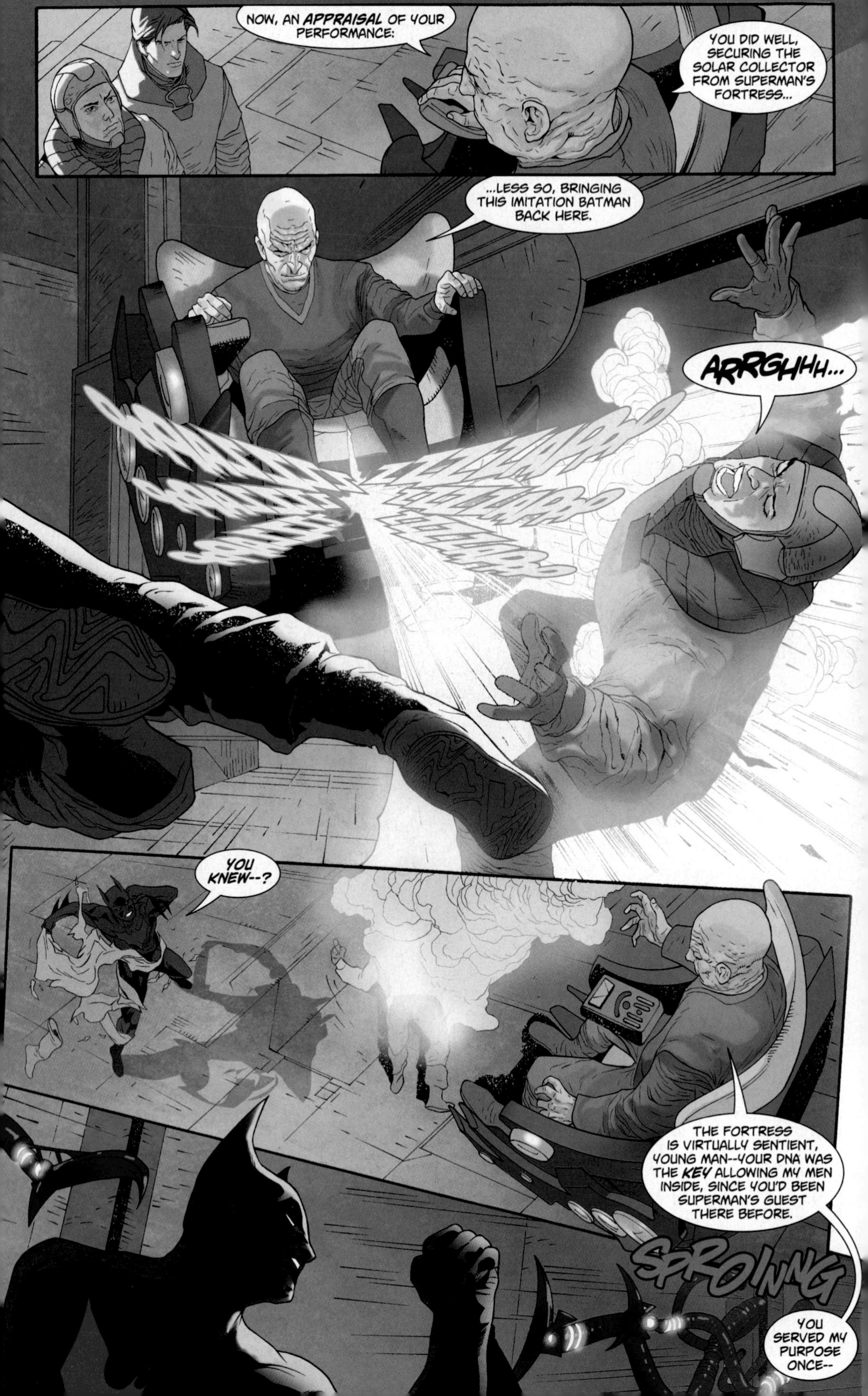
NOW, AN APPRAISAL OF YOUR PERFORMANCE:
YOU DID WELL, SECURING THE SOLAR COLLECTOR FROM SUPERMAN'S FORTRESS...
...LESS SO, BRINGING THIS IMITATION BATMAN BACK HERE.
ARRGHHH...
YOU KNEW--?
THE FORTRESS IS VIRTUALLY SENTIENT, YOUNG MAN--YOUR DNA WAS THE KEY ALLOWING MY MEN INSIDE, SINCE YOU'D BEEN SUPERMAN'S GUEST THERE BEFORE.
SPROINNG
YOU SERVED MY PURPOSE ONCE--

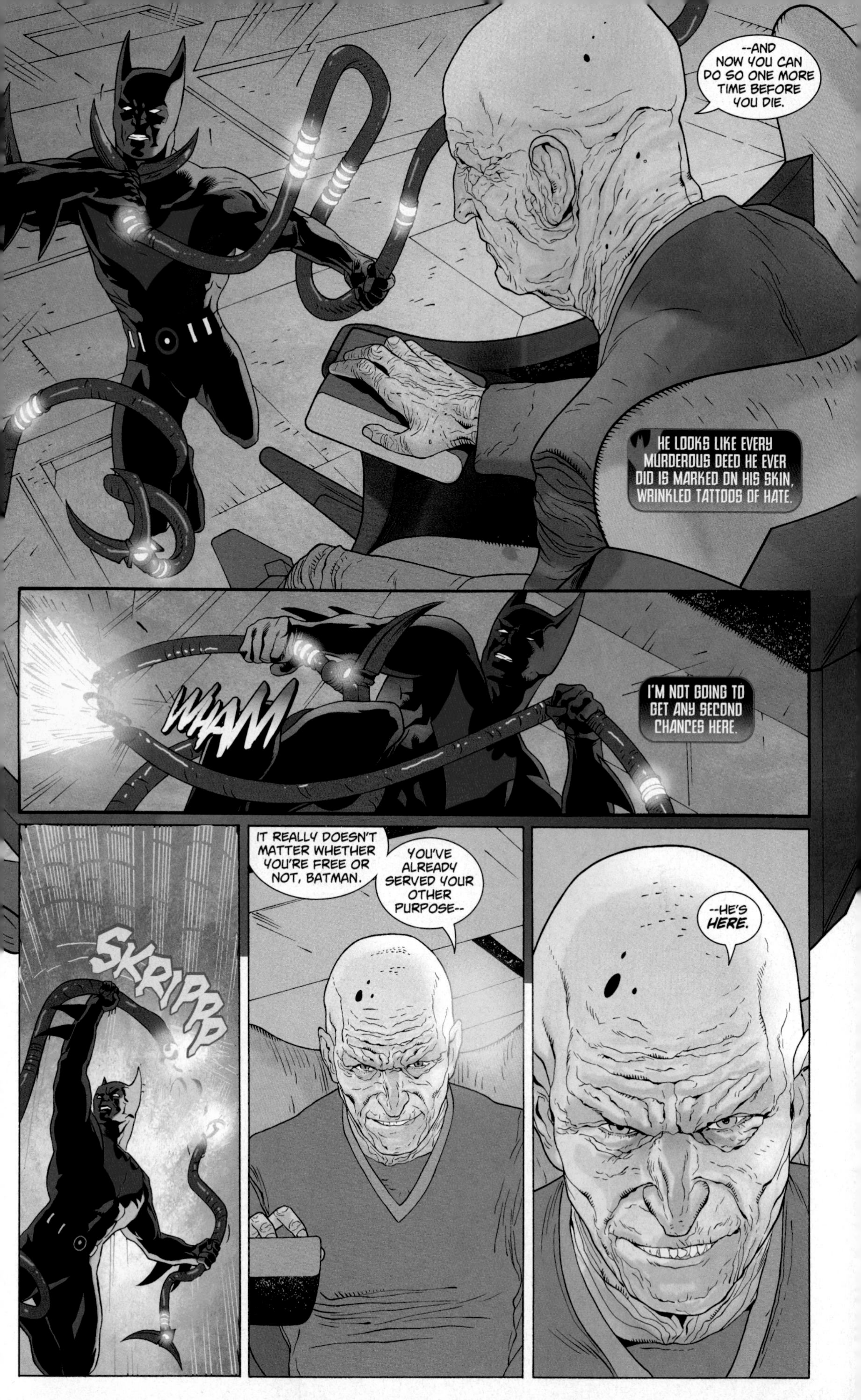
--AND NOW YOU CAN DO SO ONE MORE TIME BEFORE YOU DIE.
HE LOOKS LIKE EVERY MURDEROUS DEED HE EVER DID IS MARKED ON HIS SKIN, WRINKLED TATTOOS OF HATE.
WHAM
I'M NOT GOING TO GET ANY SECOND CHANCES HERE.
SKRIPPP
IT REALLY DOESN'T MATTER WHETHER YOU'RE FREE OR NOT, BATMAN.
YOU'VE ALREADY SERVED YOUR OTHER PURPOSE--
--HE'S HERE.

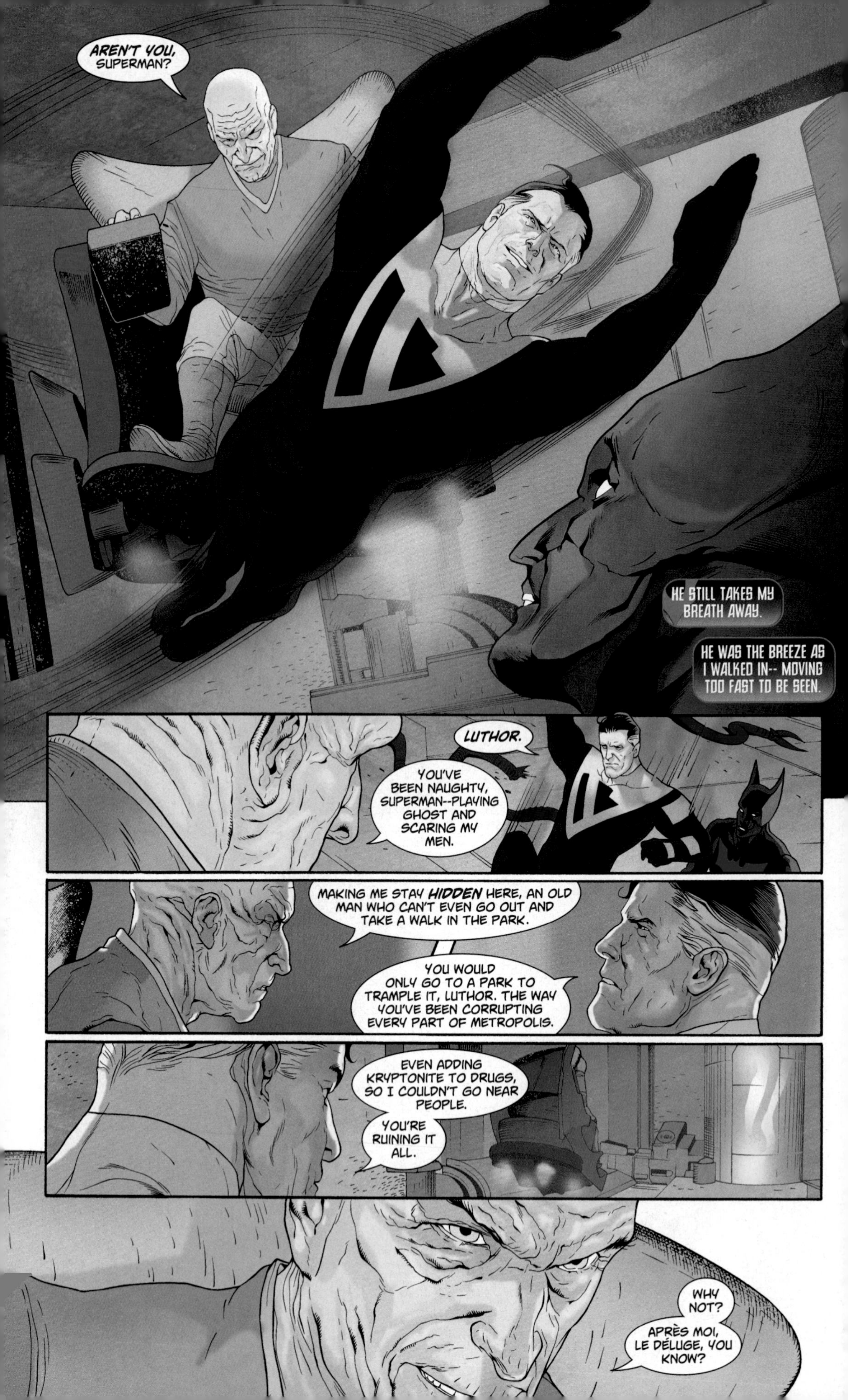
AREN'T YOU, SUPERMAN?
HE STILL TAKES MY BREATH AWAY.
HE WAS THE BREEZE AS I WALKED IN-- MOVING TOO FAST TO BE SEEN.
LUTHOR.
YOU'VE BEEN NAUGHTY, SUPERMAN--PLAYING GHOST AND SCARING MY MEN.
MAKING ME STAY HIDDEN HERE, AN OLD MAN WHO CAN'T EVEN GO OUT AND TAKE A WALK IN THE PARK.
YOU WOULD ONLY GO TO A PARK TO TRAMPLE IT, LUTHOR. THE WAY YOU'VE BEEN CORRUPTING EVERY PART OF METROPOLIS.
EVEN ADDING KRYPTONITE TO DRUGS, SO I COULDN'T GO NEAR PEOPLE.
YOU'RE RUINING IT ALL.
WHY NOT?
APRÈS MOI, LE DÉLUGE, YOU KNOW?

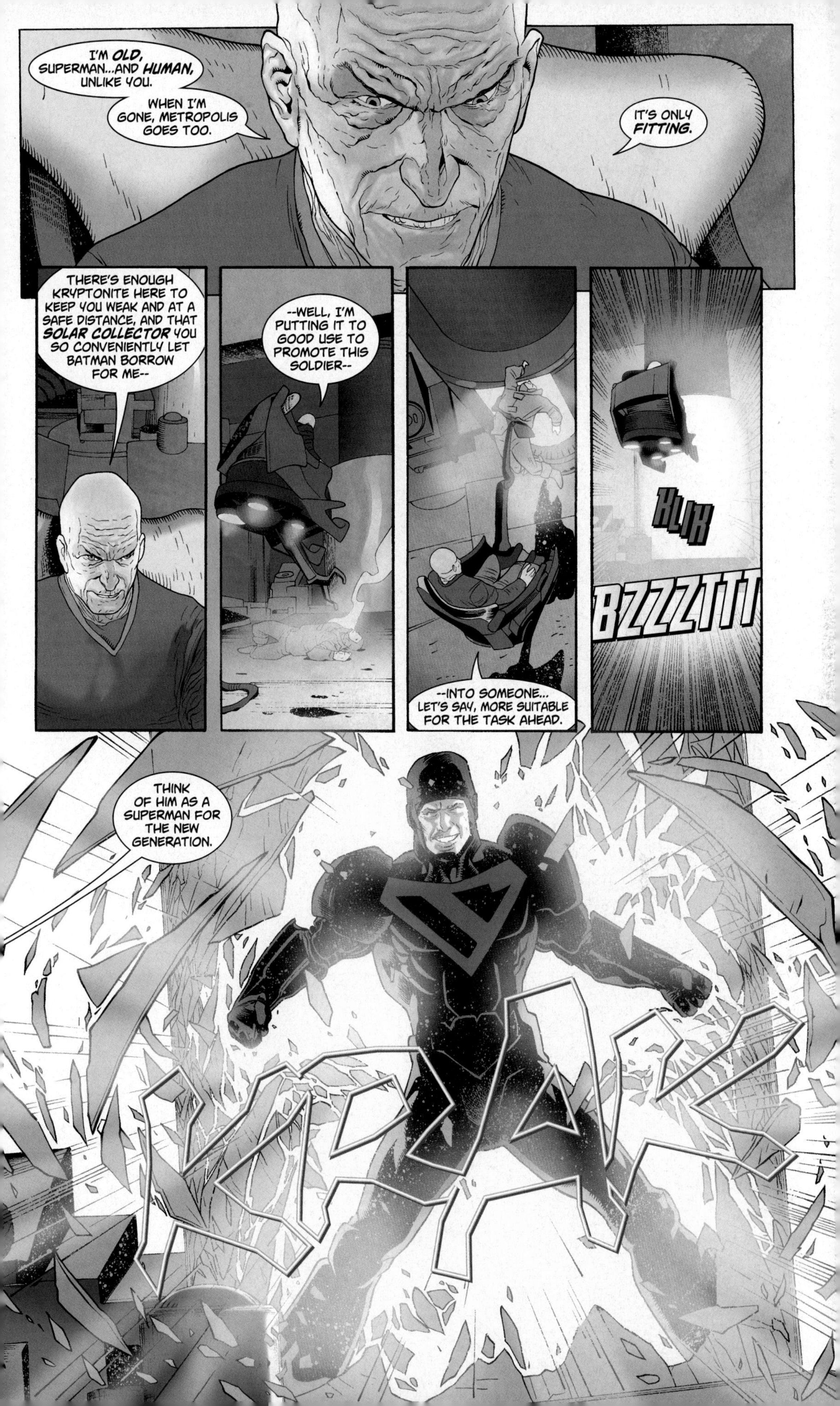
I'M OLD, SUPERMAN...AND HUMAN, UNLIKE YOU.
WHEN I'M GONE, METROPOLIS GOES TOO.
IT'S ONLY FITTING.
THERE'S ENOUGH KRYPTONITE HERE TO KEEP YOU WEAK AND AT A SAFE DISTANCE, AND THAT SOLAR COLLECTOR YOU SO CONVENIENTLY LET BATMAN BORROW FOR ME--
--WELL, I'M PUTTING IT TO GOOD USE TO PROMOTE THIS SOLDIER--
--INTO SOMEONE... LET'S SAY, MORE SUITABLE FOR THE TASK AHEAD.
KLIK
BZZZTTT
THINK OF HIM AS A SUPERMAN FOR THE NEW GENERATION.

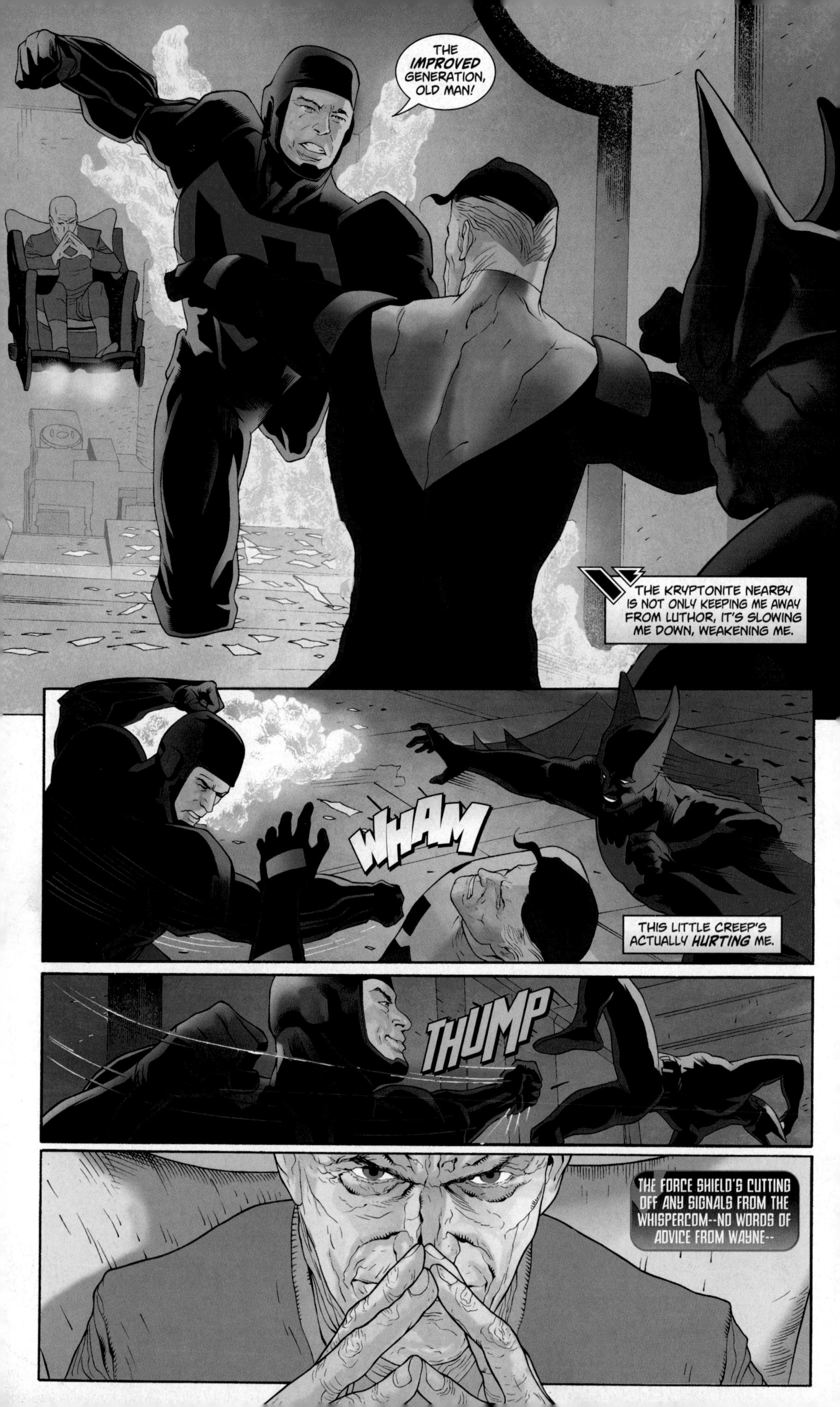
THE IMPROVED GENERATION, OLD MAN!
THE KRYPTONITE NEARBY IS NOT ONLY KEEPING ME AWAY FROM LUTHOR, IT'S SLOWING ME DOWN, WEAKENING ME.
WHAM
THIS LITTLE CREEP'S ACTUALLY HURTING ME.
THUMP
THE FORCE SHIELD'S CUTTING OFF ANY SIGNALS FROM THE WHISPERCOM--NO WORDS OF ADVICE FROM WAYNE--

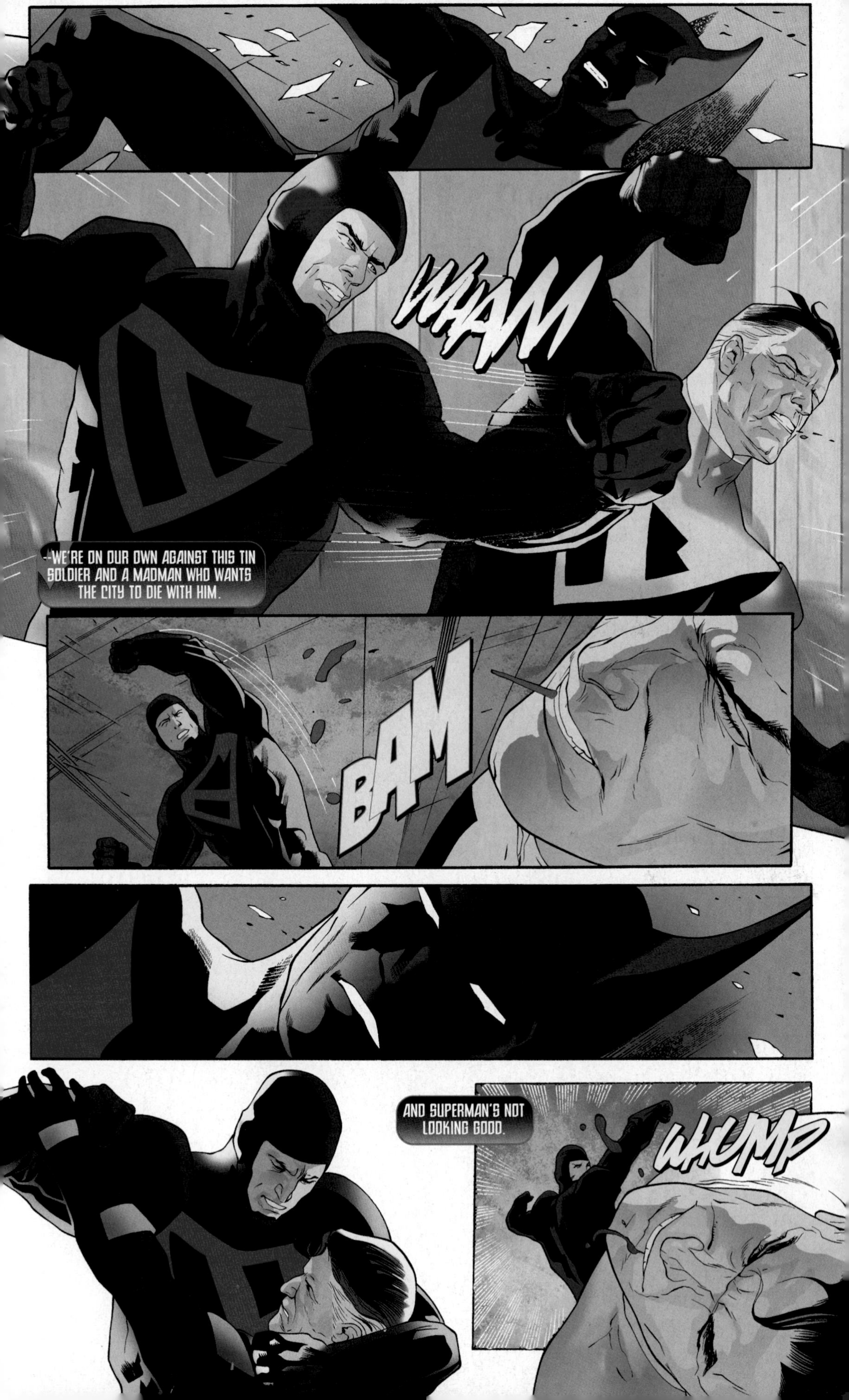

WHAM
--WE'RE ON OUR OWN AGAINST THIS TIN SOLDIER AND A MADMAN WHO WANTS THE CITY TO DIE WITH HIM.
BAM
AND SUPERMAN'S NOT LOOKING GOOD.
WHUMP

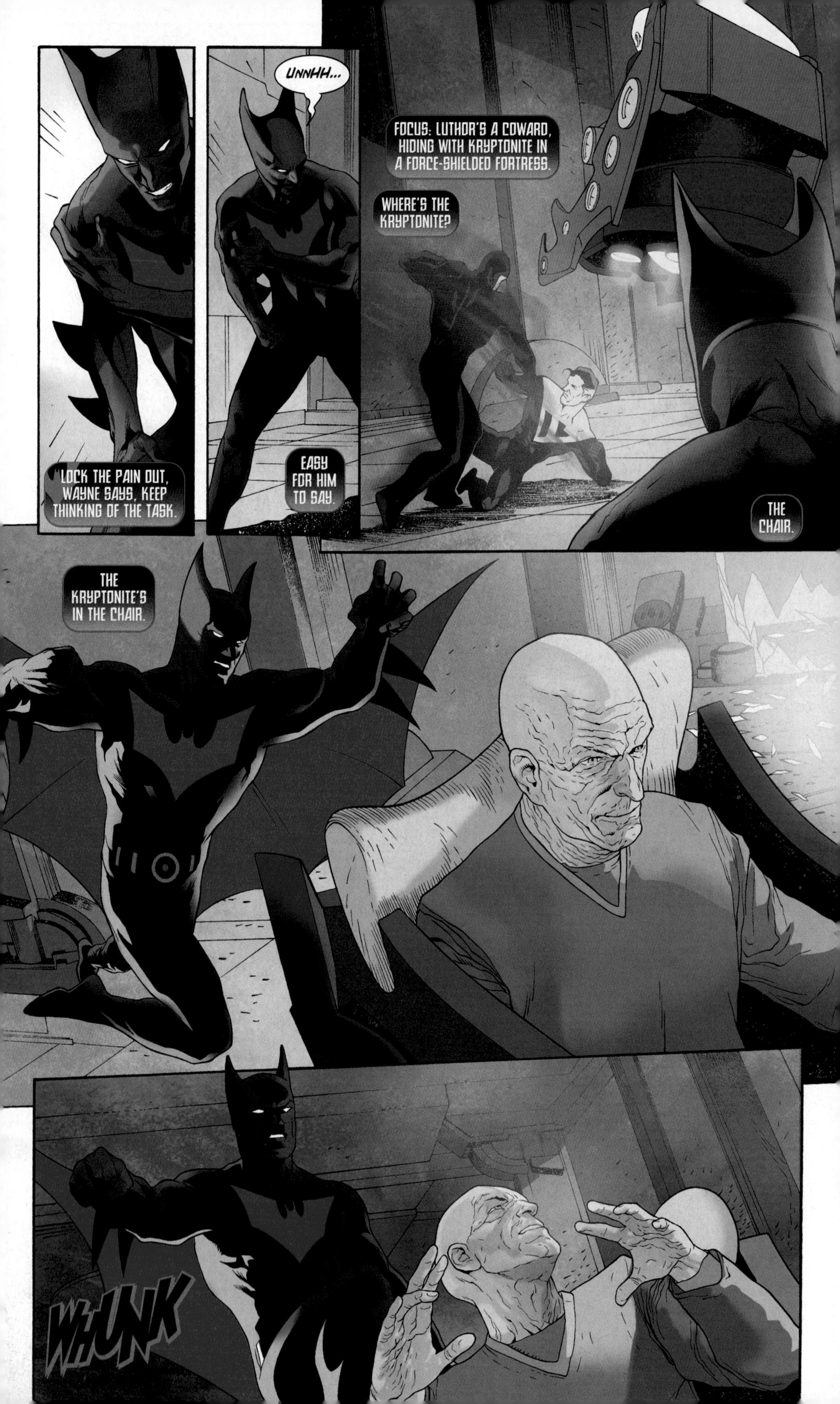
LOCK THE PAIN OUT, WAYNE SAYS, KEEP THINKING OF THE TASK.
UNNHH...
EASY FOR HIM TO SAY.
FOCUS: LUTHOR'S A COWARD, HIDING WITH KRYPTONITE IN A FORCE-SHIELDED FORTRESS.
WHERE'S THE KRYPTONITE?
THE CHAIR.
THE KRYPTONITE'S IN THE CHAIR.
WHUNK

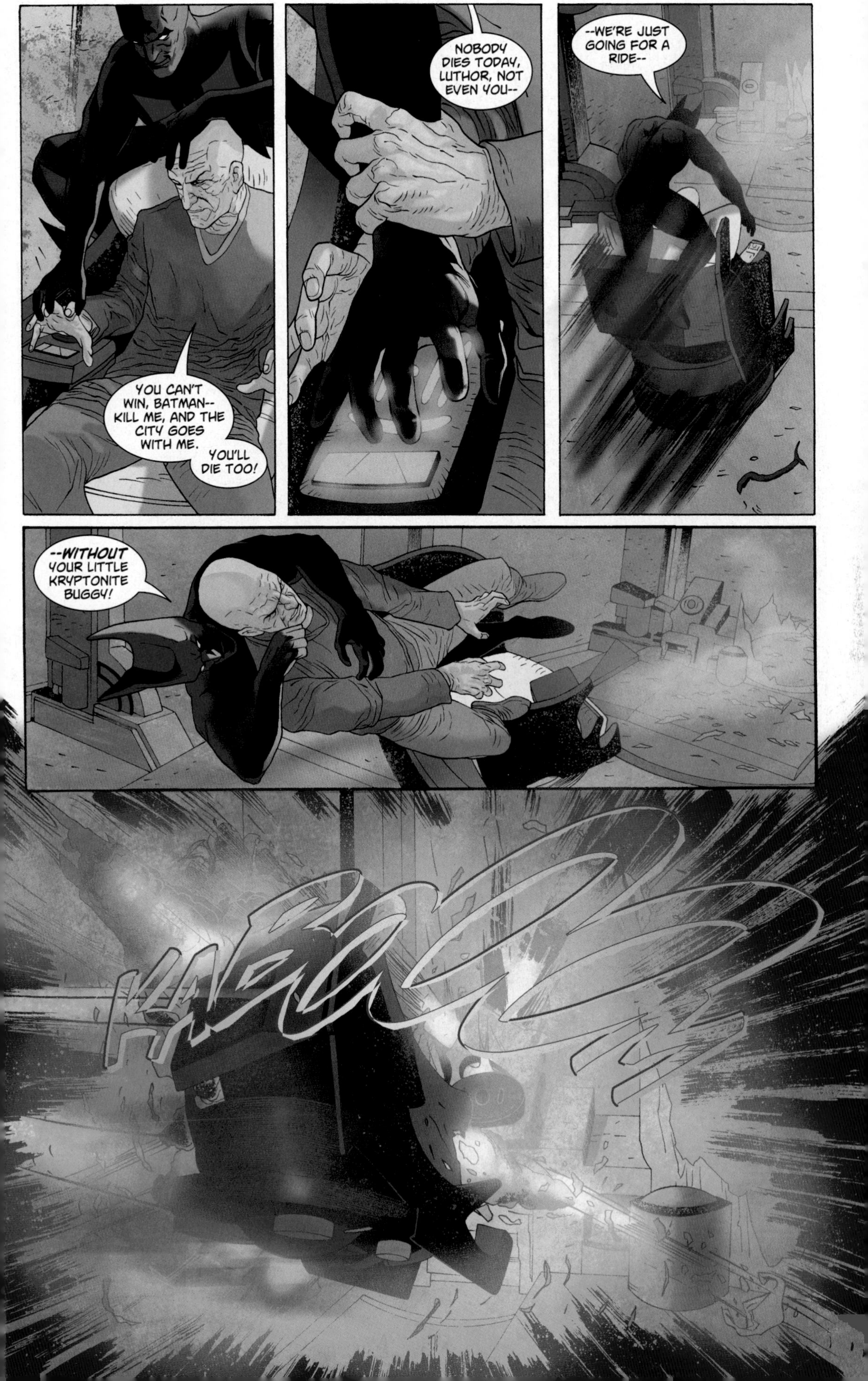
YOU CAN'T WIN, BATMAN-- KILL ME, AND THE CITY GOES WITH ME.
YOU'LL DIE TOO!
NOBODY DIES TODAY, LUTHOR, NOT EVEN YOU--
--WE'RE JUST GOING FOR A RIDE--
--WITHOUT YOUR LITTLE KRYPTONITE BUGGY!

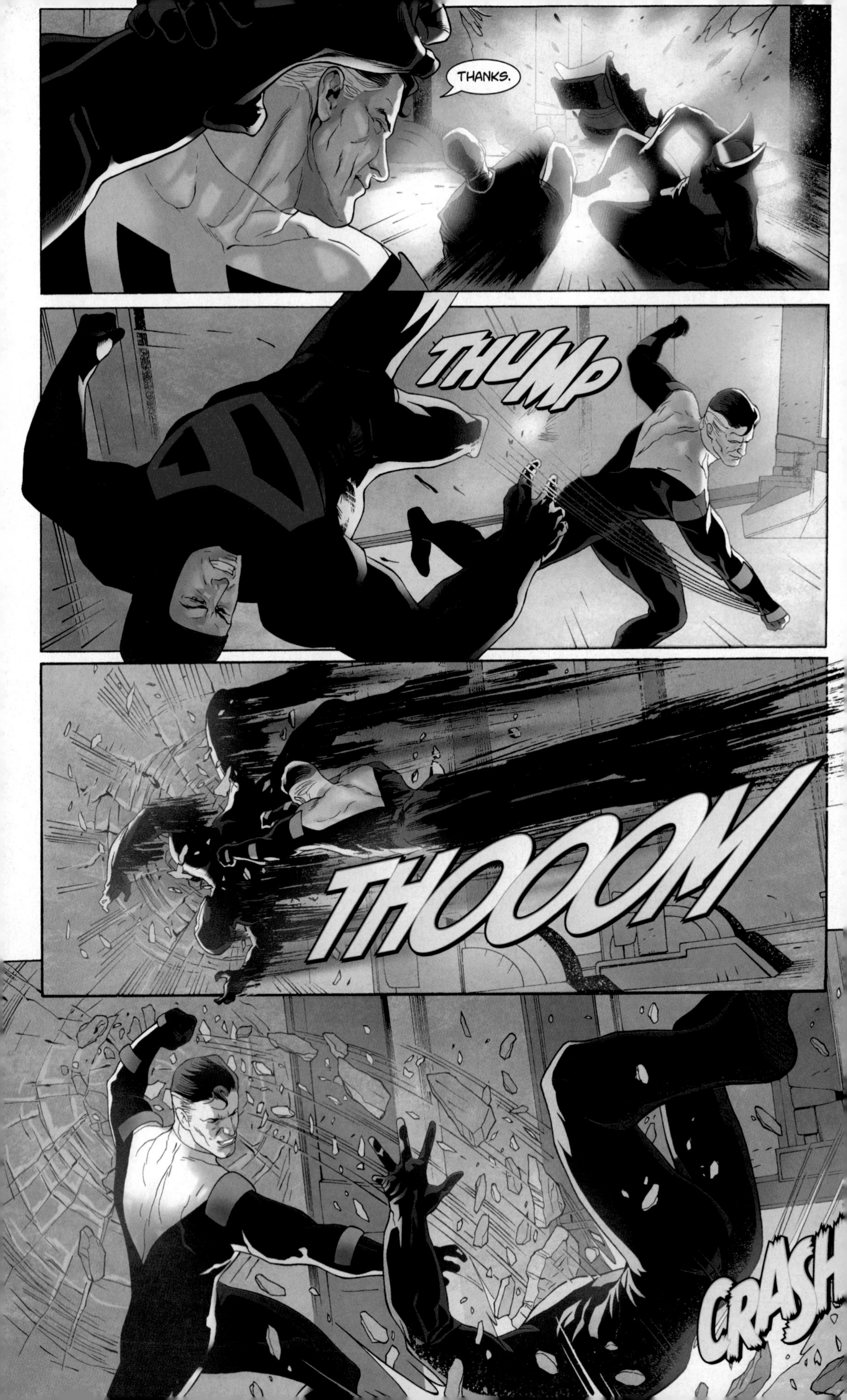
THANKS.
THUMP
THOOOM
CRASH

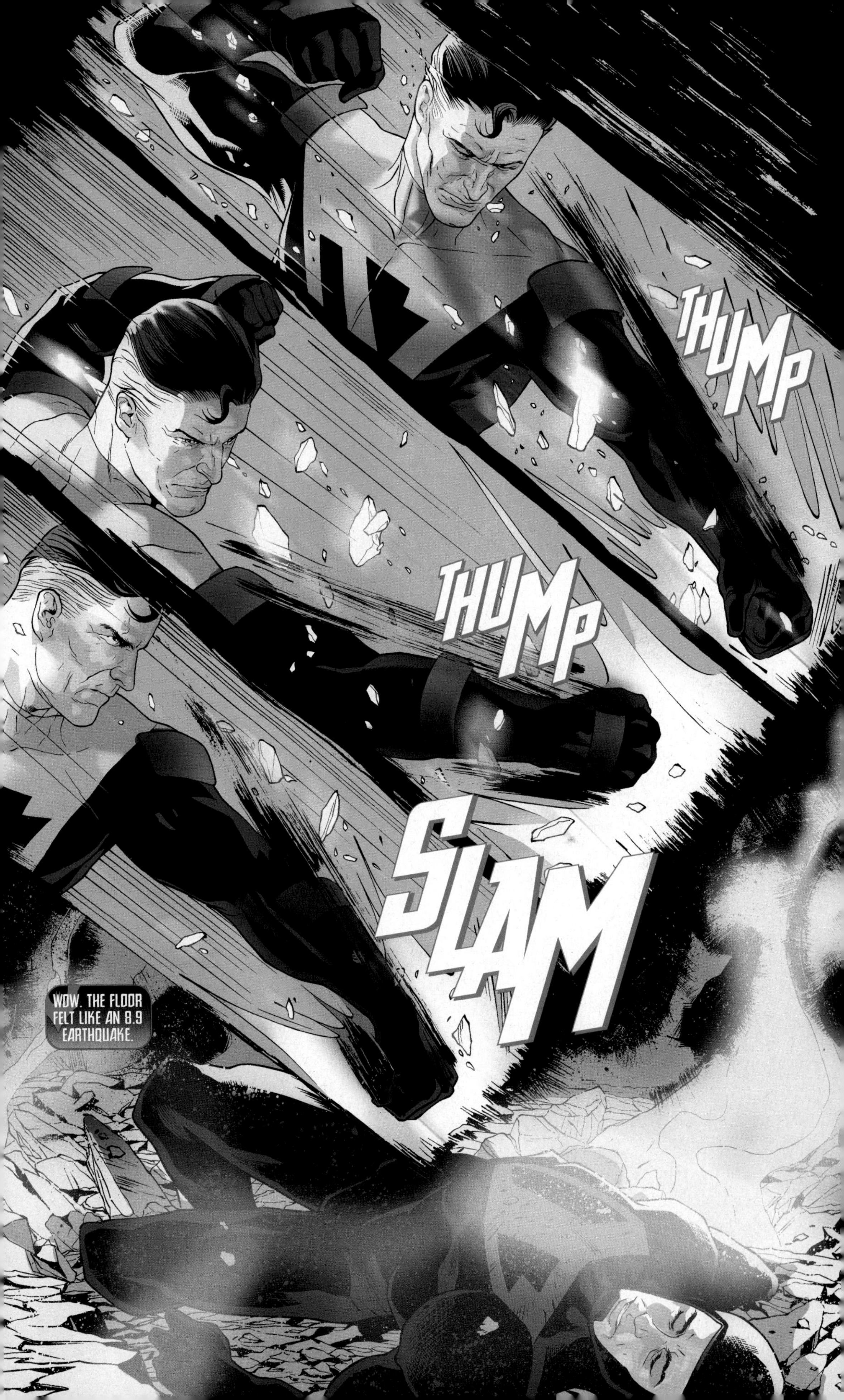
THUMP
THUMP
SLAM
WOW. THE FLOOR FELT LIKE AN 8.9 EARTHQUAKE.

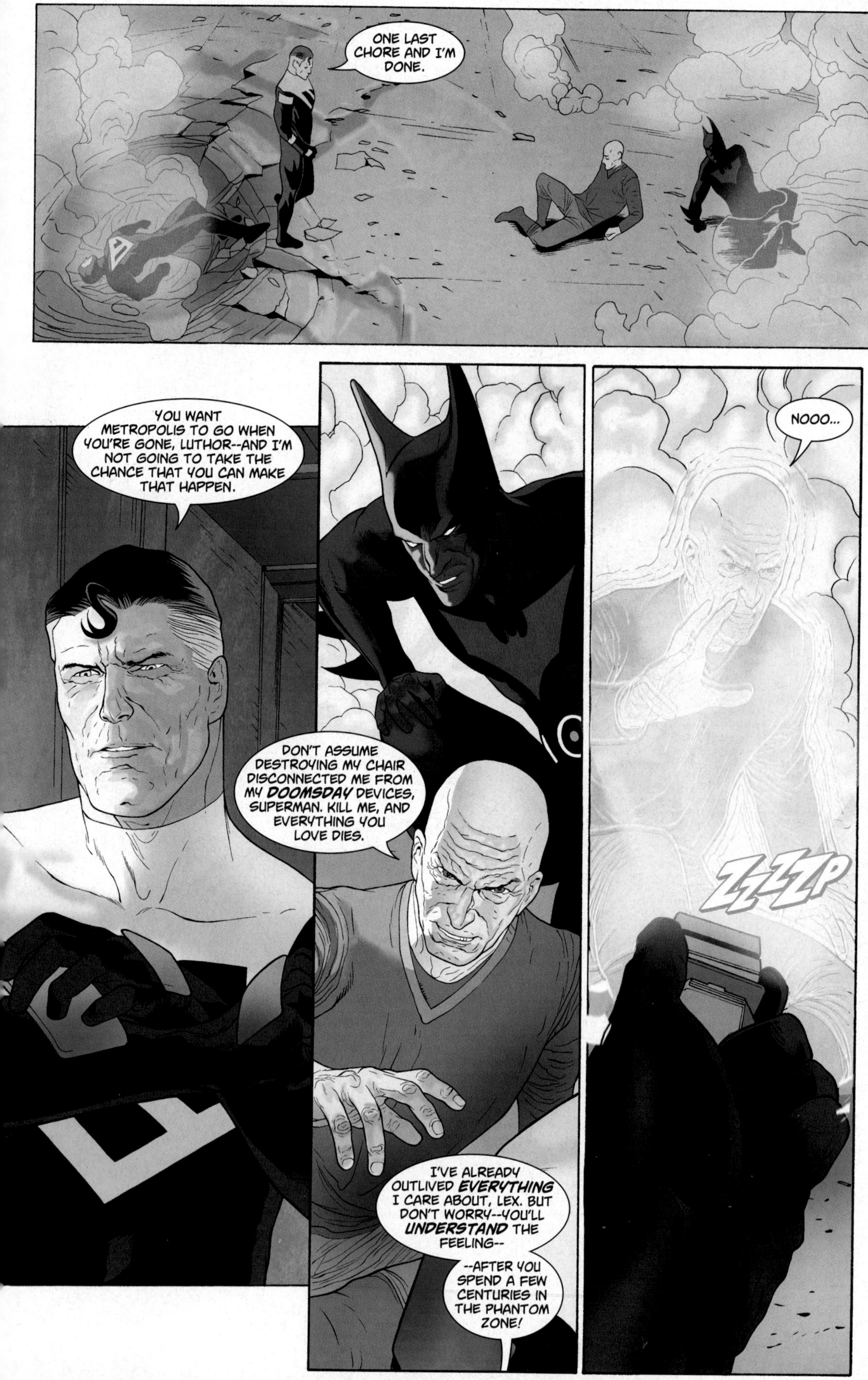
ONE LAST CHORE AND I'M DONE.
YOU WANT METROPOLIS TO GO WHEN YOU'RE GONE, LUTHOR--AND I'M NOT GOING TO TAKE THE CHANCE THAT YOU CAN MAKE THAT HAPPEN.
DON'T ASSUME DESTROYING MY CHAIR DISCONNECTED ME FROM MY DOOMSDAY DEVICES, SUPERMAN. KILL ME, AND EVERYTHING YOU LOVE DIES.
I'VE ALREADY OUTLIVED EVERYTHING I CARE ABOUT, LEX. BUT DON'T WORRY--YOU'LL UNDERSTAND THE FEELING--
--AFTER YOU SPEND A FEW CENTURIES IN THE PHANTOM ZONE!
NOOO...
ZZZZP

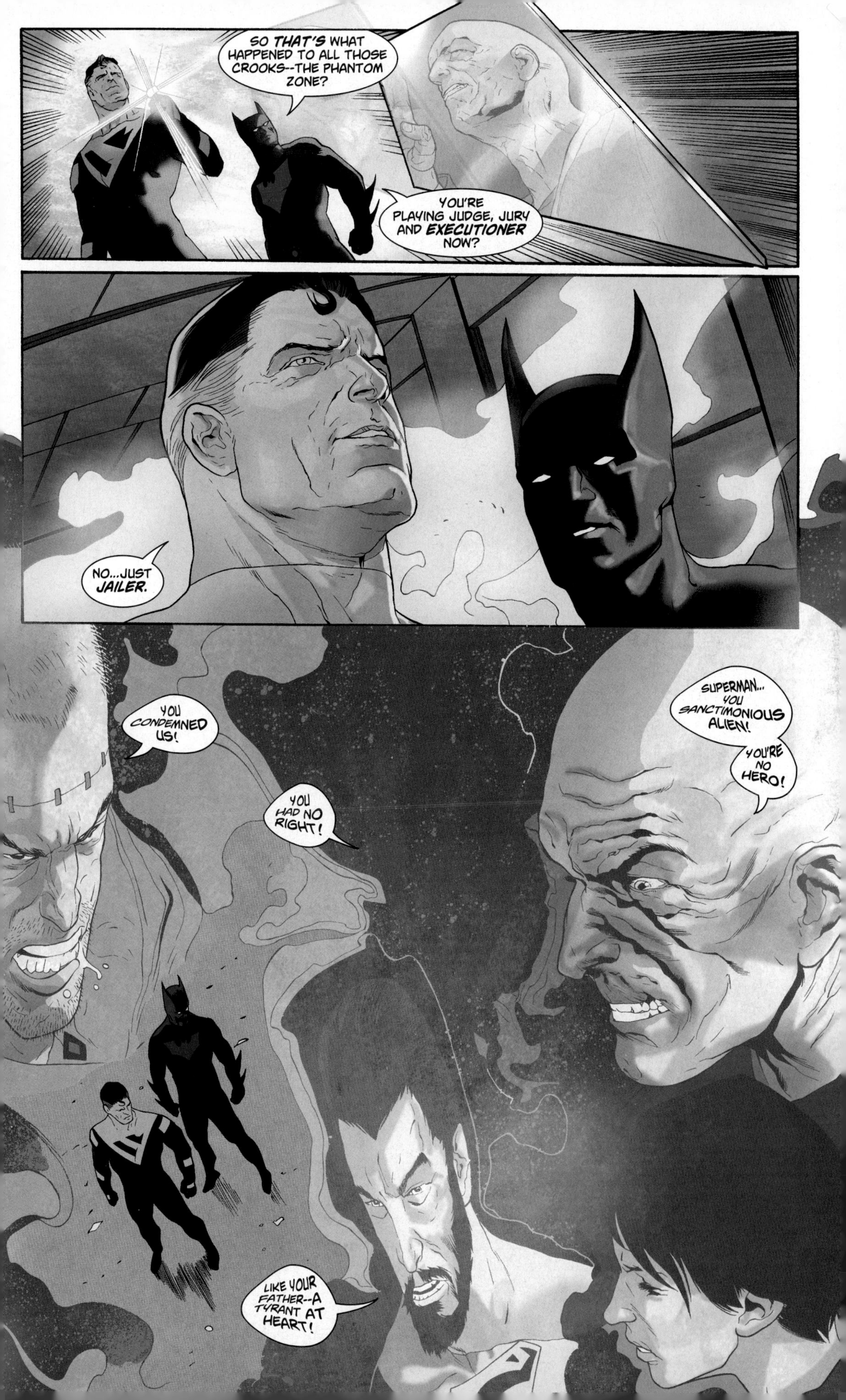
SO THAT'S WHAT HAPPENED TO ALL THOSE CROOKS--THE PHANTOM ZONE?
YOU'RE PLAYING JUDGE, JURY AND EXECUTIONER NOW?
NO...JUST JAILER.
YOU CONDEMNED US!
YOU HAD NO RIGHT!
SUPERMAN... YOU SANCTIMONIOUS ALIEN!
YOU'RE NO HERO!
LIKE YOUR FATHER--A TYRANT AT HEART!

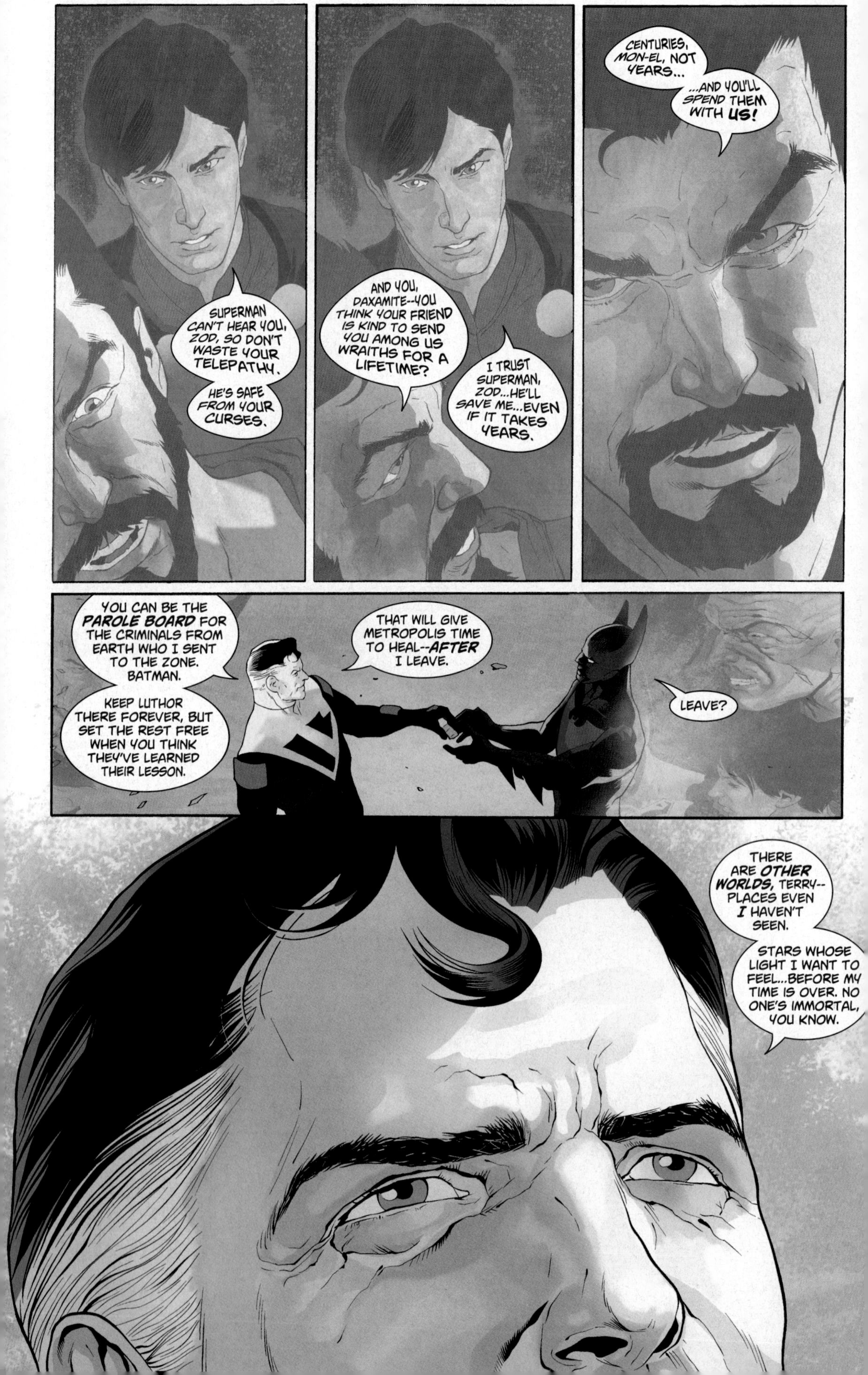
SUPERMAN CAN'T HEAR YOU, ZOD, SO DON'T WASTE YOUR TELEPATHY.
HE'S SAFE FROM YOUR CURSES.
AND YOU, DAXAMITE--YOU THINK YOUR FRIEND IS KIND TO SEND YOU AMONG US WRAITHS FOR A LIFETIME?
I TRUST SUPERMAN, ZOD...HE'LL SAVE ME...EVEN IF IT TAKES YEARS.
CENTURIES, MON-EL, NOT YEARS...
...AND YOU'LL SPEND THEM WITH US!
YOU CAN BE THE PAROLE BOARD FOR THE CRIMINALS FROM EARTH WHO I SENT TO THE ZONE. BATMAN.
KEEP LUTHOR THERE FOREVER, BUT SET THE REST FREE WHEN YOU THINK THEY'VE LEARNED THEIR LESSON.
THAT WILL GIVE METROPOLIS TIME TO HEAL--AFTER I LEAVE.
LEAVE?
THERE ARE OTHER WORLDS, TERRY--PLACES EVEN I HAVEN'T SEEN.
STARS WHOSE LIGHT I WANT TO FEEL...BEFORE MY TIME IS OVER. NO ONE'S IMMORTAL, YOU KNOW.

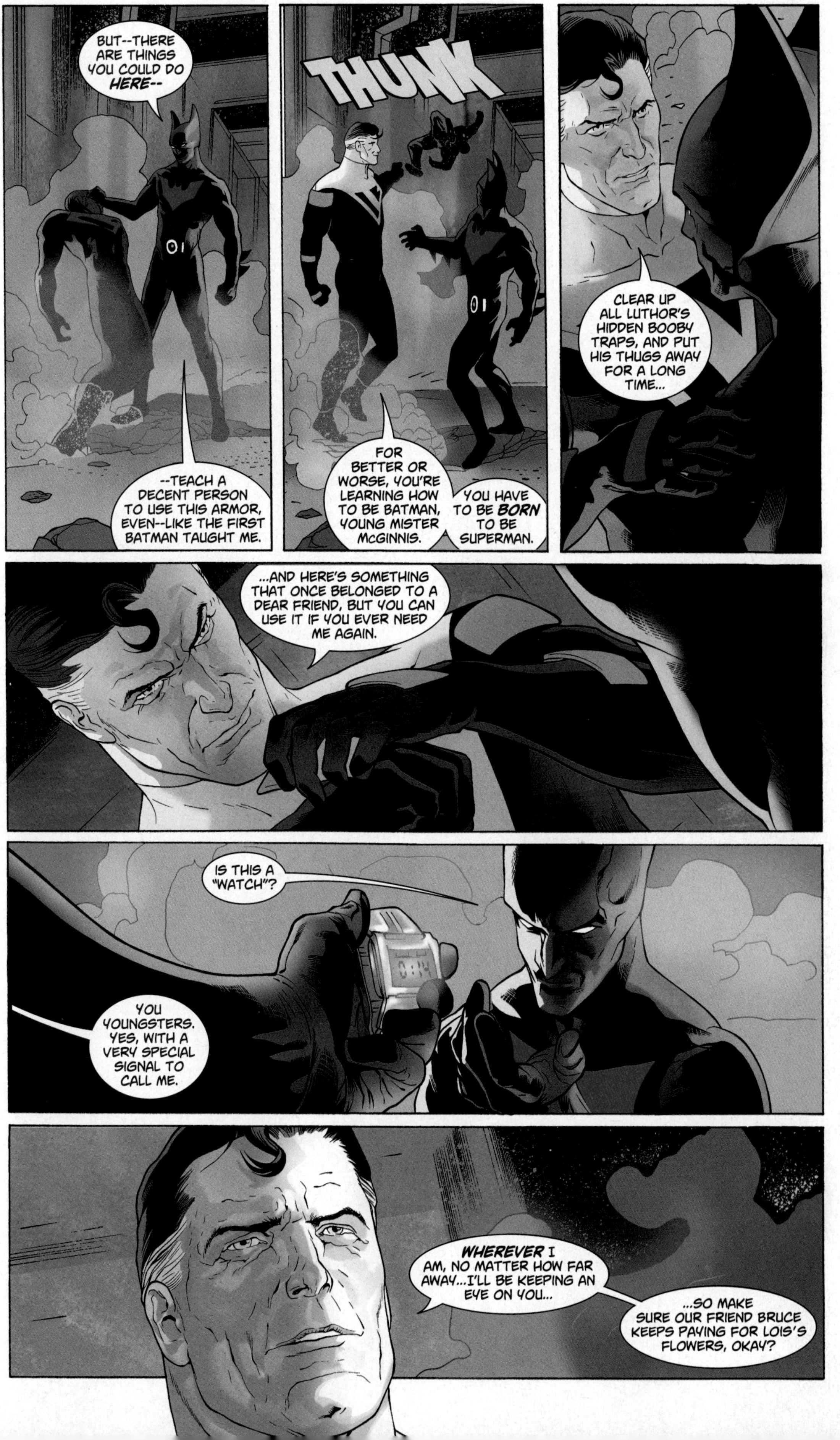

BUT--THERE ARE THINGS YOU COULD DO *HERE*--
--TEACH A DECENT PERSON TO USE THIS ARMOR, EVEN--LIKE THE FIRST BATMAN TAUGHT ME.
THUNK
FOR BETTER OR WORSE, YOU'RE LEARNING HOW TO BE BATMAN, YOUNG MISTER McGINNIS.
YOU HAVE TO BE *BORN* TO BE SUPERMAN.
CLEAR UP ALL LUTHOR'S HIDDEN BOOBY TRAPS, AND PUT HIS THUGS AWAY FOR A LONG TIME...
...AND HERE'S SOMETHING THAT ONCE BELONGED TO A DEAR FRIEND, BUT YOU CAN USE IT IF YOU EVER NEED ME AGAIN.
IS THIS A "WATCH"?
YOU YOUNGSTERS. YES, WITH A VERY SPECIAL SIGNAL TO CALL ME.
WHEREVER I AM, NO MATTER HOW FAR AWAY...I'LL BE KEEPING AN EYE ON YOU...
...SO MAKE SURE OUR FRIEND BRUCE KEEPS PAYING FOR LOIS'S FLOWERS, OKAY?

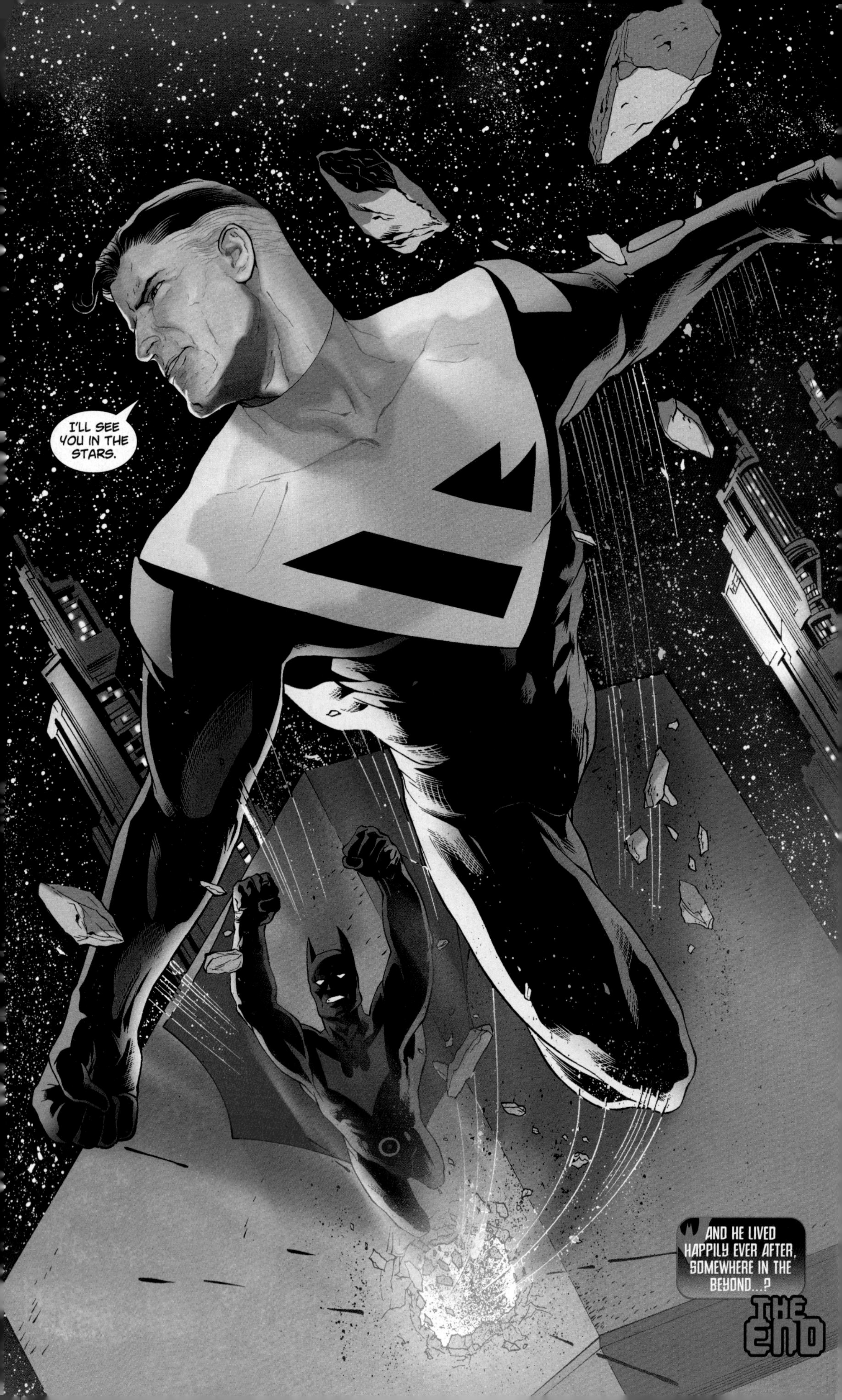
I'LL SEE YOU IN THE STARS.
AND HE LIVED HAPPILY EVER AFTER, SOMEWHERE IN THE BEYOND...?
THE END

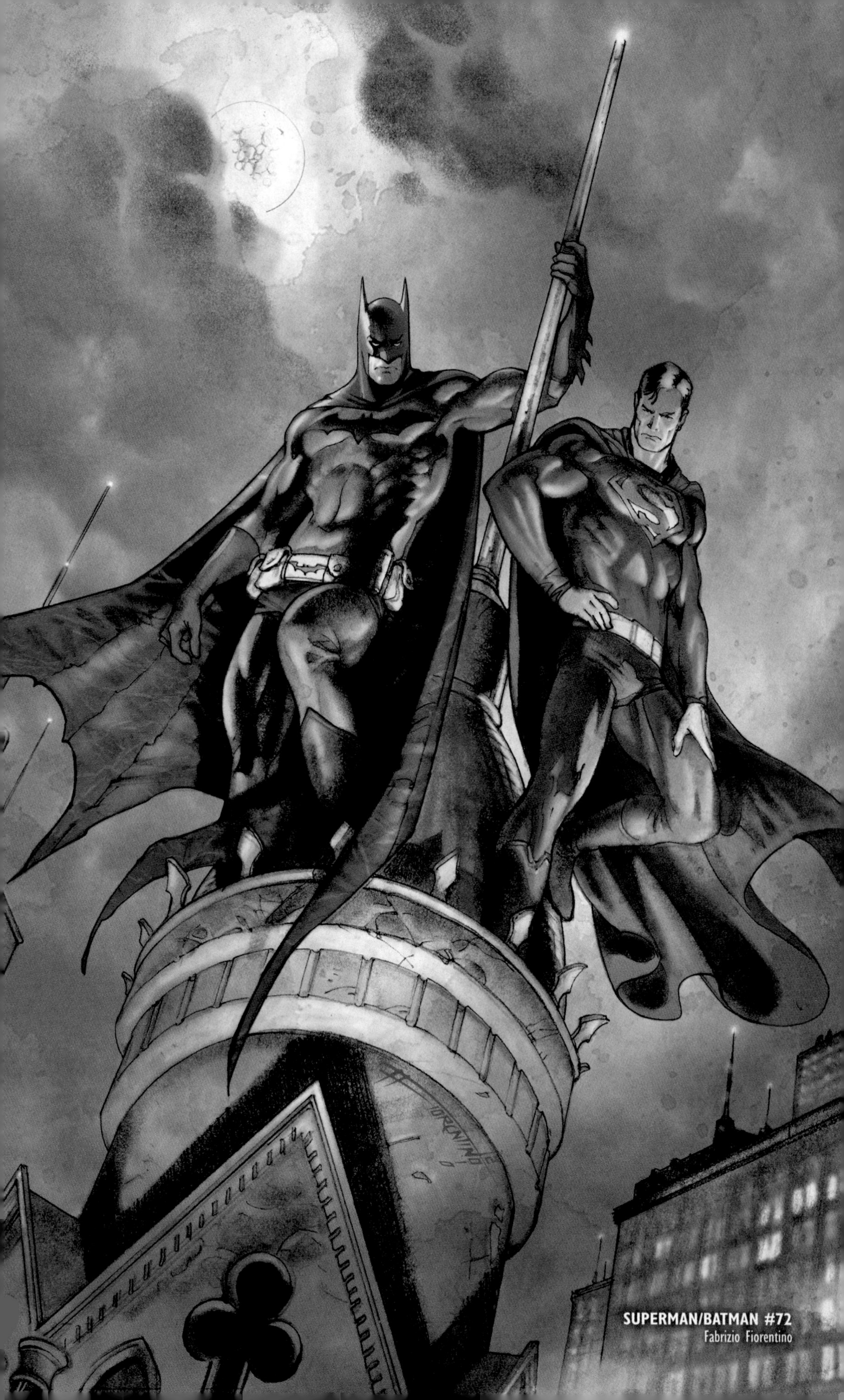

SUPERMAN/BATMAN #72
Fabrizio Fiorentino

WORSHIP

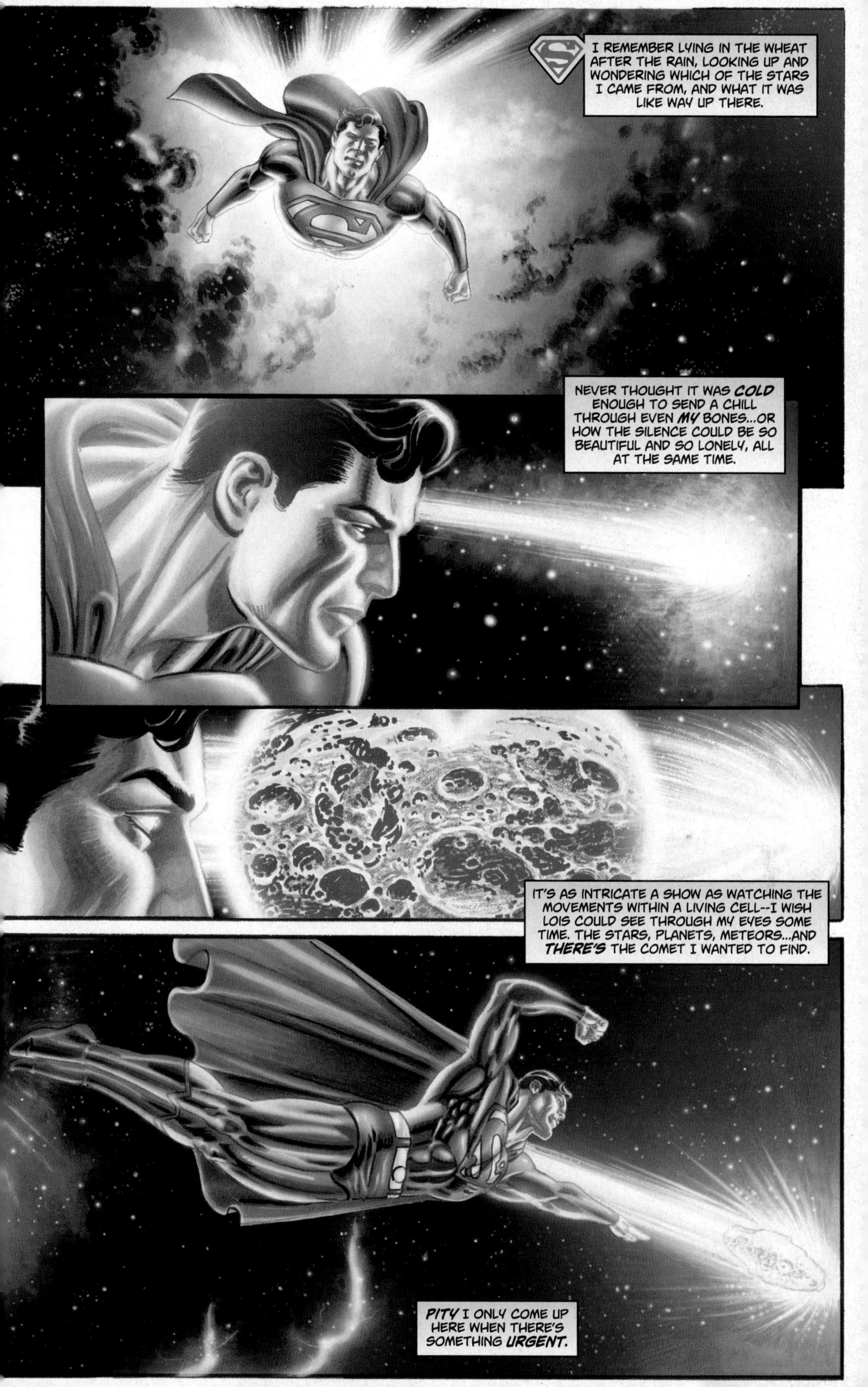
I REMEMBER LYING IN THE WHEAT AFTER THE RAIN, LOOKING UP AND WONDERING WHICH OF THE STARS I CAME FROM, AND WHAT IT WAS LIKE WAY UP THERE.
NEVER THOUGHT IT WAS *COLD* ENOUGH TO SEND A CHILL THROUGH EVEN *MY* BONES...OR HOW THE SILENCE COULD BE SO BEAUTIFUL AND SO LONELY, ALL AT THE SAME TIME.
IT'S AS INTRICATE A SHOW AS WATCHING THE MOVEMENTS WITHIN A LIVING CELL--I WISH LOIS COULD SEE THROUGH MY EYES SOME TIME. THE STARS, PLANETS, METEORS...AND *THERE'S* THE COMET I WANTED TO FIND.
PITY I ONLY COME UP HERE WHEN THERE'S SOMETHING *URGENT*.

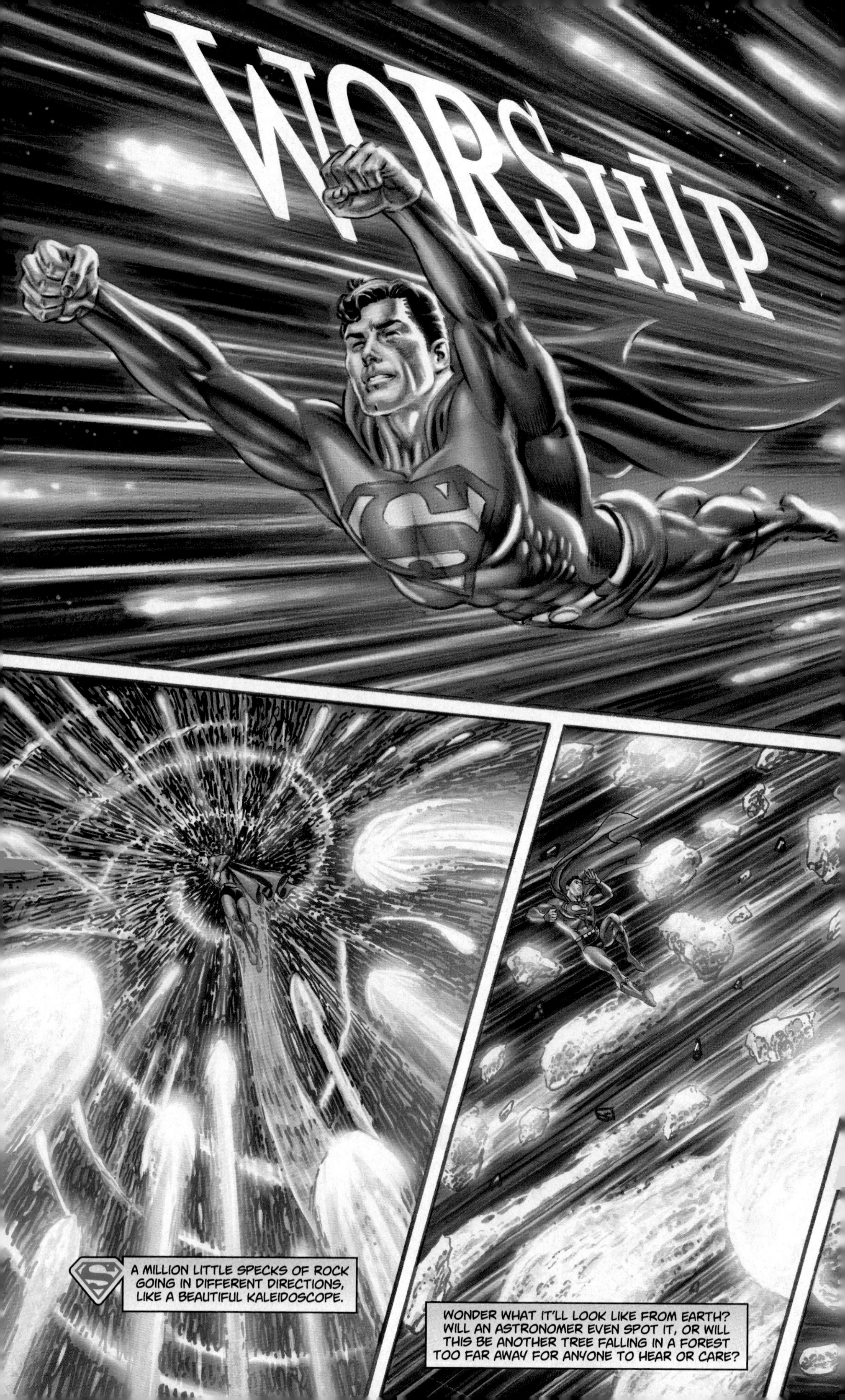
WORSHIP
A MILLION LITTLE SPECKS OF ROCK GOING IN DIFFERENT DIRECTIONS, LIKE A BEAUTIFUL KALEIDOSCOPE.
WONDER WHAT IT'LL LOOK LIKE FROM EARTH? WILL AN ASTRONOMER EVEN SPOT IT, OR WILL THIS BE ANOTHER TREE FALLING IN A FOREST TOO FAR AWAY FOR ANYONE TO HEAR OR CARE?

Paul Levitz Writer Jerry Ordway Artist

Steve Wands Letterer Pete Pantazis Colorist Fabrizio Fiorentino Cover Rex Ogle Assistant Editor Eddie Berganza Editor

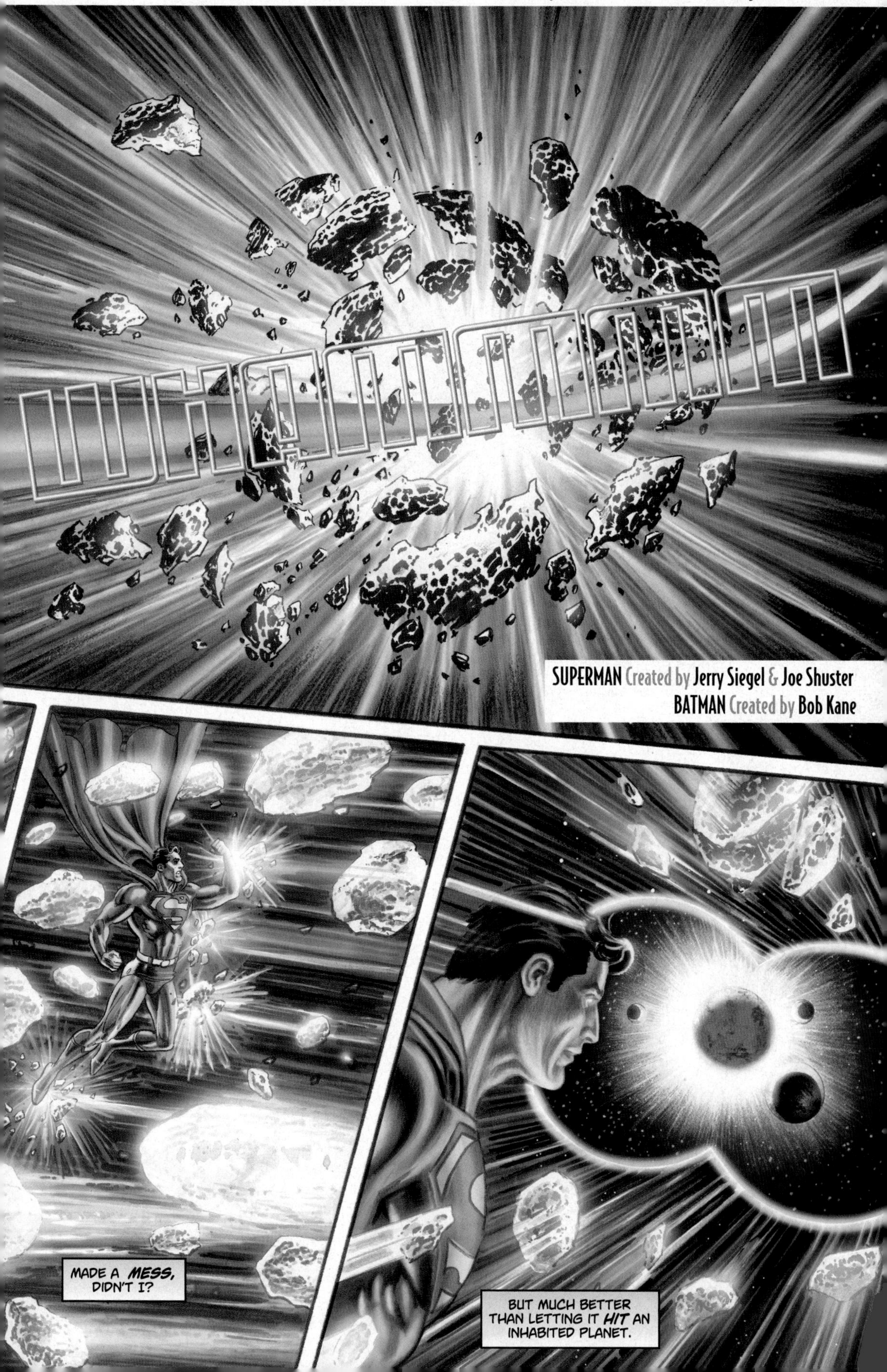
SUPERMAN Created by Jerry Siegel & Joe Shuster
BATMAN Created by Bob Kane
MADE A MESS, DIDN'T I?
BUT MUCH BETTER THAN LETTING IT HIT AN INHABITED PLANET.

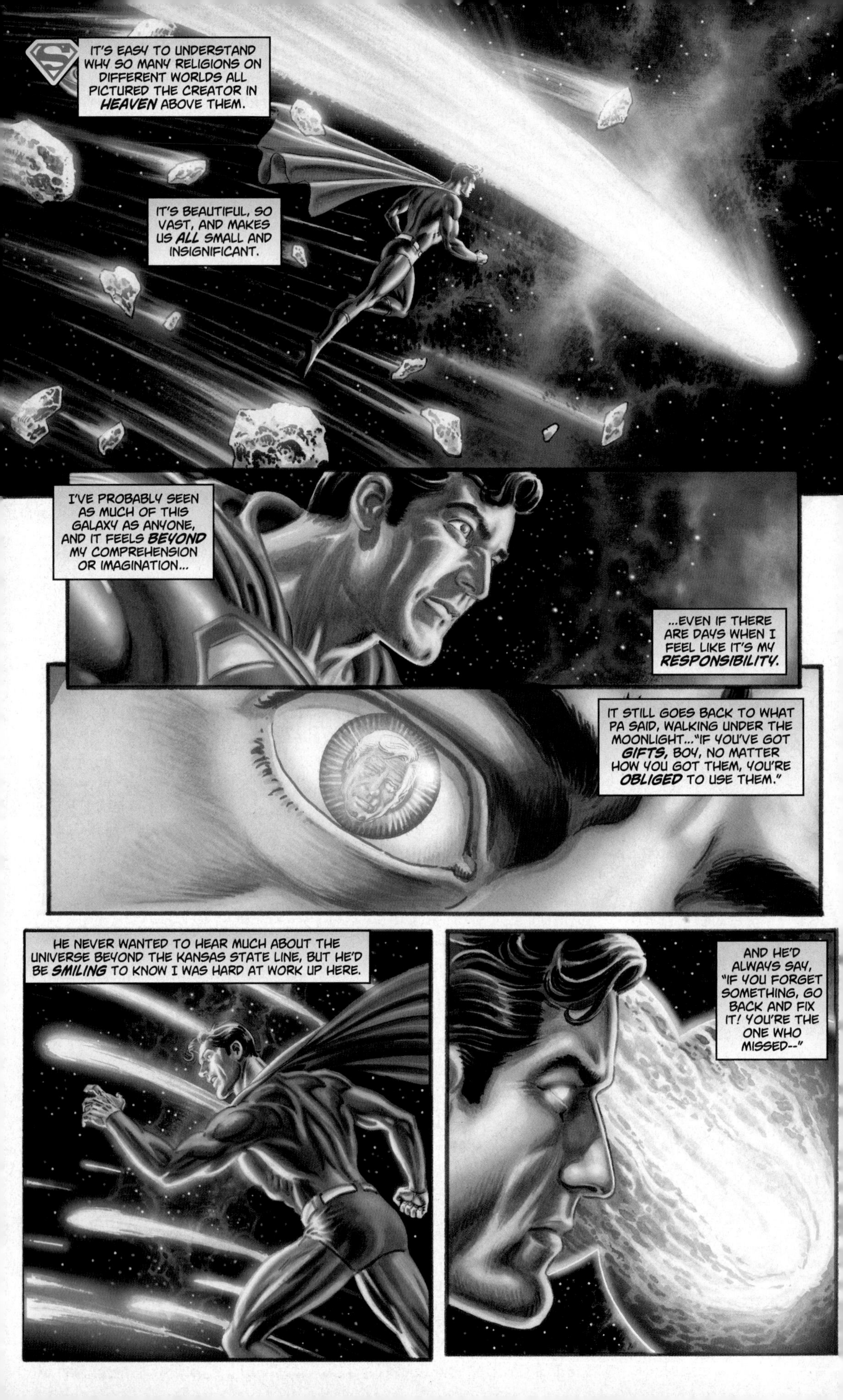
IT'S EASY TO UNDERSTAND WHY SO MANY RELIGIONS ON DIFFERENT WORLDS ALL PICTURED THE CREATOR IN HEAVEN ABOVE THEM.
IT'S BEAUTIFUL, SO VAST, AND MAKES US ALL SMALL AND INSIGNIFICANT.
I'VE PROBABLY SEEN AS MUCH OF THIS GALAXY AS ANYONE, AND IT FEELS BEYOND MY COMPREHENSION OR IMAGINATION...
...EVEN IF THERE ARE DAYS WHEN I FEEL LIKE IT'S MY RESPONSIBILITY.
IT STILL GOES BACK TO WHAT PA SAID, WALKING UNDER THE MOONLIGHT..."IF YOU'VE GOT GIFTS, BOY, NO MATTER HOW YOU GOT THEM, YOU'RE OBLIGED TO USE THEM."
HE NEVER WANTED TO HEAR MUCH ABOUT THE UNIVERSE BEYOND THE KANSAS STATE LINE, BUT HE'D BE SMILING TO KNOW I WAS HARD AT WORK UP HERE.
AND HE'D ALWAYS SAY, "IF YOU FORGET SOMETHING, GO BACK AND FIX IT! YOU'RE THE ONE WHO MISSED--"

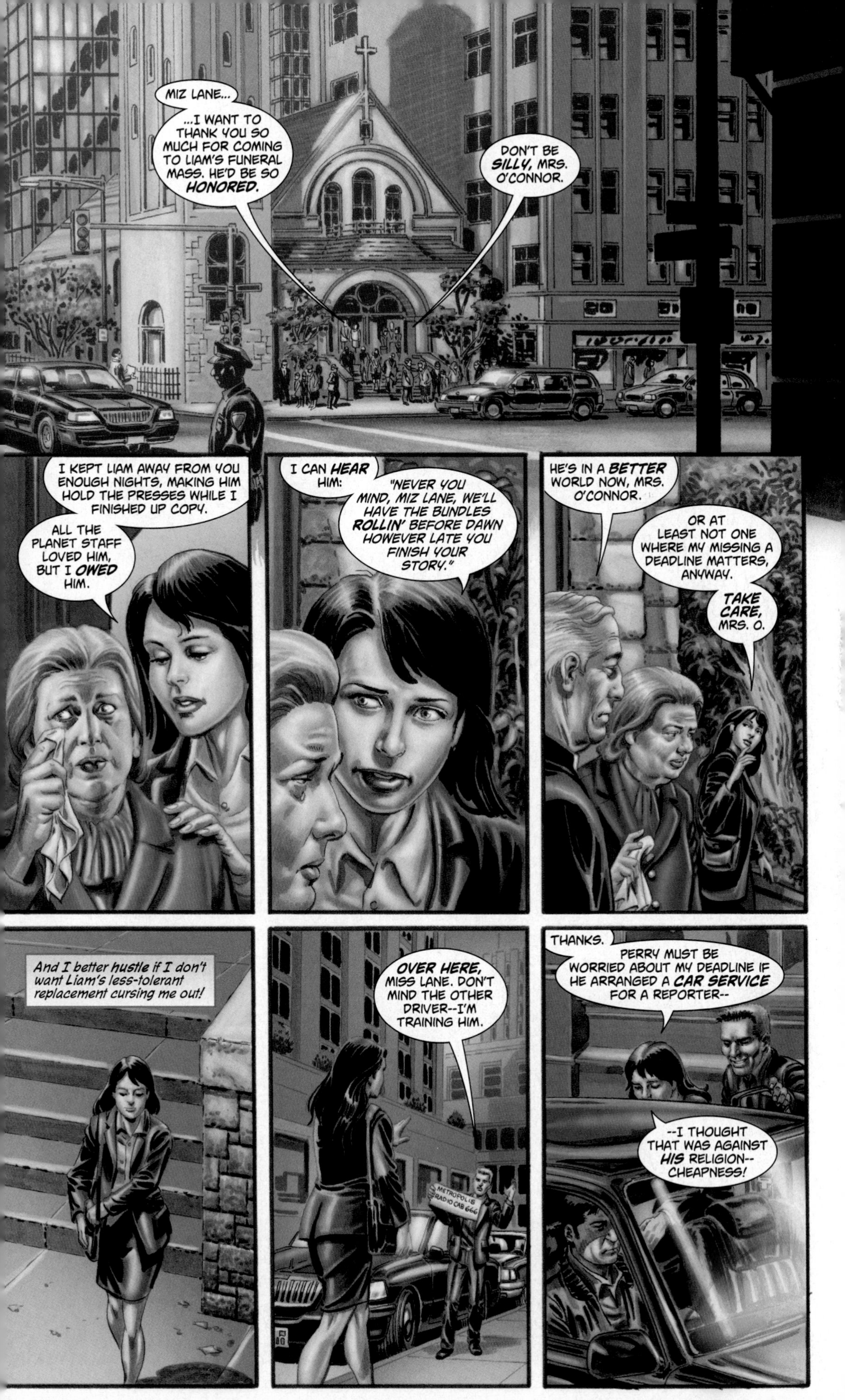
MIZ LANE...
...I WANT TO THANK YOU SO MUCH FOR COMING TO LIAM'S FUNERAL MASS. HE'D BE SO HONORED.
DON'T BE SILLY, MRS. O'CONNOR.
I KEPT LIAM AWAY FROM YOU ENOUGH NIGHTS, MAKING HIM HOLD THE PRESSES WHILE I FINISHED UP COPY.
ALL THE PLANET STAFF LOVED HIM, BUT I OWED HIM.
I CAN HEAR HIM:
"NEVER YOU MIND, MIZ LANE, WE'LL HAVE THE BUNDLES ROLLIN' BEFORE DAWN HOWEVER LATE YOU FINISH YOUR STORY."
HE'S IN A BETTER WORLD NOW, MRS. O'CONNOR.
OR AT LEAST NOT ONE WHERE MY MISSING A DEADLINE MATTERS, ANYWAY.
TAKE CARE, MRS. O.
And I better hustle if I don't want Liam's less-tolerant replacement cursing me out!
OVER HERE, MISS LANE. DON'T MIND THE OTHER DRIVER--I'M TRAINING HIM.
METROPOLIS RADIO CAB 666
THANKS.
PERRY MUST BE WORRIED ABOUT MY DEADLINE IF HE ARRANGED A CAR SERVICE FOR A REPORTER--
--I THOUGHT THAT WAS AGAINST HIS RELIGION--CHEAPNESS!

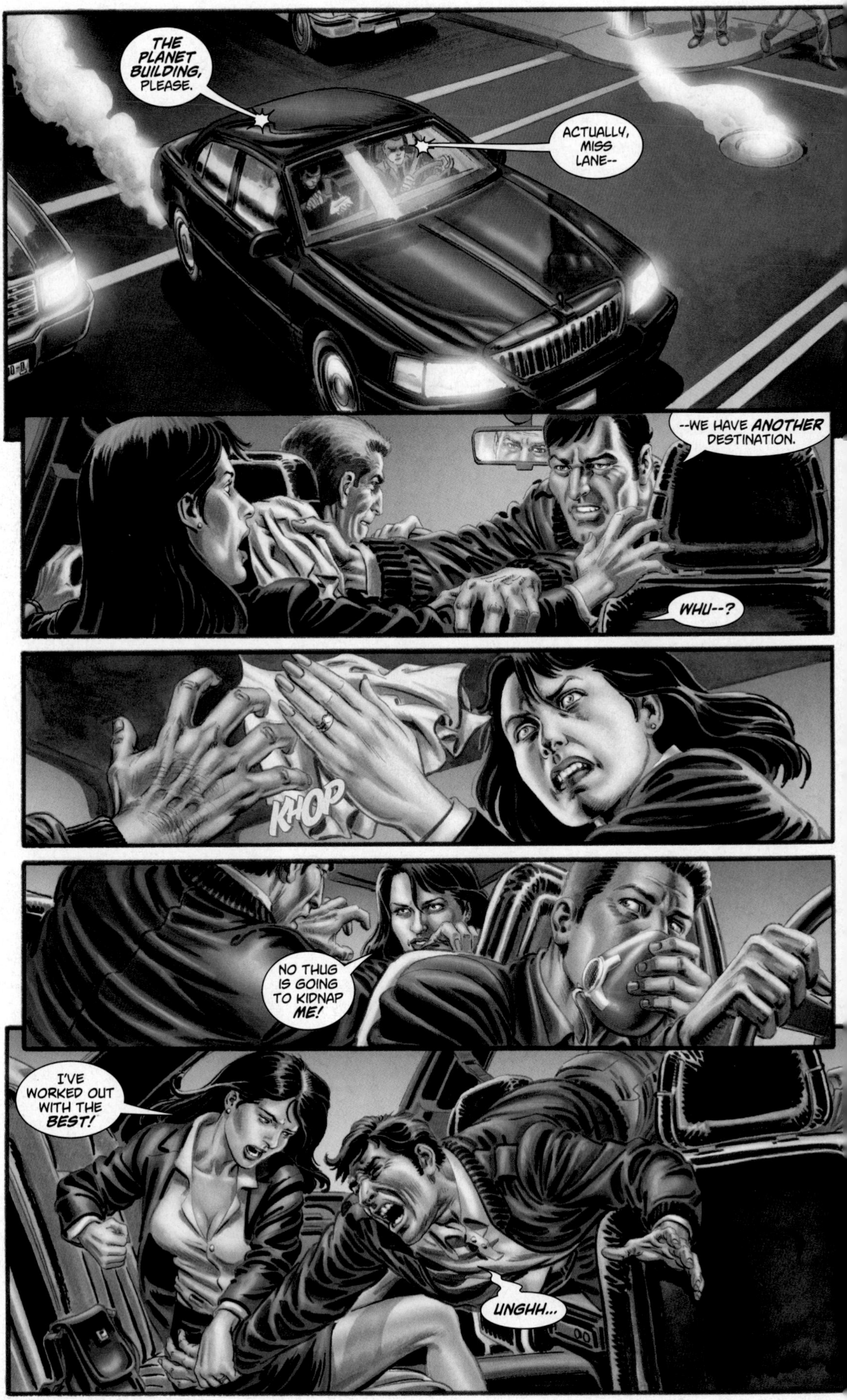

THE PLANET BUILDING, PLEASE.
ACTUALLY, MISS LANE--
--WE HAVE ANOTHER DESTINATION.
WHU--?
KHOP
NO THUG IS GOING TO KIDNAP ME!
I'VE WORKED OUT WITH THE BEST!
UNGHH...

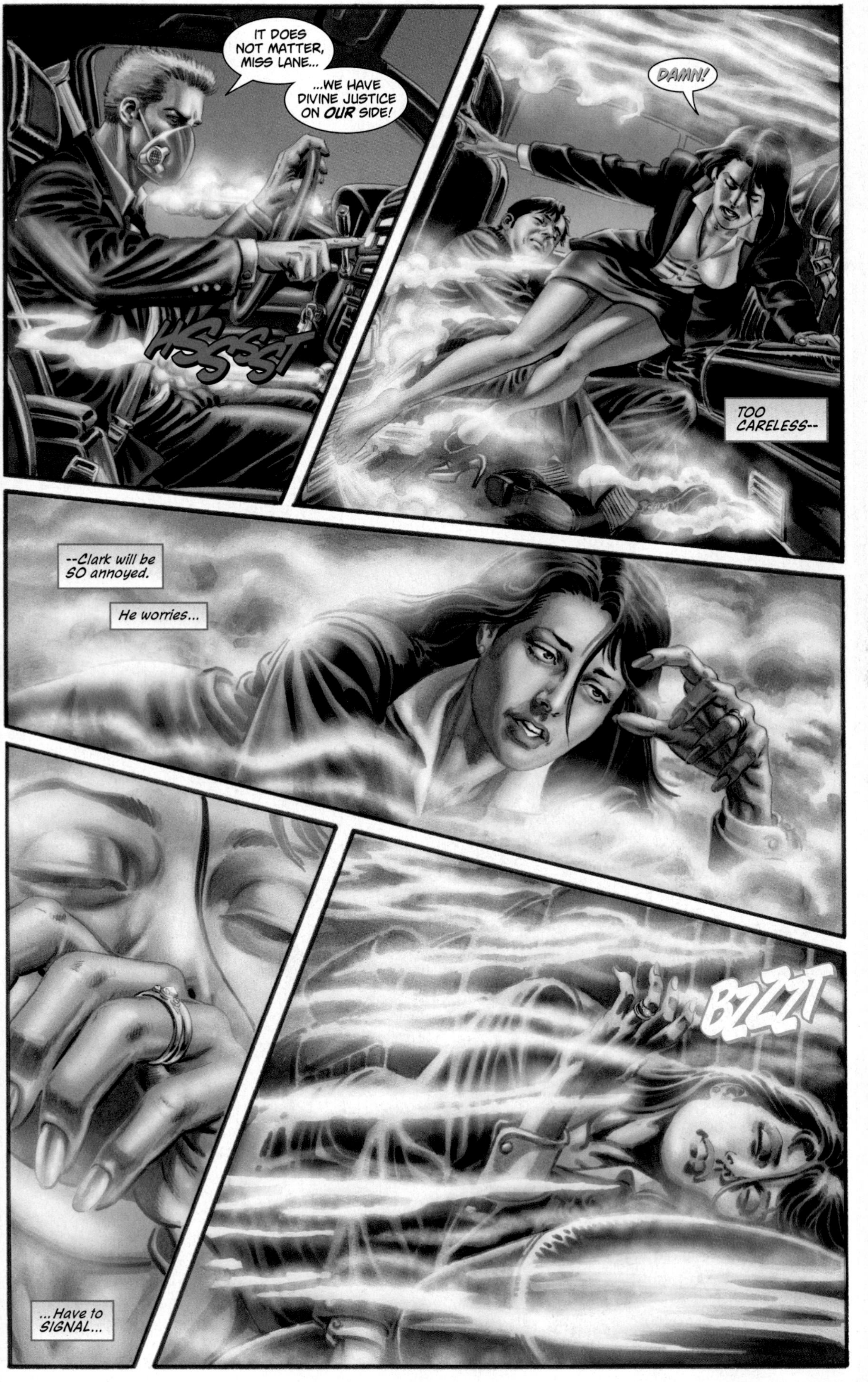
IT DOES NOT MATTER, MISS LANE...
...WE HAVE DIVINE JUSTICE ON OUR SIDE!
HSSSST
DAMN!
TOO CARELESS--
--Clark will be SO annoyed.
He worries...
...Have to SIGNAL...
BZZZT

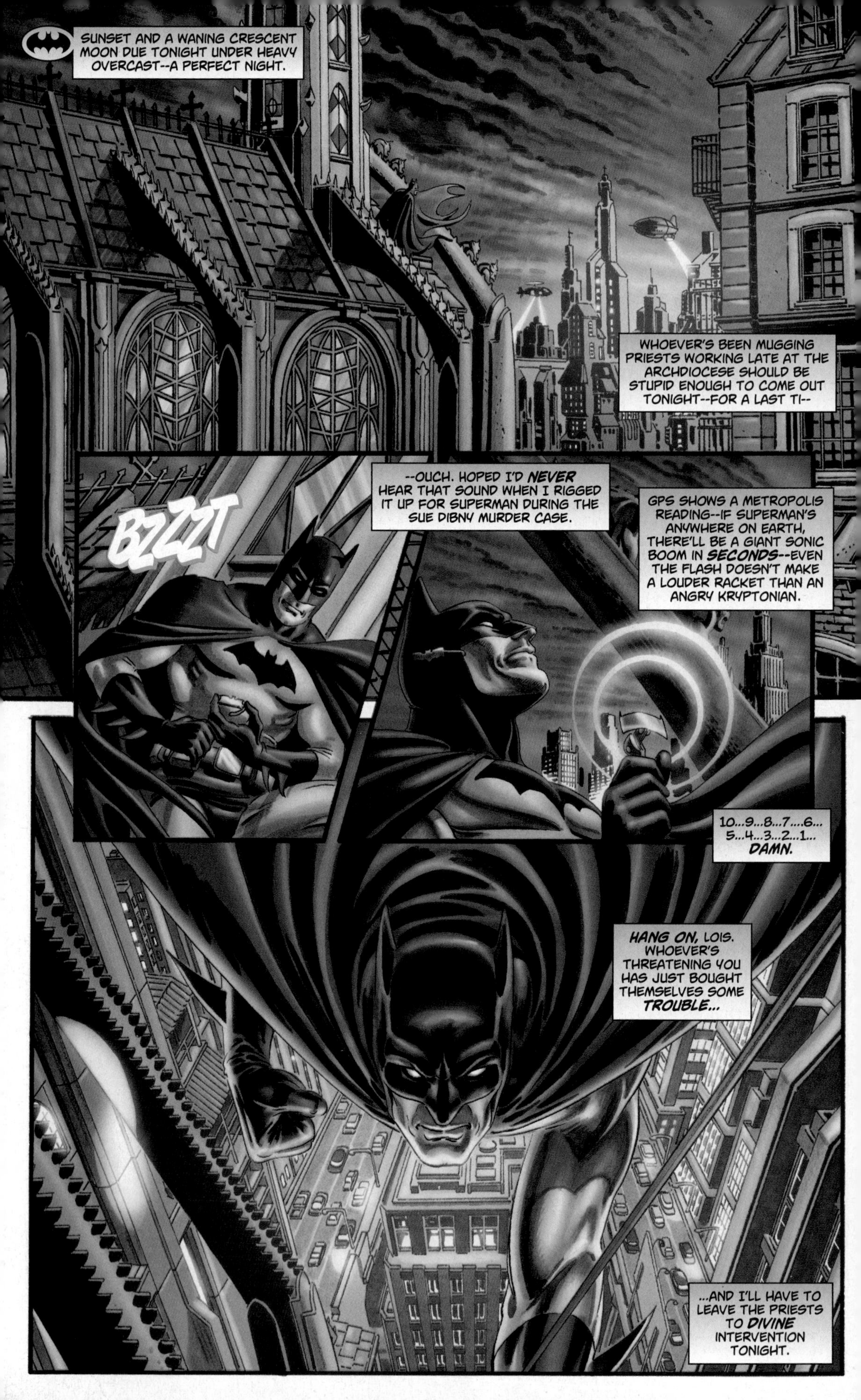
SUNSET AND A WANING CRESCENT MOON DUE TONIGHT UNDER HEAVY OVERCAST--A PERFECT NIGHT.
WHOEVER'S BEEN MUGGING PRIESTS WORKING LATE AT THE ARCHDIOCESE SHOULD BE STUPID ENOUGH TO COME OUT TONIGHT--FOR A LAST TI--
BZZZT
--OUCH. HOPED I'D NEVER HEAR THAT SOUND WHEN I RIGGED IT UP FOR SUPERMAN DURING THE SUE DIBNY MURDER CASE.
GPS SHOWS A METROPOLIS READING--IF SUPERMAN'S ANYWHERE ON EARTH, THERE'LL BE A GIANT SONIC BOOM IN SECONDS--EVEN THE FLASH DOESN'T MAKE A LOUDER RACKET THAN AN ANGRY KRYPTONIAN.
10...9...8...7....6... 5...4...3...2...1... DAMN.
HANG ON, LOIS. WHOEVER'S THREATENING YOU HAS JUST BOUGHT THEMSELVES SOME TROUBLE...
...AND I'LL HAVE TO LEAVE THE PRIESTS TO DIVINE INTERVENTION TONIGHT.

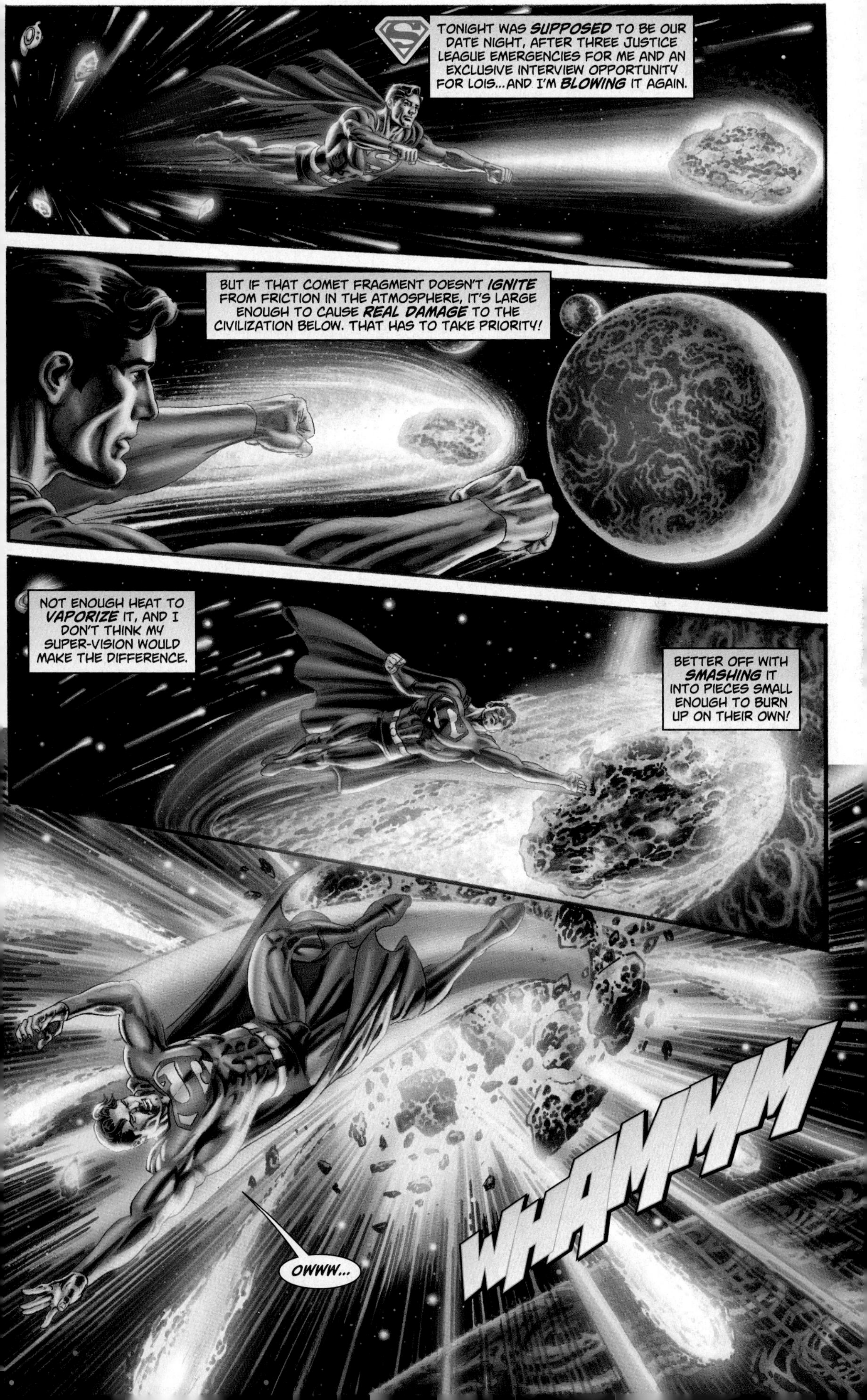

TONIGHT WAS SUPPOSED TO BE OUR DATE NIGHT, AFTER THREE JUSTICE LEAGUE EMERGENCIES FOR ME AND AN EXCLUSIVE INTERVIEW OPPORTUNITY FOR LOIS...AND I'M BLOWING IT AGAIN.
BUT IF THAT COMET FRAGMENT DOESN'T IGNITE FROM FRICTION IN THE ATMOSPHERE, IT'S LARGE ENOUGH TO CAUSE REAL DAMAGE TO THE CIVILIZATION BELOW. THAT HAS TO TAKE PRIORITY!
NOT ENOUGH HEAT TO VAPORIZE IT, AND I DON'T THINK MY SUPER-VISION WOULD MAKE THE DIFFERENCE.
BETTER OFF WITH SMASHING IT INTO PIECES SMALL ENOUGH TO BURN UP ON THEIR OWN!
WHAMMMM
OWWW...

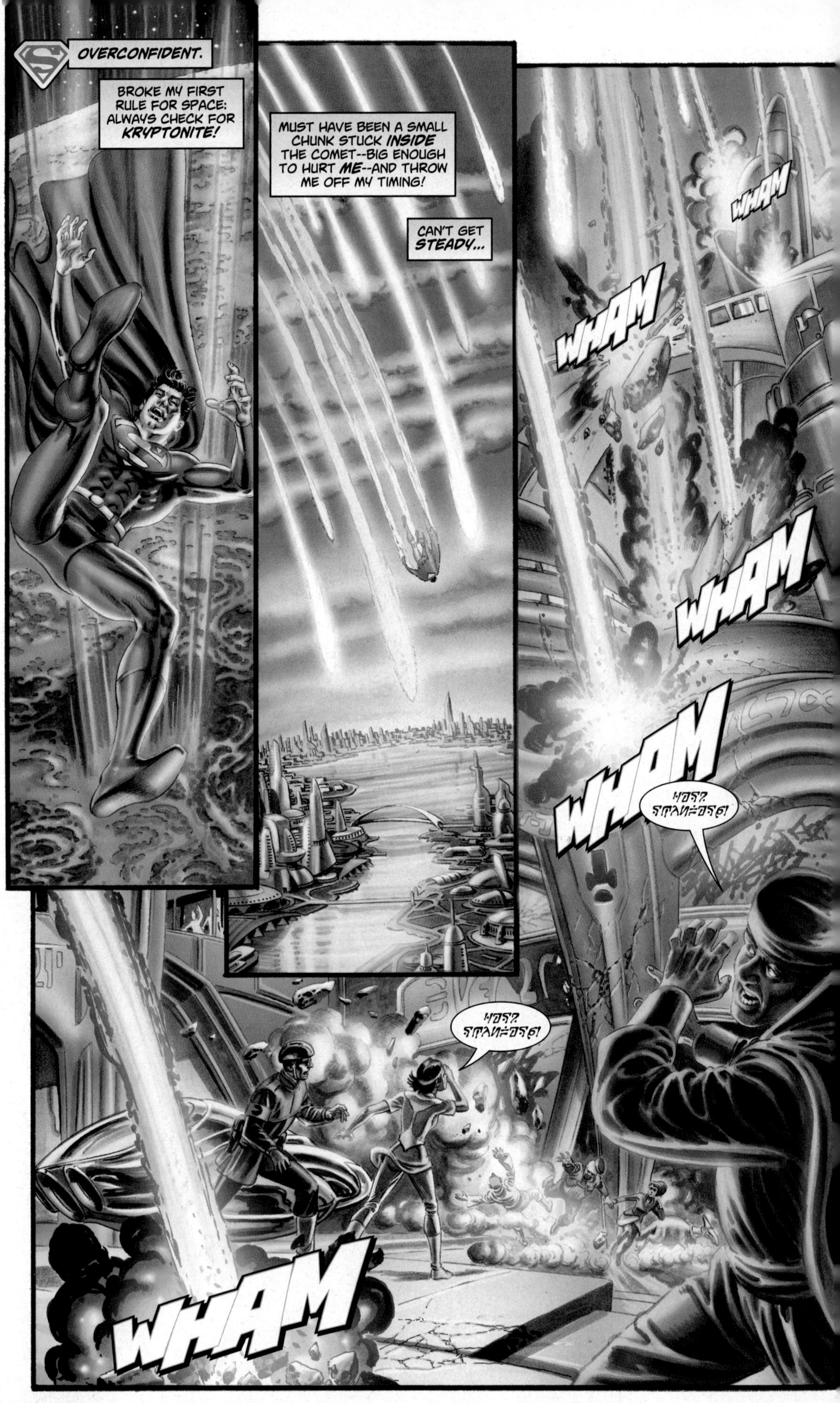
OVERCONFIDENT.
BROKE MY FIRST RULE FOR SPACE: ALWAYS CHECK FOR KRYPTONITE!
MUST HAVE BEEN A SMALL CHUNK STUCK INSIDE THE COMET--BIG ENOUGH TO HURT ME--AND THROW ME OFF MY TIMING!
CAN'T GET STEADY...
WHAM
WHAM
WHAM
WHAM
WHAM

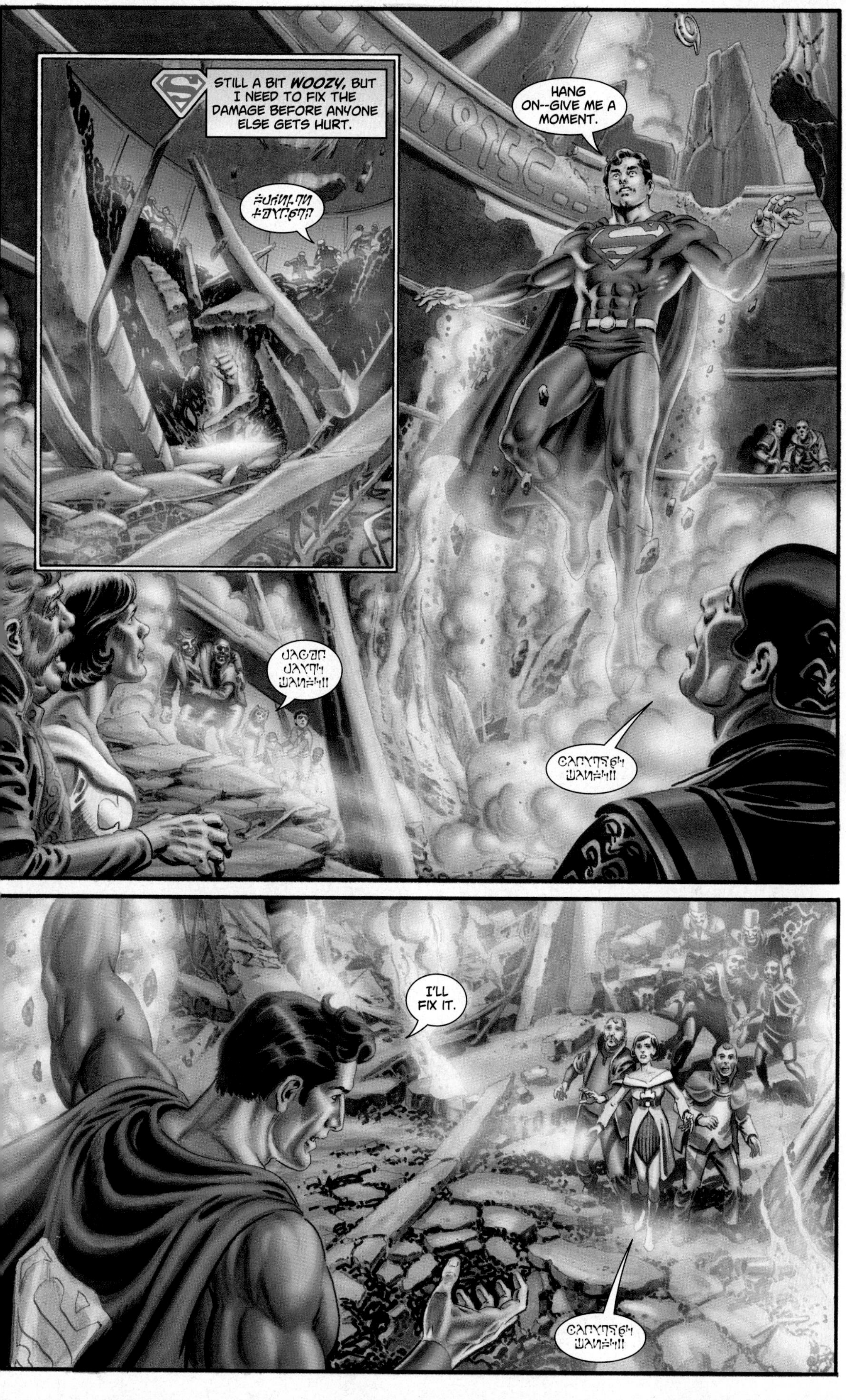
STILL A BIT WOOZY, BUT I NEED TO FIX THE DAMAGE BEFORE ANYONE ELSE GETS HURT.
HANG ON--GIVE ME A MOMENT.
I'LL FIX IT.

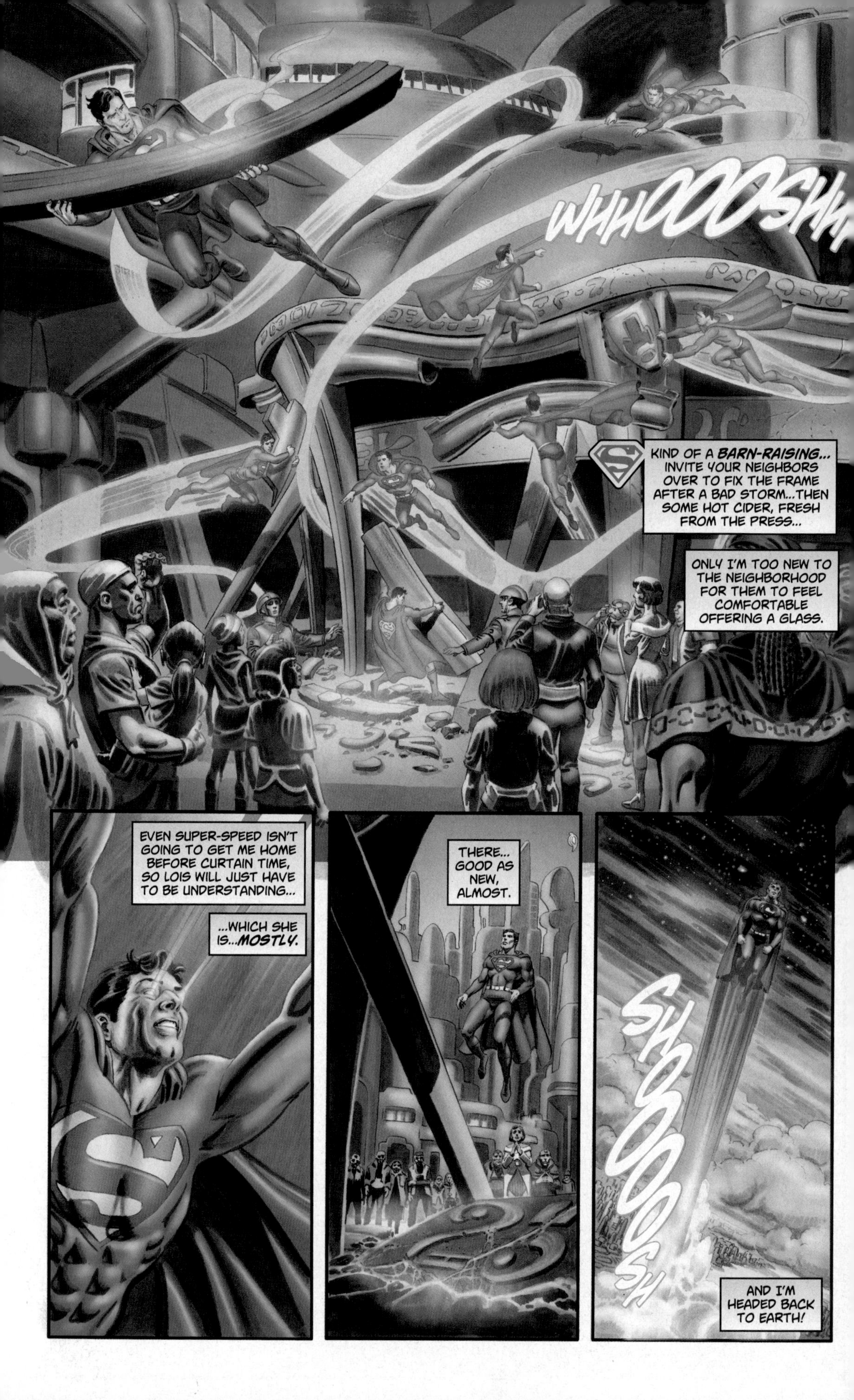
WHHOOOOSHH
KIND OF A BARN-RAISING... INVITE YOUR NEIGHBORS OVER TO FIX THE FRAME AFTER A BAD STORM...THEN SOME HOT CIDER, FRESH FROM THE PRESS...
ONLY I'M TOO NEW TO THE NEIGHBORHOOD FOR THEM TO FEEL COMFORTABLE OFFERING A GLASS.
EVEN SUPER-SPEED ISN'T GOING TO GET ME HOME BEFORE CURTAIN TIME, SO LOIS WILL JUST HAVE TO BE UNDERSTANDING...
...WHICH SHE IS...MOSTLY.
THERE... GOOD AS NEW, ALMOST.
SHOOOOOSH
AND I'M HEADED BACK TO EARTH!

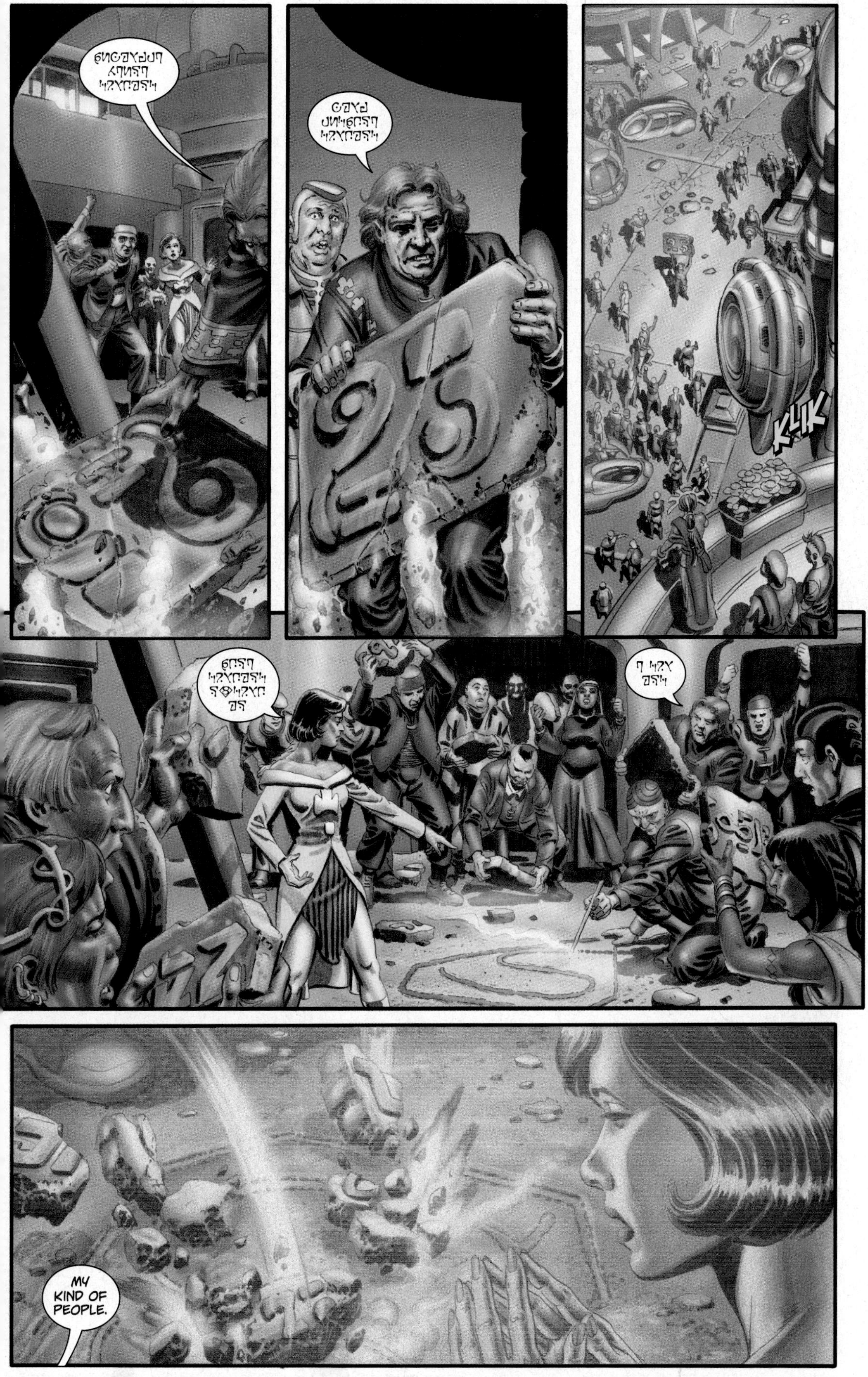
KLIK
MY KIND OF PEOPLE.

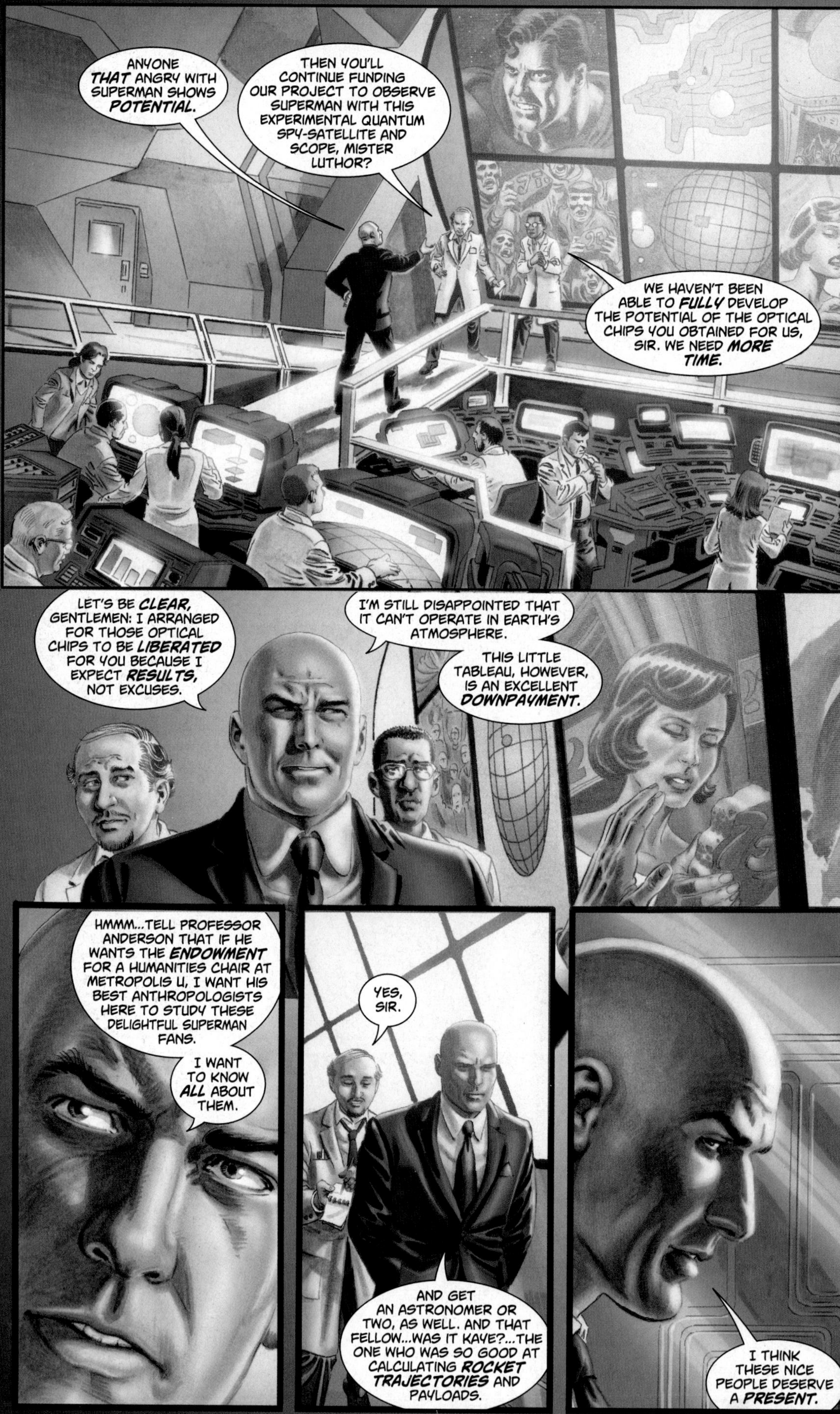
ANYONE THAT ANGRY WITH SUPERMAN SHOWS POTENTIAL.
THEN YOU'LL CONTINUE FUNDING OUR PROJECT TO OBSERVE SUPERMAN WITH THIS EXPERIMENTAL QUANTUM SPY-SATELLITE AND SCOPE, MISTER LUTHOR?
WE HAVEN'T BEEN ABLE TO FULLY DEVELOP THE POTENTIAL OF THE OPTICAL CHIPS YOU OBTAINED FOR US, SIR. WE NEED MORE TIME.
LET'S BE CLEAR, GENTLEMEN: I ARRANGED FOR THOSE OPTICAL CHIPS TO BE LIBERATED FOR YOU BECAUSE I EXPECT RESULTS, NOT EXCUSES.
I'M STILL DISAPPOINTED THAT IT CAN'T OPERATE IN EARTH'S ATMOSPHERE.
THIS LITTLE TABLEAU, HOWEVER, IS AN EXCELLENT DOWNPAYMENT.
HMMM...TELL PROFESSOR ANDERSON THAT IF HE WANTS THE ENDOWMENT FOR A HUMANITIES CHAIR AT METROPOLIS U, I WANT HIS BEST ANTHROPOLOGISTS HERE TO STUDY THESE DELIGHTFUL SUPERMAN FANS.
I WANT TO KNOW ALL ABOUT THEM.
YES, SIR.
AND GET AN ASTRONOMER OR TWO, AS WELL. AND THAT FELLOW...WAS IT KAYE?...THE ONE WHO WAS SO GOOD AT CALCULATING ROCKET TRAJECTORIES AND PAYLOADS.
I THINK THESE NICE PEOPLE DESERVE A PRESENT.

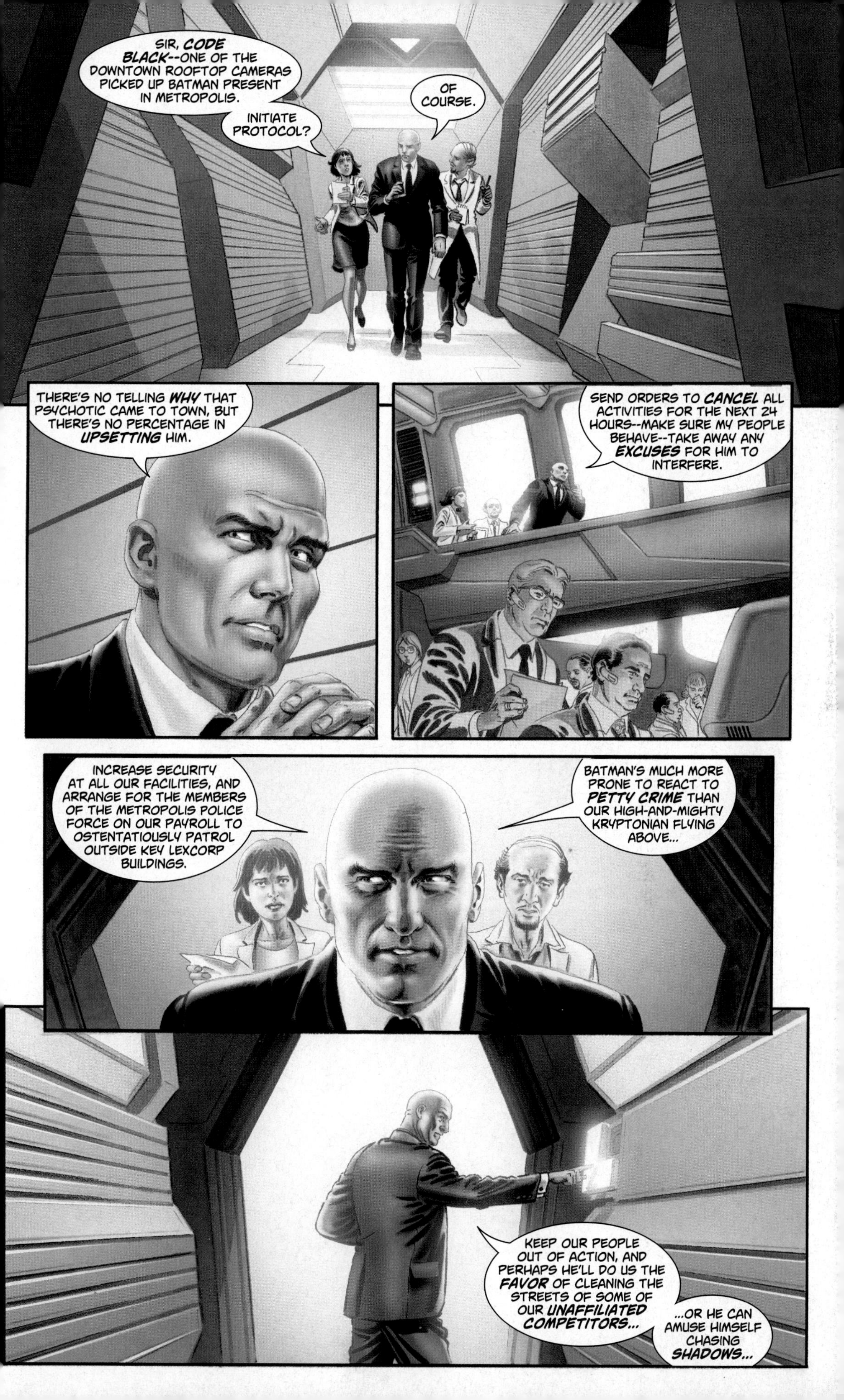
SIR, CODE BLACK--ONE OF THE DOWNTOWN ROOFTOP CAMERAS PICKED UP BATMAN PRESENT IN METROPOLIS.
INITIATE PROTOCOL?
OF COURSE.
THERE'S NO TELLING WHY THAT PSYCHOTIC CAME TO TOWN, BUT THERE'S NO PERCENTAGE IN UPSETTING HIM.
SEND ORDERS TO CANCEL ALL ACTIVITIES FOR THE NEXT 24 HOURS--MAKE SURE MY PEOPLE BEHAVE--TAKE AWAY ANY EXCUSES FOR HIM TO INTERFERE.
INCREASE SECURITY AT ALL OUR FACILITIES, AND ARRANGE FOR THE MEMBERS OF THE METROPOLIS POLICE FORCE ON OUR PAYROLL TO OSTENTATIOUSLY PATROL OUTSIDE KEY LEXCORP BUILDINGS.
BATMAN'S MUCH MORE PRONE TO REACT TO PETTY CRIME THAN OUR HIGH-AND-MIGHTY KRYPTONIAN FLYING ABOVE...
KEEP OUR PEOPLE OUT OF ACTION, AND PERHAPS HE'LL DO US THE FAVOR OF CLEANING THE STREETS OF SOME OF OUR UNAFFILIATED COMPETITORS...
...OR HE CAN AMUSE HIMSELF CHASING SHADOWS...

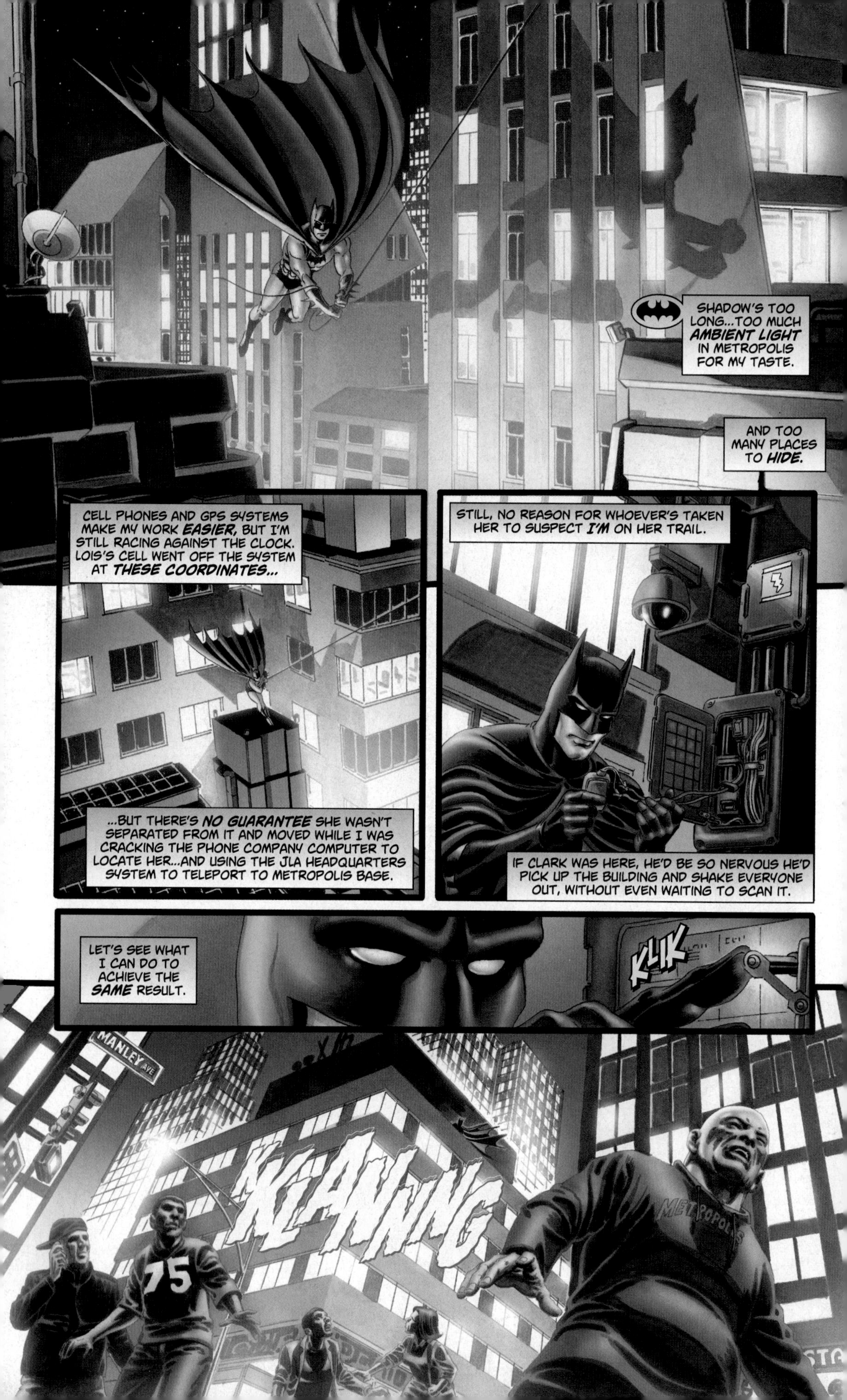
SHADOW'S TOO LONG...TOO MUCH AMBIENT LIGHT IN METROPOLIS FOR MY TASTE.
AND TOO MANY PLACES TO HIDE.
CELL PHONES AND GPS SYSTEMS MAKE MY WORK EASIER, BUT I'M STILL RACING AGAINST THE CLOCK. LOIS'S CELL WENT OFF THE SYSTEM AT THESE COORDINATES...
...BUT THERE'S NO GUARANTEE SHE WASN'T SEPARATED FROM IT AND MOVED WHILE I WAS CRACKING THE PHONE COMPANY COMPUTER TO LOCATE HER...AND USING THE JLA HEADQUARTERS SYSTEM TO TELEPORT TO METROPOLIS BASE.
STILL, NO REASON FOR WHOEVER'S TAKEN HER TO SUSPECT I'M ON HER TRAIL.
IF CLARK WAS HERE, HE'D BE SO NERVOUS HE'D PICK UP THE BUILDING AND SHAKE EVERYONE OUT, WITHOUT EVEN WAITING TO SCAN IT.
LET'S SEE WHAT I CAN DO TO ACHIEVE THE SAME RESULT.
KLIK
MANLEY AVE
KLANNG
75
METROPOLIS

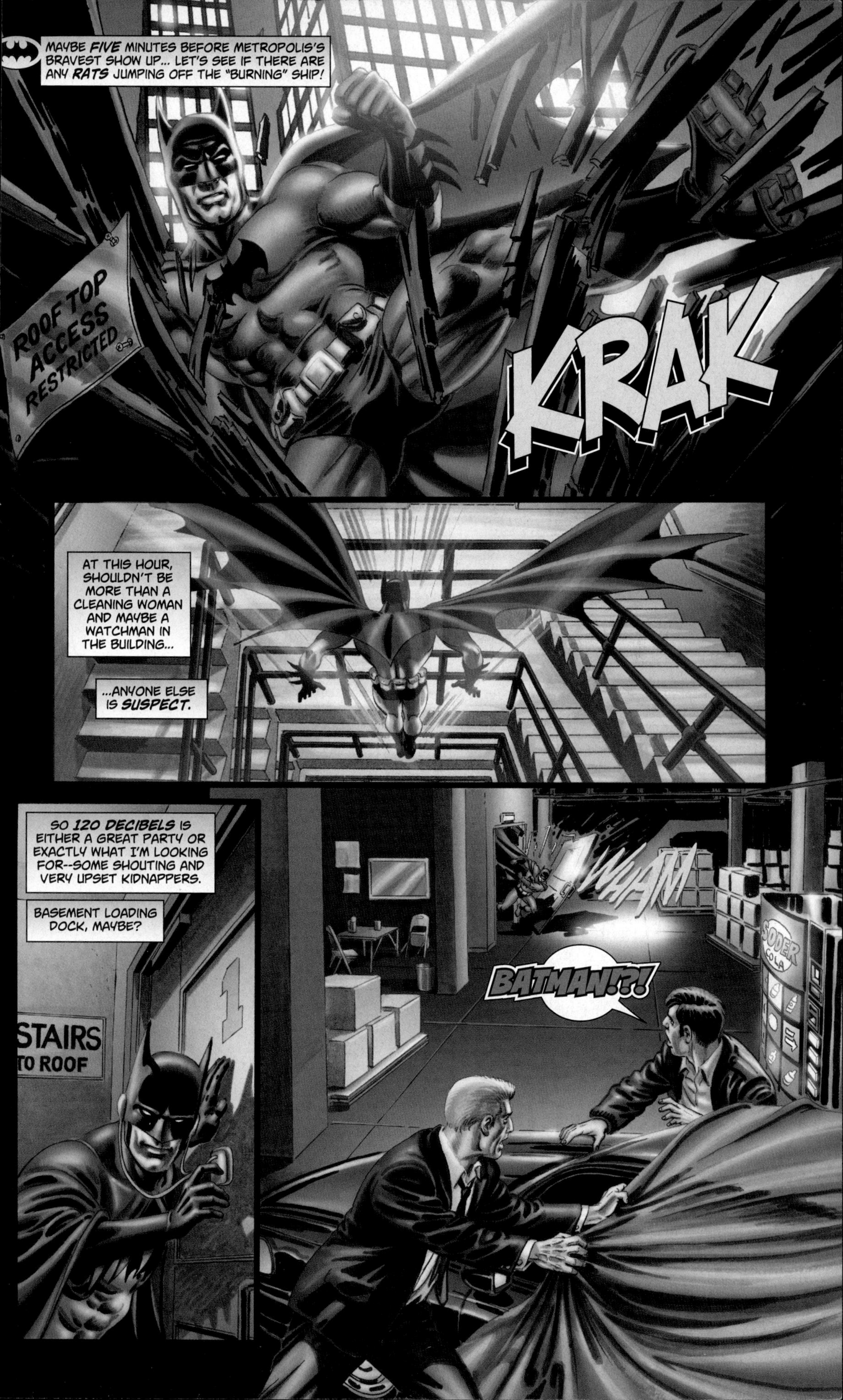
MAYBE FIVE MINUTES BEFORE METROPOLIS'S BRAVEST SHOW UP... LET'S SEE IF THERE ARE ANY RATS JUMPING OFF THE "BURNING" SHIP!
ROOF TOP ACCESS RESTRICTED
KRAK
AT THIS HOUR, SHOULDN'T BE MORE THAN A CLEANING WOMAN AND MAYBE A WATCHMAN IN THE BUILDING...
...ANYONE ELSE IS SUSPECT.
SO 120 DECIBELS IS EITHER A GREAT PARTY OR EXACTLY WHAT I'M LOOKING FOR--SOME SHOUTING AND VERY UPSET KIDNAPPERS.
BASEMENT LOADING DOCK, MAYBE?
STAIRS TO ROOF
WHAM
SODER COLA
BATMAN!?!

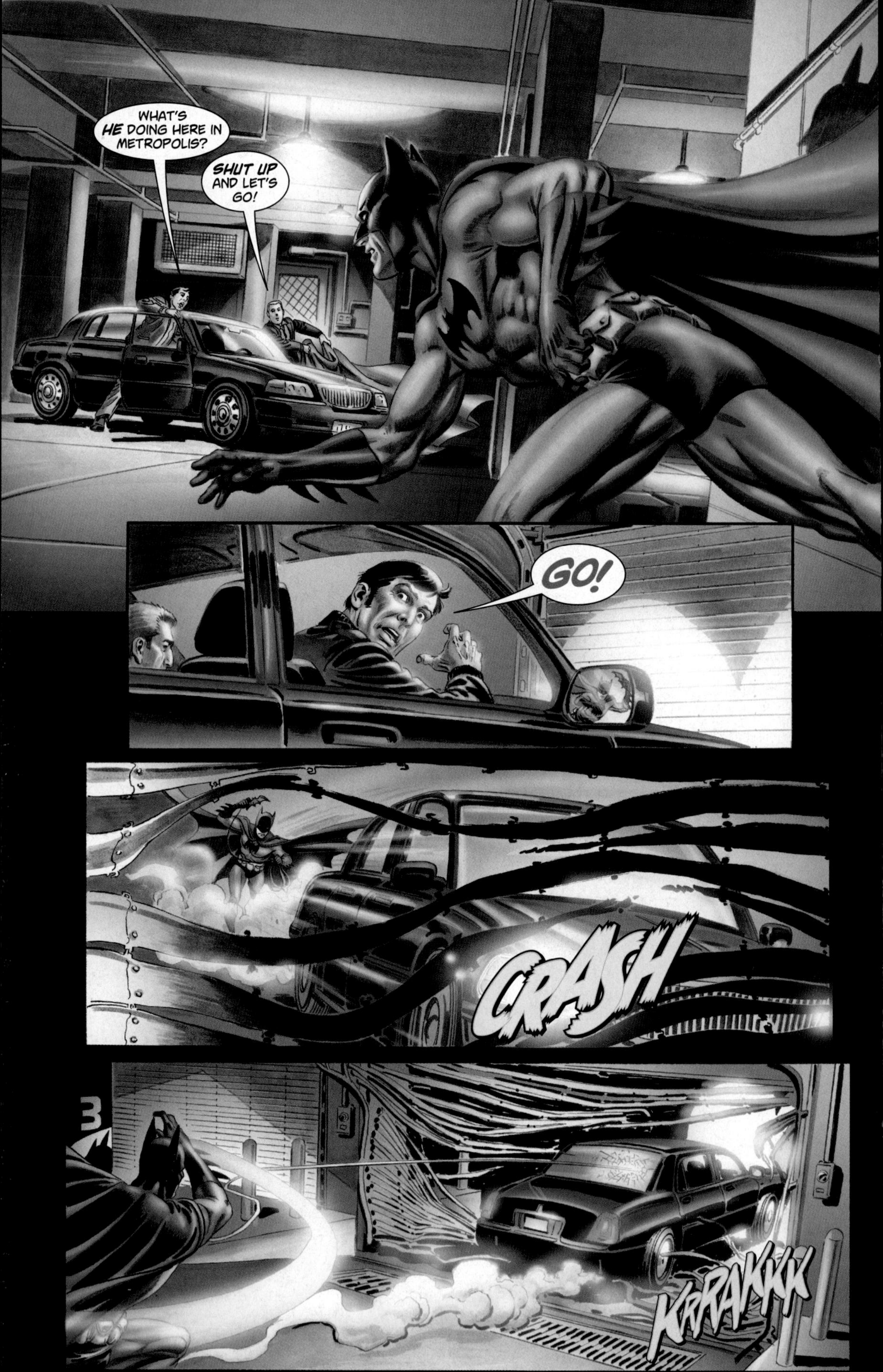
WHAT'S HE DOING HERE IN METROPOLIS?
SHUT UP AND LET'S GO!
GO!
CRASH
KRRAKKK

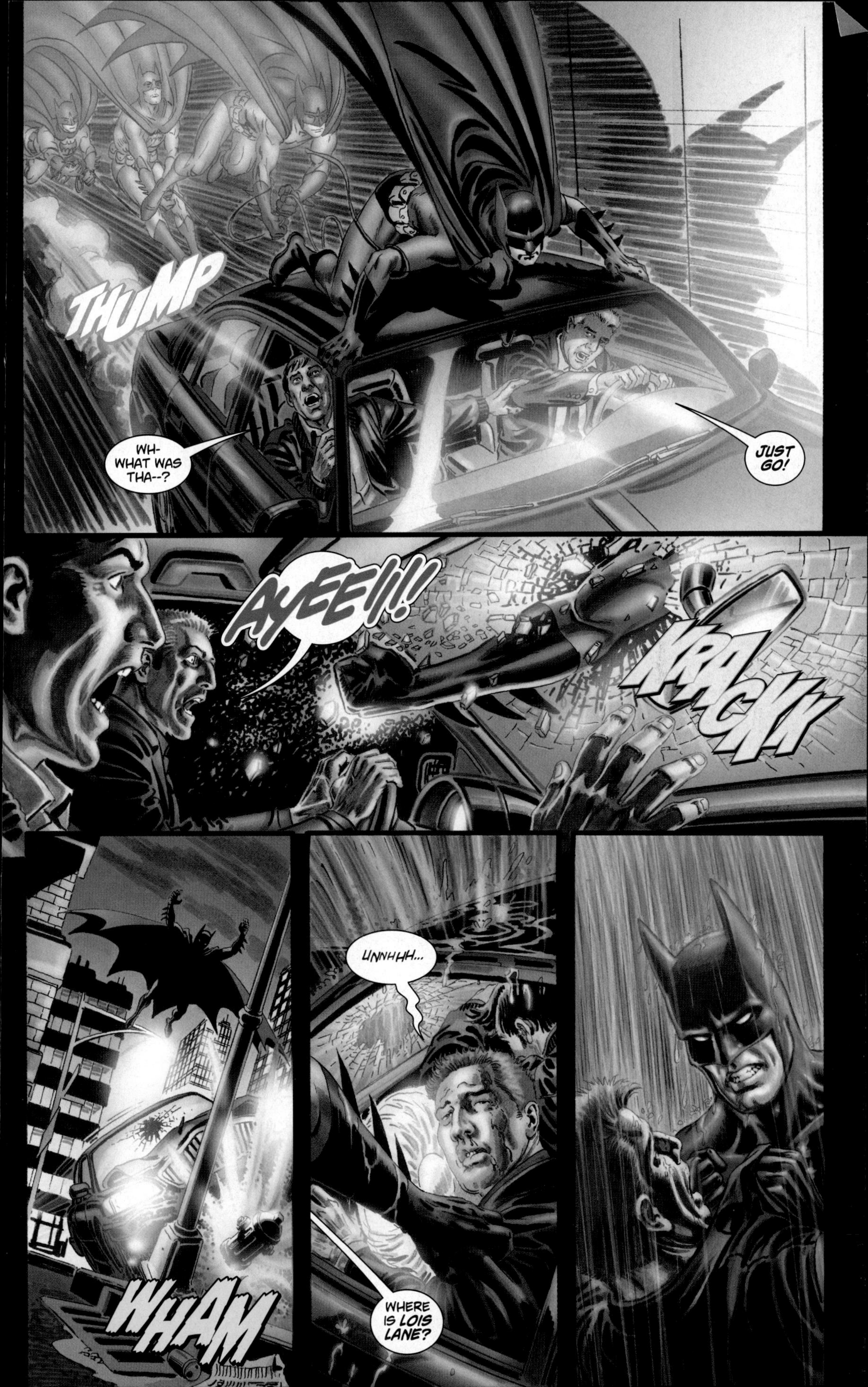
THUMP
WH- WHAT WAS THA--?
JUST GO!
AYEEII!
KRACKK
WHAM
UNNHHH...
WHERE IS LOIS LANE?

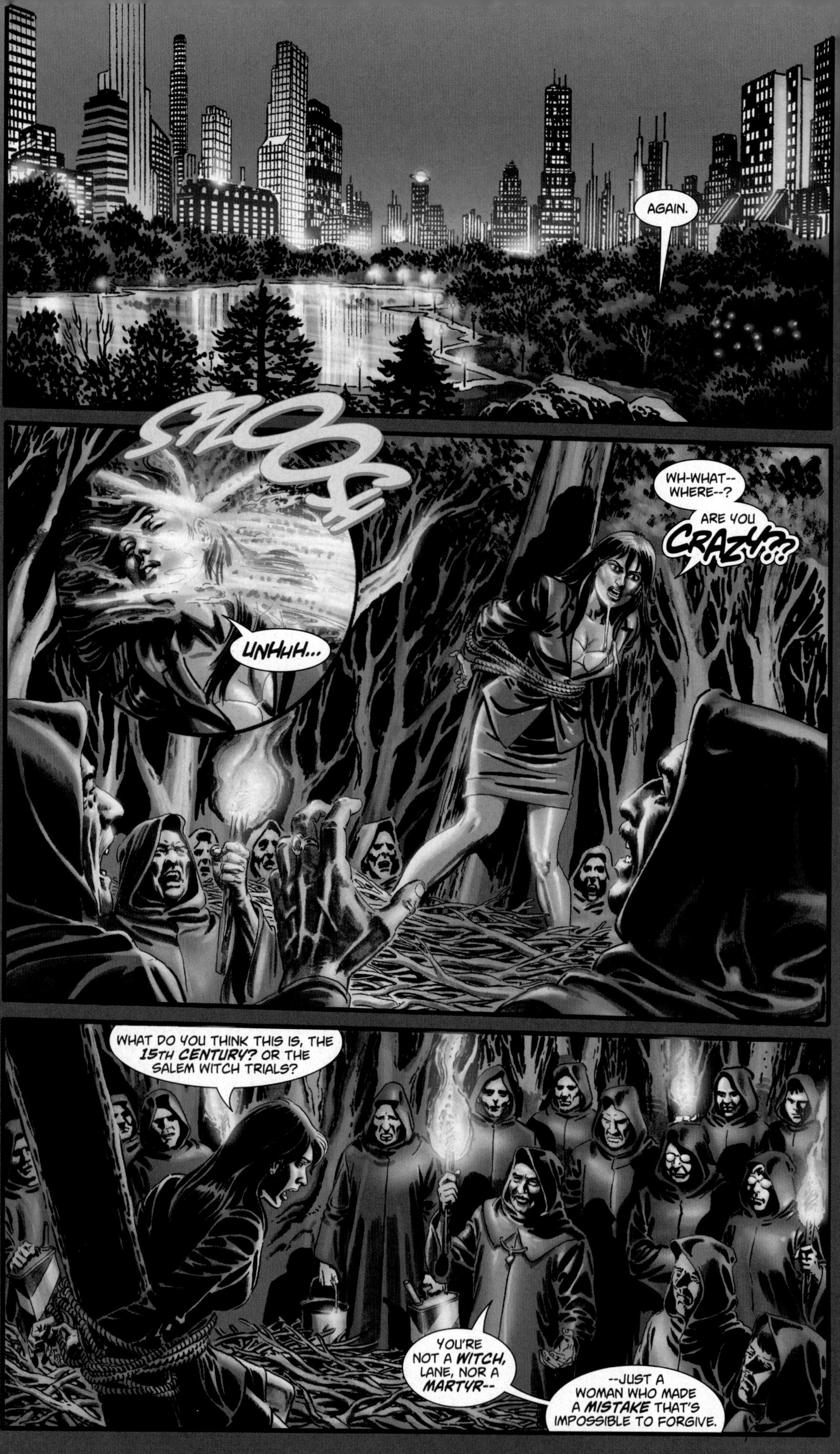
AGAIN.
WH-WHAT-- WHERE--?
ARE YOU CRAZY?!?
UNHHH...
WHAT DO YOU THINK THIS IS, THE 15TH CENTURY? OR THE SALEM WITCH TRIALS?
YOU'RE NOT A WITCH, LANE, NOR A MARTYR--
--JUST A WOMAN WHO MADE A MISTAKE THAT'S IMPOSSIBLE TO FORGIVE.

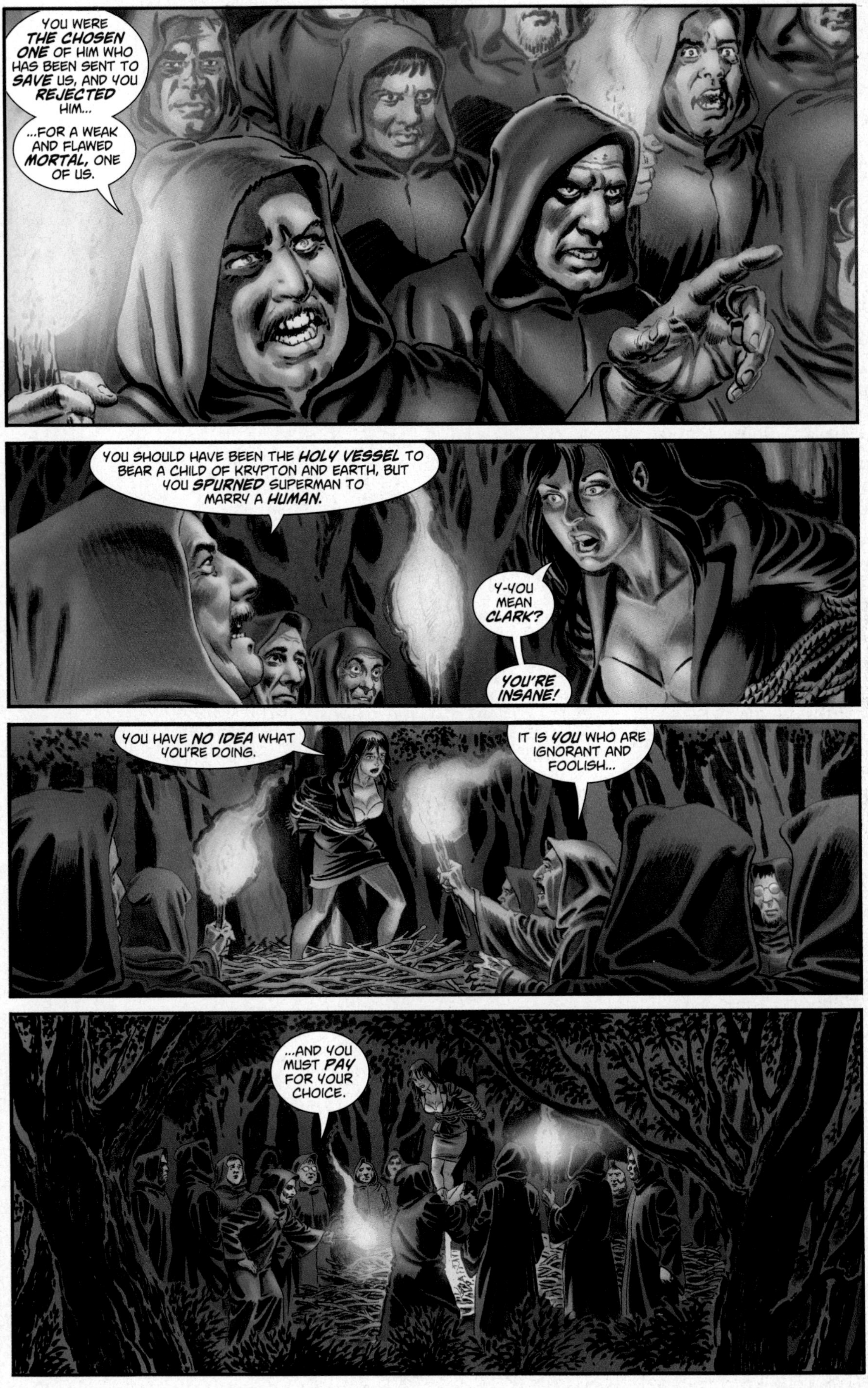
YOU WERE THE CHOSEN ONE OF HIM WHO HAS BEEN SENT TO SAVE US, AND YOU REJECTED HIM...
...FOR A WEAK AND FLAWED MORTAL, ONE OF US.
YOU SHOULD HAVE BEEN THE HOLY VESSEL TO BEAR A CHILD OF KRYPTON AND EARTH, BUT YOU SPURNED SUPERMAN TO MARRY A HUMAN.
Y-YOU MEAN CLARK?
YOU'RE INSANE!
YOU HAVE NO IDEA WHAT YOU'RE DOING.
IT IS YOU WHO ARE IGNORANT AND FOOLISH...
...AND YOU MUST PAY FOR YOUR CHOICE.

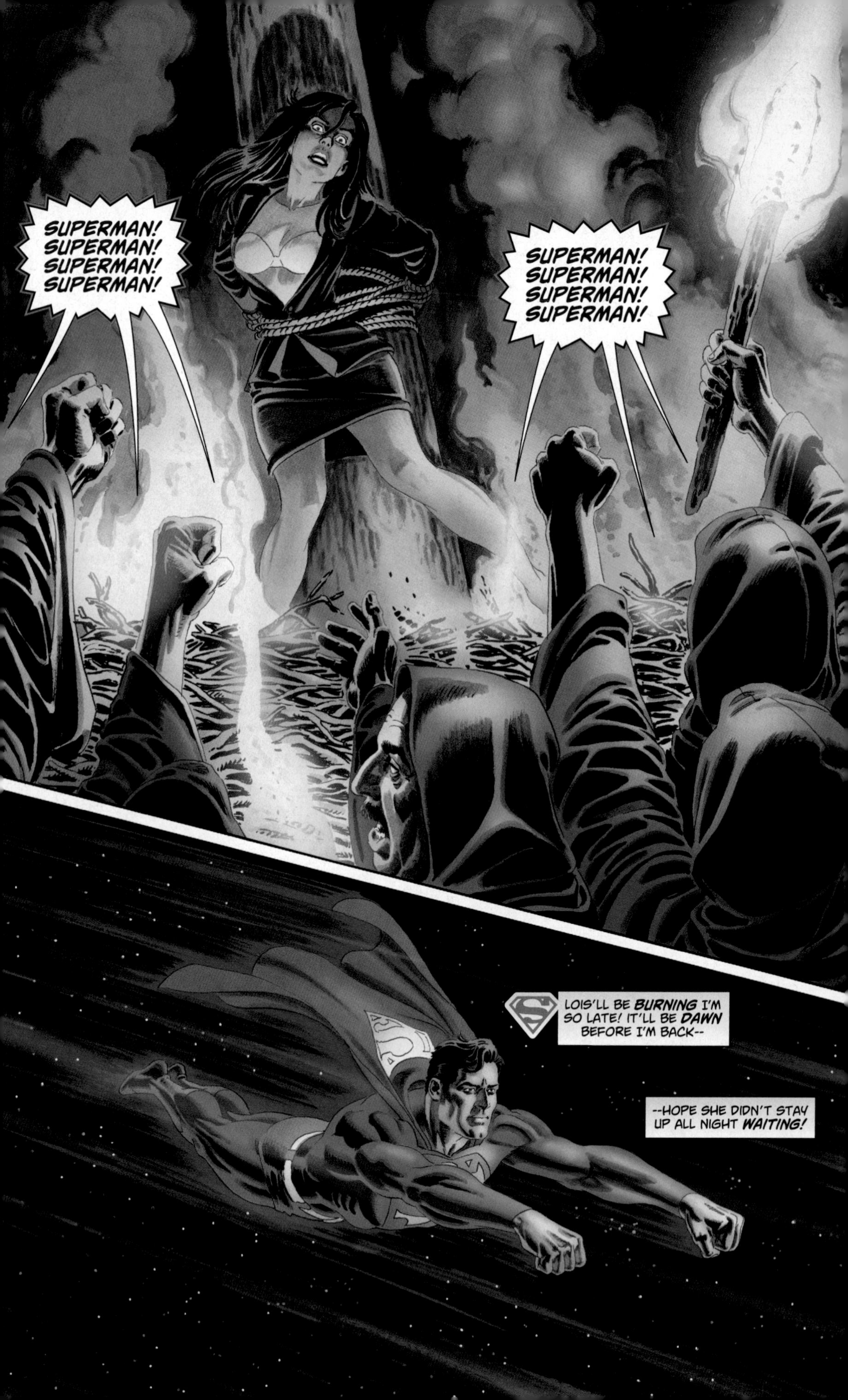
SUPERMAN! SUPERMAN! SUPERMAN! SUPERMAN!
SUPERMAN! SUPERMAN! SUPERMAN! SUPERMAN!
LOIS'LL BE BURNING I'M SO LATE! IT'LL BE DAWN BEFORE I'M BACK--
--HOPE SHE DIDN'T STAY UP ALL NIGHT WAITING!

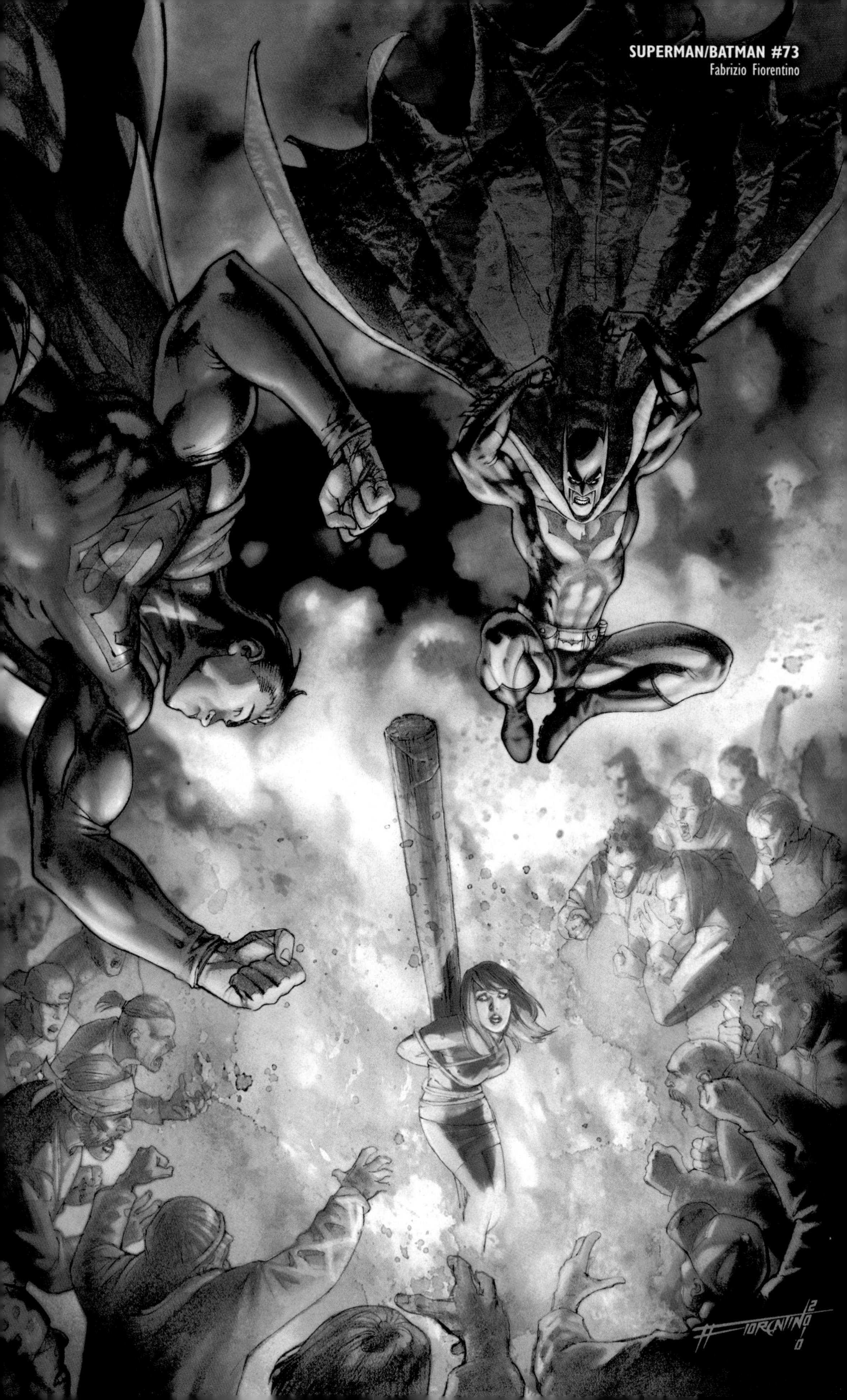

SUPERMAN/BATMAN #73
Fabrizio Fiorentino

SACRIFICE

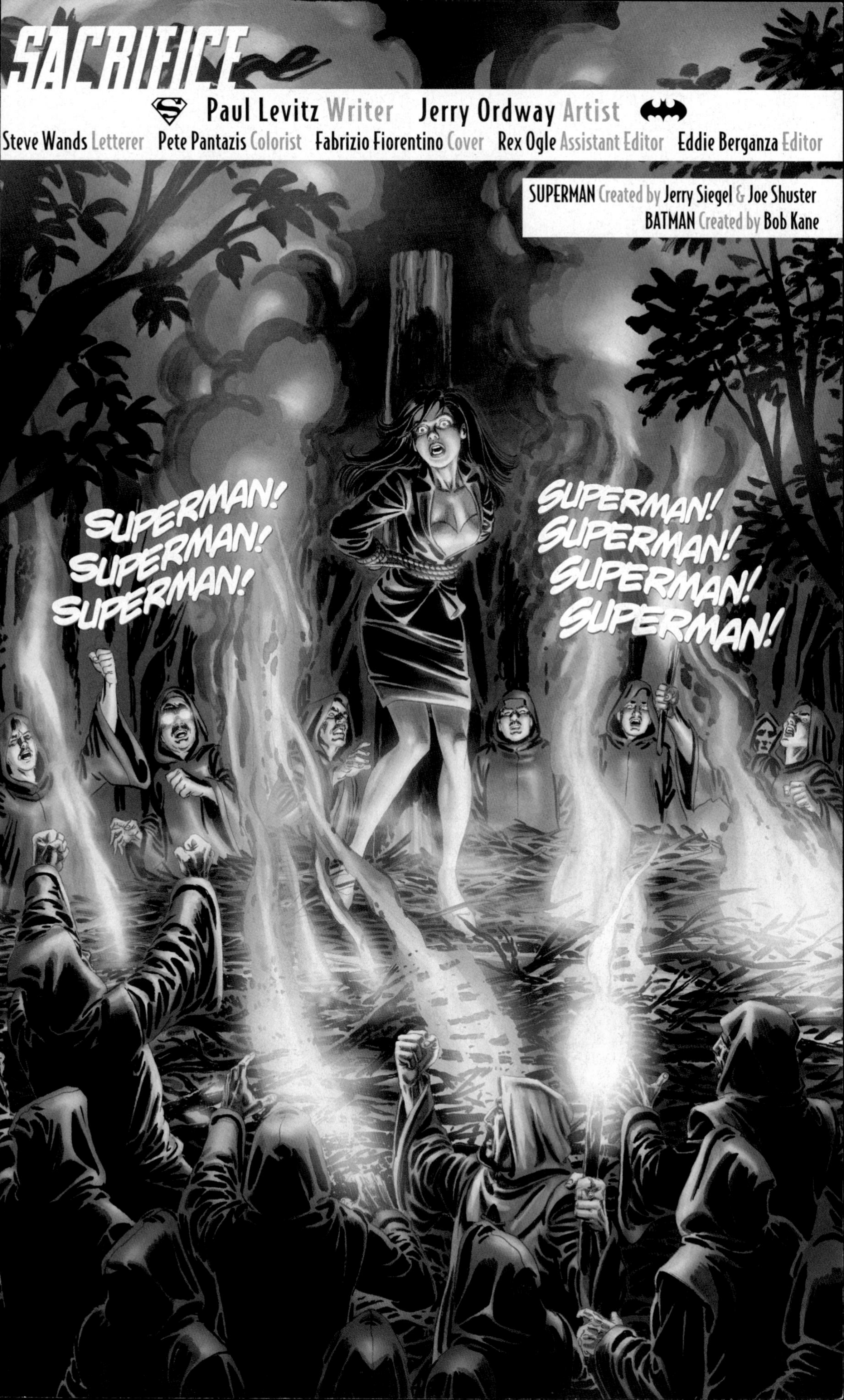
SACRIFICE
Paul Levitz Writer Jerry Ordway Artist
Steve Wands Letterer Pete Pantazis Colorist Fabrizio Fiorentino Cover Rex Ogle Assistant Editor Eddie Berganza Editor
SUPERMAN Created by Jerry Siegel & Joe Shuster
BATMAN Created by Bob Kane
SUPERMAN! SUPERMAN! SUPERMAN!
SUPERMAN! SUPERMAN! SUPERMAN! SUPERMAN!

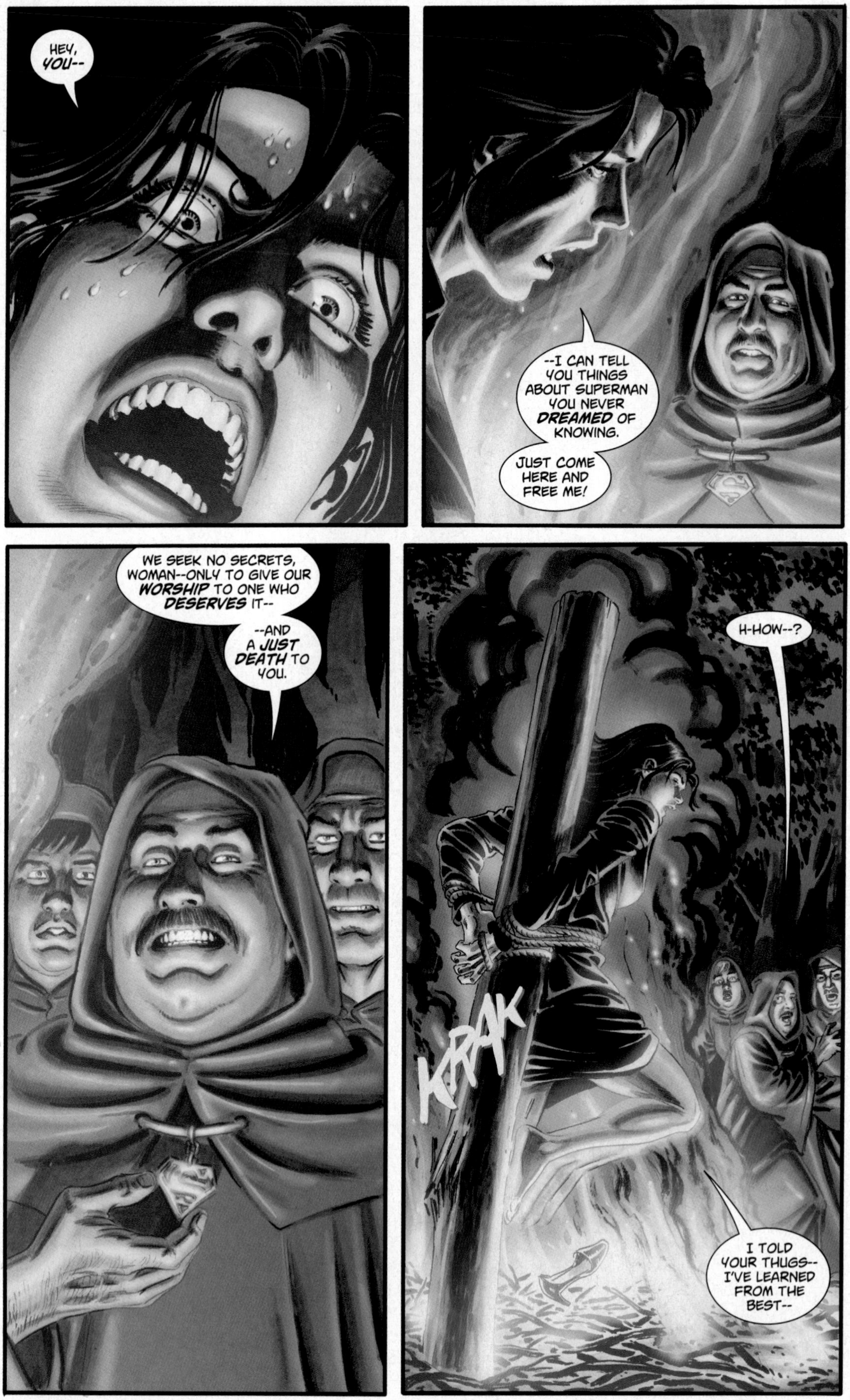
HEY, YOU--
--I CAN TELL YOU THINGS ABOUT SUPERMAN YOU NEVER DREAMED OF KNOWING.
JUST COME HERE AND FREE ME!
WE SEEK NO SECRETS, WOMAN--ONLY TO GIVE OUR WORSHIP TO ONE WHO DESERVES IT--
--AND A JUST DEATH TO YOU.
H-HOW--?
KRAK
I TOLD YOUR THUGS-- I'VE LEARNED FROM THE BEST--

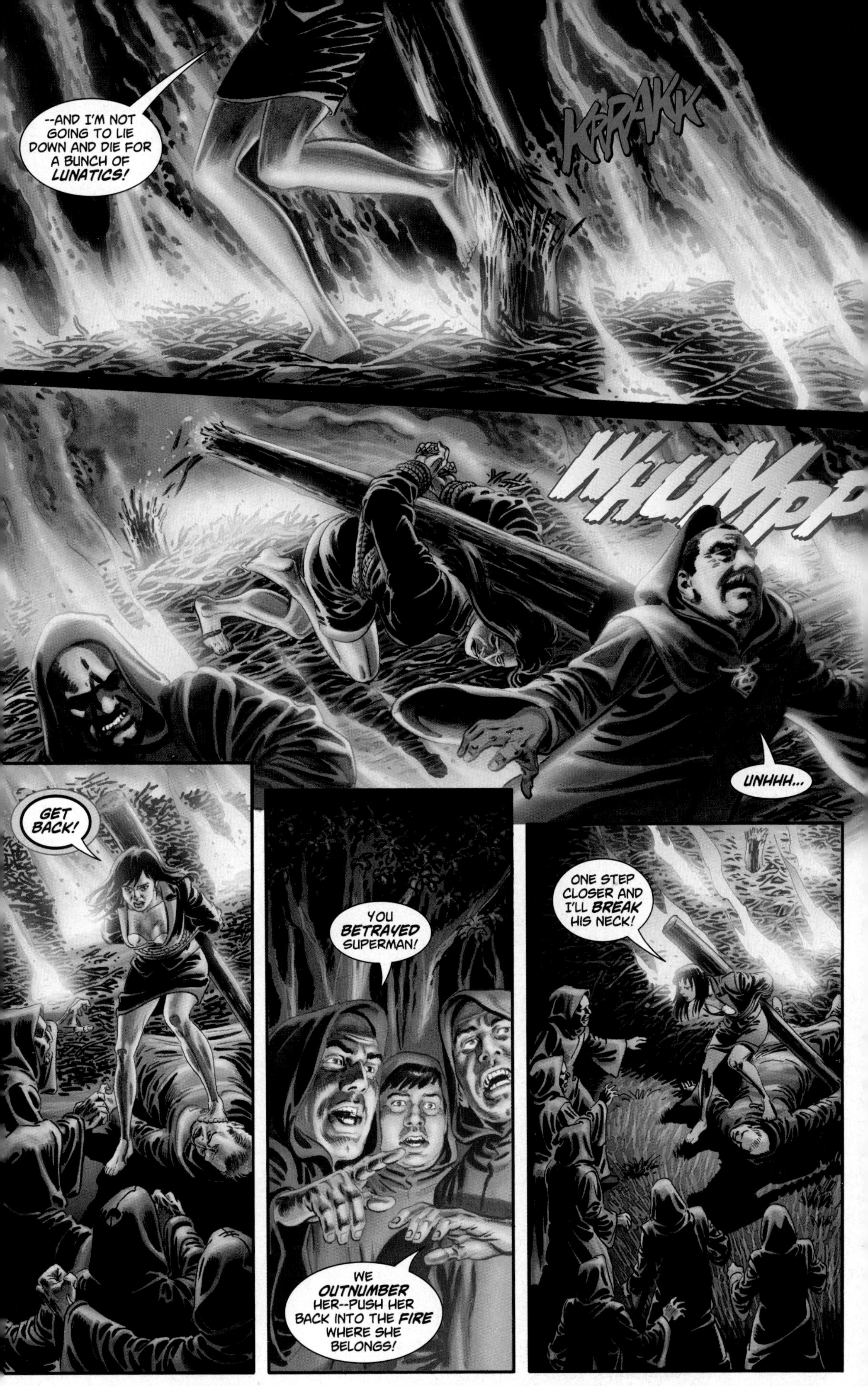
--AND I'M NOT GOING TO LIE DOWN AND DIE FOR A BUNCH OF LUNATICS!
KRAKK
WHUMPP
UNHHH...
GET BACK!
YOU BETRAYED SUPERMAN!
WE OUTNUMBER HER--PUSH HER BACK INTO THE FIRE WHERE SHE BELONGS!
ONE STEP CLOSER AND I'LL BREAK HIS NECK!

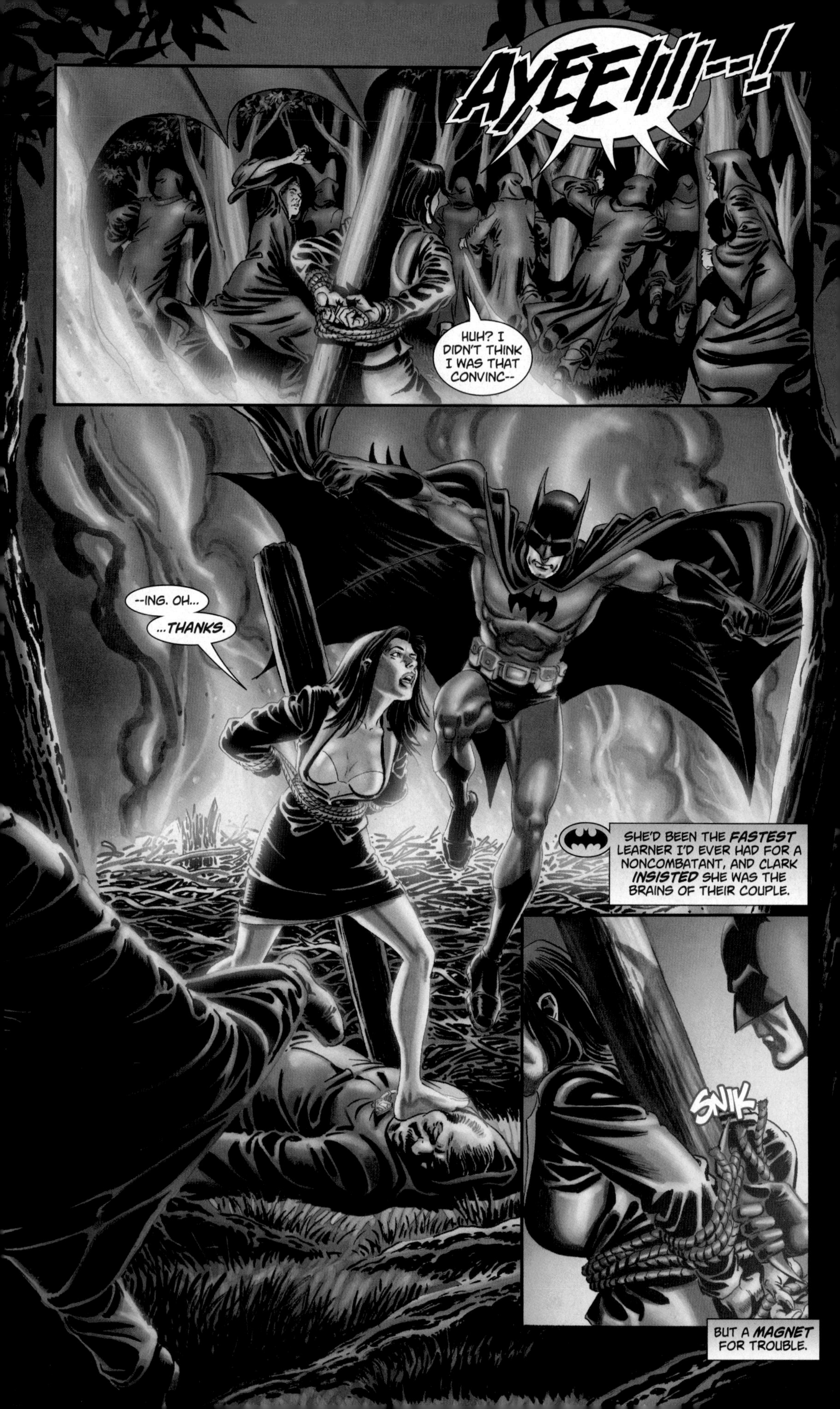
AYEEIII--!
HUH? I DIDN'T THINK I WAS THAT CONVINC--
--ING. OH...
...THANKS.
SHE'D BEEN THE FASTEST LEARNER I'D EVER HAD FOR A NONCOMBATANT, AND CLARK INSISTED SHE WAS THE BRAINS OF THEIR COUPLE.
SNIK
BUT A MAGNET FOR TROUBLE.

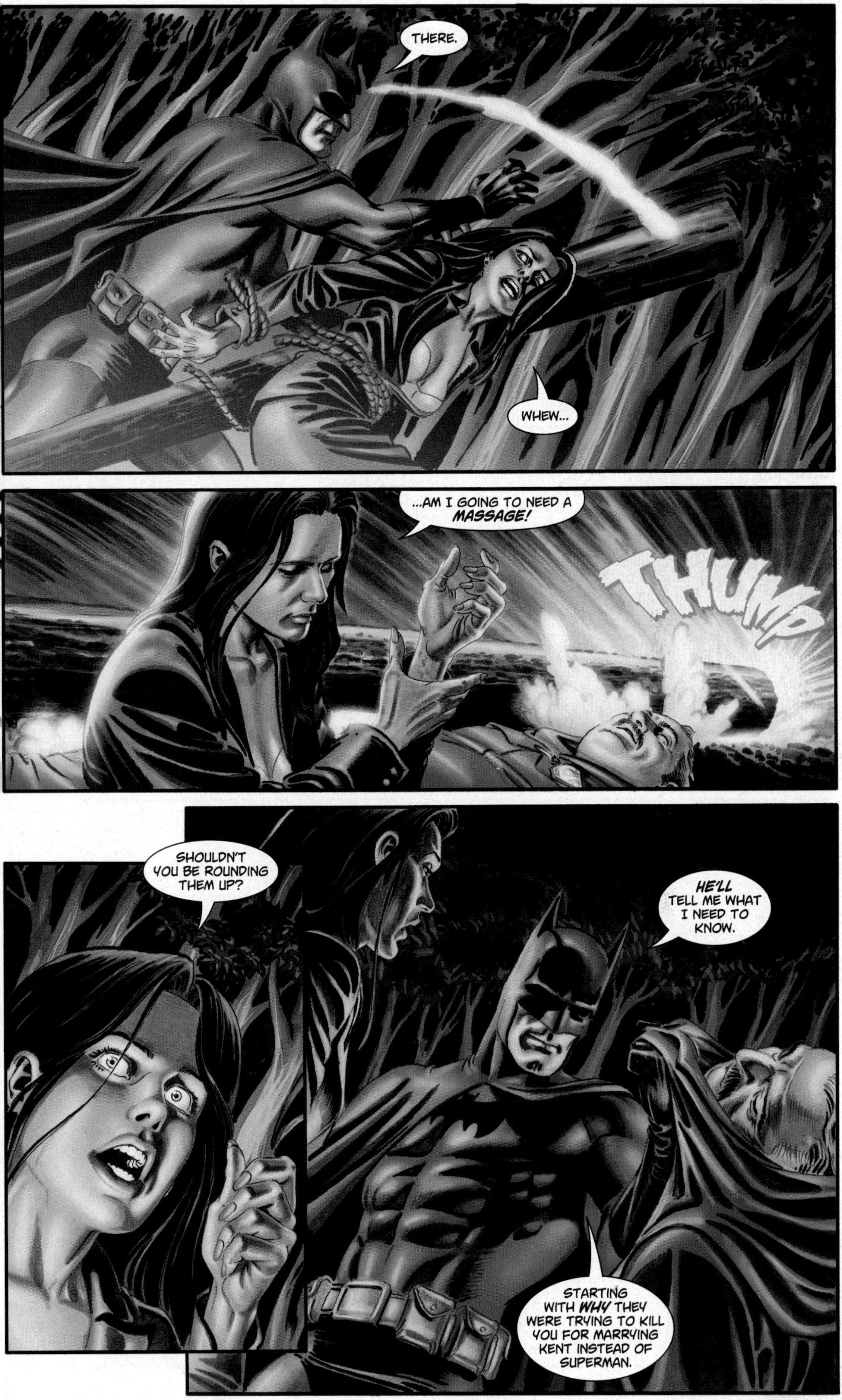
THERE.
WHEW...
...AM I GOING TO NEED A MASSAGE!
THUMP
SHOULDN'T YOU BE ROUNDING THEM UP?
HE'LL TELL ME WHAT I NEED TO KNOW.
STARTING WITH WHY THEY WERE TRYING TO KILL YOU FOR MARRYING KENT INSTEAD OF SUPERMAN.

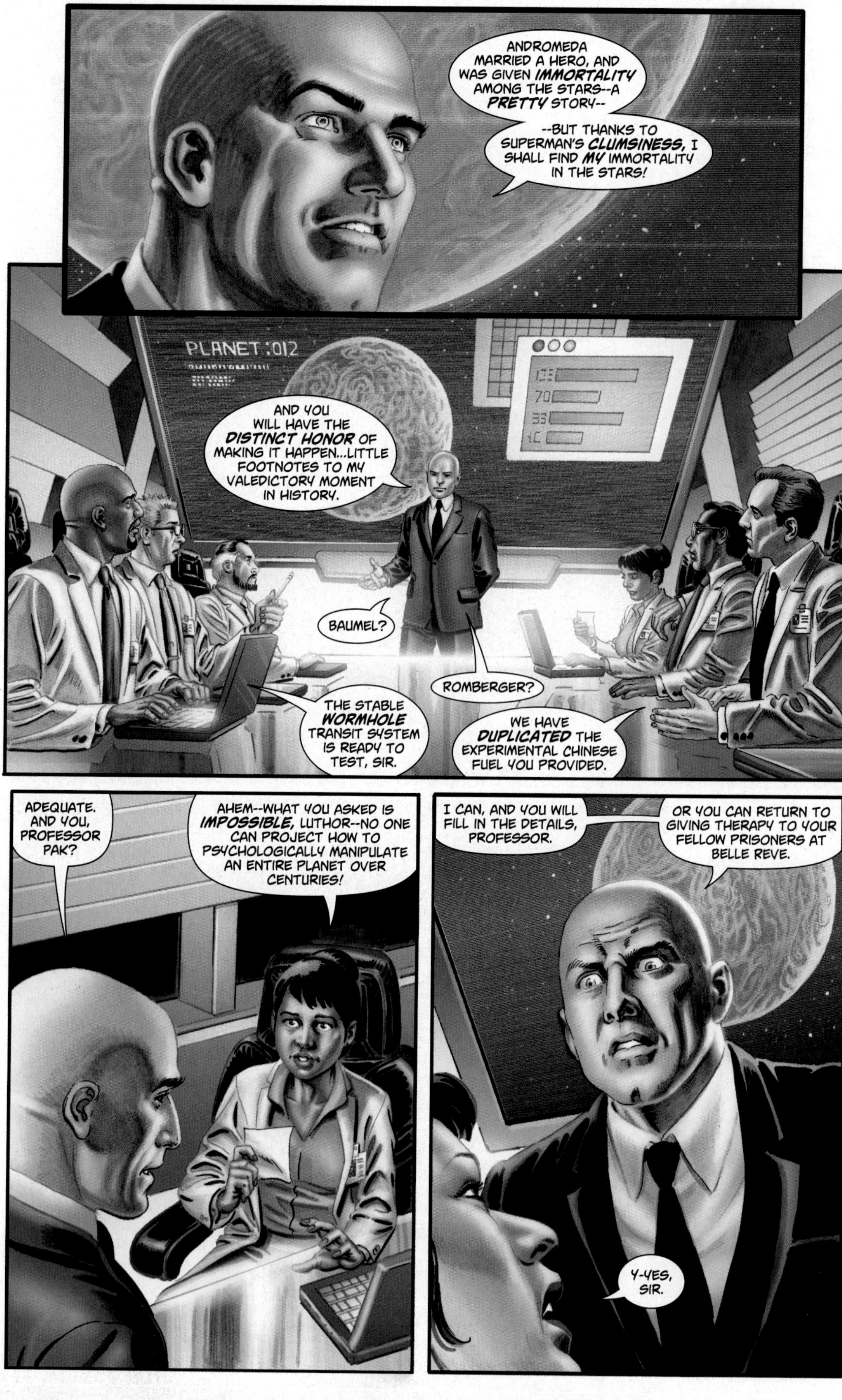

ANDROMEDA MARRIED A HERO, AND WAS GIVEN IMMORTALITY AMONG THE STARS--A PRETTY STORY--
--BUT THANKS TO SUPERMAN'S CLUMSINESS, I SHALL FIND MY IMMORTALITY IN THE STARS!
PLANET :012
AND YOU WILL HAVE THE DISTINCT HONOR OF MAKING IT HAPPEN...LITTLE FOOTNOTES TO MY VALEDICTORY MOMENT IN HISTORY.
BAUMEL?
THE STABLE WORMHOLE TRANSIT SYSTEM IS READY TO TEST, SIR.
ROMBERGER?
WE HAVE DUPLICATED THE EXPERIMENTAL CHINESE FUEL YOU PROVIDED.
ADEQUATE. AND YOU, PROFESSOR PAK?
AHEM--WHAT YOU ASKED IS IMPOSSIBLE, LUTHOR--NO ONE CAN PROJECT HOW TO PSYCHOLOGICALLY MANIPULATE AN ENTIRE PLANET OVER CENTURIES!
I CAN, AND YOU WILL FILL IN THE DETAILS, PROFESSOR.
OR YOU CAN RETURN TO GIVING THERAPY TO YOUR FELLOW PRISONERS AT BELLE REVE.
Y-YES, SIR.

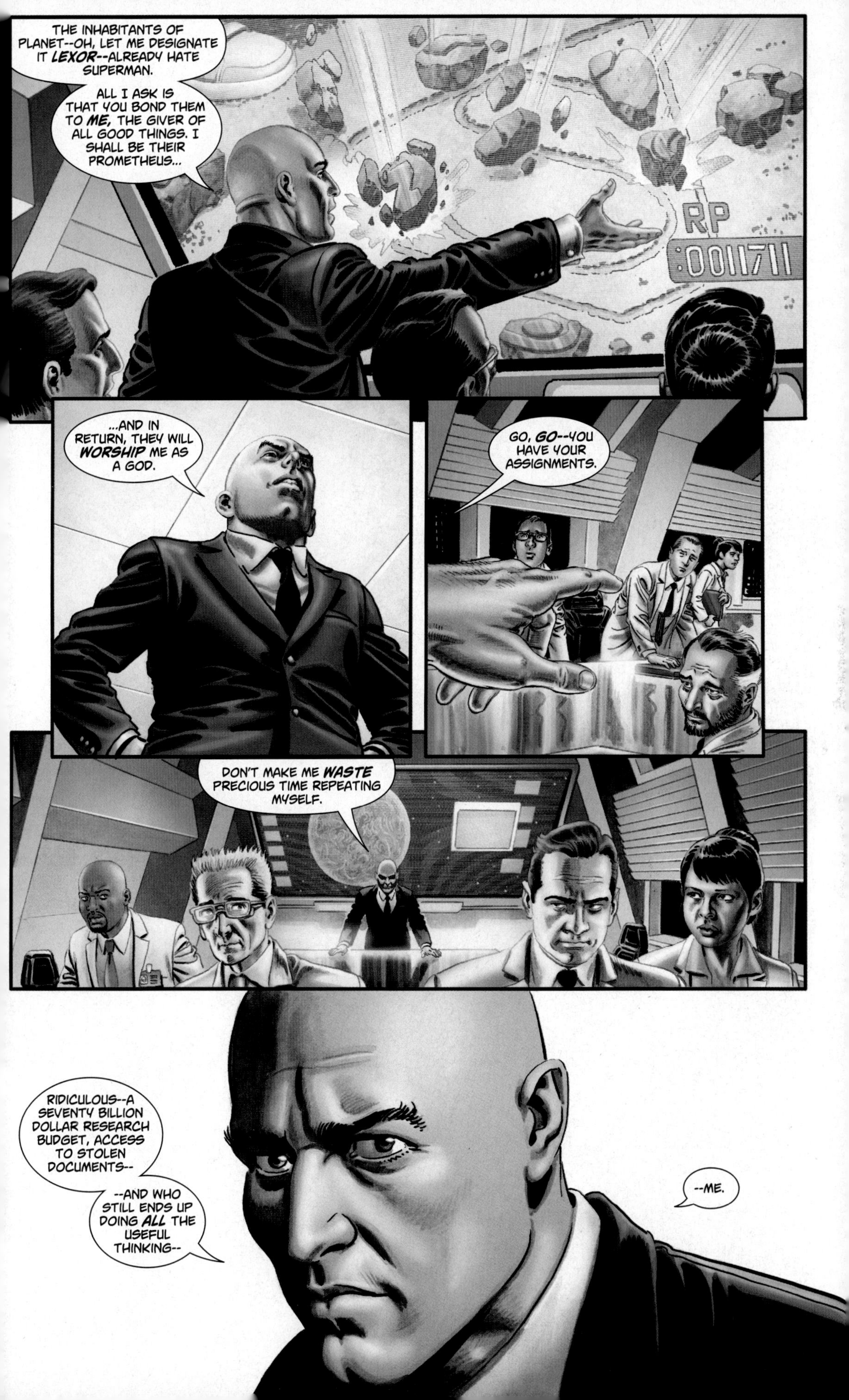
THE INHABITANTS OF PLANET--OH, LET ME DESIGNATE IT LEXOR--ALREADY HATE SUPERMAN.
ALL I ASK IS THAT YOU BOND THEM TO ME, THE GIVER OF ALL GOOD THINGS. I SHALL BE THEIR PROMETHEUS...
RP
:0011711
...AND IN RETURN, THEY WILL WORSHIP ME AS A GOD.
GO, GO--YOU HAVE YOUR ASSIGNMENTS.
DON'T MAKE ME WASTE PRECIOUS TIME REPEATING MYSELF.
RIDICULOUS--A SEVENTY BILLION DOLLAR RESEARCH BUDGET, ACCESS TO STOLEN DOCUMENTS--
--AND WHO STILL ENDS UP DOING ALL THE USEFUL THINKING--
--ME.

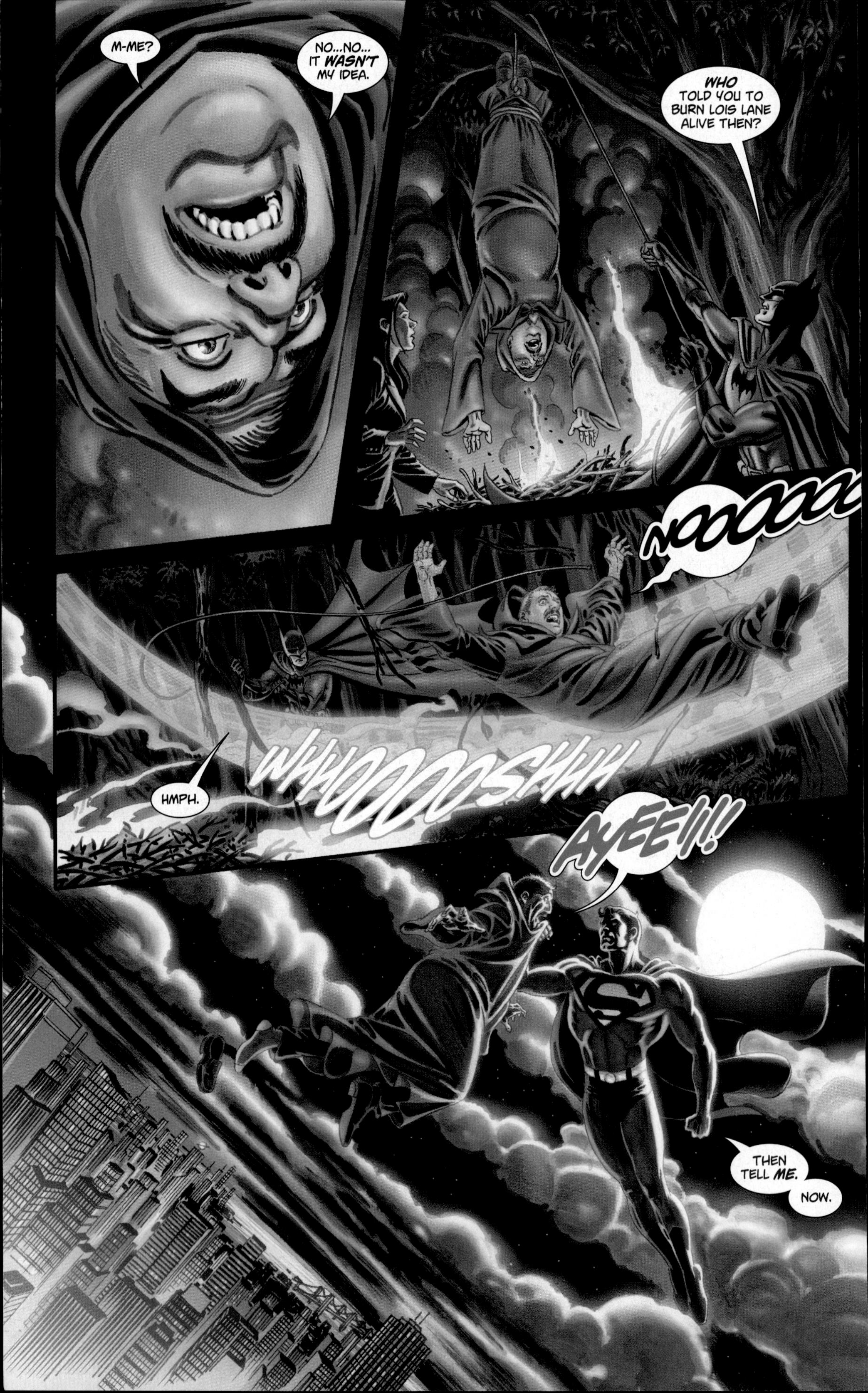
M-ME?
NO...NO... IT WASN'T MY IDEA.
WHO TOLD YOU TO BURN LOIS LANE ALIVE THEN?
NOOOOOO
WHOOOOOSHHH
HMPH.
AYEE!!!
THEN TELL ME.
NOW.

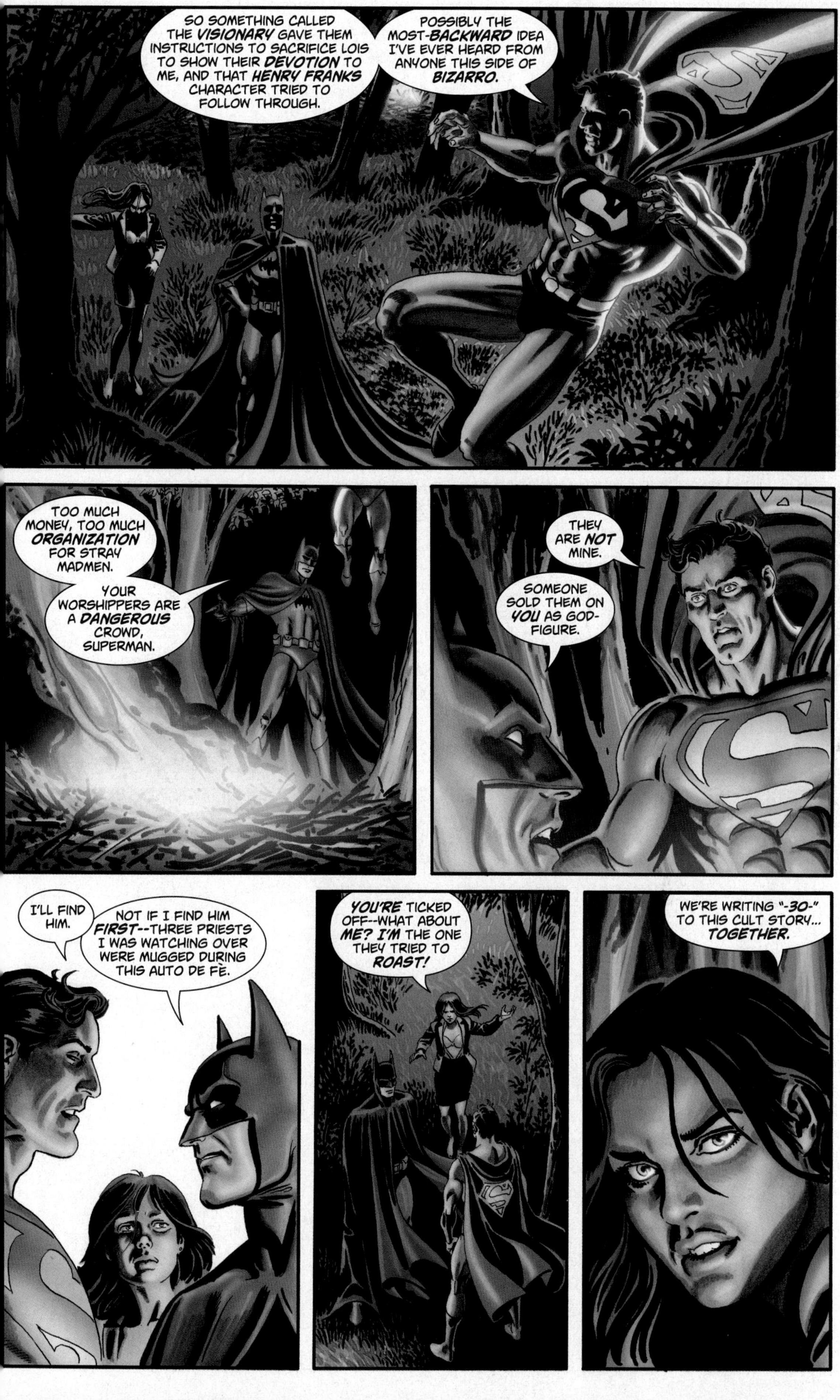
SO SOMETHING CALLED THE VISIONARY GAVE THEM INSTRUCTIONS TO SACRIFICE LOIS TO SHOW THEIR DEVOTION TO ME, AND THAT HENRY FRANKS CHARACTER TRIED TO FOLLOW THROUGH.
POSSIBLY THE MOST-BACKWARD IDEA I'VE EVER HEARD FROM ANYONE THIS SIDE OF BIZARRO.
TOO MUCH MONEY, TOO MUCH ORGANIZATION FOR STRAY MADMEN.
YOUR WORSHIPPERS ARE A DANGEROUS CROWD, SUPERMAN.
THEY ARE NOT MINE.
SOMEONE SOLD THEM ON YOU AS GOD-FIGURE.
I'LL FIND HIM.
NOT IF I FIND HIM FIRST--THREE PRIESTS I WAS WATCHING OVER WERE MUGGED DURING THIS AUTO DE FÉ.
YOU'RE TICKED OFF--WHAT ABOUT ME? I'M THE ONE THEY TRIED TO ROAST!
WE'RE WRITING "-30-" TO THIS CULT STORY... TOGETHER.

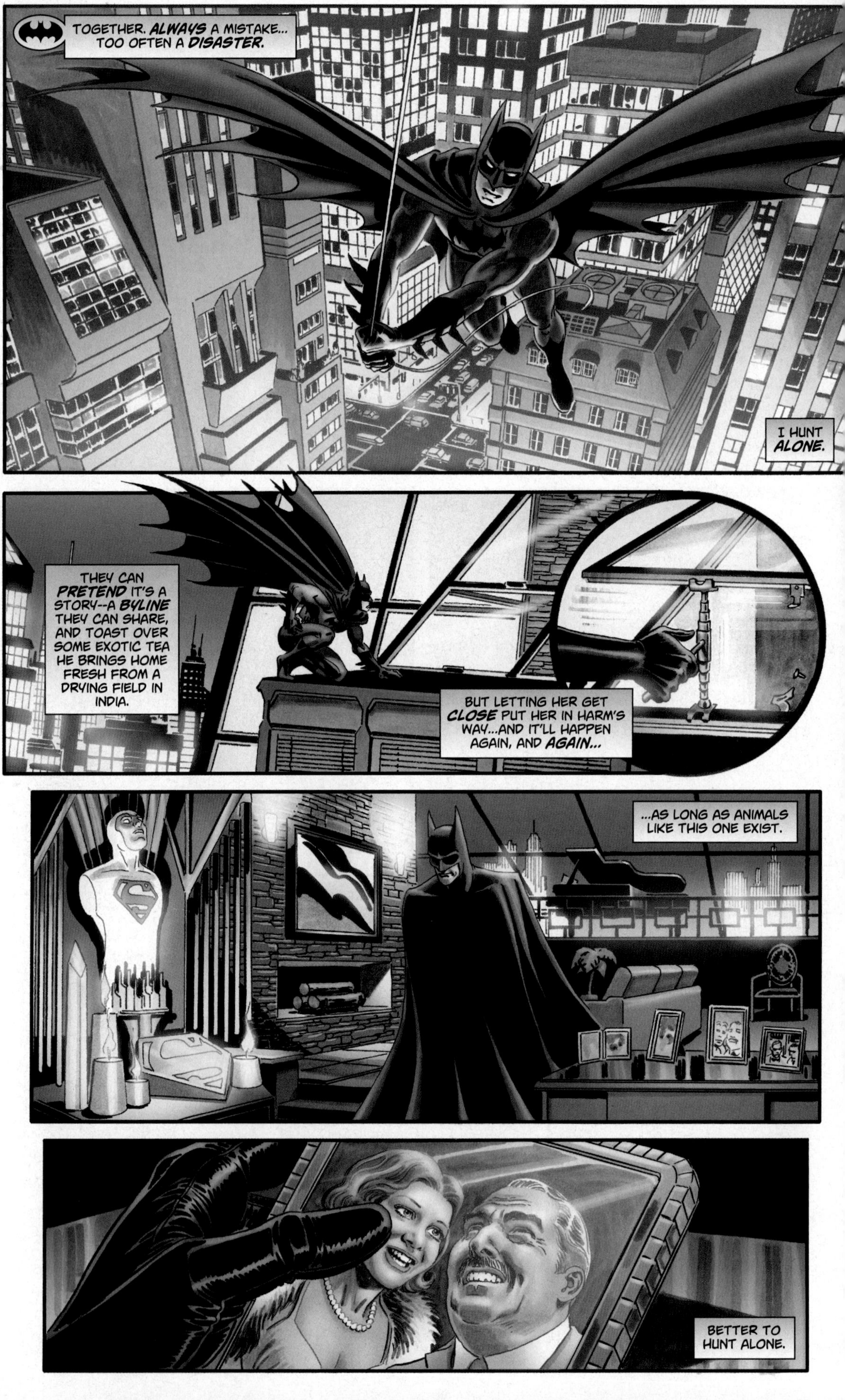
TOGETHER. ALWAYS A MISTAKE... TOO OFTEN A DISASTER.
I HUNT ALONE.
THEY CAN PRETEND IT'S A STORY--A BYLINE THEY CAN SHARE, AND TOAST OVER SOME EXOTIC TEA HE BRINGS HOME FRESH FROM A DRYING FIELD IN INDIA.
BUT LETTING HER GET CLOSE PUT HER IN HARM'S WAY...AND IT'LL HAPPEN AGAIN, AND AGAIN...
...AS LONG AS ANIMALS LIKE THIS ONE EXIST.
BETTER TO HUNT ALONE.

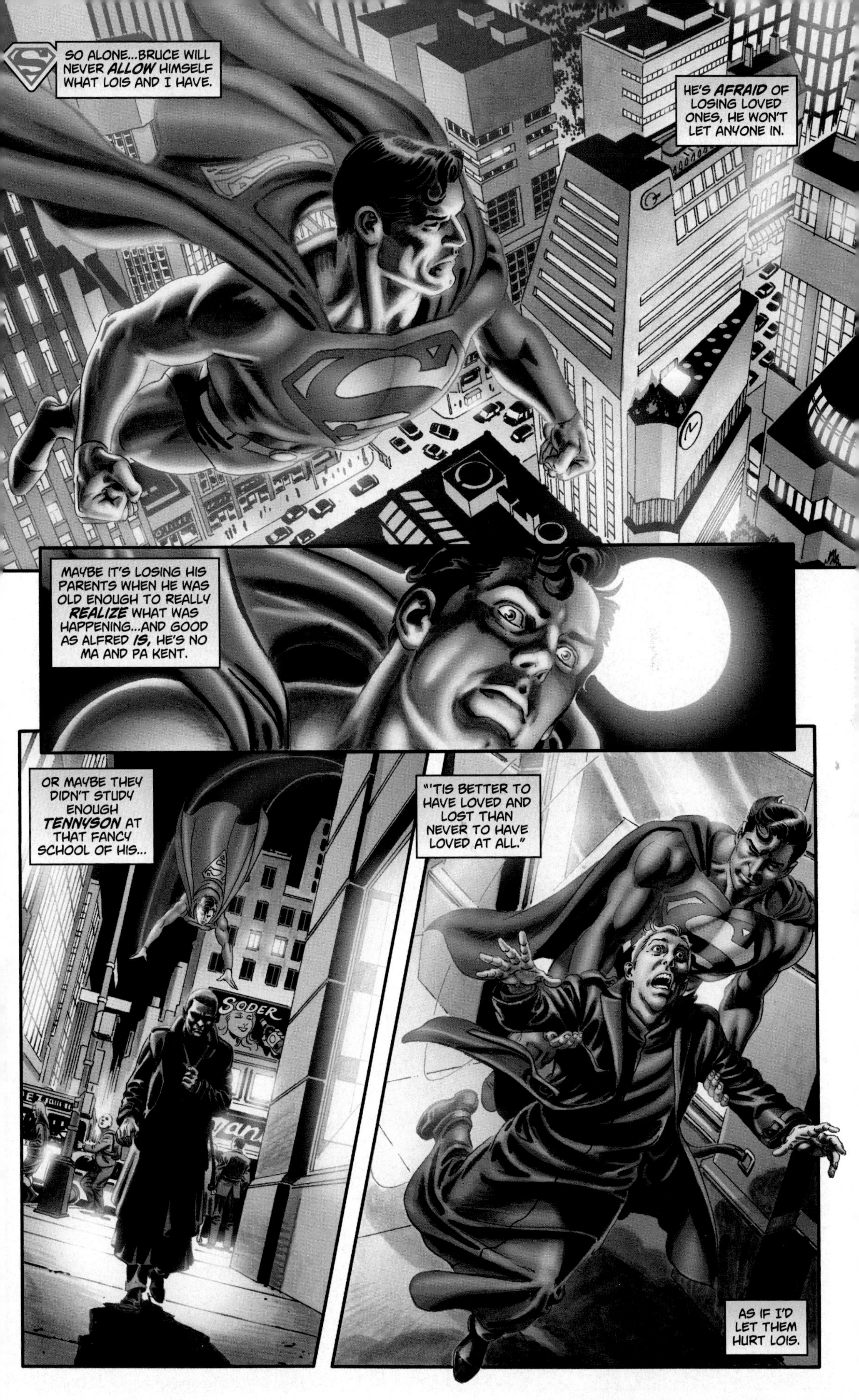
SO ALONE...BRUCE WILL NEVER ALLOW HIMSELF WHAT LOIS AND I HAVE.
HE'S AFRAID OF LOSING LOVED ONES, HE WON'T LET ANYONE IN.
MAYBE IT'S LOSING HIS PARENTS WHEN HE WAS OLD ENOUGH TO REALLY REALIZE WHAT WAS HAPPENING...AND GOOD AS ALFRED IS, HE'S NO MA AND PA KENT.
OR MAYBE THEY DIDN'T STUDY ENOUGH TENNYSON AT THAT FANCY SCHOOL OF HIS...
SODER
"'TIS BETTER TO HAVE LOVED AND LOST THAN NEVER TO HAVE LOVED AT ALL."
AS IF I'D LET THEM HURT LOIS.

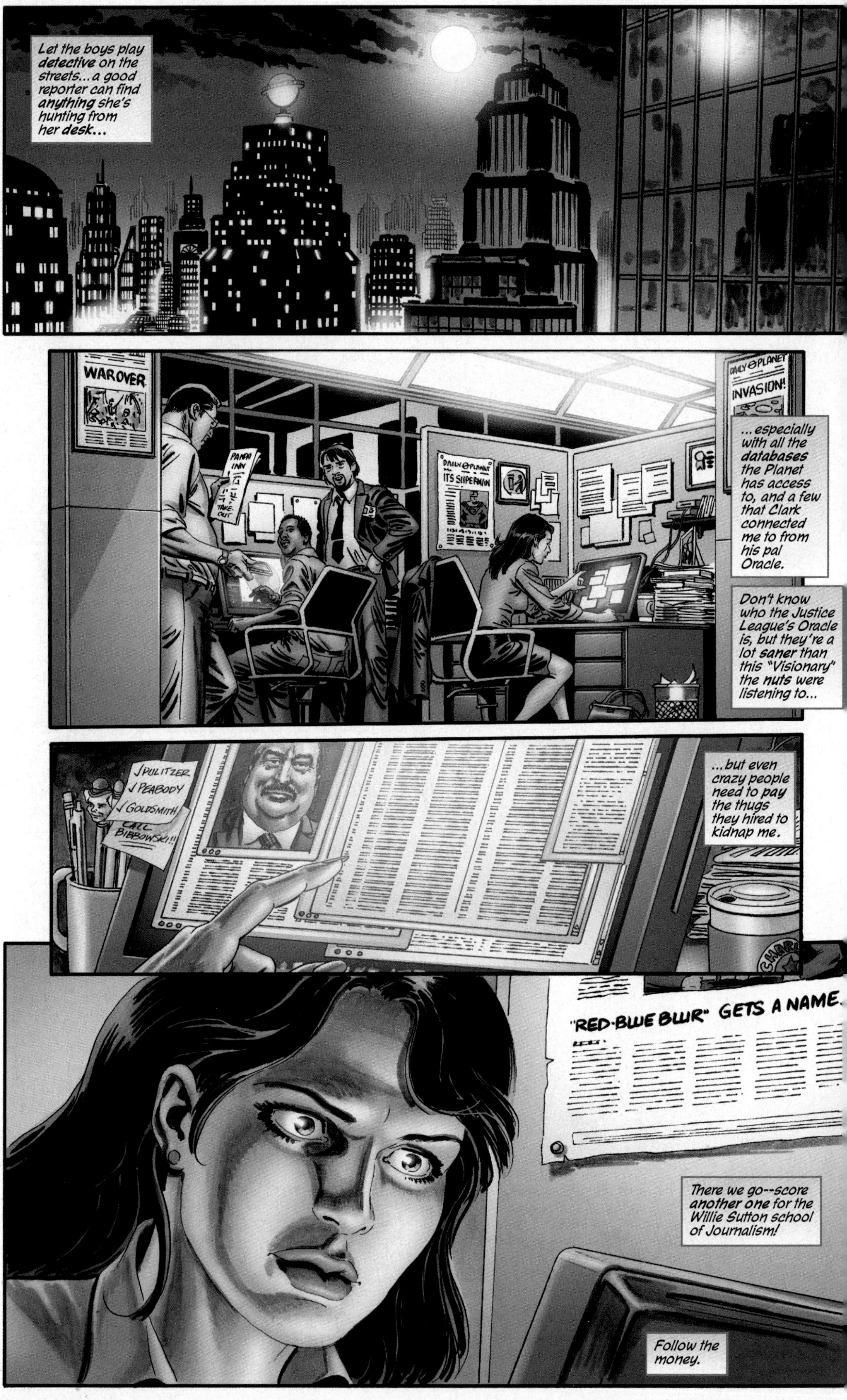

Let the boys play detective on the streets... a good reporter can find anything she's hunting from her desk...
WAR OVER
PANDA INN
TAKE-OUT
DAILY PLANET
ITS SUPERMAN
DAILY PLANET
INVASION!
...especially with all the databases the Planet has access to, and a few that Clark connected me to from his pal Oracle.
Don't know who the Justice League's Oracle is, but they're a lot saner than this "Visionary" the nuts were listening to...
√PULITZER
√PEABODY
√GOLDSMITH
CALL BIBBOWSKI!!
...but even crazy people need to pay the thugs they hired to kidnap me.
"RED-BLUE BLUR" GETS A NAME.
There we go--score another one for the Willie Sutton school of Journalism!
Follow the money.

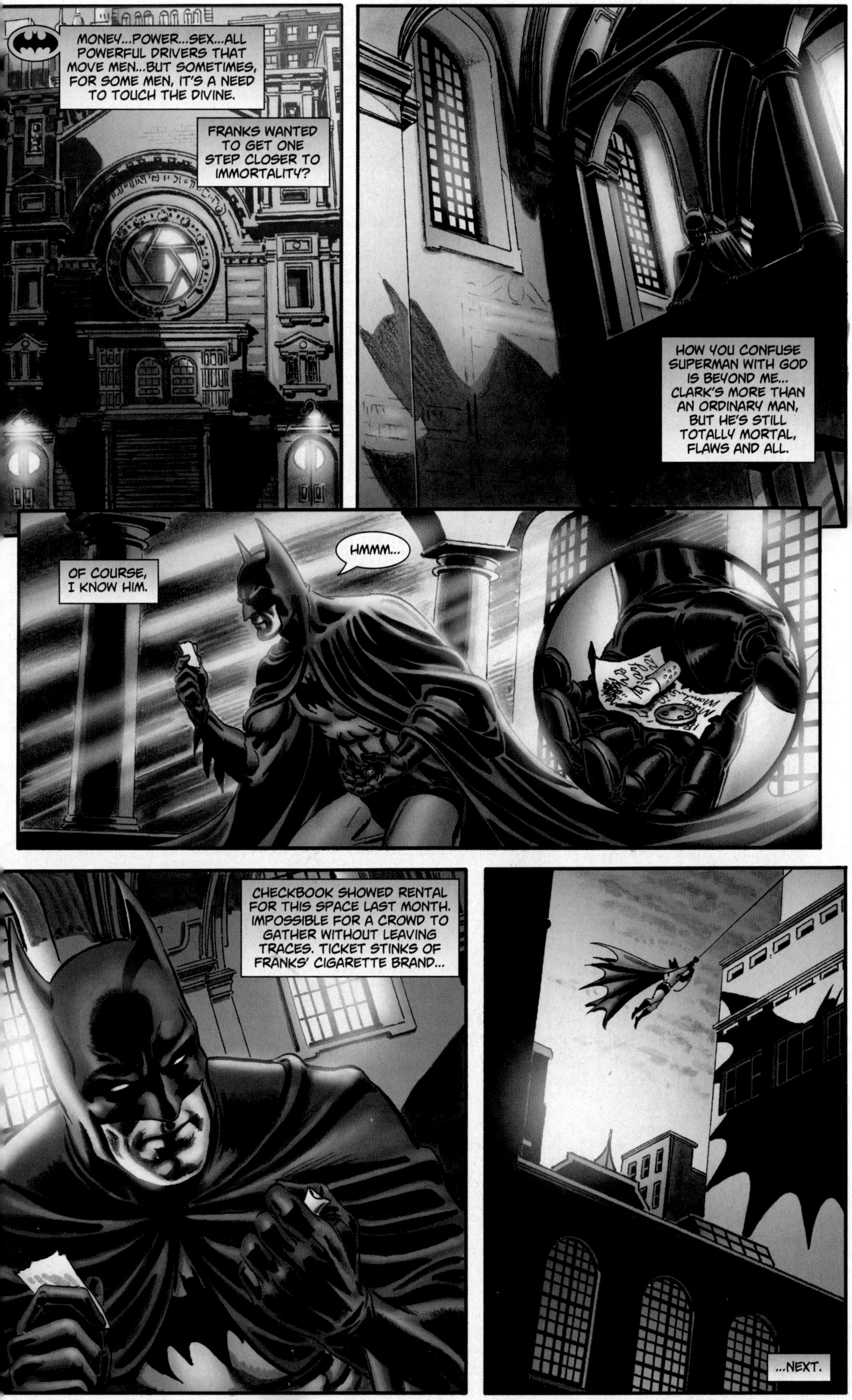
MONEY...POWER...SEX...ALL POWERFUL DRIVERS THAT MOVE MEN...BUT SOMETIMES, FOR SOME MEN, IT'S A NEED TO TOUCH THE DIVINE.
FRANKS WANTED TO GET ONE STEP CLOSER TO IMMORTALITY?
HOW YOU CONFUSE SUPERMAN WITH GOD IS BEYOND ME... CLARK'S MORE THAN AN ORDINARY MAN, BUT HE'S STILL TOTALLY MORTAL, FLAWS AND ALL.
OF COURSE, I KNOW HIM.
HMMM...
CHECKBOOK SHOWED RENTAL FOR THIS SPACE LAST MONTH. IMPOSSIBLE FOR A CROWD TO GATHER WITHOUT LEAVING TRACES. TICKET STINKS OF FRANKS' CIGARETTE BRAND...
...NEXT.

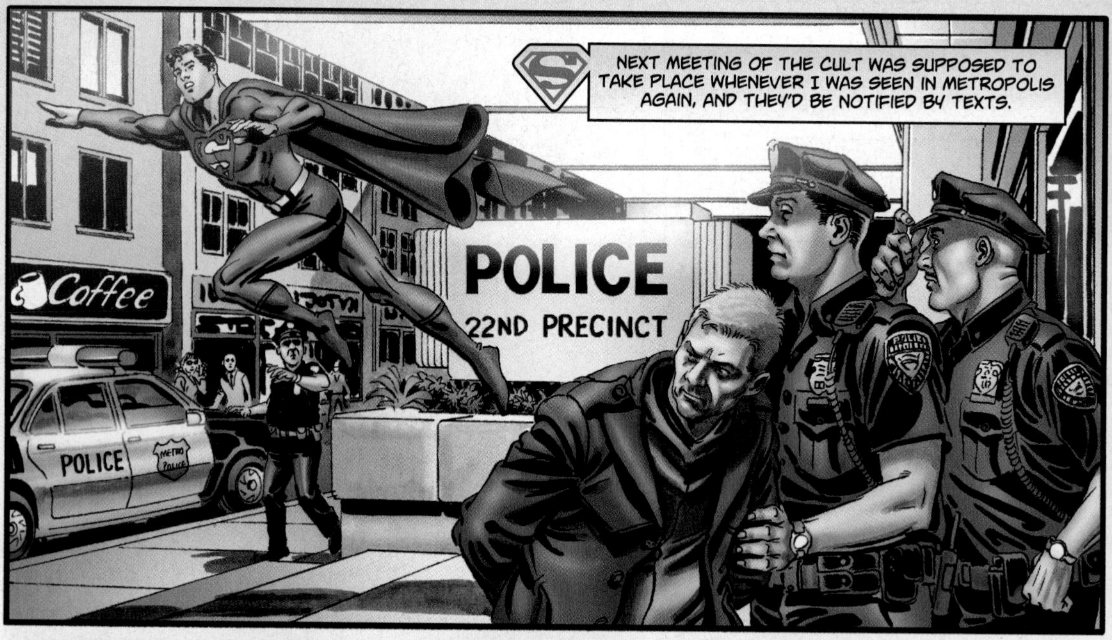
NEXT MEETING OF THE CULT WAS SUPPOSED TO TAKE PLACE WHENEVER I WAS SEEN IN METROPOLIS AGAIN, AND THEY'D BE NOTIFIED BY TEXTS.
POLICE
22ND PRECINCT
Coffee
POLICE

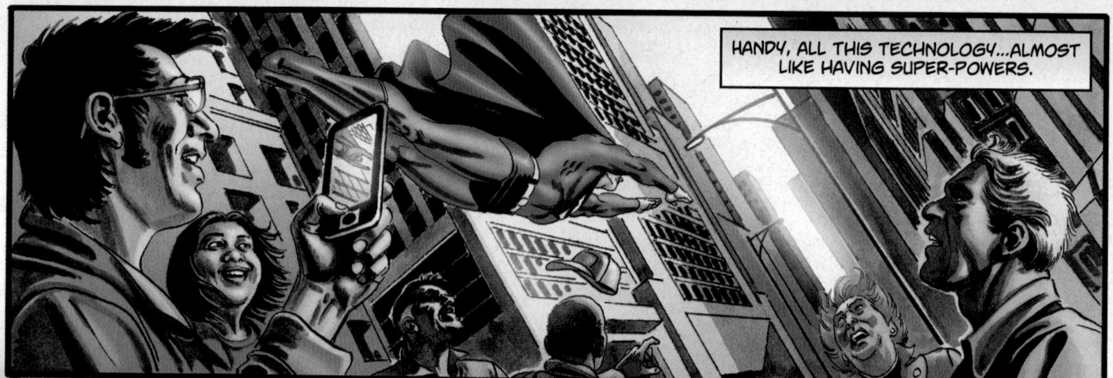
HANDY, ALL THIS TECHNOLOGY...ALMOST LIKE HAVING SUPER-POWERS.

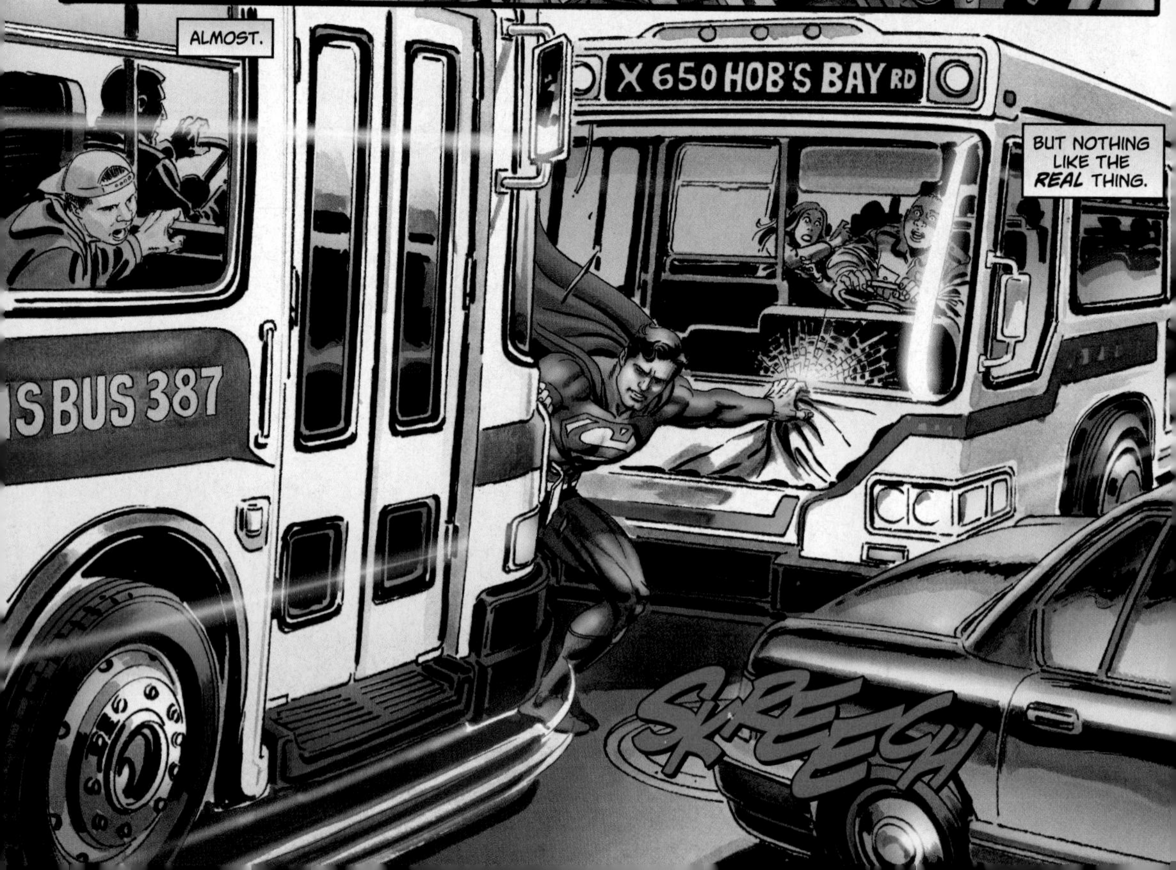
ALMOST.
X 650 HOB'S BAY RD
BUT NOTHING LIKE THE *REAL* THING.
S BUS 387
SKREECH

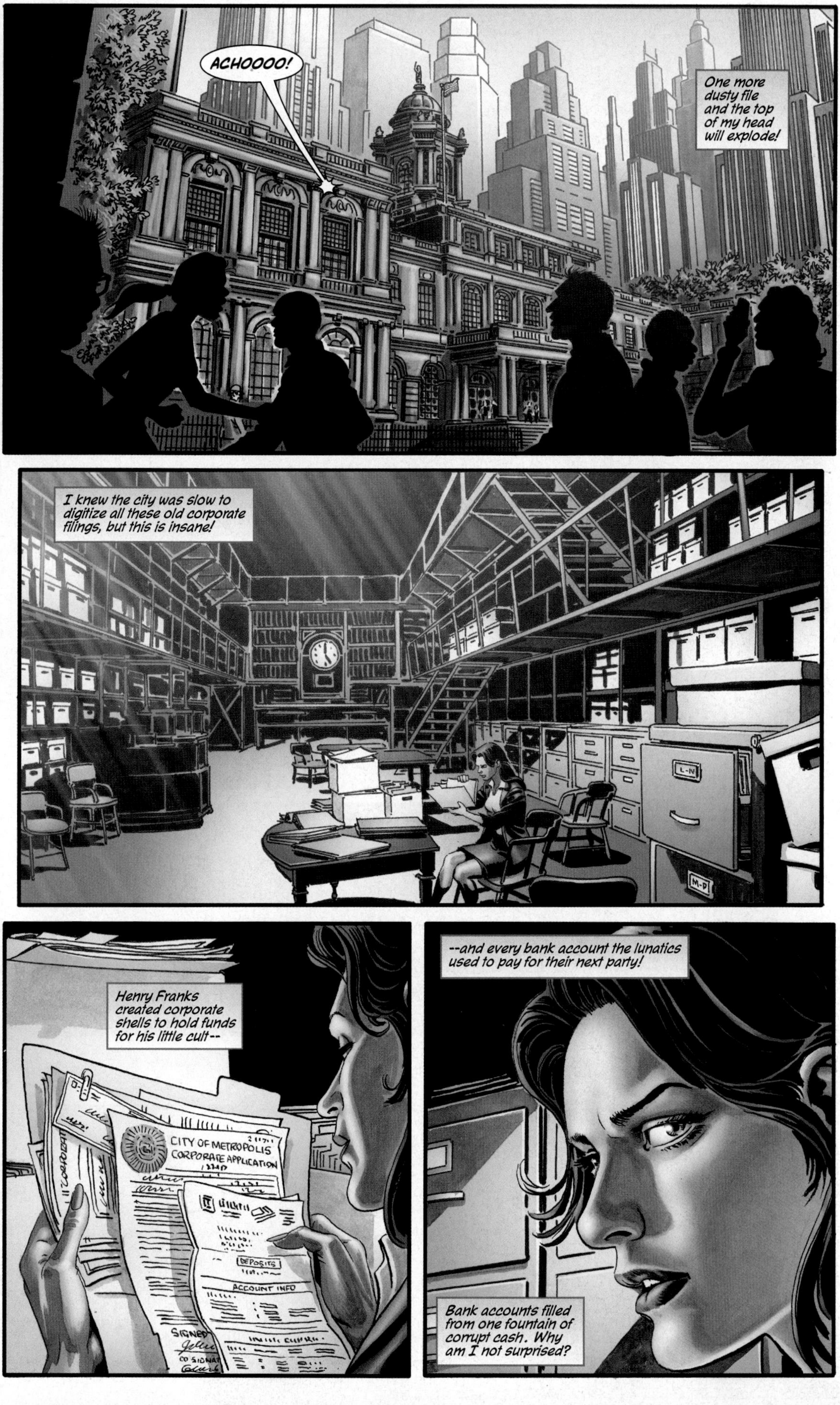
ACHOOOO!
One more dusty file and the top of my head will explode!
I knew the city was slow to digitize all these old corporate filings, but this is insane!
L-N
M-P
Henry Franks created corporate shells to hold funds for his little cult--
CITY OF METROPOLIS CORPORATE APPLICATION
DEPOSITS
ACCOUNT INFO
--and every bank account the lunatics used to pay for their next party!
Bank accounts filled from one fountain of corrupt cash. Why am I not surprised?

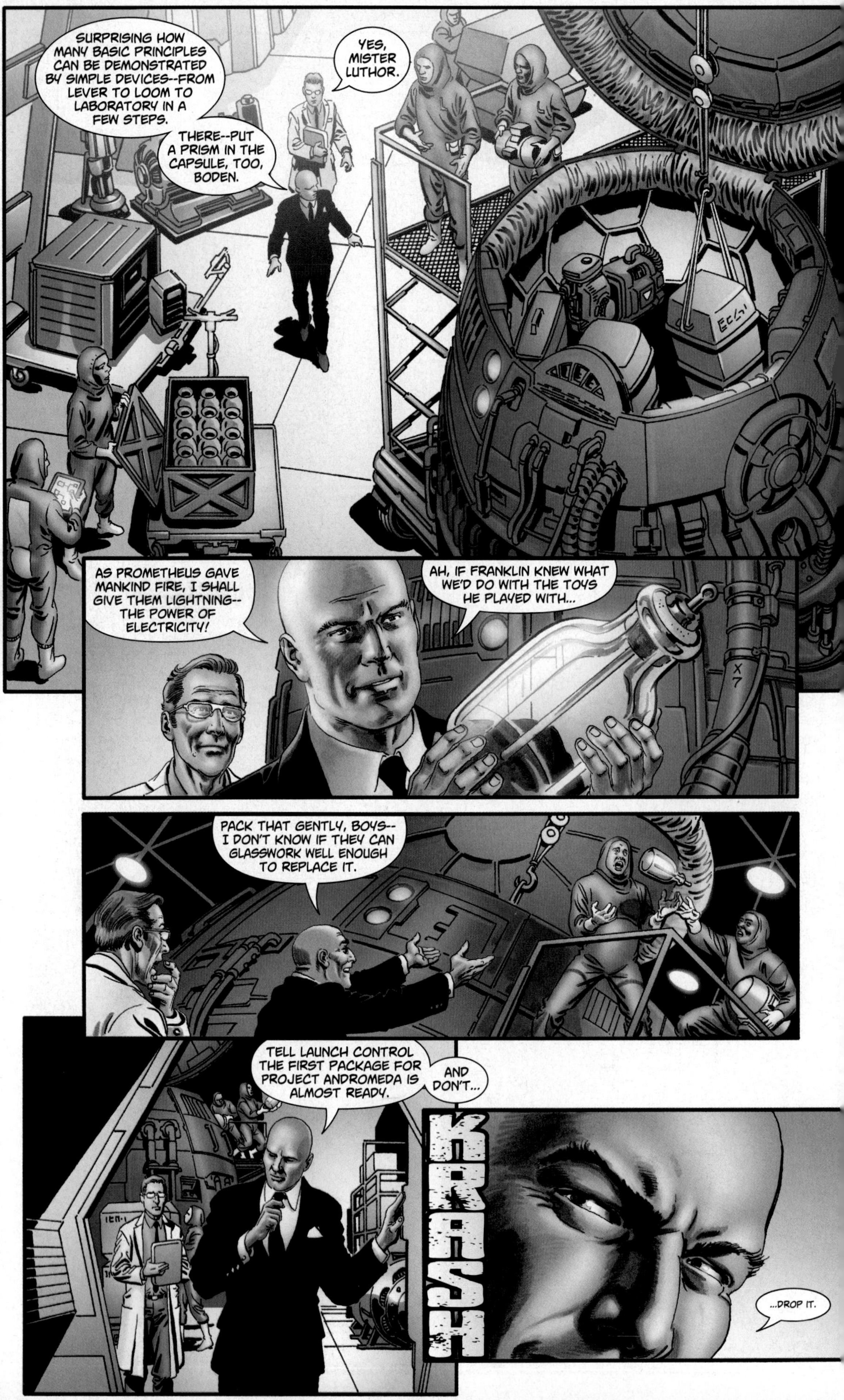
SURPRISING HOW MANY BASIC PRINCIPLES CAN BE DEMONSTRATED BY SIMPLE DEVICES--FROM LEVER TO LOOM TO LABORATORY IN A FEW STEPS.
YES, MISTER LUTHOR.
THERE--PUT A PRISM IN THE CAPSULE, TOO, BODEN.
AS PROMETHEUS GAVE MANKIND FIRE, I SHALL GIVE THEM LIGHTNING-- THE POWER OF ELECTRICITY!
AH, IF FRANKLIN KNEW WHAT WE'D DO WITH THE TOYS HE PLAYED WITH...
X 7
PACK THAT GENTLY, BOYS-- I DON'T KNOW IF THEY CAN GLASSWORK WELL ENOUGH TO REPLACE IT.
TELL LAUNCH CONTROL THE FIRST PACKAGE FOR PROJECT ANDROMEDA IS ALMOST READY.
AND DON'T...
KRASH
...DROP IT.

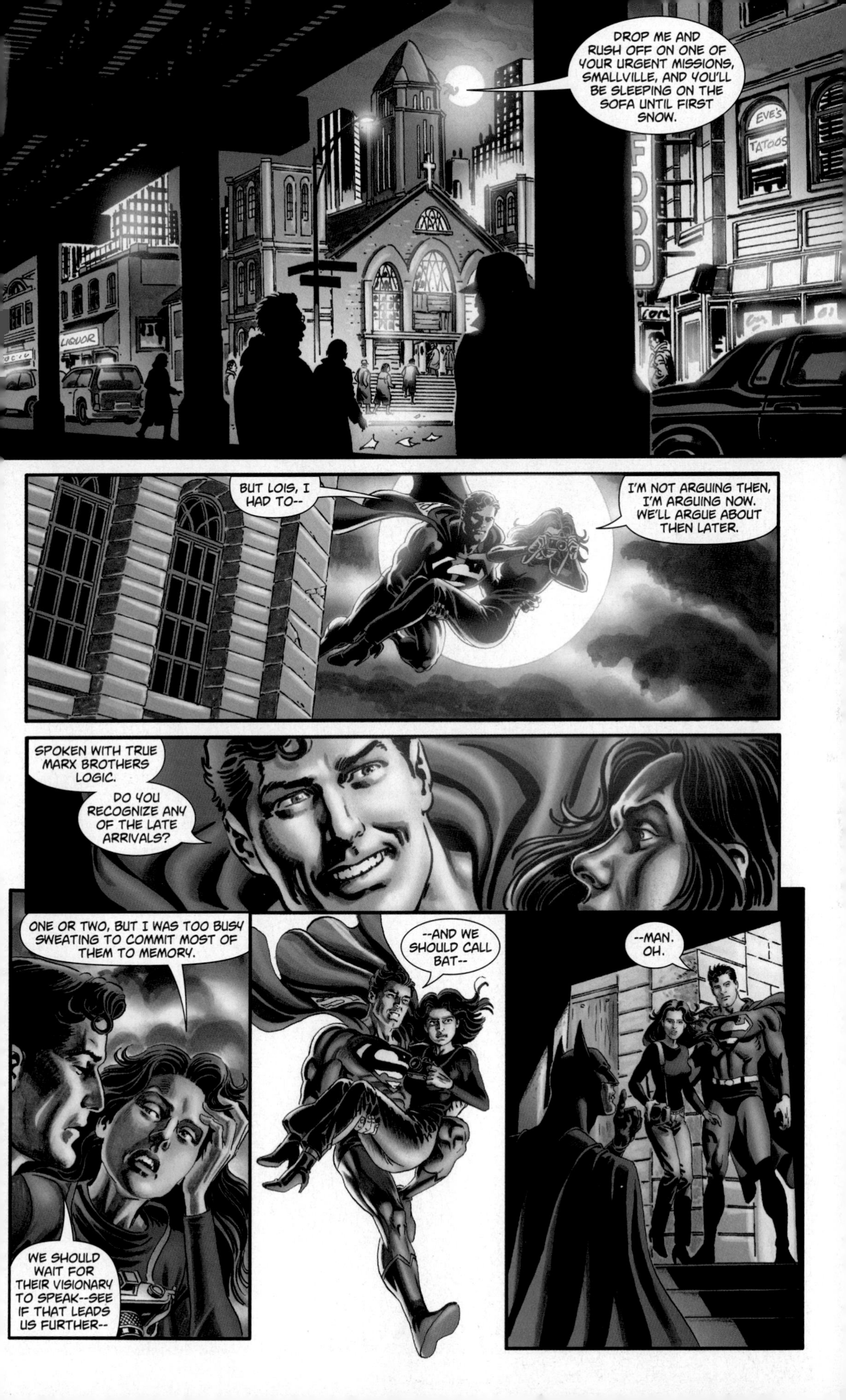
DROP ME AND RUSH OFF ON ONE OF YOUR URGENT MISSIONS, SMALLVILLE, AND YOU'LL BE SLEEPING ON THE SOFA UNTIL FIRST SNOW.
EVE'S TATOOS
FOOD
LIQUOR
BUT LOIS, I HAD TO--
I'M NOT ARGUING THEN, I'M ARGUING NOW. WE'LL ARGUE ABOUT THEN LATER.
SPOKEN WITH TRUE MARX BROTHERS LOGIC.
DO YOU RECOGNIZE ANY OF THE LATE ARRIVALS?
ONE OR TWO, BUT I WAS TOO BUSY SWEATING TO COMMIT MOST OF THEM TO MEMORY.
WE SHOULD WAIT FOR THEIR VISIONARY TO SPEAK--SEE IF THAT LEADS US FURTHER--
--AND WE SHOULD CALL BAT--
--MAN. OH.

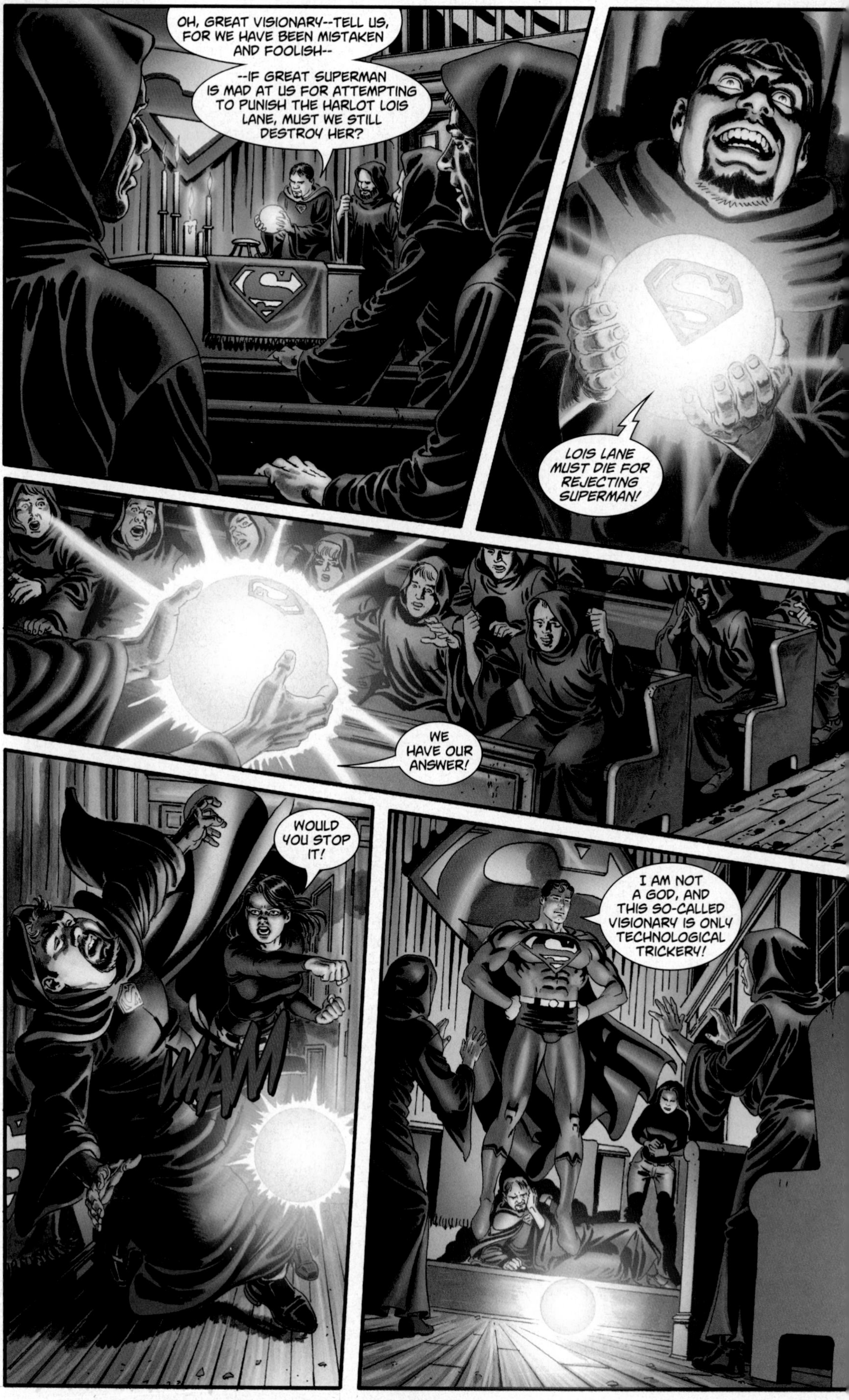
OH, GREAT VISIONARY--TELL US, FOR WE HAVE BEEN MISTAKEN AND FOOLISH--
--IF GREAT SUPERMAN IS MAD AT US FOR ATTEMPTING TO PUNISH THE HARLOT LOIS LANE, MUST WE STILL DESTROY HER?
LOIS LANE MUST DIE FOR REJECTING SUPERMAN!
WE HAVE OUR ANSWER!
WOULD YOU STOP IT!
WHAM
I AM NOT A GOD, AND THIS SO-CALLED VISIONARY IS ONLY TECHNOLOGICAL TRICKERY!

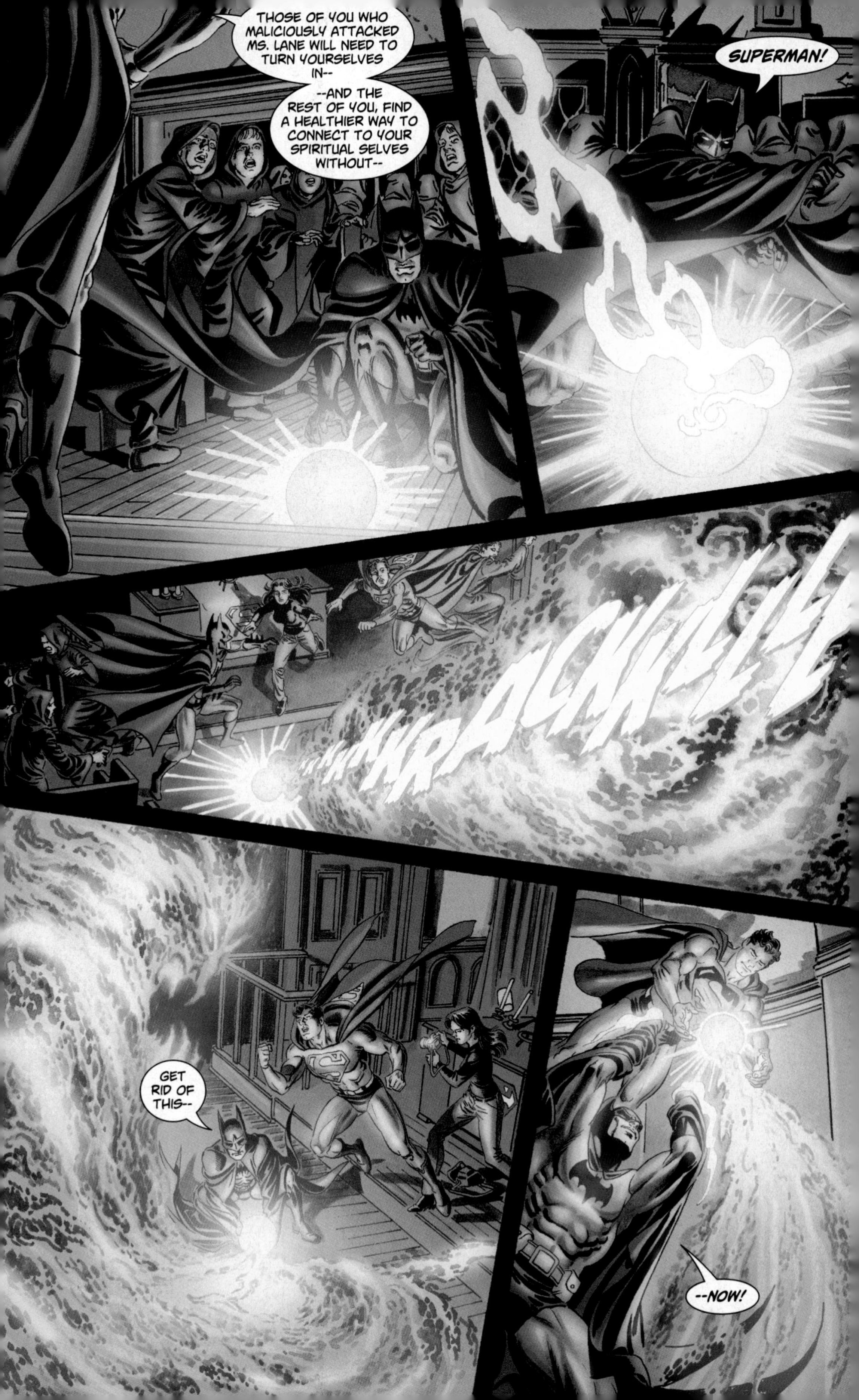
THOSE OF YOU WHO MALICIOUSLY ATTACKED MS. LANE WILL NEED TO TURN YOURSELVES IN--
--AND THE REST OF YOU, FIND A HEALTHIER WAY TO CONNECT TO YOUR SPIRITUAL SELVES WITHOUT--
SUPERMAN!
KRACKKK
GET RID OF THIS--
--NOW!

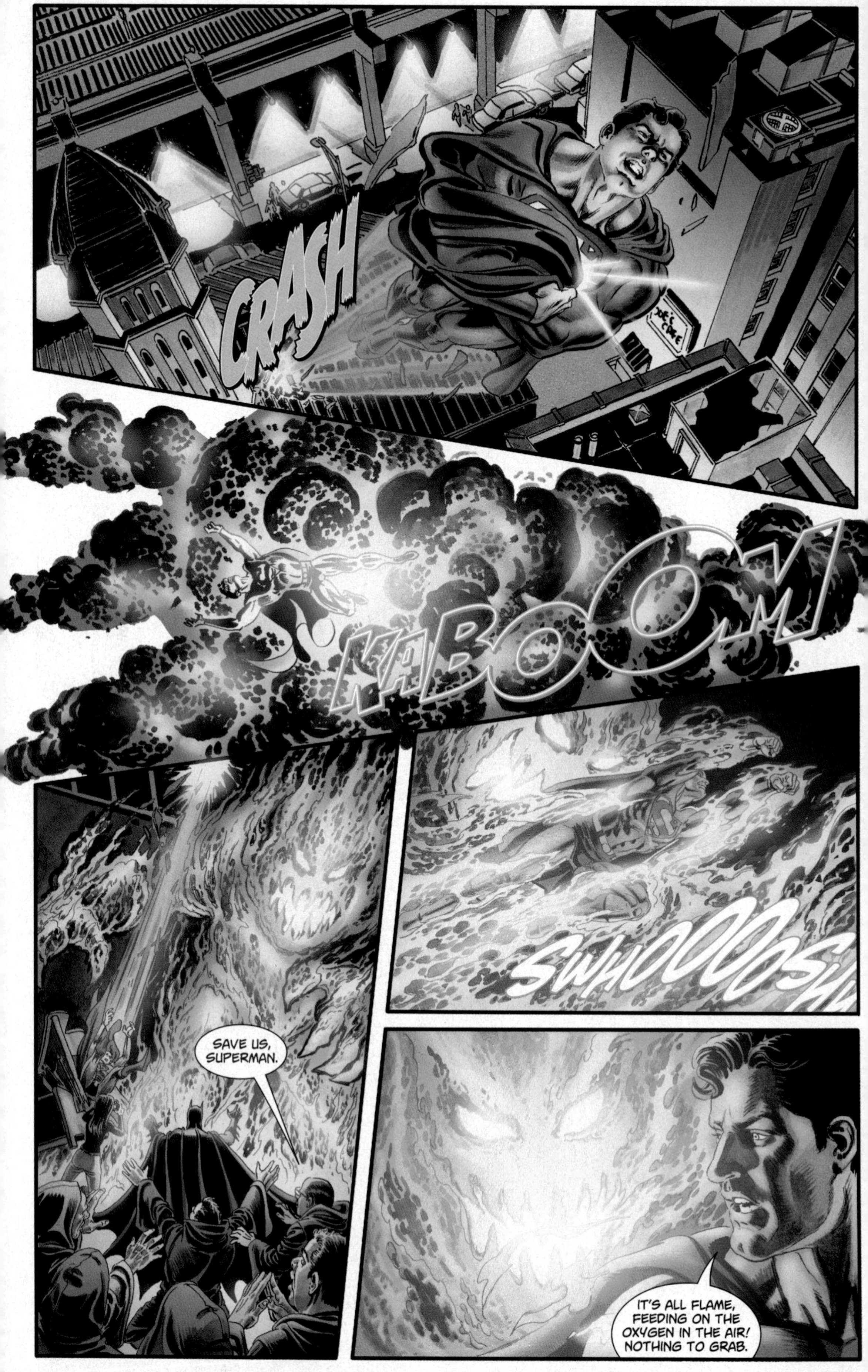
CRASH
JOE'S CAFE
KABOOOM
SWHOOOOSH
SAVE US, SUPERMAN.
IT'S ALL FLAME, FEEDING ON THE OXYGEN IN THE AIR! NOTHING TO GRAB.

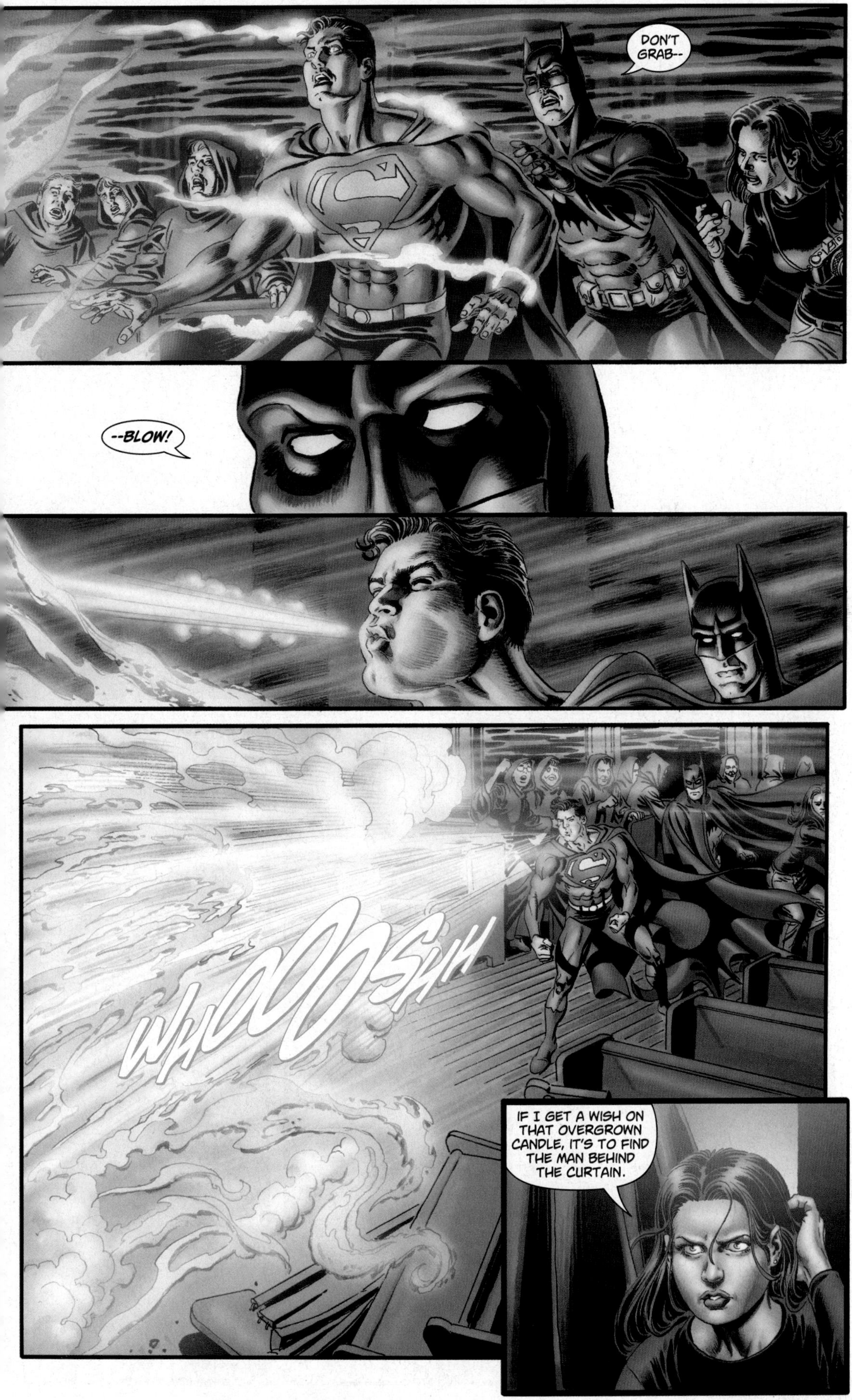
DON'T GRAB--
--BLOW!
WHOOOOSHH
IF I GET A WISH ON THAT OVERGROWN CANDLE, IT'S TO FIND THE MAN BEHIND THE CURTAIN.

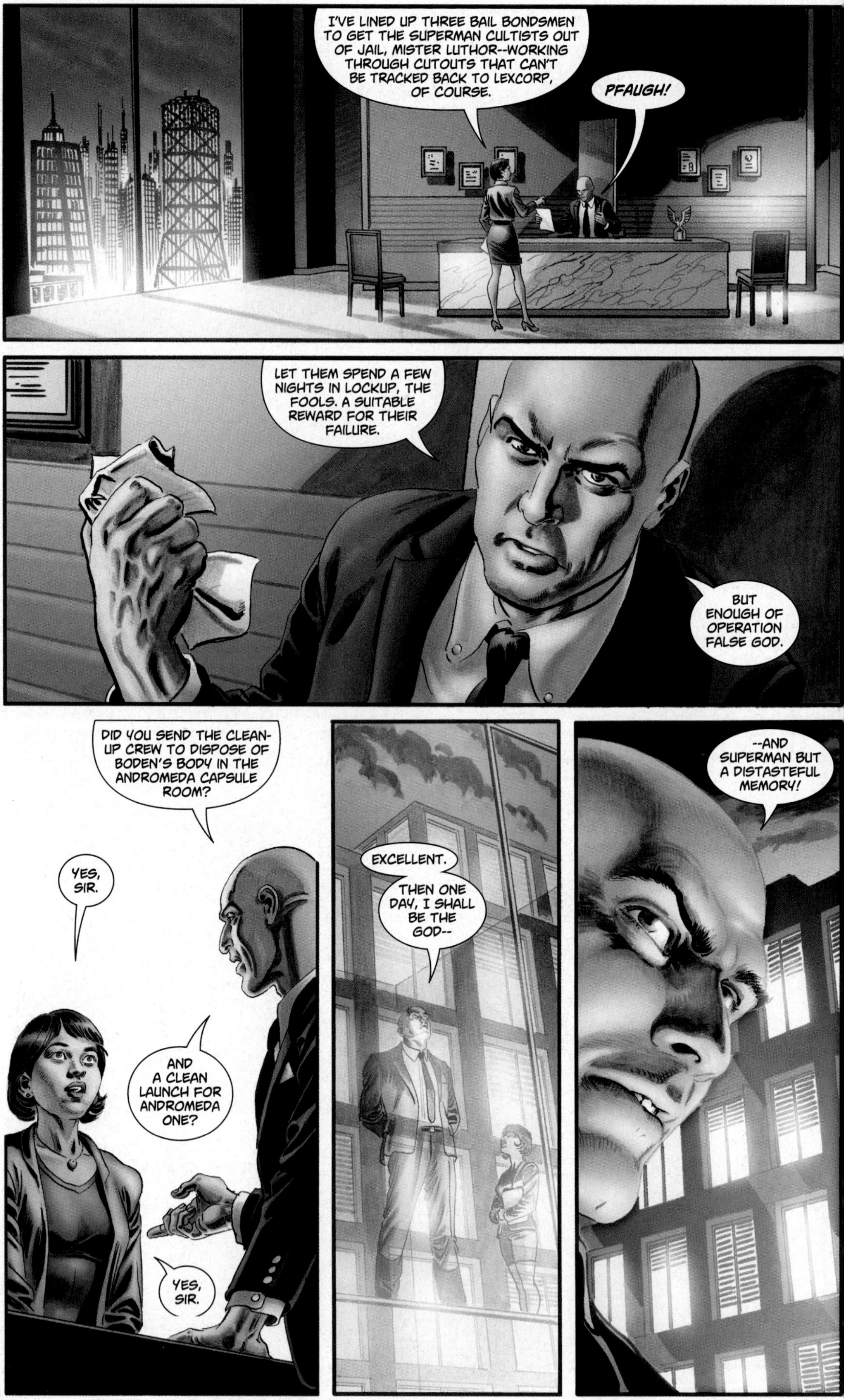
I'VE LINED UP THREE BAIL BONDSMEN TO GET THE SUPERMAN CULTISTS OUT OF JAIL, MISTER LUTHOR--WORKING THROUGH CUTOUTS THAT CAN'T BE TRACKED BACK TO LEXCORP, OF COURSE.
PFAUGH!
LET THEM SPEND A FEW NIGHTS IN LOCKUP, THE FOOLS. A SUITABLE REWARD FOR THEIR FAILURE.
BUT ENOUGH OF OPERATION FALSE GOD.
DID YOU SEND THE CLEAN-UP CREW TO DISPOSE OF BODEN'S BODY IN THE ANDROMEDA CAPSULE ROOM?
YES, SIR.
AND A CLEAN LAUNCH FOR ANDROMEDA ONE?
YES, SIR.
EXCELLENT.
THEN ONE DAY, I SHALL BE THE GOD--
--AND SUPERMAN BUT A DISTASTEFUL MEMORY!

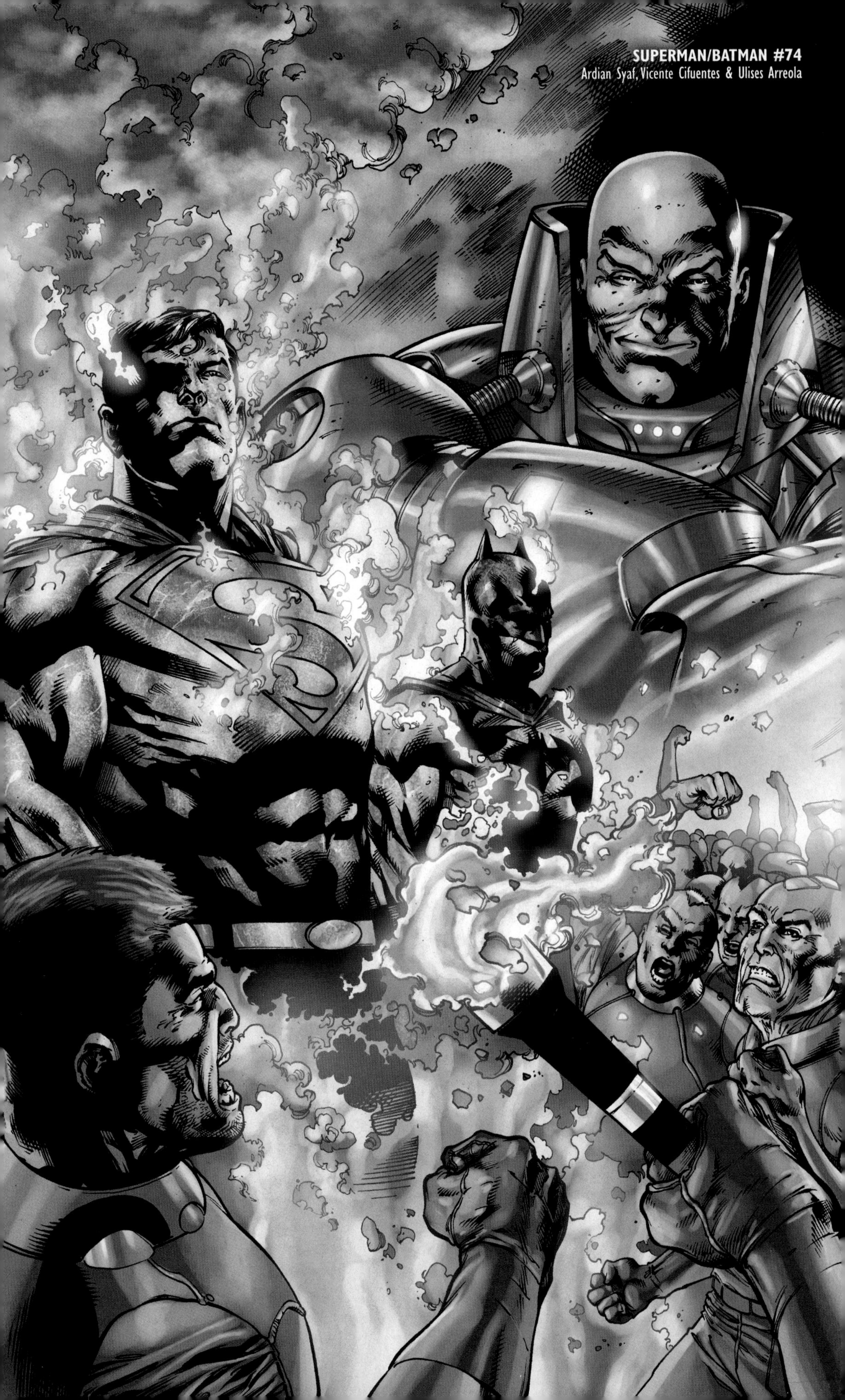

SUPERMAN/BATMAN #74
Ardian Syaf, Vicente Cifuentes & Ulises Arreola

ASCENSION

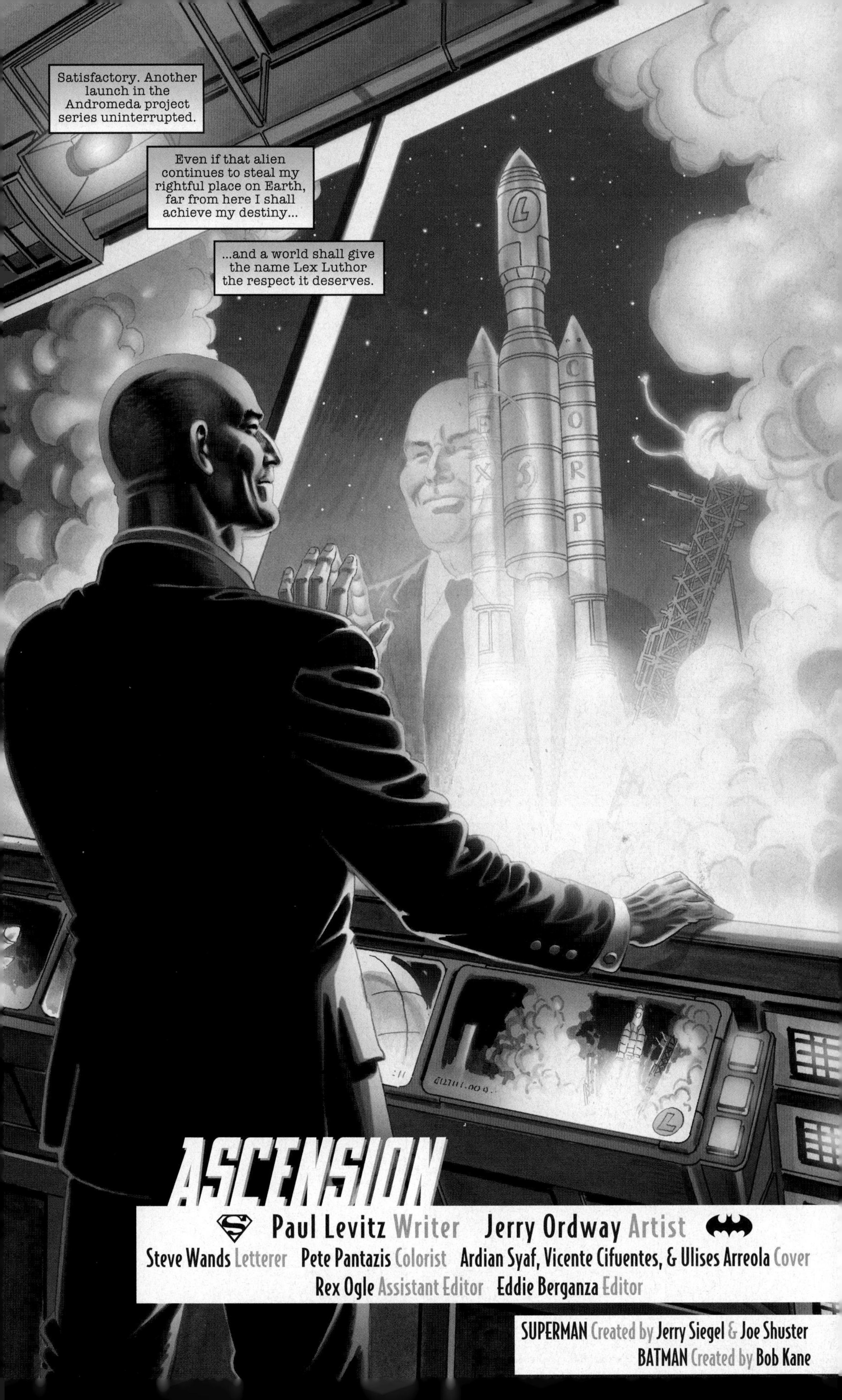
Satisfactory. Another launch in the Andromeda project series uninterrupted.
Even if that alien continues to steal my rightful place on Earth, far from here I shall achieve my destiny...
...and a world shall give the name Lex Luthor the respect it deserves.
L
C
O
R
P
ASCENSION
Paul Levitz Writer Jerry Ordway Artist
Steve Wands Letterer Pete Pantazis Colorist Ardian Syaf, Vicente Cifuentes, & Ulises Arreola Cover
Rex Ogle Assistant Editor Eddie Berganza Editor
SUPERMAN Created by Jerry Siegel & Joe Shuster
BATMAN Created by Bob Kane

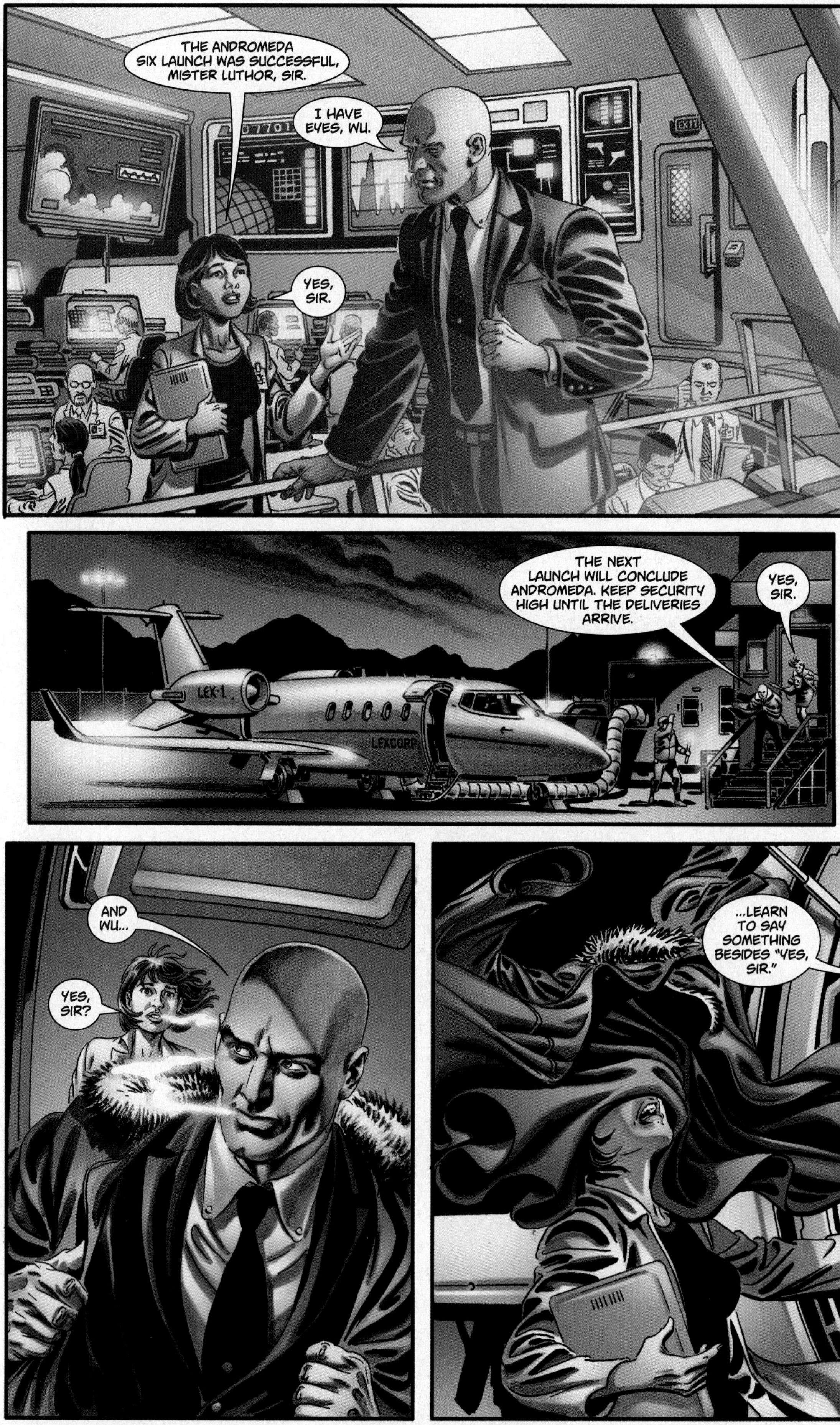
THE ANDROMEDA SIX LAUNCH WAS SUCCESSFUL, MISTER LUTHOR, SIR.
I HAVE EYES, WU.
YES, SIR.
LEX-1
LEXCORP
THE NEXT LAUNCH WILL CONCLUDE ANDROMEDA. KEEP SECURITY HIGH UNTIL THE DELIVERIES ARRIVE.
YES, SIR.
AND WU...
YES, SIR?
...LEARN TO SAY SOMETHING BESIDES "YES, SIR."

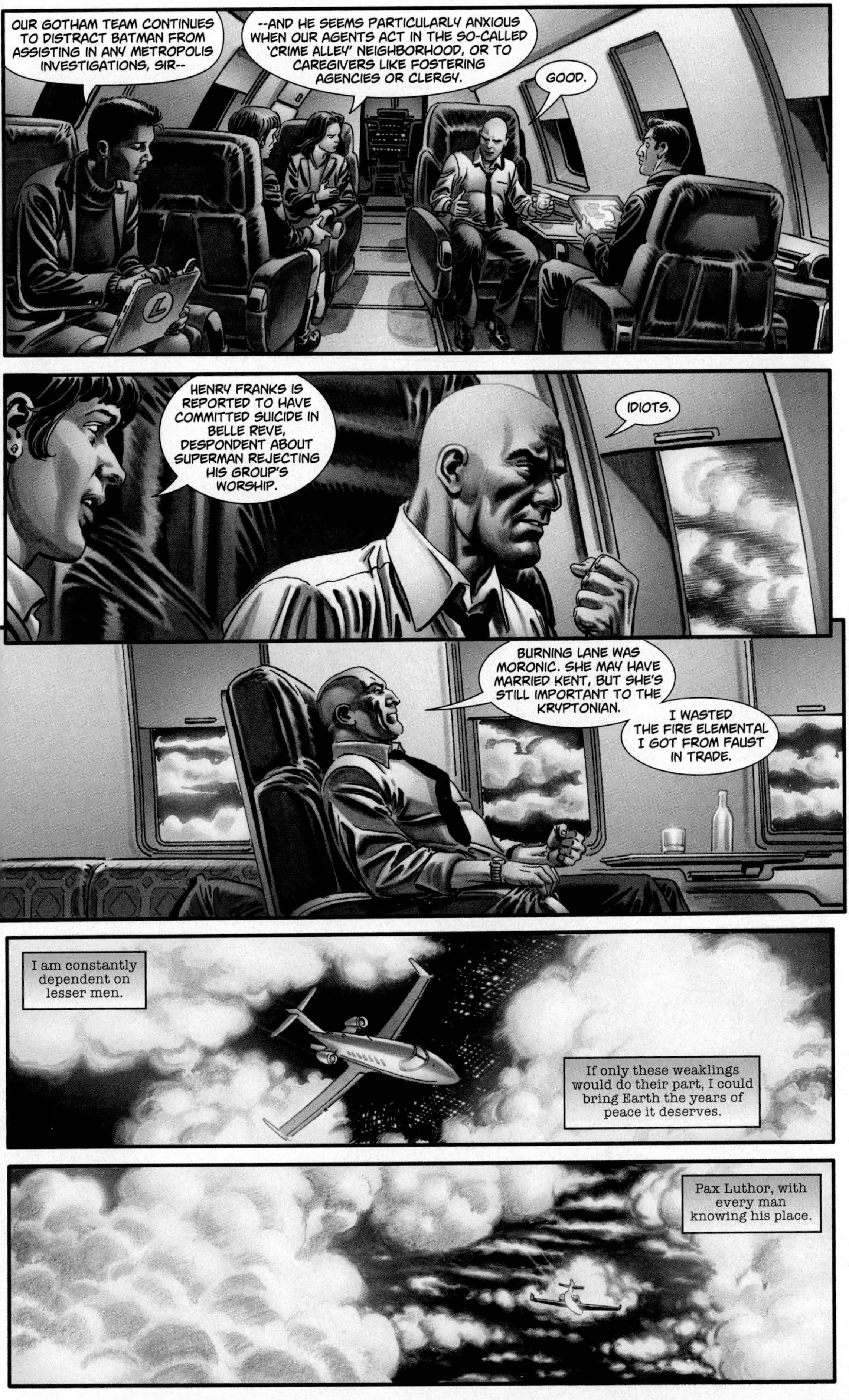

OUR GOTHAM TEAM CONTINUES TO DISTRACT BATMAN FROM ASSISTING IN ANY METROPOLIS INVESTIGATIONS, SIR--
--AND HE SEEMS PARTICULARLY ANXIOUS WHEN OUR AGENTS ACT IN THE SO-CALLED 'CRIME ALLEY' NEIGHBORHOOD, OR TO CAREGIVERS LIKE FOSTERING AGENCIES OR CLERGY.
GOOD.
HENRY FRANKS IS REPORTED TO HAVE COMMITTED SUICIDE IN BELLE REVE, DESPONDENT ABOUT SUPERMAN REJECTING HIS GROUP'S WORSHIP.
IDIOTS.
BURNING LANE WAS MORONIC. SHE MAY HAVE MARRIED KENT, BUT SHE'S STILL IMPORTANT TO THE KRYPTONIAN.
I WASTED THE FIRE ELEMENTAL I GOT FROM FAUST IN TRADE.
I am constantly dependent on lesser men.
If only these weaklings would do their part, I could bring Earth the years of peace it deserves.
Pax Luthor, with every man knowing his place.

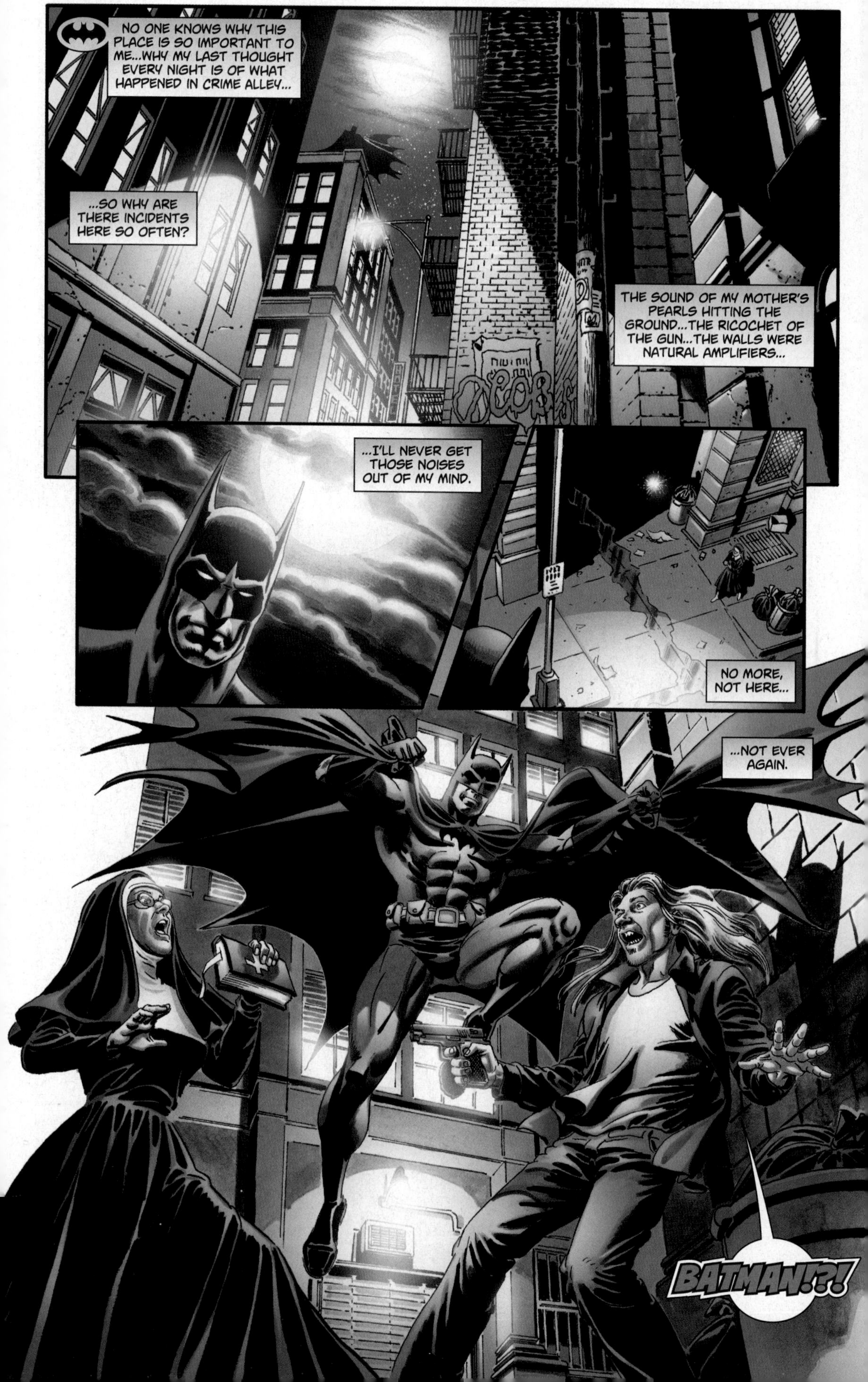
NO ONE KNOWS WHY THIS PLACE IS SO IMPORTANT TO ME...WHY MY LAST THOUGHT EVERY NIGHT IS OF WHAT HAPPENED IN CRIME ALLEY...
...SO WHY ARE THERE INCIDENTS HERE SO OFTEN?
THE SOUND OF MY MOTHER'S PEARLS HITTING THE GROUND...THE RICOCHET OF THE GUN...THE WALLS WERE NATURAL AMPLIFIERS...
...I'LL NEVER GET THOSE NOISES OUT OF MY MIND.
NO MORE, NOT HERE...
...NOT EVER AGAIN.
BATMAN!?!

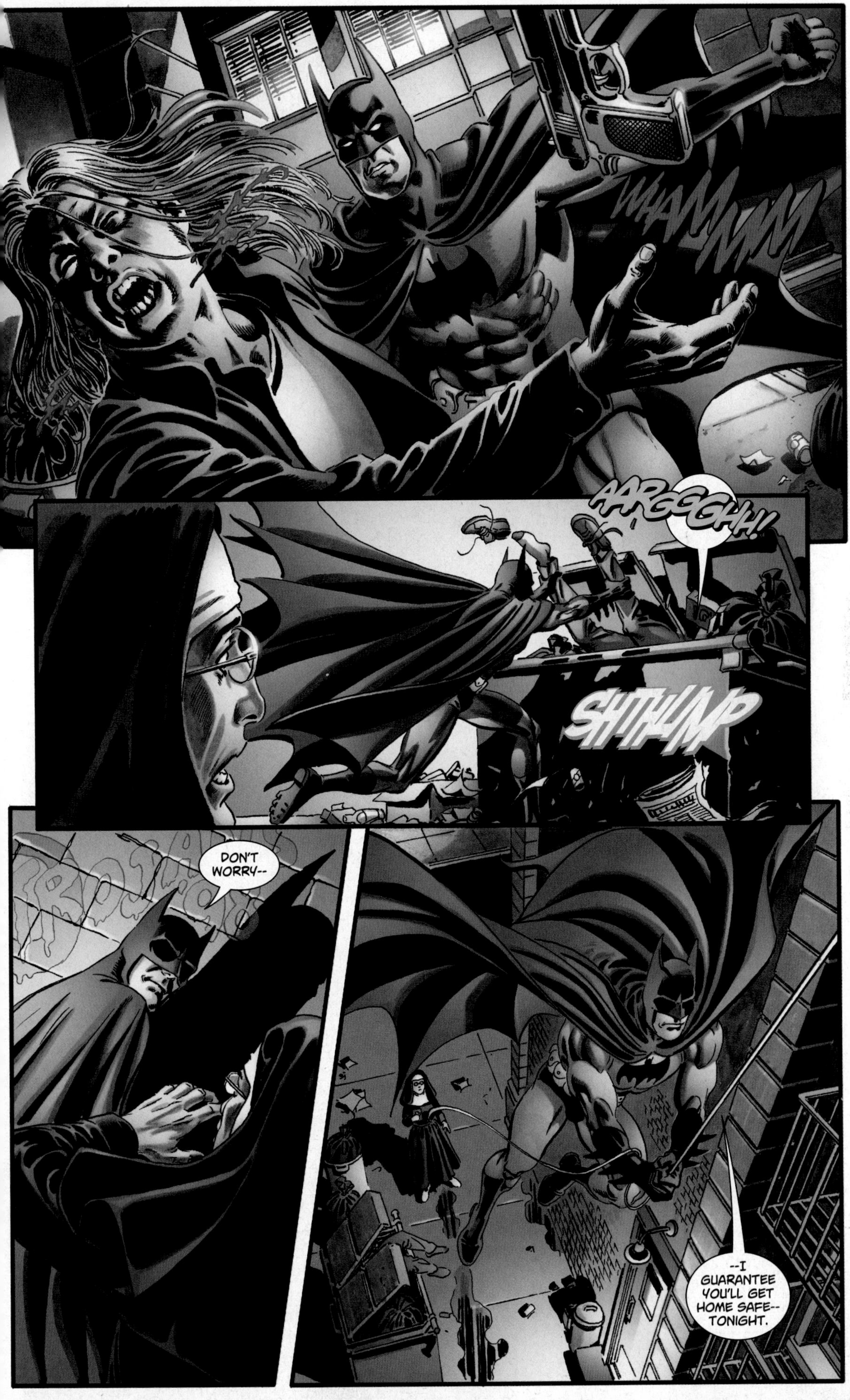
WHAMMM
AARGGGHH!
SHTHUMP
DON'T WORRY--
--I GUARANTEE YOU'LL GET HOME SAFE--TONIGHT.

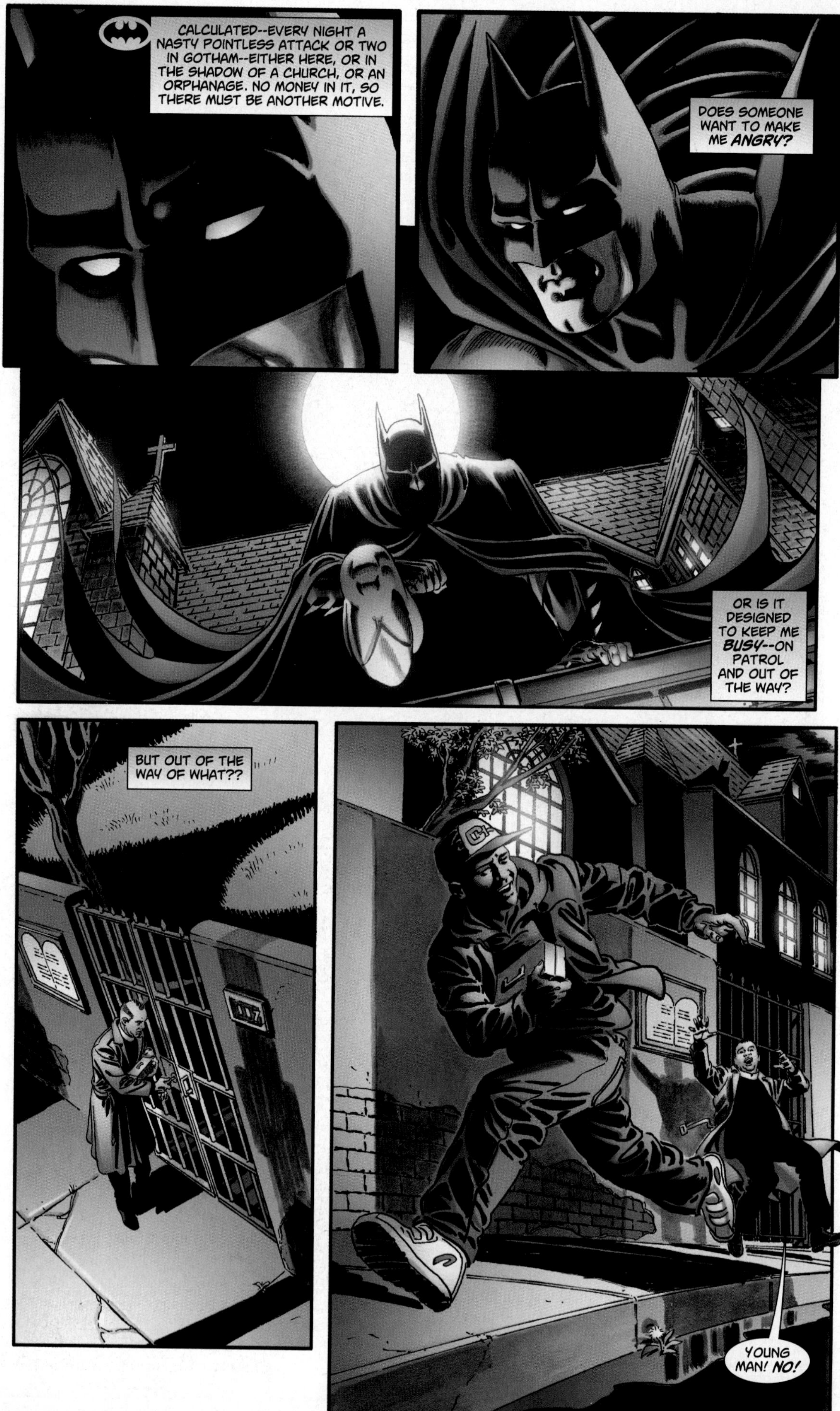

CALCULATED--EVERY NIGHT A NASTY POINTLESS ATTACK OR TWO IN GOTHAM--EITHER HERE, OR IN THE SHADOW OF A CHURCH, OR AN ORPHANAGE. NO MONEY IN IT, SO THERE MUST BE ANOTHER MOTIVE.
DOES SOMEONE WANT TO MAKE ME ANGRY?
OR IS IT DESIGNED TO KEEP ME BUSY--ON PATROL AND OUT OF THE WAY?
BUT OUT OF THE WAY OF WHAT??
YOUNG MAN! NO!

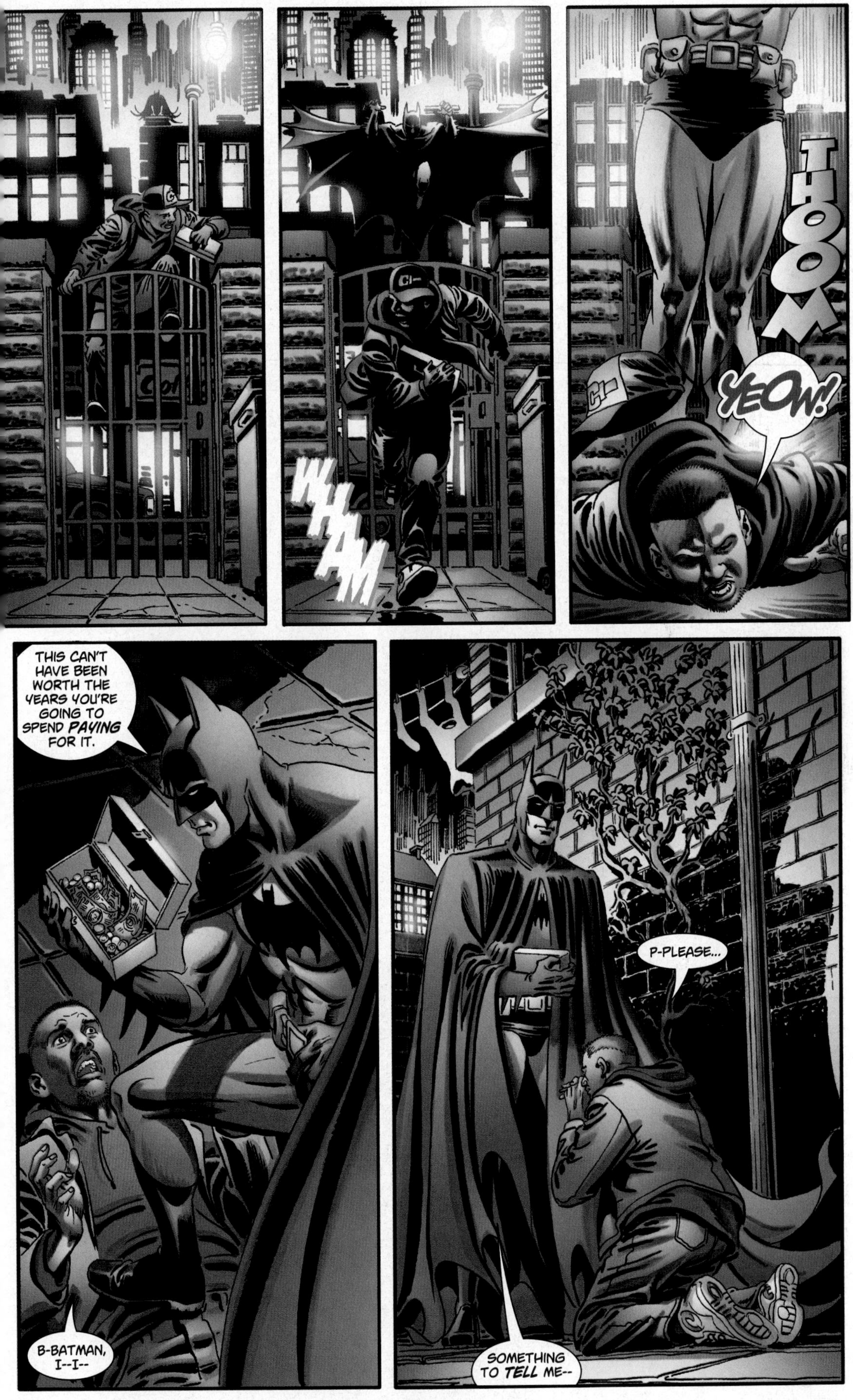
WHAM
THOOM
YEOW!
THIS CAN'T HAVE BEEN WORTH THE YEARS YOU'RE GOING TO SPEND *PAYING* FOR IT.
B-BATMAN, I--I--
P-PLEASE...
SOMETHING TO *TELL* ME--

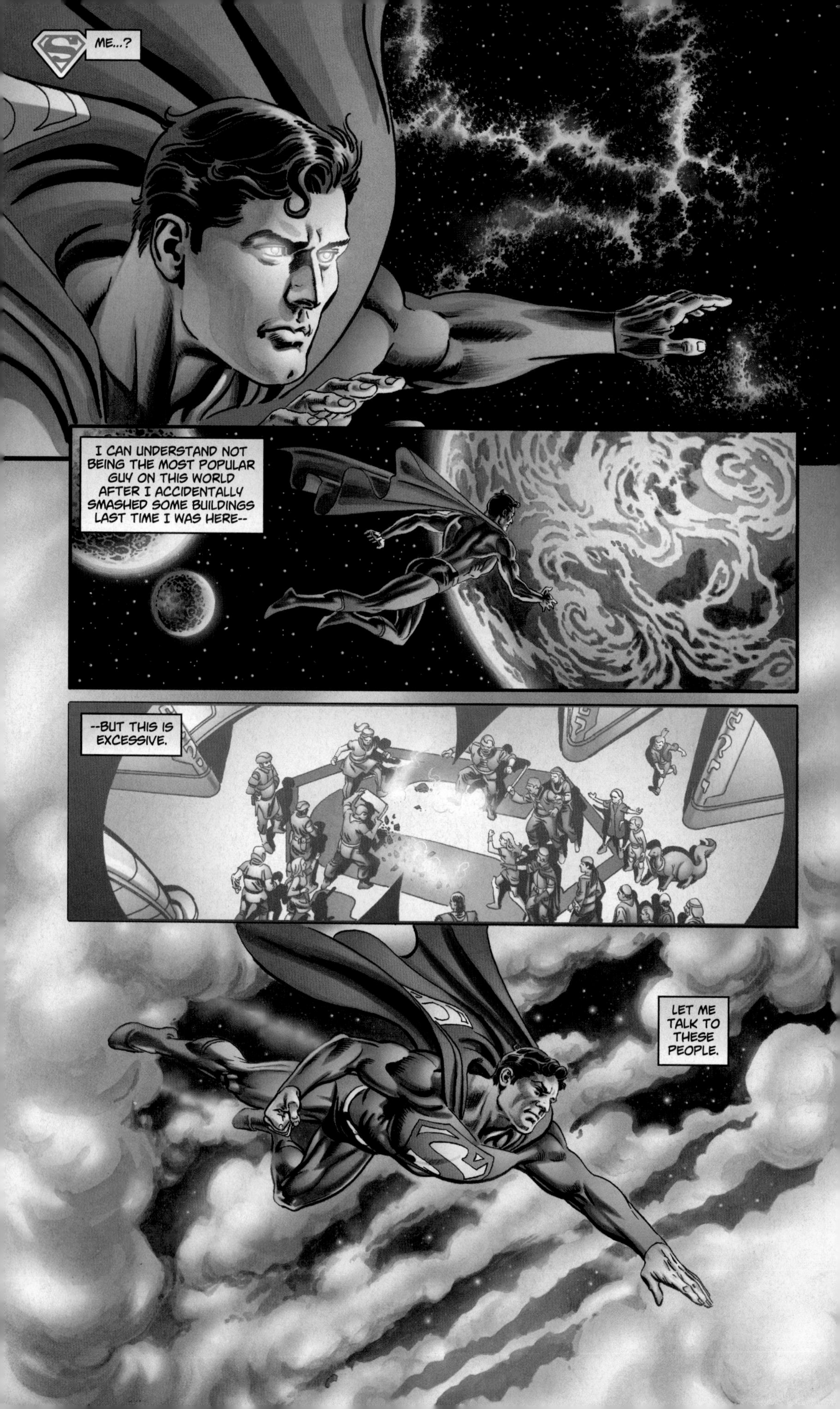
ME...?
I CAN UNDERSTAND NOT BEING THE MOST POPULAR GUY ON THIS WORLD AFTER I ACCIDENTALLY SMASHED SOME BUILDINGS LAST TIME I WAS HERE--
--BUT THIS IS EXCESSIVE.
LET ME TALK TO THESE PEOPLE.

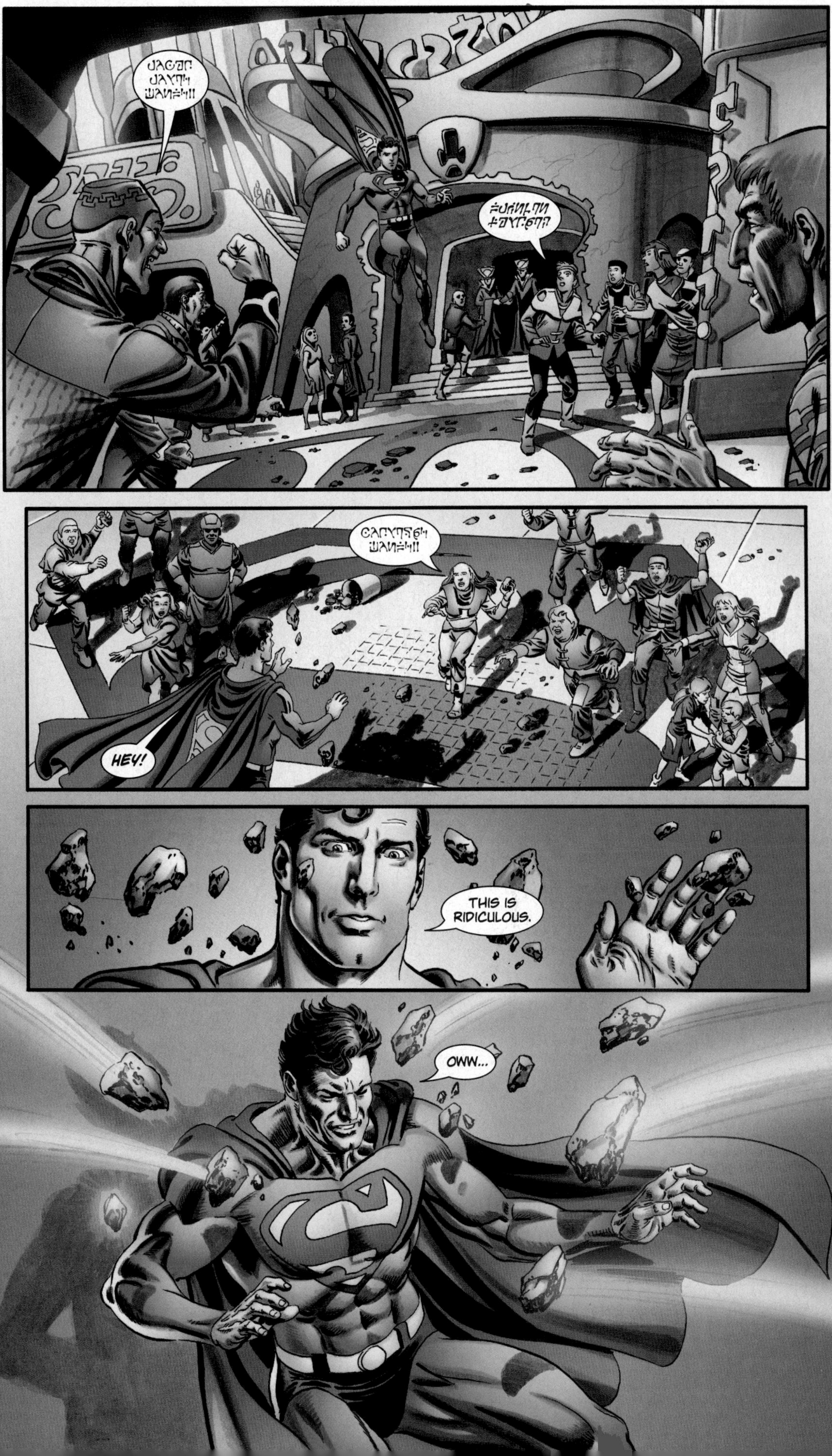
HEY!
THIS IS RIDICULOUS.
OWW...

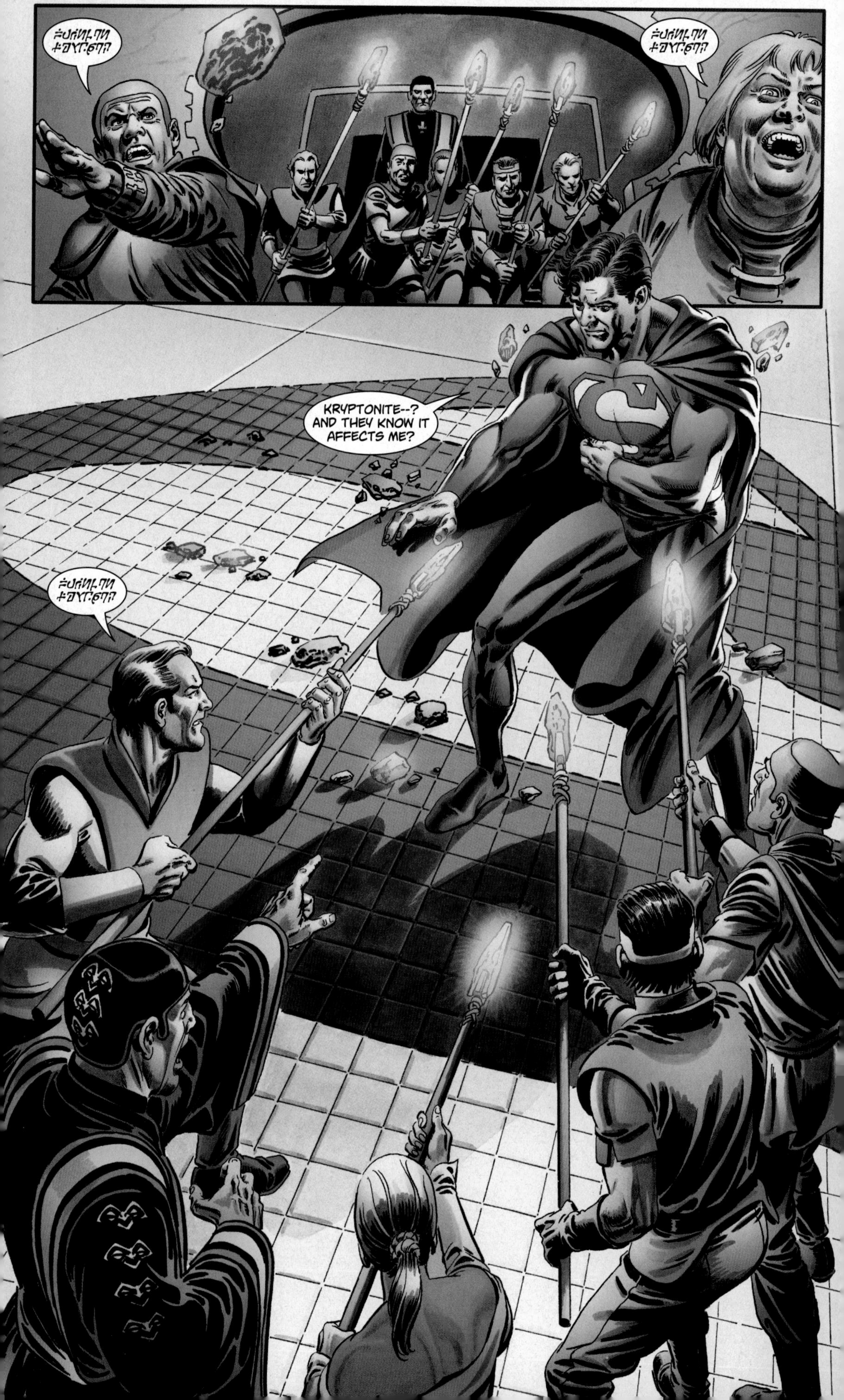
KRYPTONITE--? AND THEY KNOW IT AFFECTS ME?

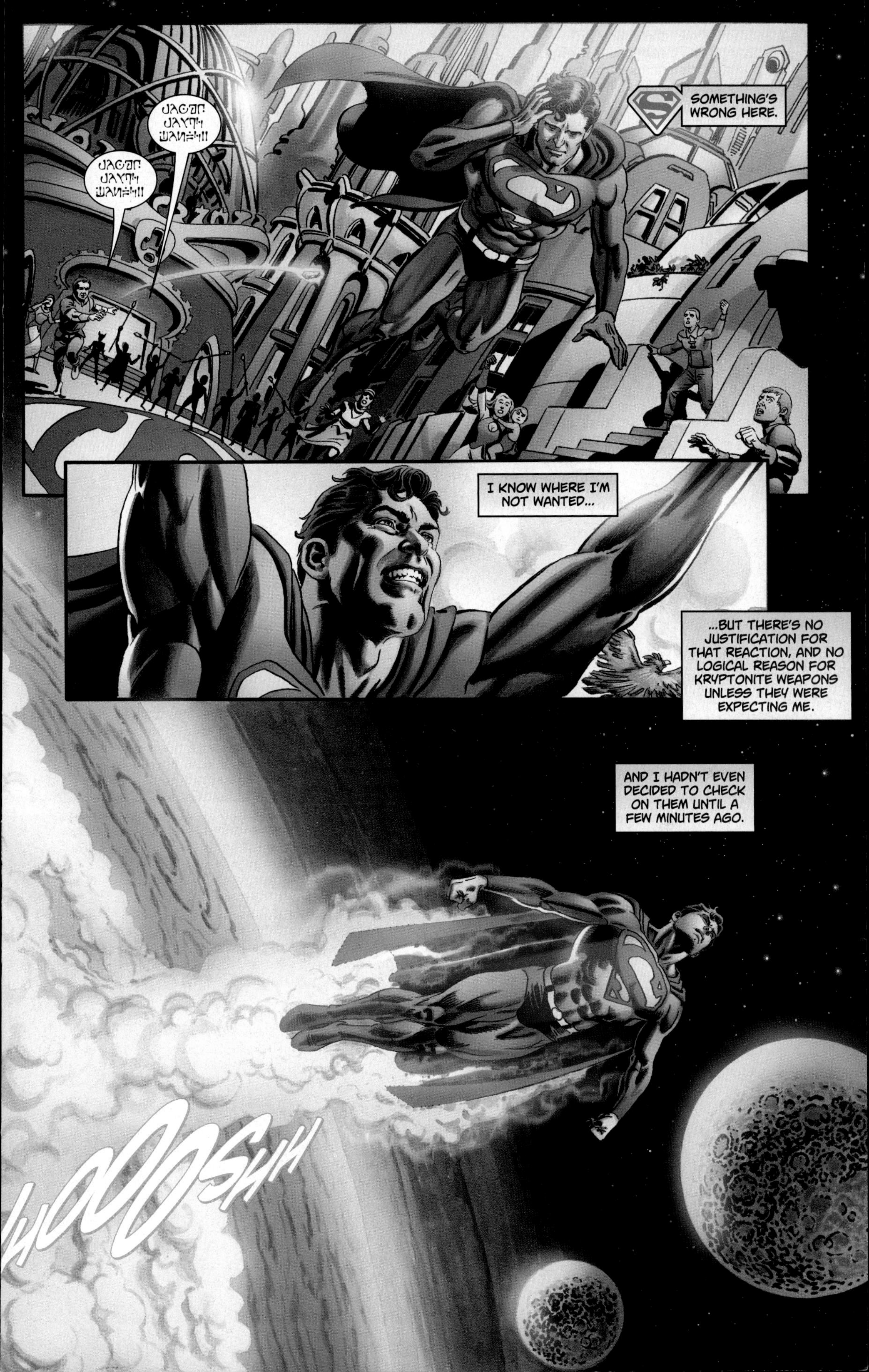
SOMETHING'S WRONG HERE.
I KNOW WHERE I'M NOT WANTED...
...BUT THERE'S NO JUSTIFICATION FOR THAT REACTION, AND NO LOGICAL REASON FOR KRYPTONITE WEAPONS UNLESS THEY WERE EXPECTING ME.
AND I HADN'T EVEN DECIDED TO CHECK ON THEM UNTIL A FEW MINUTES AGO.

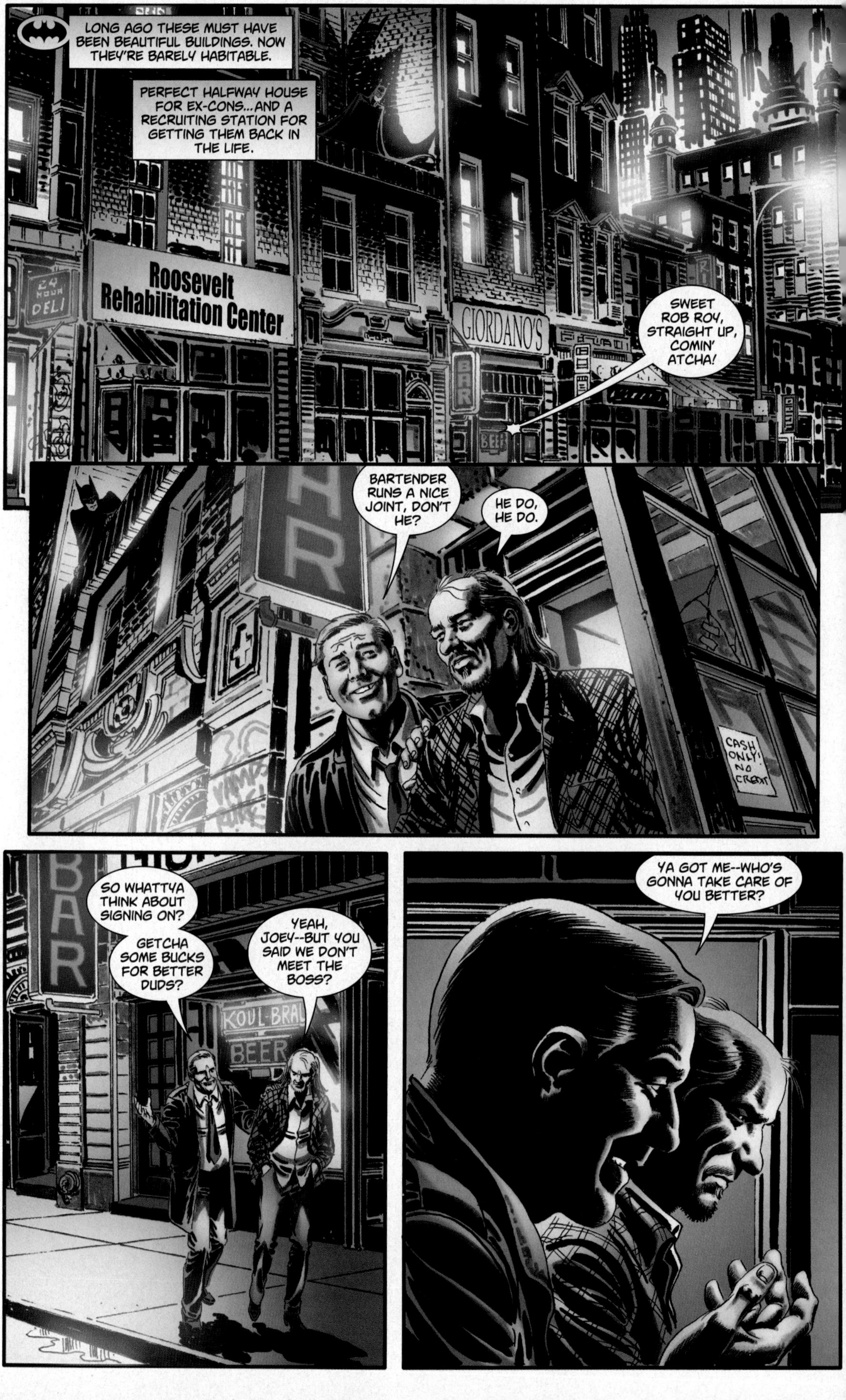
LONG AGO THESE MUST HAVE BEEN BEAUTIFUL BUILDINGS. NOW THEY'RE BARELY HABITABLE.
PERFECT HALFWAY HOUSE FOR EX-CONS...AND A RECRUITING STATION FOR GETTING THEM BACK IN THE LIFE.
24 HOUR DELI
Roosevelt Rehabilitation Center
GIORDANO'S
BAR
BEER
SWEET ROB ROY, STRAIGHT UP, COMIN' ATCHA!
BARTENDER RUNS A NICE JOINT, DON'T HE?
HE DO, HE DO.
CASH ONLY! NO CREDIT
SO WHATTYA THINK ABOUT SIGNING ON?
GETCHA SOME BUCKS FOR BETTER DUDS?
YEAH, JOEY--BUT YOU SAID WE DON'T MEET THE BOSS?
BAR
KOUL-BRAU
BEER
YA GOT ME--WHO'S GONNA TAKE CARE OF YOU BETTER?

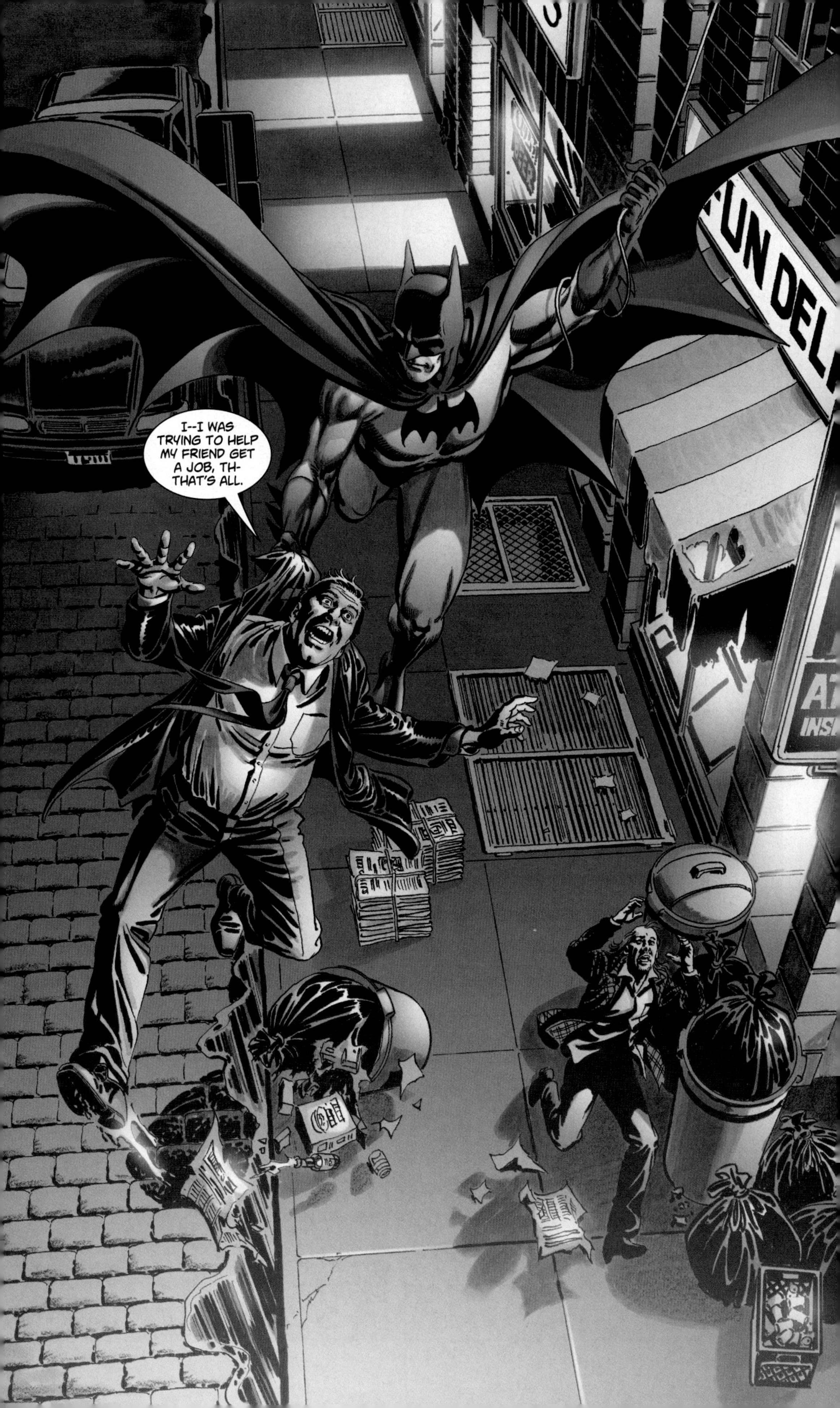
I--I WAS TRYING TO HELP MY FRIEND GET A JOB, TH-THAT'S ALL.

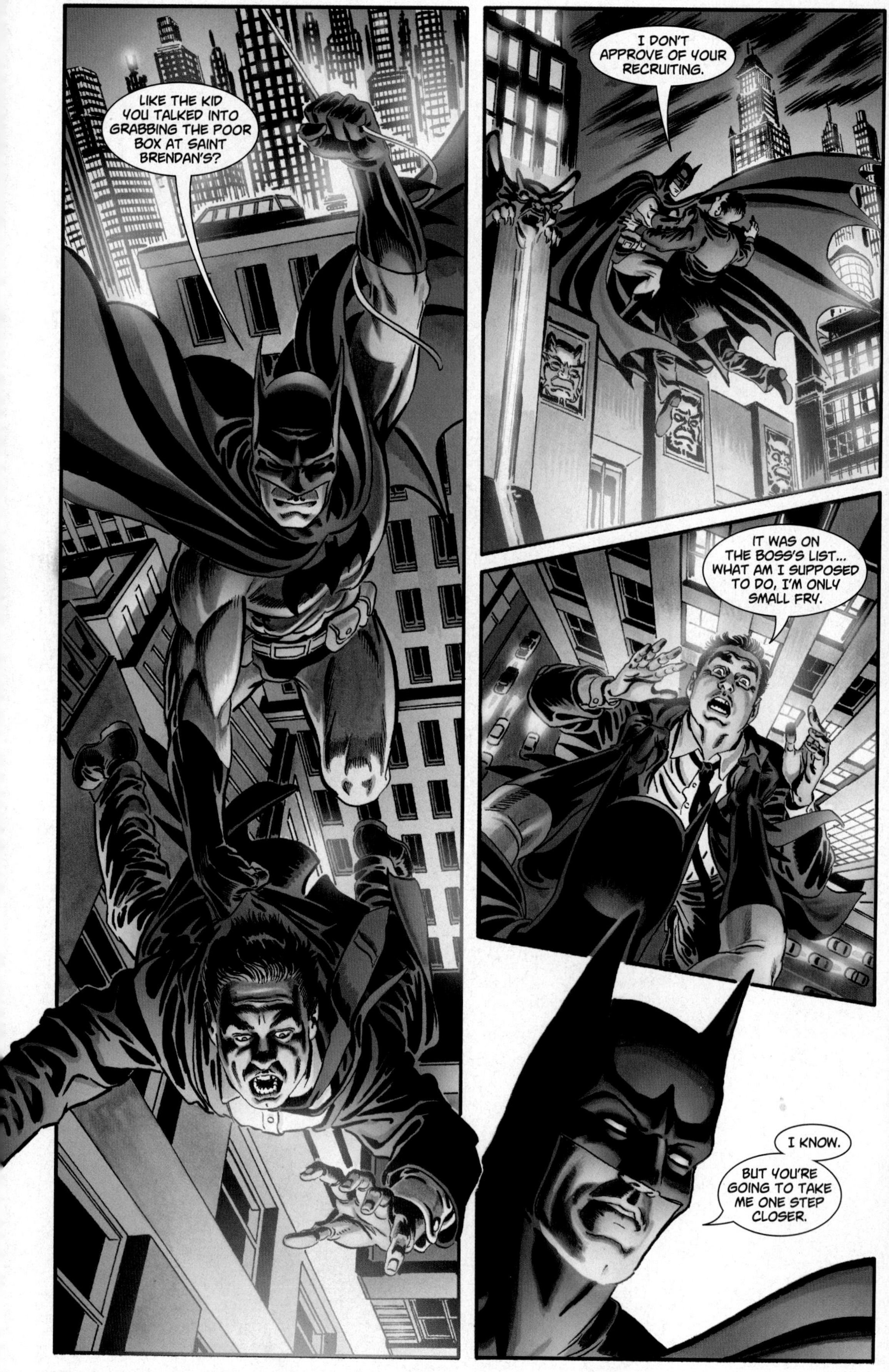
LIKE THE KID YOU TALKED INTO GRABBING THE POOR BOX AT SAINT BRENDAN'S?
I DON'T APPROVE OF YOUR RECRUITING.
IT WAS ON THE BOSS'S LIST... WHAT AM I SUPPOSED TO DO, I'M ONLY SMALL FRY.
I KNOW.
BUT YOU'RE GOING TO TAKE ME ONE STEP CLOSER.

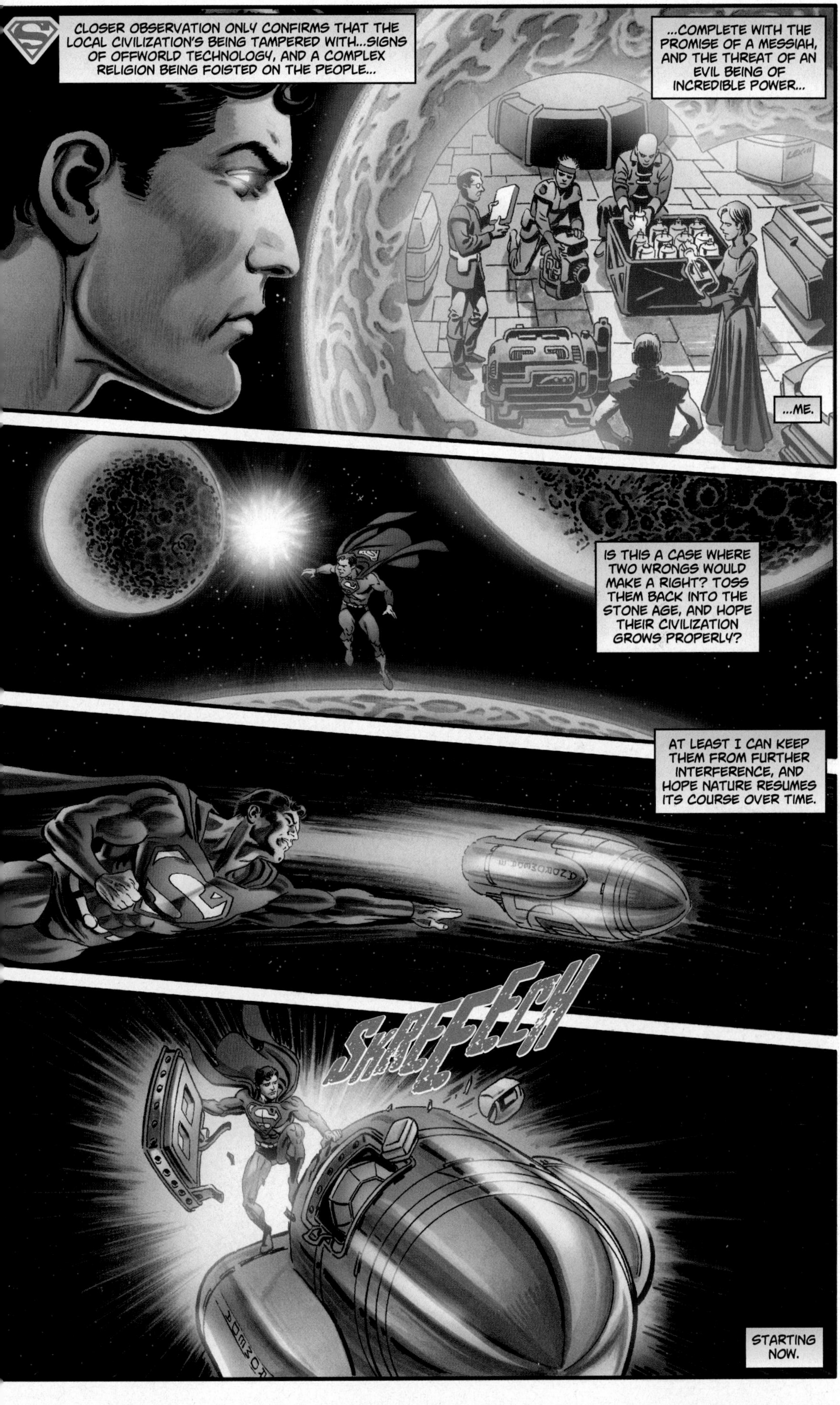
CLOSER OBSERVATION ONLY CONFIRMS THAT THE LOCAL CIVILIZATION'S BEING TAMPERED WITH...SIGNS OF OFFWORLD TECHNOLOGY, AND A COMPLEX RELIGION BEING FOISTED ON THE PEOPLE...
...COMPLETE WITH THE PROMISE OF A MESSIAH, AND THE THREAT OF AN EVIL BEING OF INCREDIBLE POWER...
...ME.
IS THIS A CASE WHERE TWO WRONGS WOULD MAKE A RIGHT? TOSS THEM BACK INTO THE STONE AGE, AND HOPE THEIR CIVILIZATION GROWS PROPERLY?
AT LEAST I CAN KEEP THEM FROM FURTHER INTERFERENCE, AND HOPE NATURE RESUMES ITS COURSE OVER TIME.
SKREEECH
STARTING NOW.

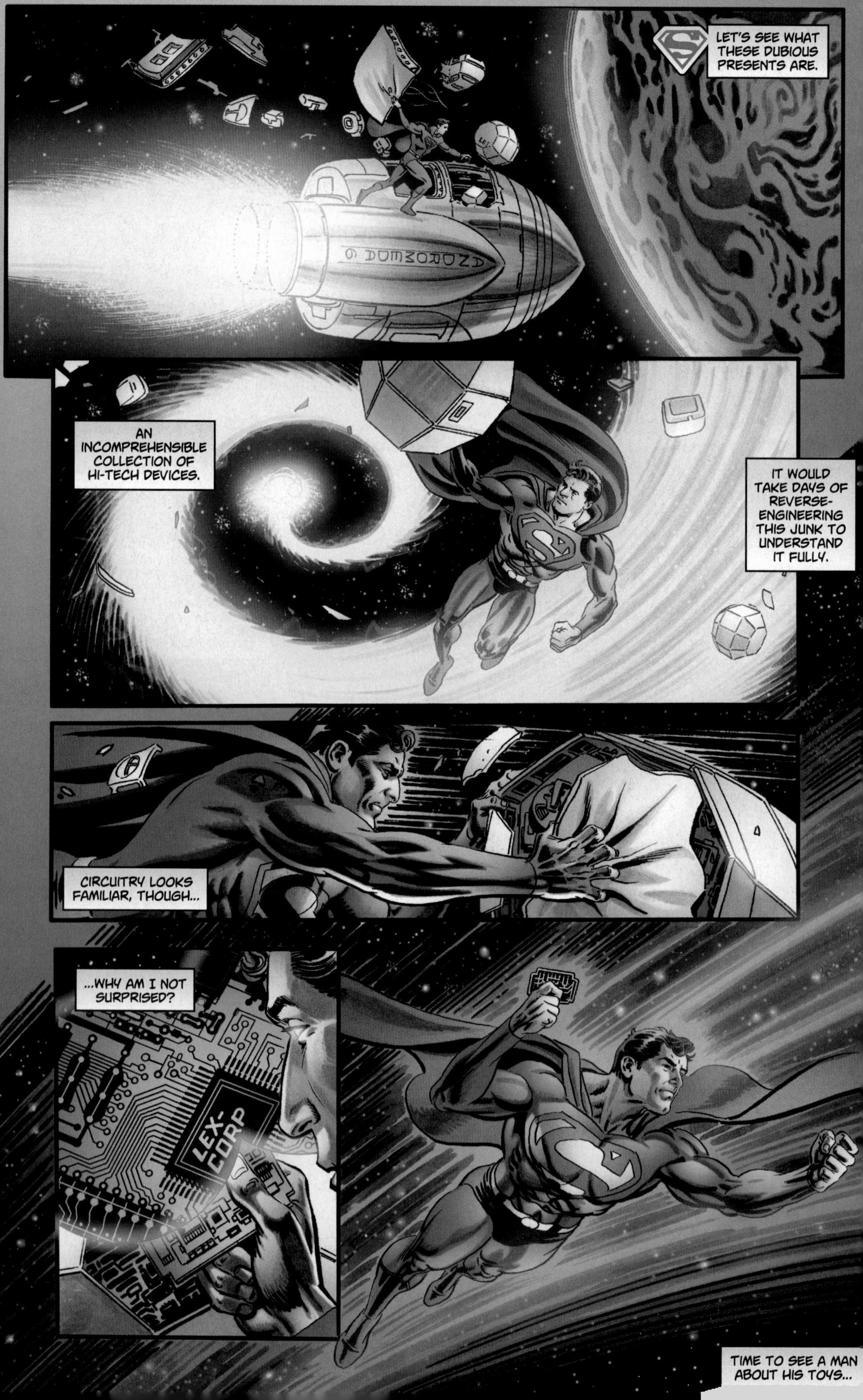
LET'S SEE WHAT THESE DUBIOUS PRESENTS ARE.
AN INCOMPREHENSIBLE COLLECTION OF HI-TECH DEVICES.
IT WOULD TAKE DAYS OF REVERSE-ENGINEERING THIS JUNK TO UNDERSTAND IT FULLY.
CIRCUITRY LOOKS FAMILIAR, THOUGH...
...WHY AM I NOT SURPRISED?
LEX-CORP
TIME TO SEE A MAN ABOUT HIS TOYS...

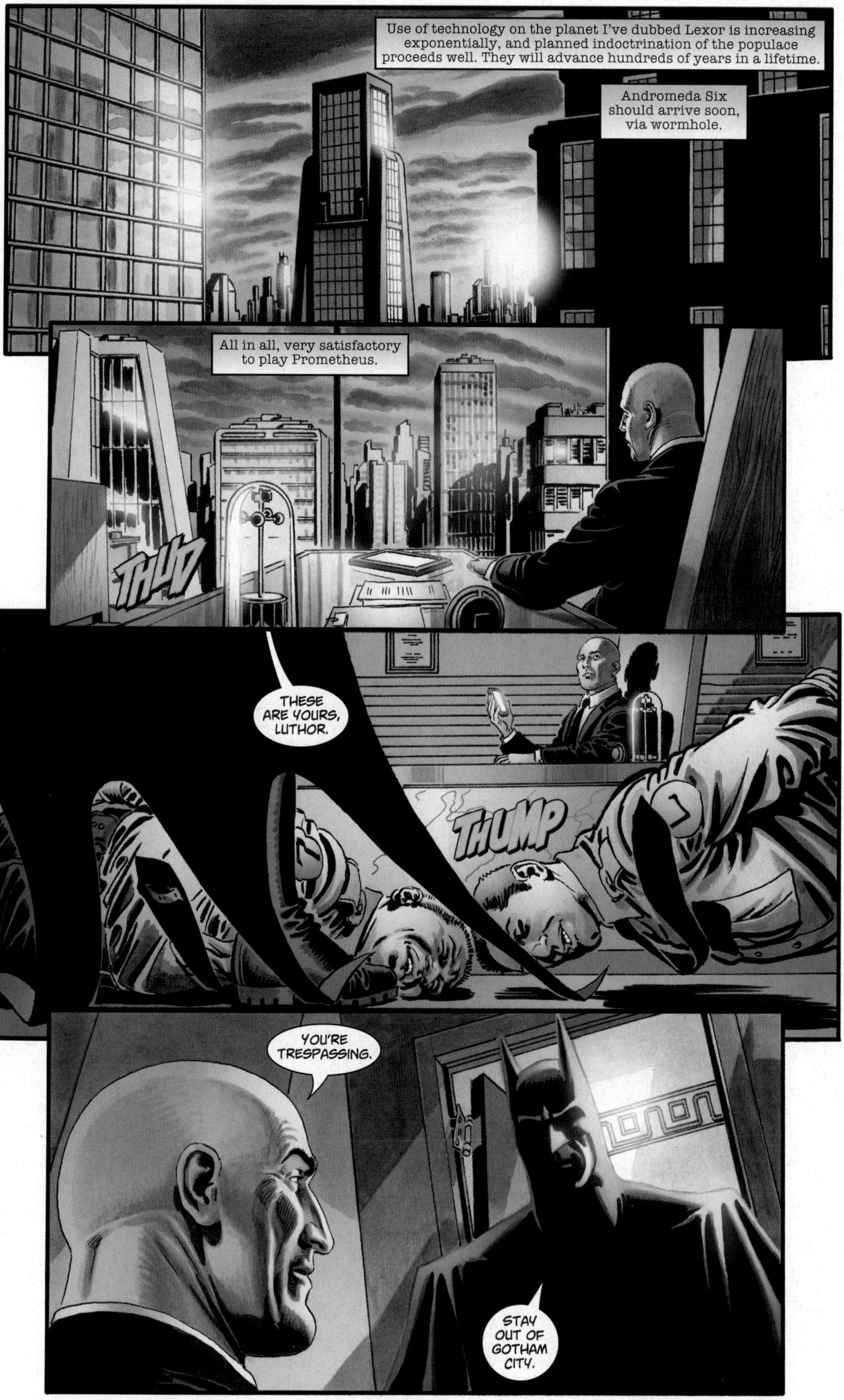
Use of technology on the planet I've dubbed Lexor is increasing exponentially, and planned indoctrination of the populace proceeds well. They will advance hundreds of years in a lifetime.
Andromeda Six should arrive soon, via wormhole.
All in all, very satisfactory to play Prometheus.
THUD
THESE ARE YOURS, LUTHOR.
THUMP
YOU'RE TRESPASSING.
STAY OUT OF GOTHAM CITY.

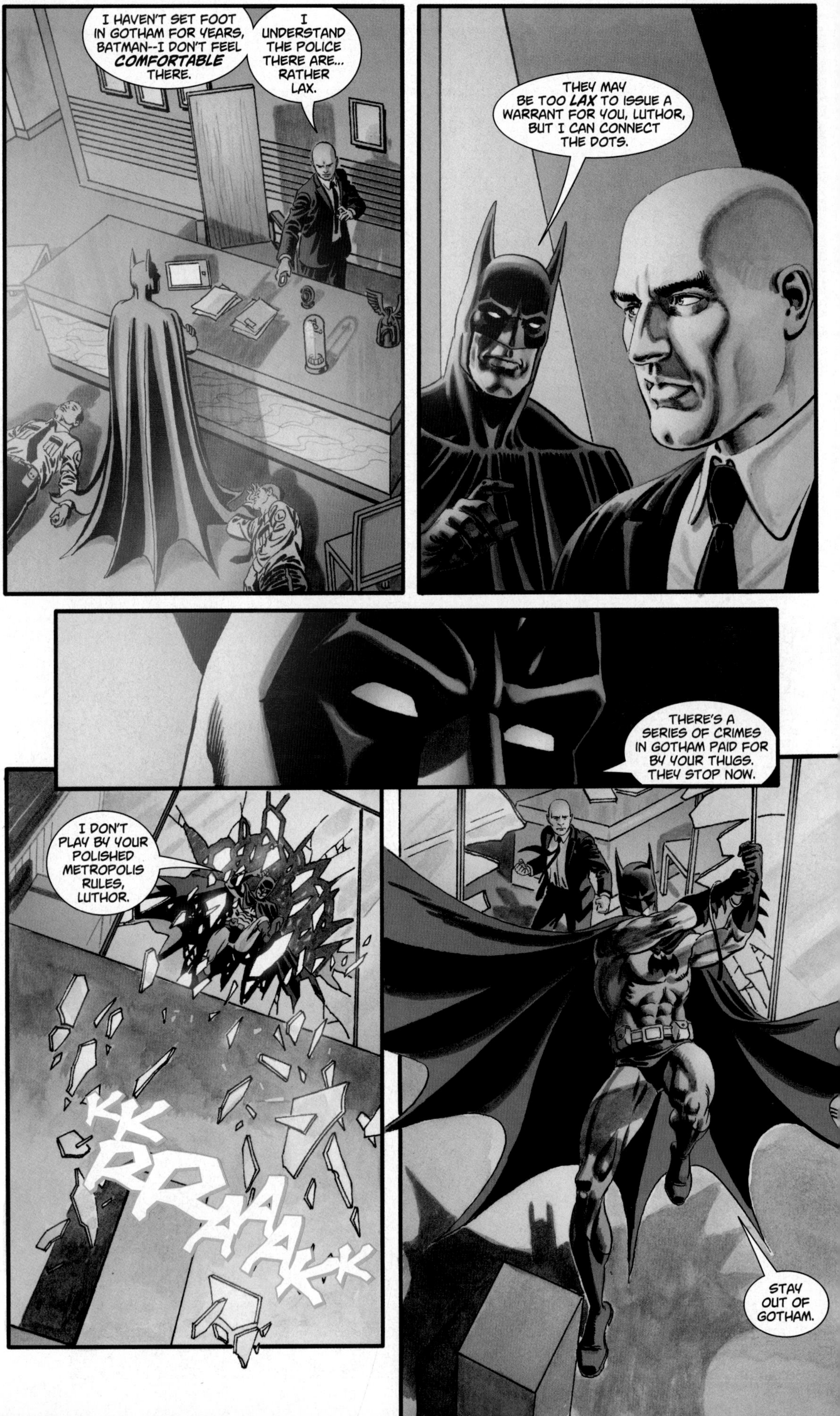
I HAVEN'T SET FOOT IN GOTHAM FOR YEARS, BATMAN--I DON'T FEEL COMFORTABLE THERE.
I UNDERSTAND THE POLICE THERE ARE... RATHER LAX.
THEY MAY BE TOO LAX TO ISSUE A WARRANT FOR YOU, LUTHOR, BUT I CAN CONNECT THE DOTS.
THERE'S A SERIES OF CRIMES IN GOTHAM PAID FOR BY YOUR THUGS. THEY STOP NOW.
I DON'T PLAY BY YOUR POLISHED METROPOLIS RULES, LUTHOR.
KKRRAAAKKK
STAY OUT OF GOTHAM.

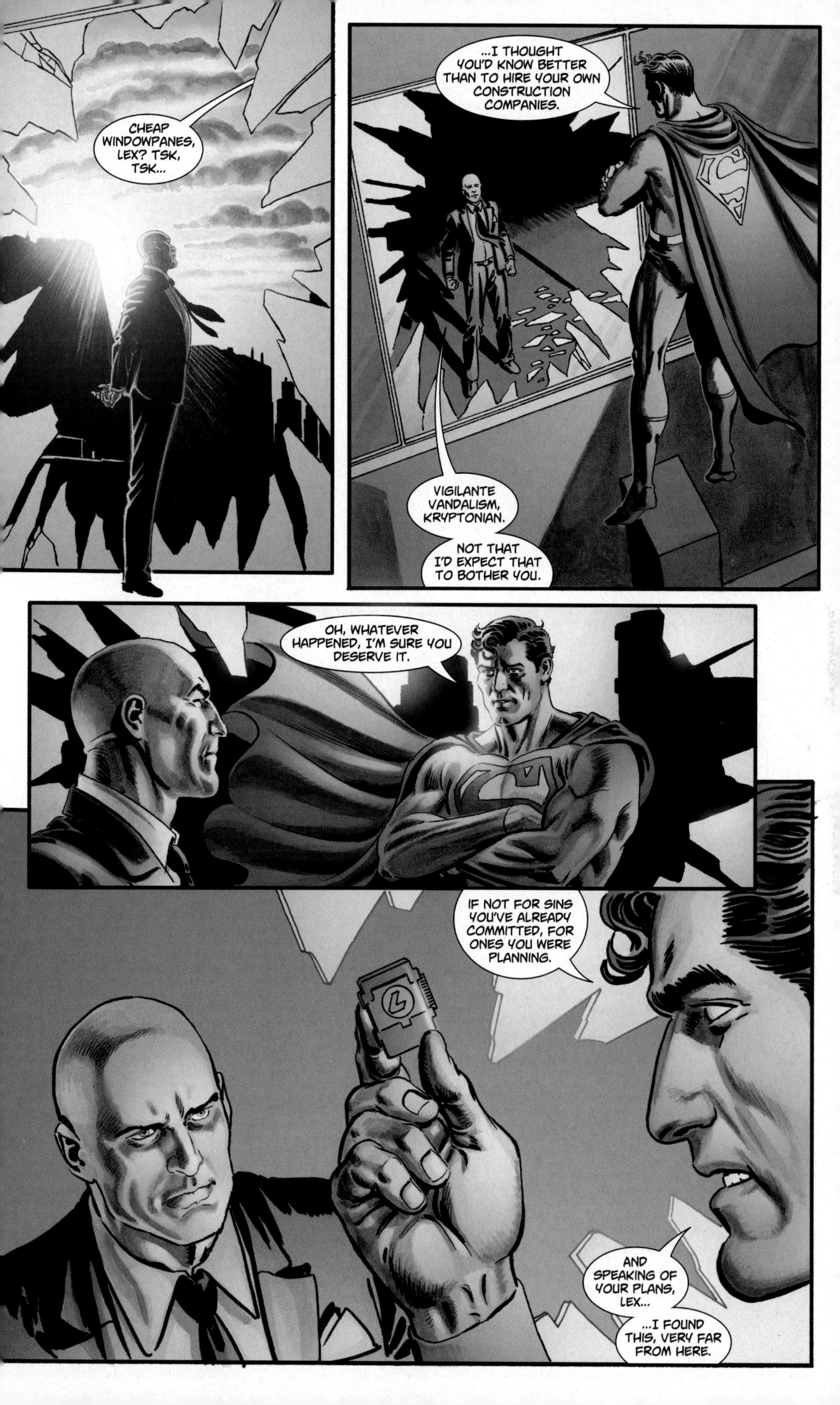
CHEAP WINDOWPANES, LEX? TSK, TSK...
...I THOUGHT YOU'D KNOW BETTER THAN TO HIRE YOUR OWN CONSTRUCTION COMPANIES.
VIGILANTE VANDALISM, KRYPTONIAN.
NOT THAT I'D EXPECT THAT TO BOTHER YOU.
OH, WHATEVER HAPPENED, I'M SURE YOU DESERVE IT.
IF NOT FOR SINS YOU'VE ALREADY COMMITTED, FOR ONES YOU WERE PLANNING.
AND SPEAKING OF YOUR PLANS, LEX...
...I FOUND THIS, VERY FAR FROM HERE.

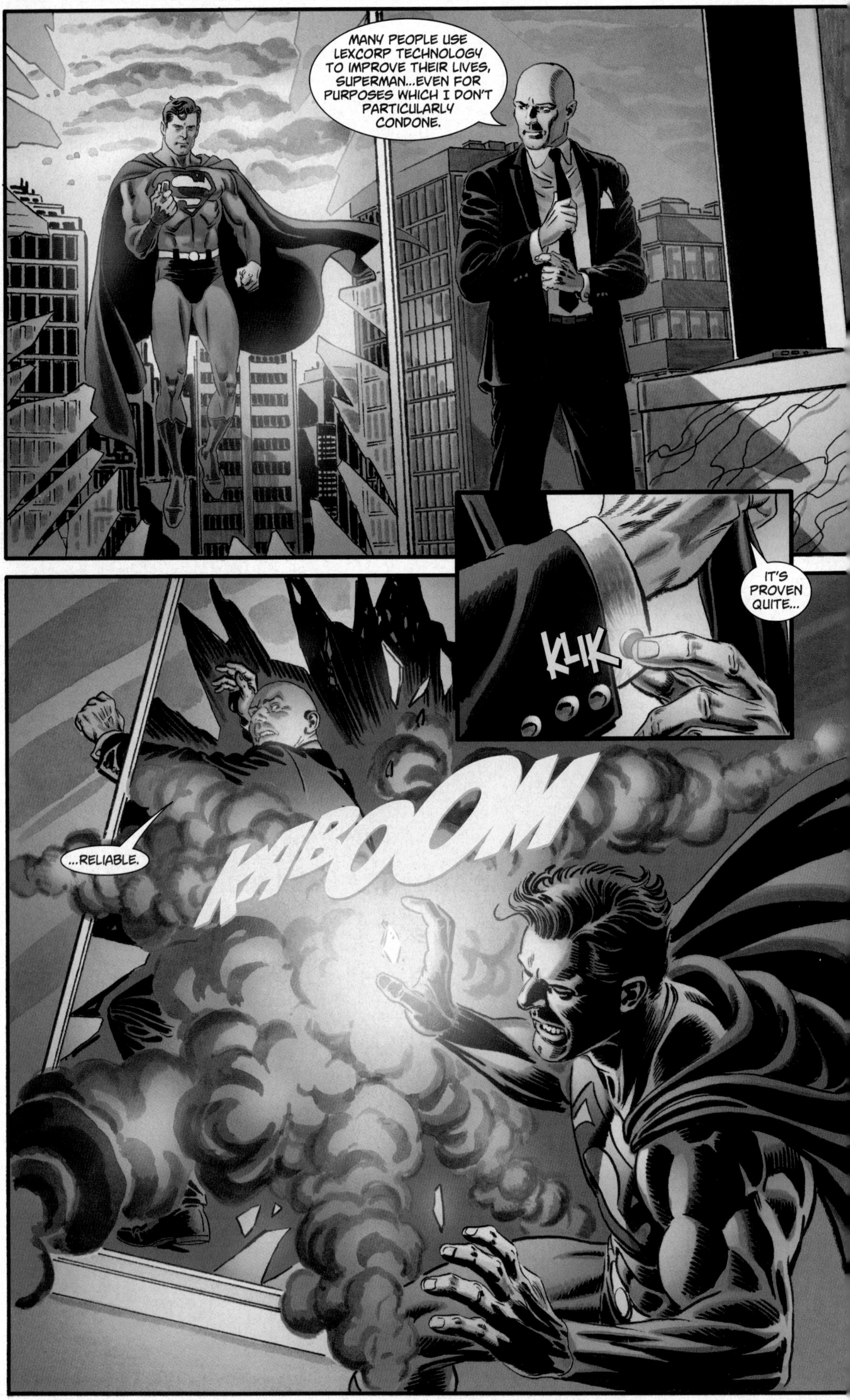

MANY PEOPLE USE LEXCORP TECHNOLOGY TO IMPROVE THEIR LIVES, SUPERMAN...EVEN FOR PURPOSES WHICH I DON'T PARTICULARLY CONDONE.
IT'S PROVEN QUITE...
KLIK
...RELIABLE.
KABOOM

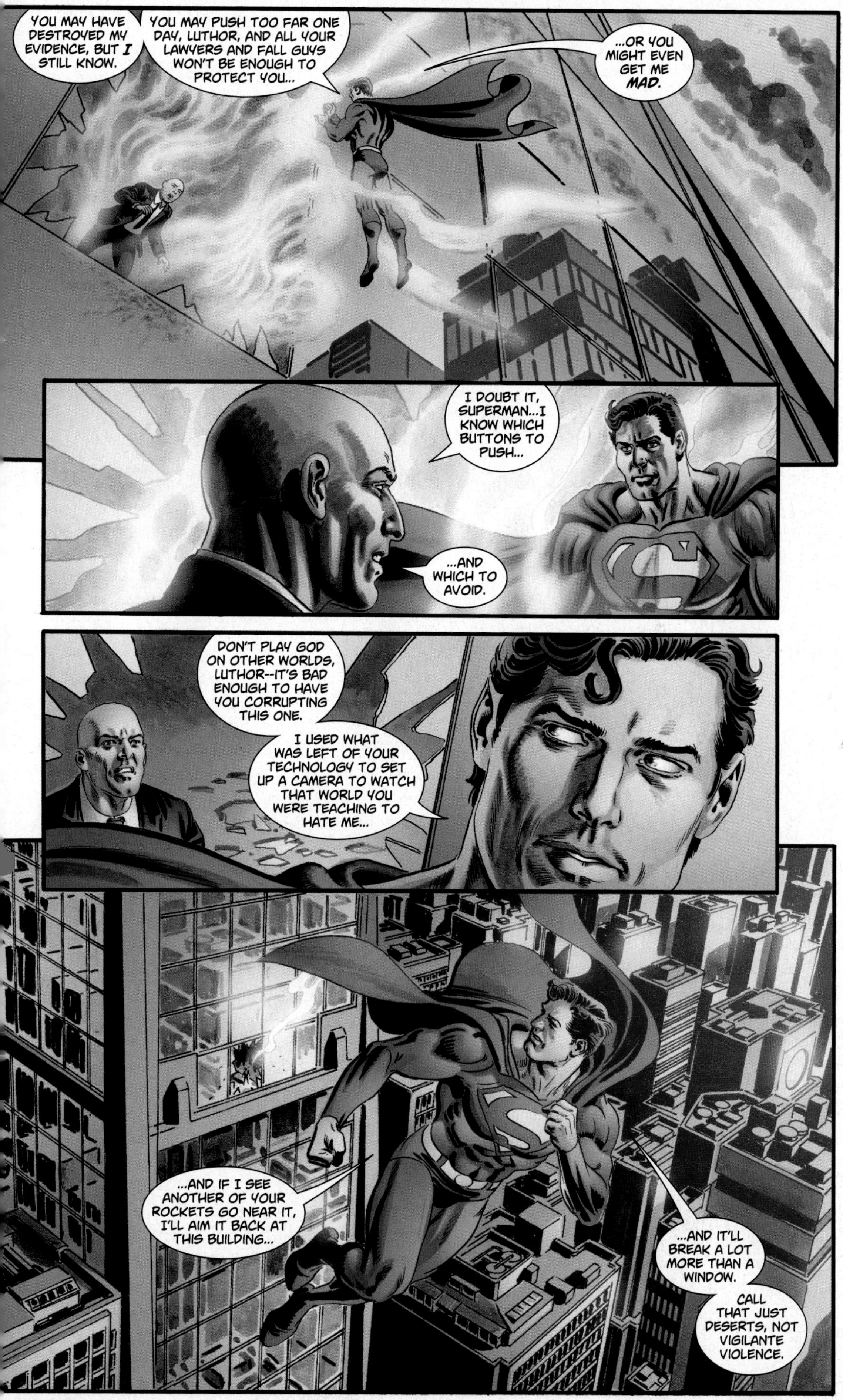
YOU MAY HAVE DESTROYED MY EVIDENCE, BUT *I* STILL KNOW.
YOU MAY PUSH TOO FAR ONE DAY, LUTHOR, AND ALL YOUR LAWYERS AND FALL GUYS WON'T BE ENOUGH TO PROTECT YOU...
...OR YOU MIGHT EVEN GET ME **MAD.**
I DOUBT IT, SUPERMAN...I KNOW WHICH BUTTONS TO PUSH...
...AND WHICH TO AVOID.
DON'T PLAY GOD ON OTHER WORLDS, LUTHOR--IT'S BAD ENOUGH TO HAVE YOU CORRUPTING THIS ONE.
I USED WHAT WAS LEFT OF YOUR TECHNOLOGY TO SET UP A CAMERA TO WATCH THAT WORLD YOU WERE TEACHING TO HATE ME...
...AND IF I SEE ANOTHER OF YOUR ROCKETS GO NEAR IT, I'LL AIM IT BACK AT THIS BUILDING...
...AND IT'LL BREAK A LOT MORE THAN A WINDOW.
CALL THAT JUST DESERTS, NOT VIGILANTE VIOLENCE.

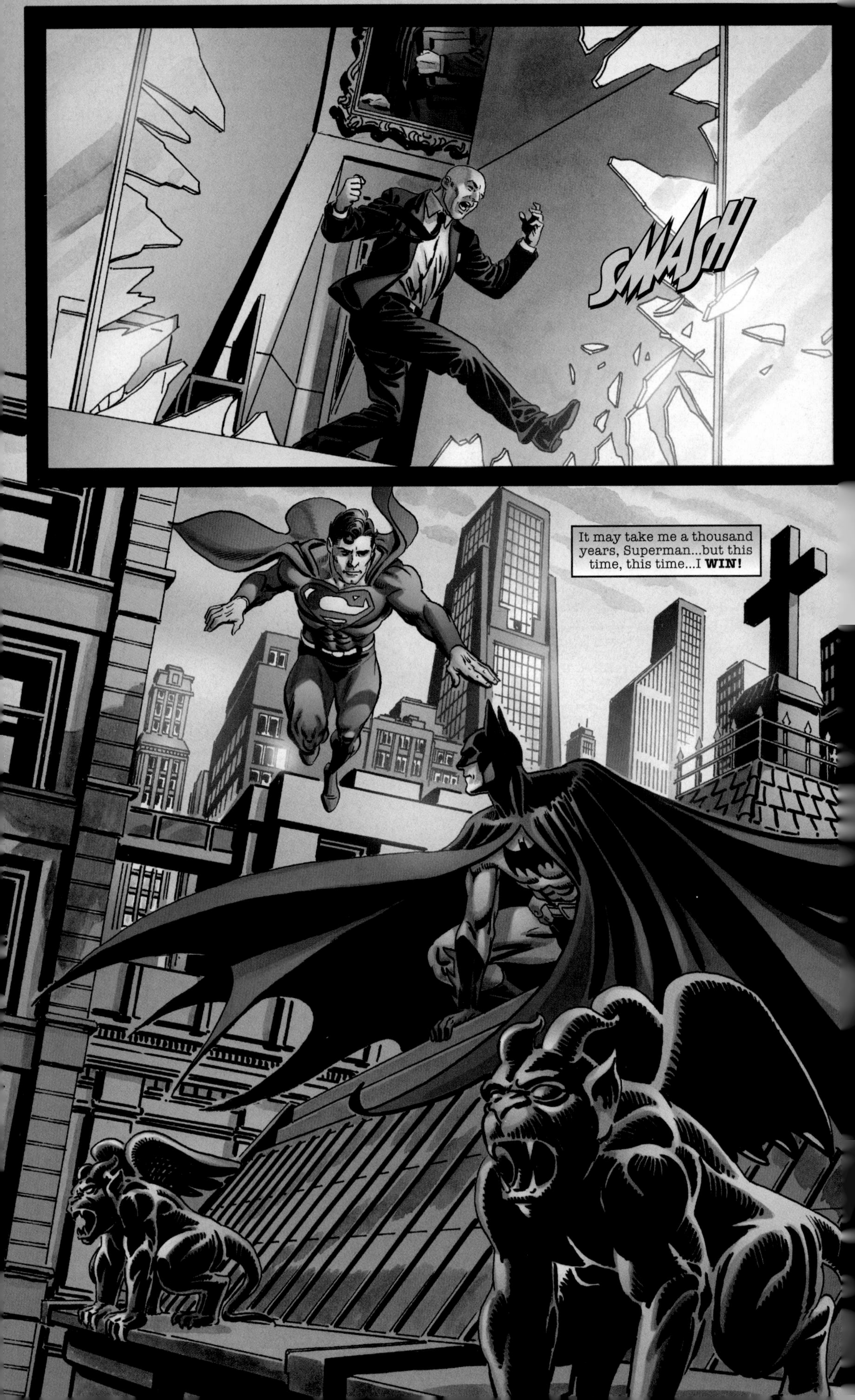
SMASH
It may take me a thousand years, Superman...but this time, this time...I **WIN!**

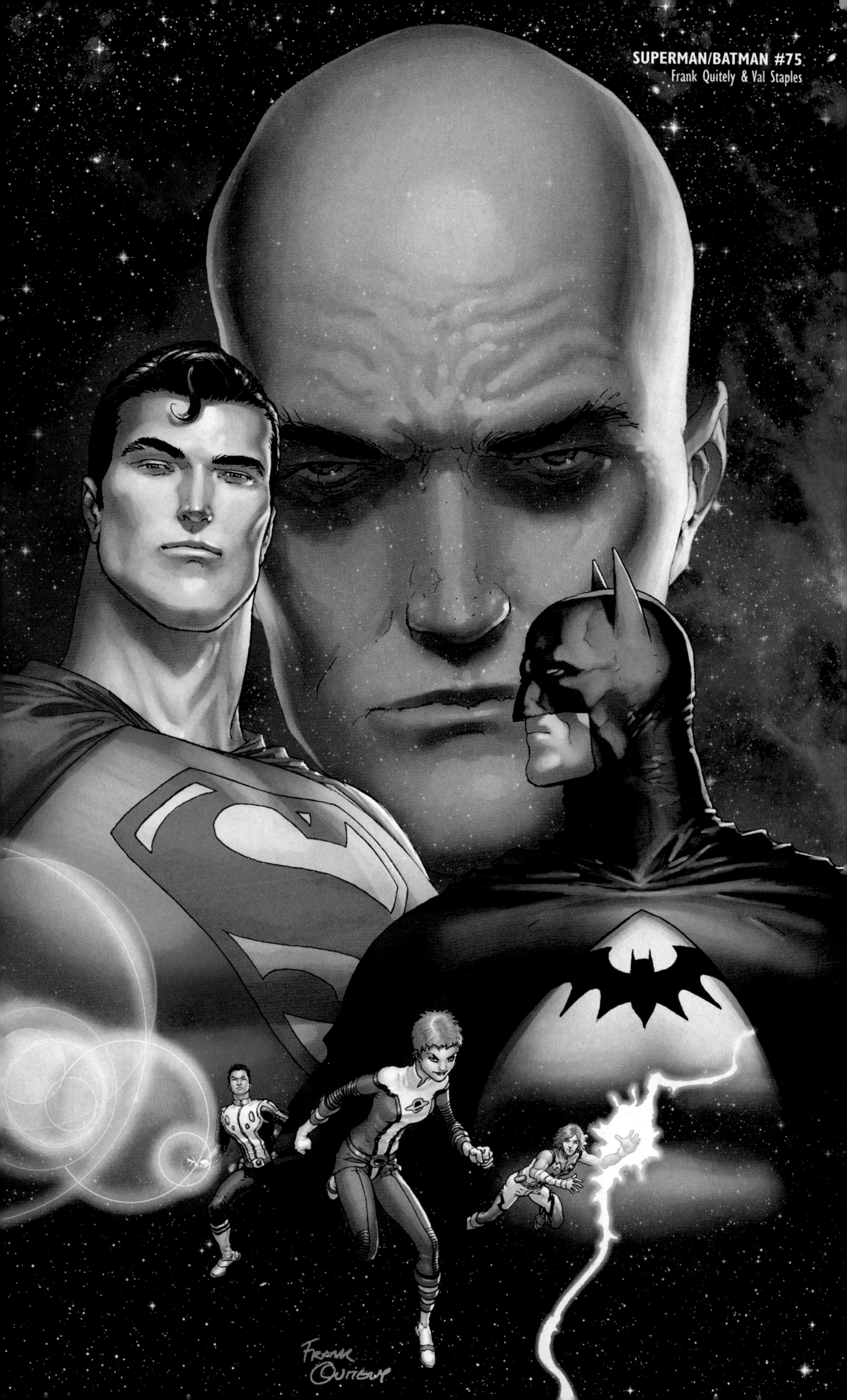

SUPERMAN/BATMAN #75
Frank Quitely & Val Staples

RESURRECTION

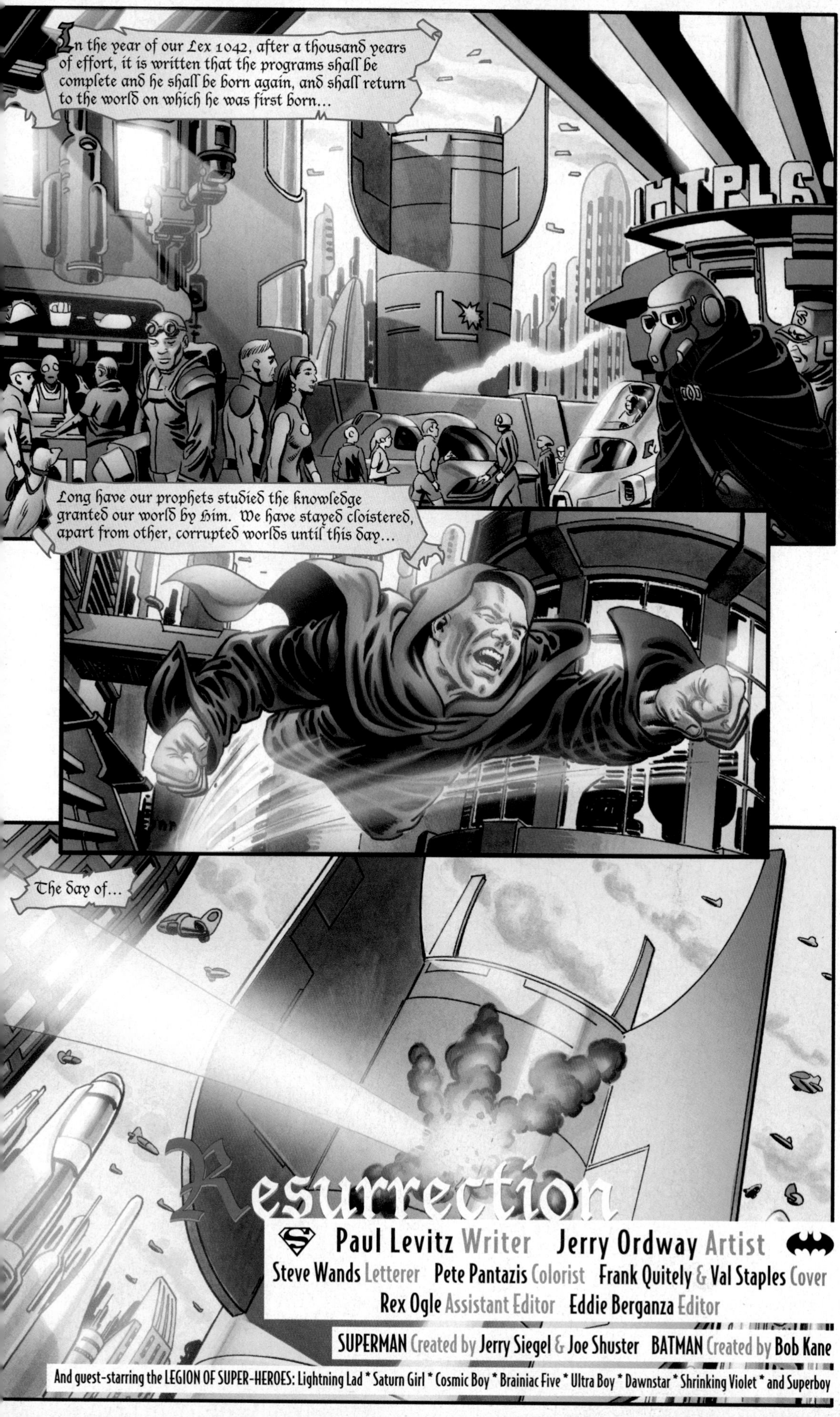
In the year of our Lex 1042, after a thousand years of effort, it is written that the programs shall be complete and he shall be born again, and shall return to the world on which he was first born...
HTPLS
Long have our prophets studied the knowledge granted our world by Him. We have stayed cloistered, apart from other, corrupted worlds until this day...
The day of...
Resurrection
Paul Levitz Writer Jerry Ordway Artist
Steve Wands Letterer Pete Pantazis Colorist Frank Quitely & Val Staples Cover
Rex Ogle Assistant Editor Eddie Berganza Editor
SUPERMAN Created by Jerry Siegel & Joe Shuster BATMAN Created by Bob Kane
And guest-starring the LEGION OF SUPER-HEROES: Lightning Lad * Saturn Girl * Cosmic Boy * Brainiac Five * Ultra Boy * Dawnstar * Shrinking Violet * and Superboy

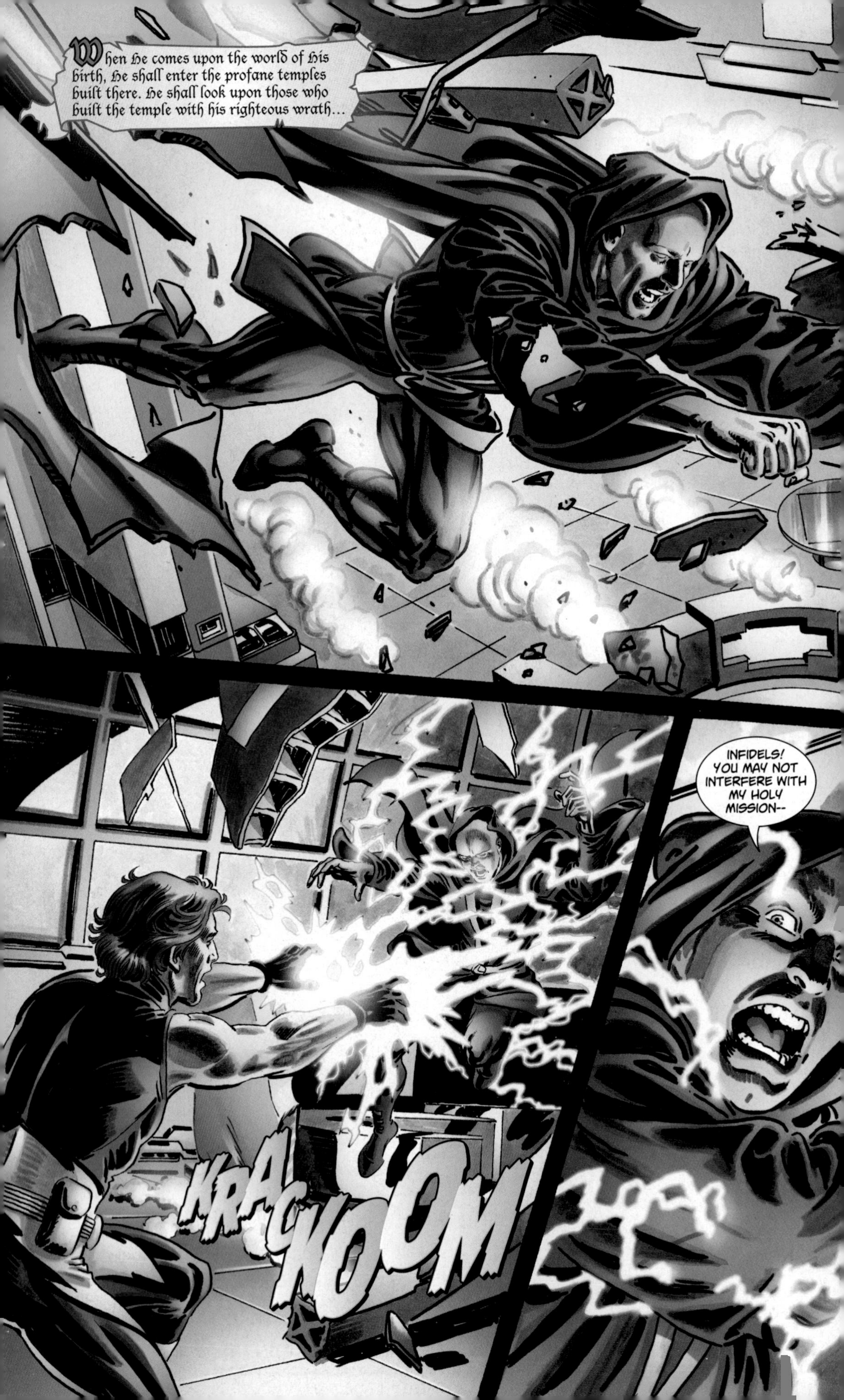
When He comes upon the world of His birth, He shall enter the profane temples built there. He shall look upon those who built the temple with his righteous wrath...
KRACKOOM
INFIDELS! YOU MAY NOT INTERFERE WITH MY HOLY MISSION--

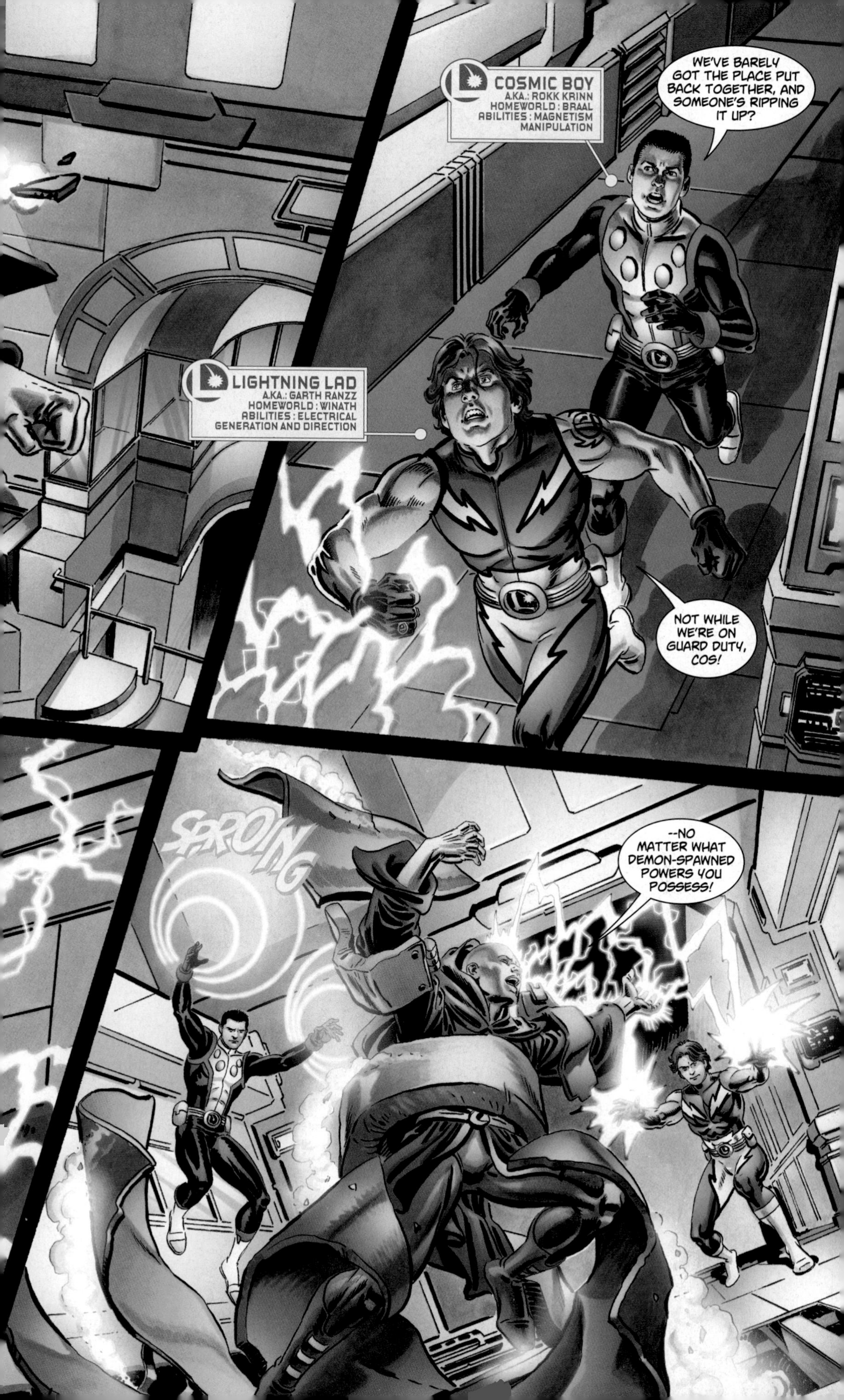
COSMIC BOY
A.KA.: ROKK KRINN
HOMEWORLD: BRAAL
ABILITIES: MAGNETISM MANIPULATION
WE'VE BARELY GOT THE PLACE PUT BACK TOGETHER, AND SOMEONE'S RIPPING IT UP?
LIGHTNING LAD
A.K.A.: GARTH RANZZ
HOMEWORLD: WINATH
ABILITIES: ELECTRICAL GENERATION AND DIRECTION
NOT WHILE WE'RE ON GUARD DUTY, COS!
SPROING
--NO MATTER WHAT DEMON-SPAWNED POWERS YOU POSSESS!

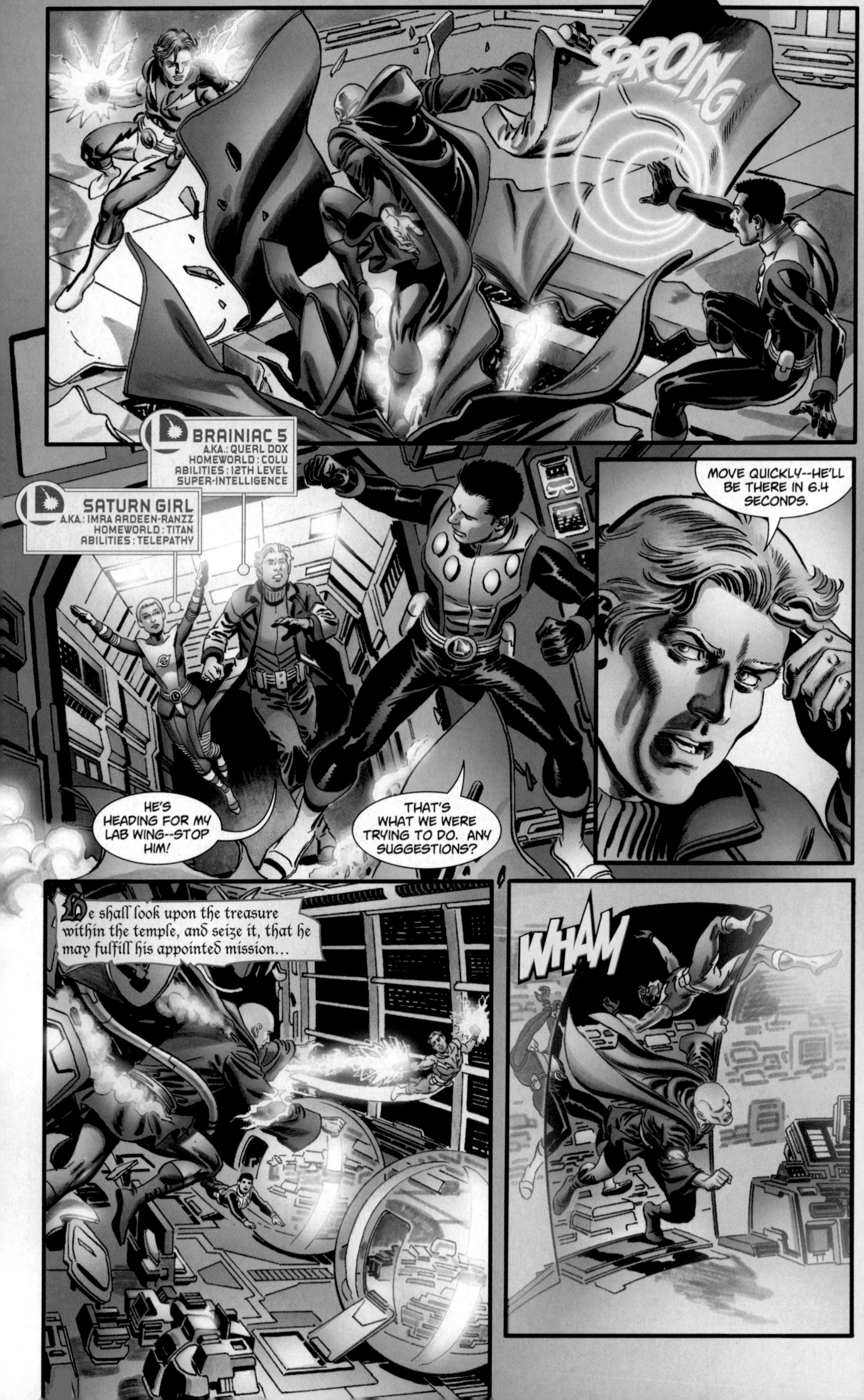
SPROING
BRAINIAC 5
A.K.A.: QUERL DOX
HOMEWORLD: COLU
ABILITIES: 12TH LEVEL SUPER-INTELLIGENCE
SATURN GIRL
A.K.A.: IMRA ARDEEN-RANZZ
HOMEWORLD: TITAN
ABILITIES: TELEPATHY
HE'S HEADING FOR MY LAB WING--STOP HIM!
THAT'S WHAT WE WERE TRYING TO DO. ANY SUGGESTIONS?
MOVE QUICKLY--HE'LL BE THERE IN 6.4 SECONDS.
He shall look upon the treasure within the temple, and seize it, that he may fulfill his appointed mission…
WHAM

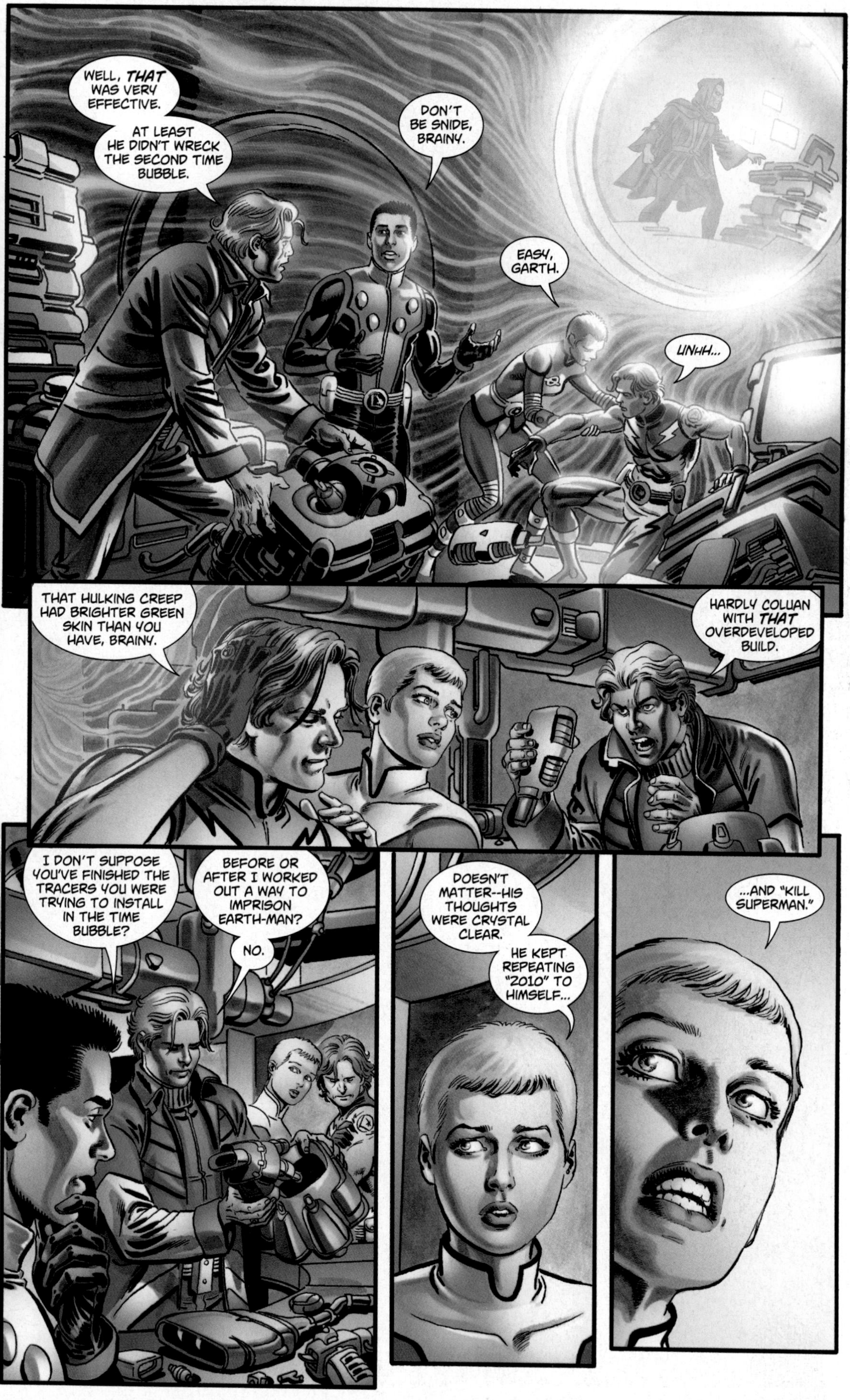
WELL, *THAT* WAS VERY EFFECTIVE.
AT LEAST HE DIDN'T WRECK THE SECOND TIME BUBBLE.
DON'T BE SNIDE, BRAINY.
EASY, GARTH.
UNHH...
THAT HULKING CREEP HAD BRIGHTER GREEN SKIN THAN YOU HAVE, BRAINY.
HARDLY COLUAN WITH *THAT* OVERDEVELOPED BUILD.
I DON'T SUPPOSE YOU'VE FINISHED THE TRACERS YOU WERE TRYING TO INSTALL IN THE TIME BUBBLE?
BEFORE OR AFTER I WORKED OUT A WAY TO IMPRISON EARTH-MAN?
NO.
DOESN'T MATTER--HIS THOUGHTS WERE CRYSTAL CLEAR.
HE KEPT REPEATING "2010" TO HIMSELF...
...AND "KILL SUPERMAN."

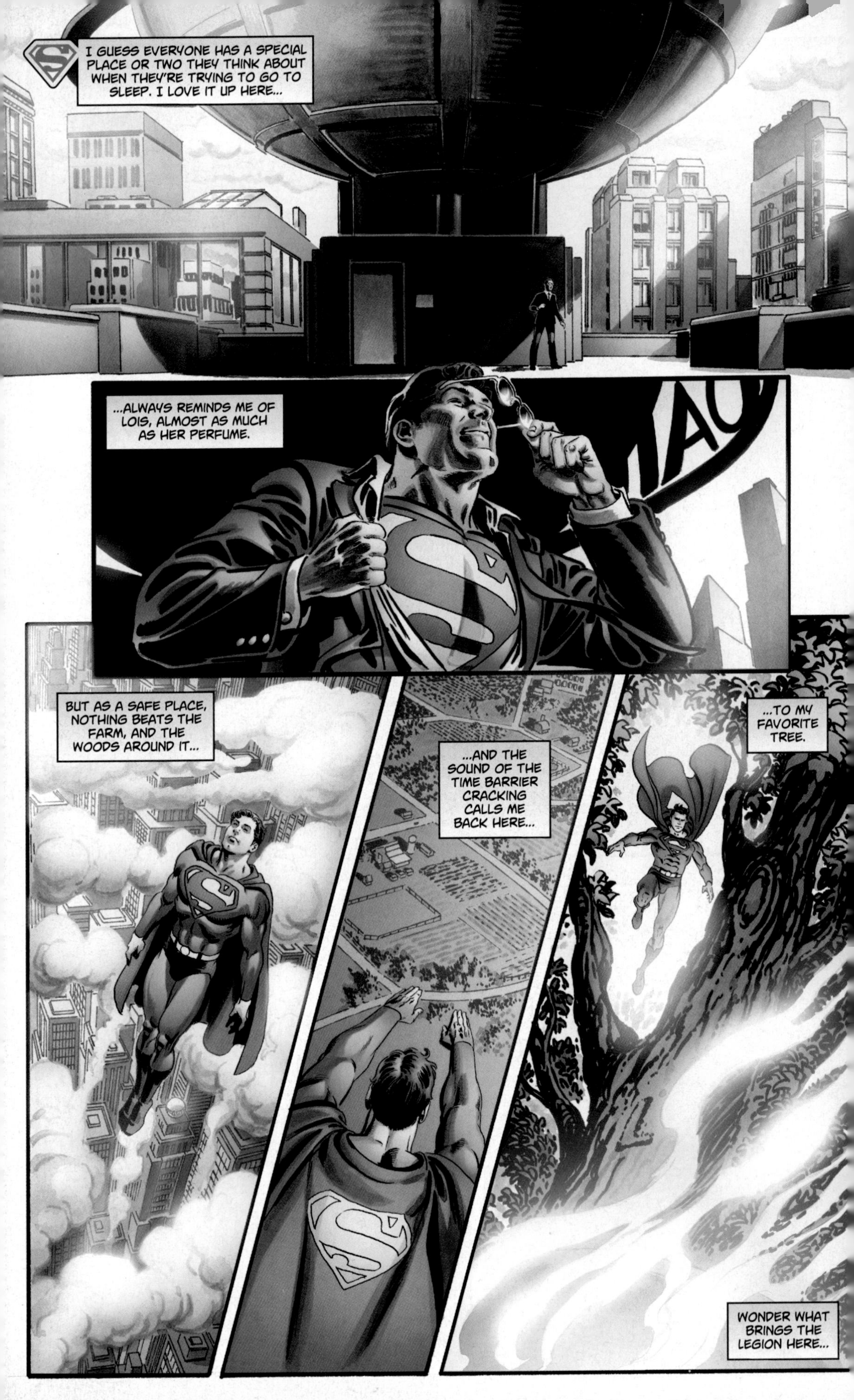
I GUESS EVERYONE HAS A SPECIAL PLACE OR TWO THEY THINK ABOUT WHEN THEY'RE TRYING TO GO TO SLEEP. I LOVE IT UP HERE...
...ALWAYS REMINDS ME OF LOIS, ALMOST AS MUCH AS HER PERFUME.
BUT AS A SAFE PLACE, NOTHING BEATS THE FARM, AND THE WOODS AROUND IT...
...AND THE SOUND OF THE TIME BARRIER CRACKING CALLS ME BACK HERE...
...TO MY FAVORITE TREE.
WONDER WHAT BRINGS THE LEGION HERE...

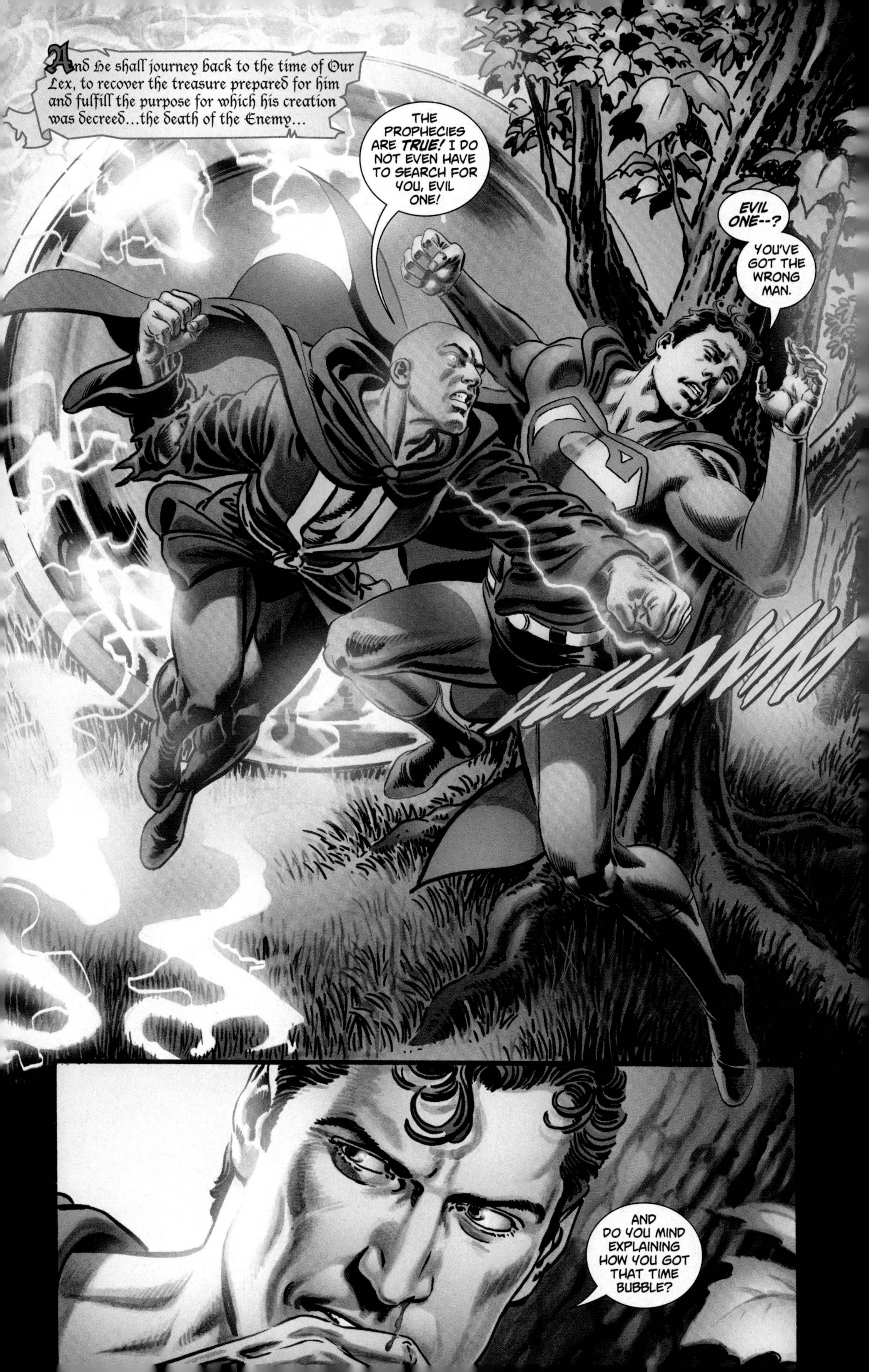
And He shall journey back to the time of Our Lex, to recover the treasure prepared for him and fulfill the purpose for which his creation was decreed...the death of the Enemy...
THE PROPHECIES ARE TRUE! I DO NOT EVEN HAVE TO SEARCH FOR YOU, EVIL ONE!
EVIL ONE--?
YOU'VE GOT THE WRONG MAN.
WHHAMM
AND DO YOU MIND EXPLAINING HOW YOU GOT THAT TIME BUBBLE?

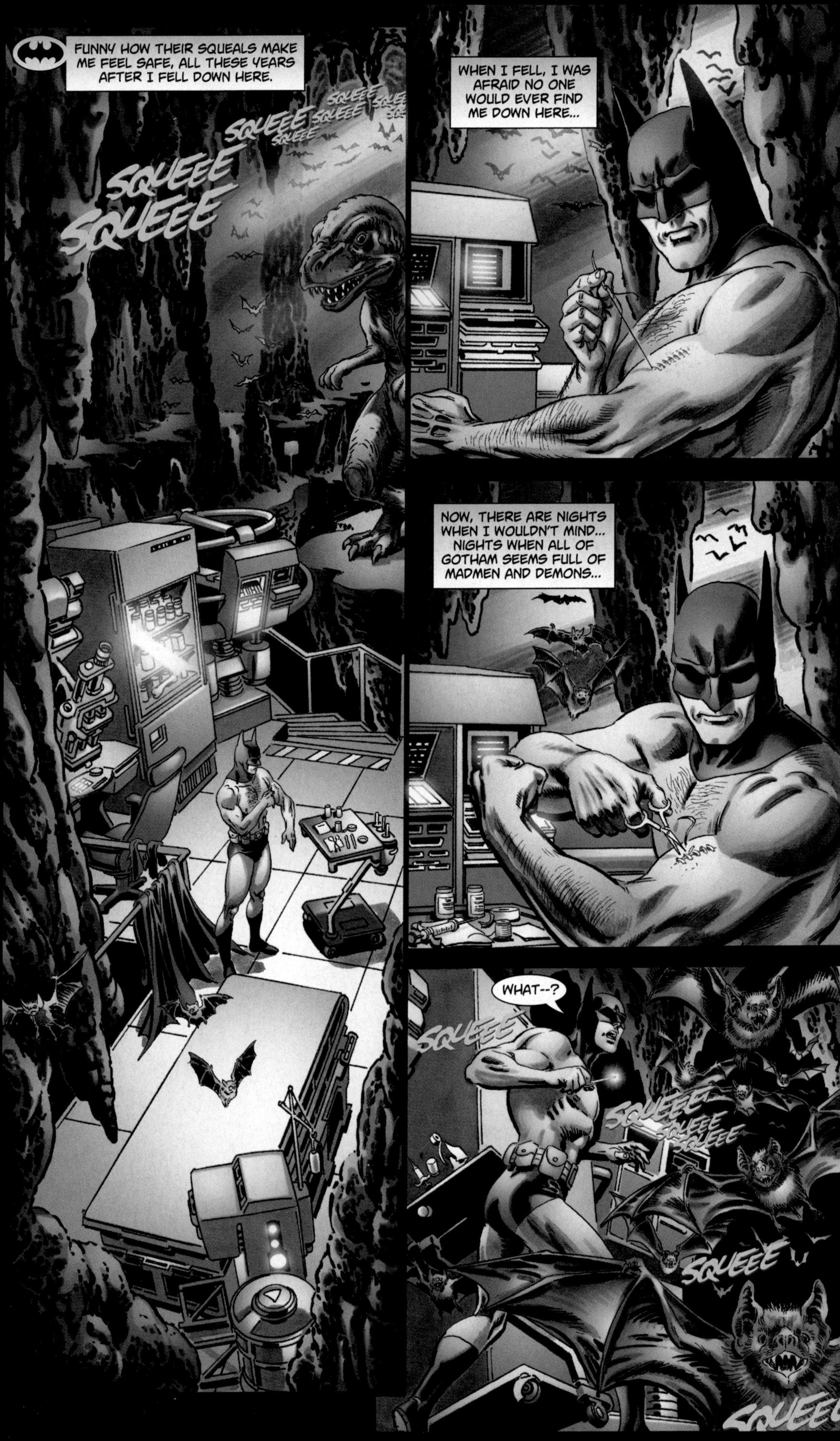
FUNNY HOW THEIR SQUEALS MAKE ME FEEL SAFE, ALL THESE YEARS AFTER I FELL DOWN HERE.
SQUEEE SQUEEE
SQUEEE SQUEEE
WHEN I FELL, I WAS AFRAID NO ONE WOULD EVER FIND ME DOWN HERE...
NOW, THERE ARE NIGHTS WHEN I WOULDN'T MIND... NIGHTS WHEN ALL OF GOTHAM SEEMS FULL OF MADMEN AND DEMONS...
WHAT--?
SQUEEE
SQUEEE SQUEEE SQUEEE
SQUEEE

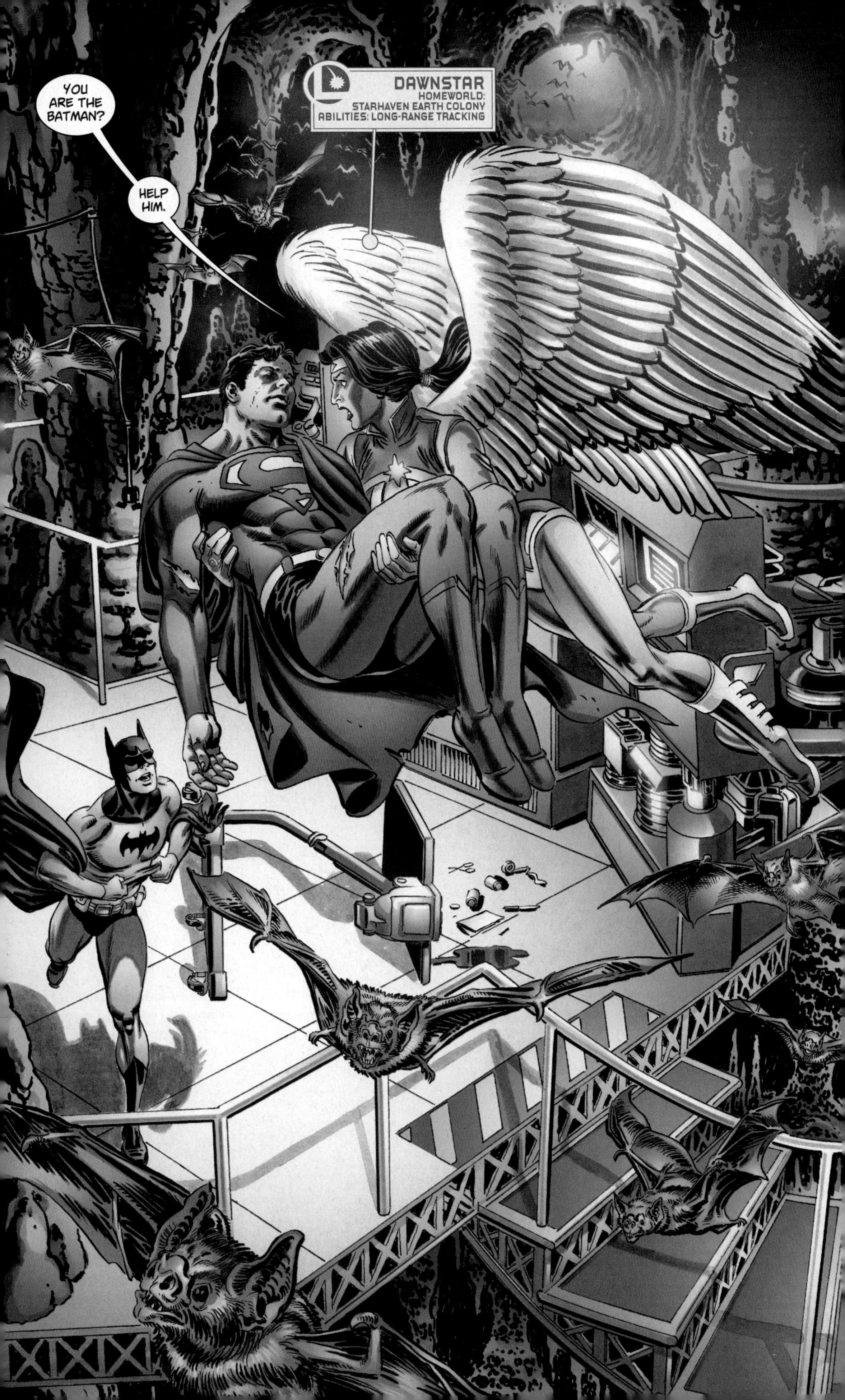
YOU ARE THE BATMAN?
HELP HIM.
DAWNSTAR
HOMEWORLD: STARHAVEN EARTH COLONY
ABILITIES: LONG-RANGE TRACKING

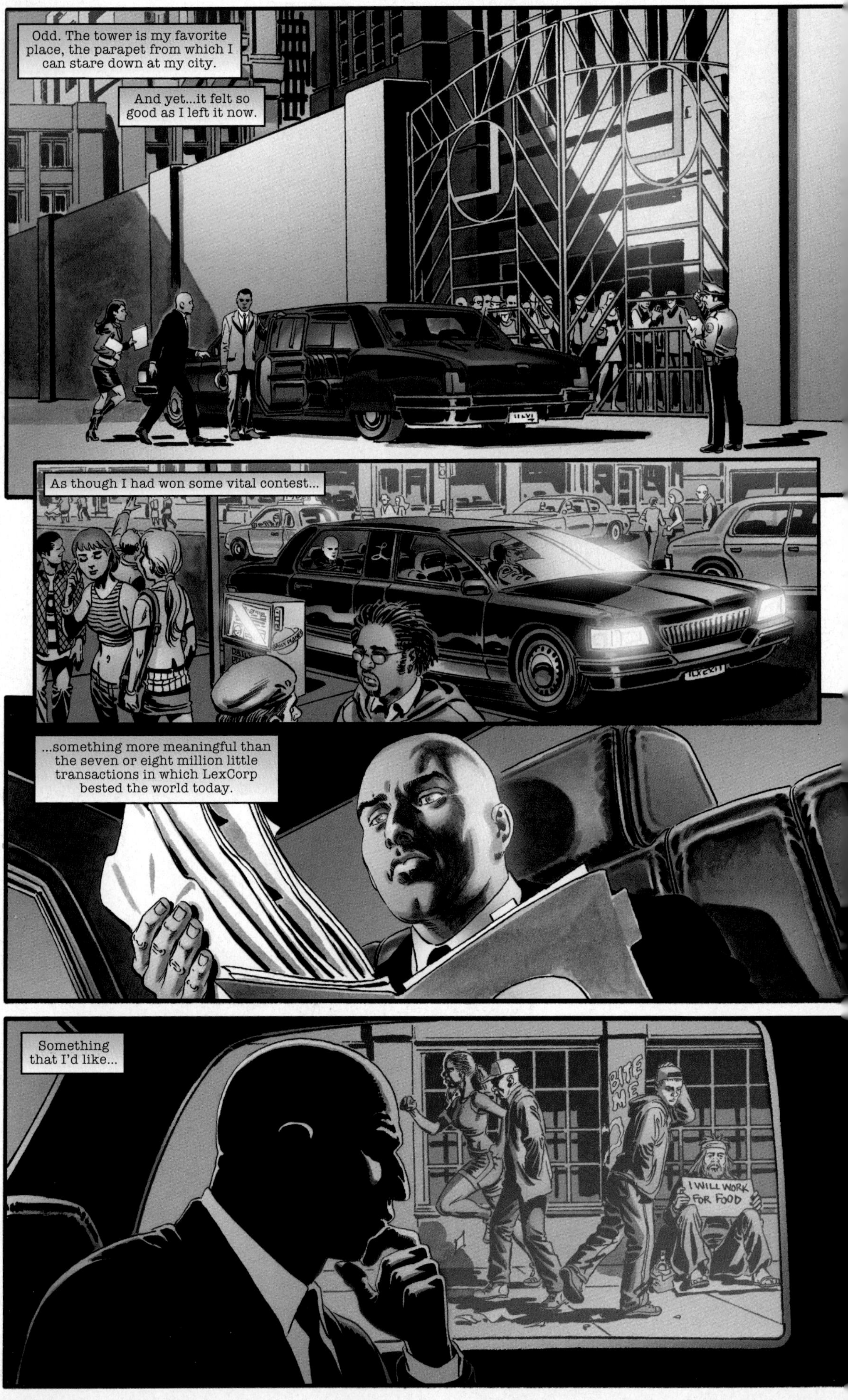

Odd. The tower is my favorite place, the parapet from which I can stare down at my city.
And yet...it felt so good as I left it now.
As though I had won some vital contest...
...something more meaningful than the seven or eight million little transactions in which LexCorp bested the world today.
Something that I'd like...
BITE ME
I WILL WORK FOR FOOD

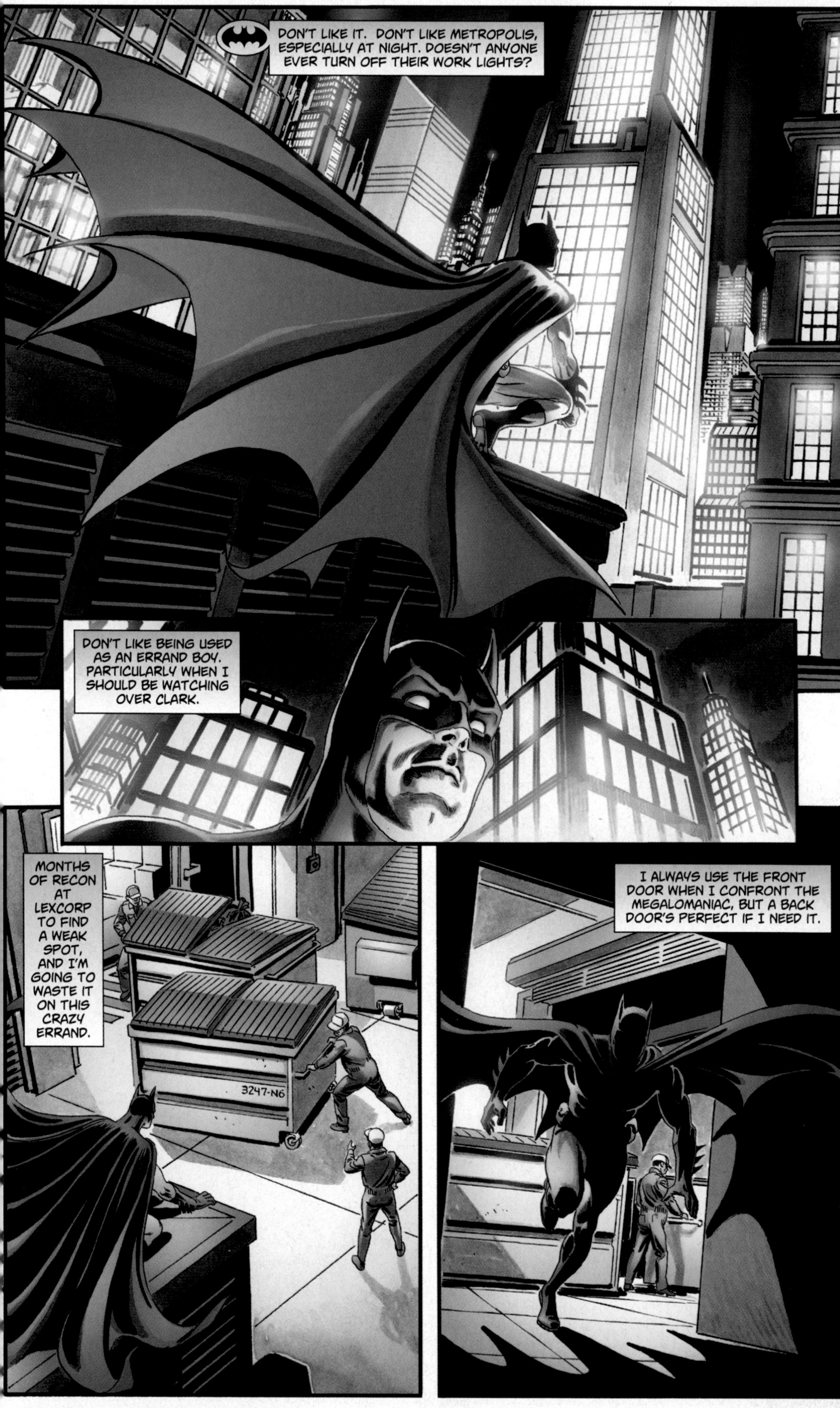
DON'T LIKE IT. DON'T LIKE METROPOLIS, ESPECIALLY AT NIGHT. DOESN'T ANYONE EVER TURN OFF THEIR WORK LIGHTS?
DON'T LIKE BEING USED AS AN ERRAND BOY. PARTICULARLY WHEN I SHOULD BE WATCHING OVER CLARK.
MONTHS OF RECON AT LEXCORP TO FIND A WEAK SPOT, AND I'M GOING TO WASTE IT ON THIS CRAZY ERRAND.
3247-N6
I ALWAYS USE THE FRONT DOOR WHEN I CONFRONT THE MEGALOMANIAC, BUT A BACK DOOR'S PERFECT IF I NEED IT.

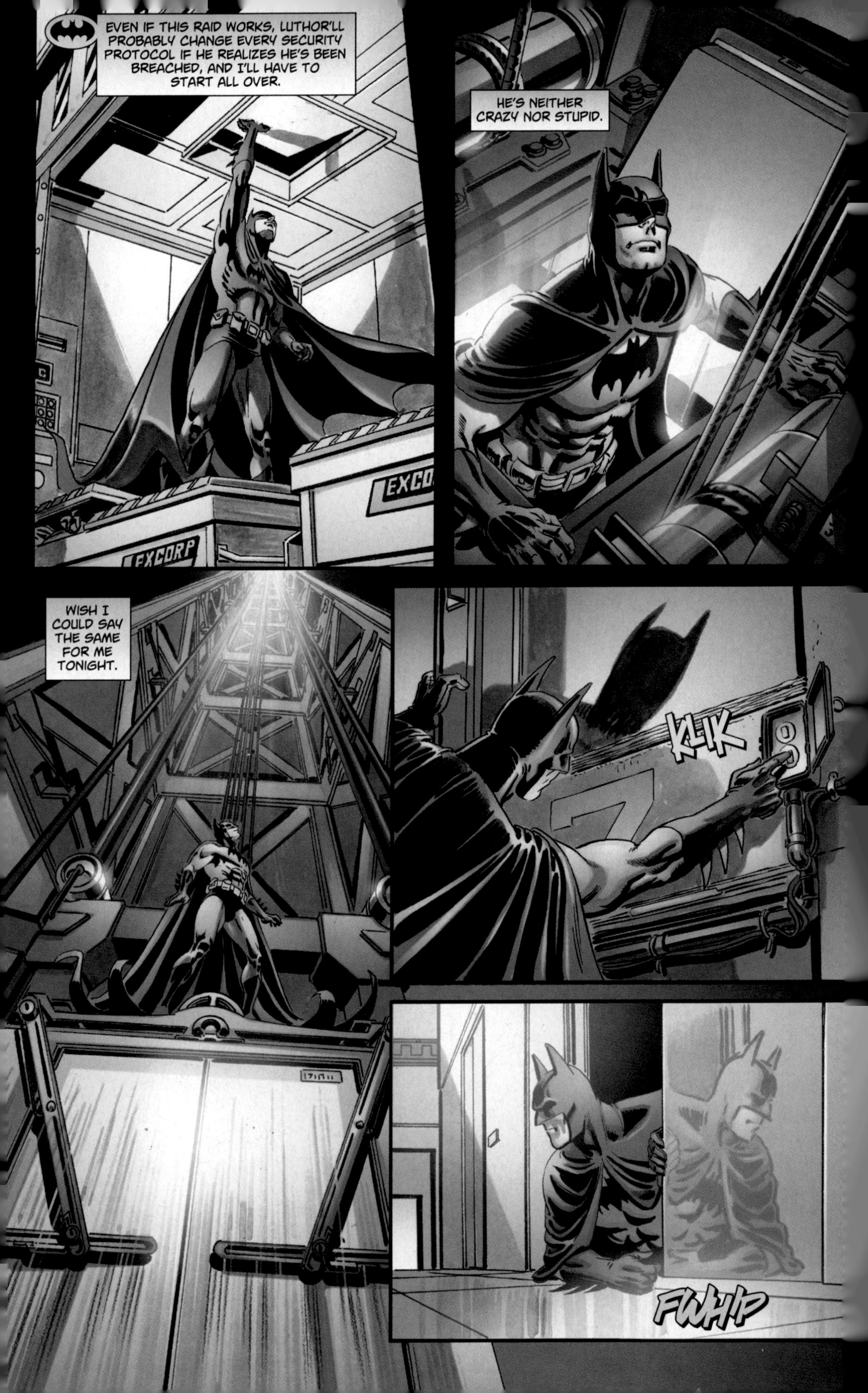
EVEN IF THIS RAID WORKS, LUTHOR'LL PROBABLY CHANGE EVERY SECURITY PROTOCOL IF HE REALIZES HE'S BEEN BREACHED, AND I'LL HAVE TO START ALL OVER.
LEXCORP
HE'S NEITHER CRAZY NOR STUPID.
WISH I COULD SAY THE SAME FOR ME TONIGHT.
KLIK
FWHIP

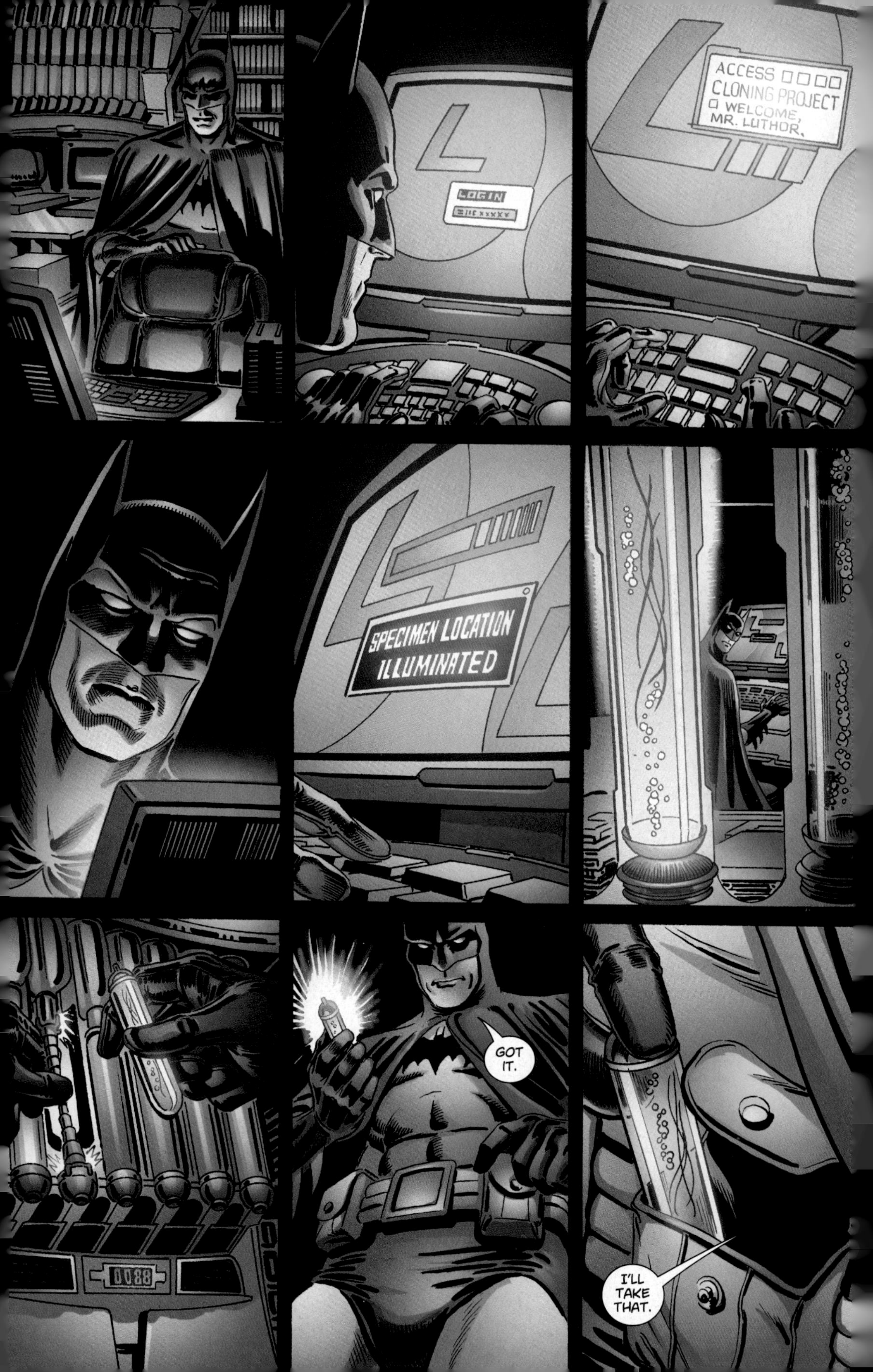
LOGIN
ACCESS
CLONING PROJECT
WELCOME, MR. LUTHOR.
SPECIMEN LOCATION ILLUMINATED
0088
GOT IT.
I'LL TAKE THAT.

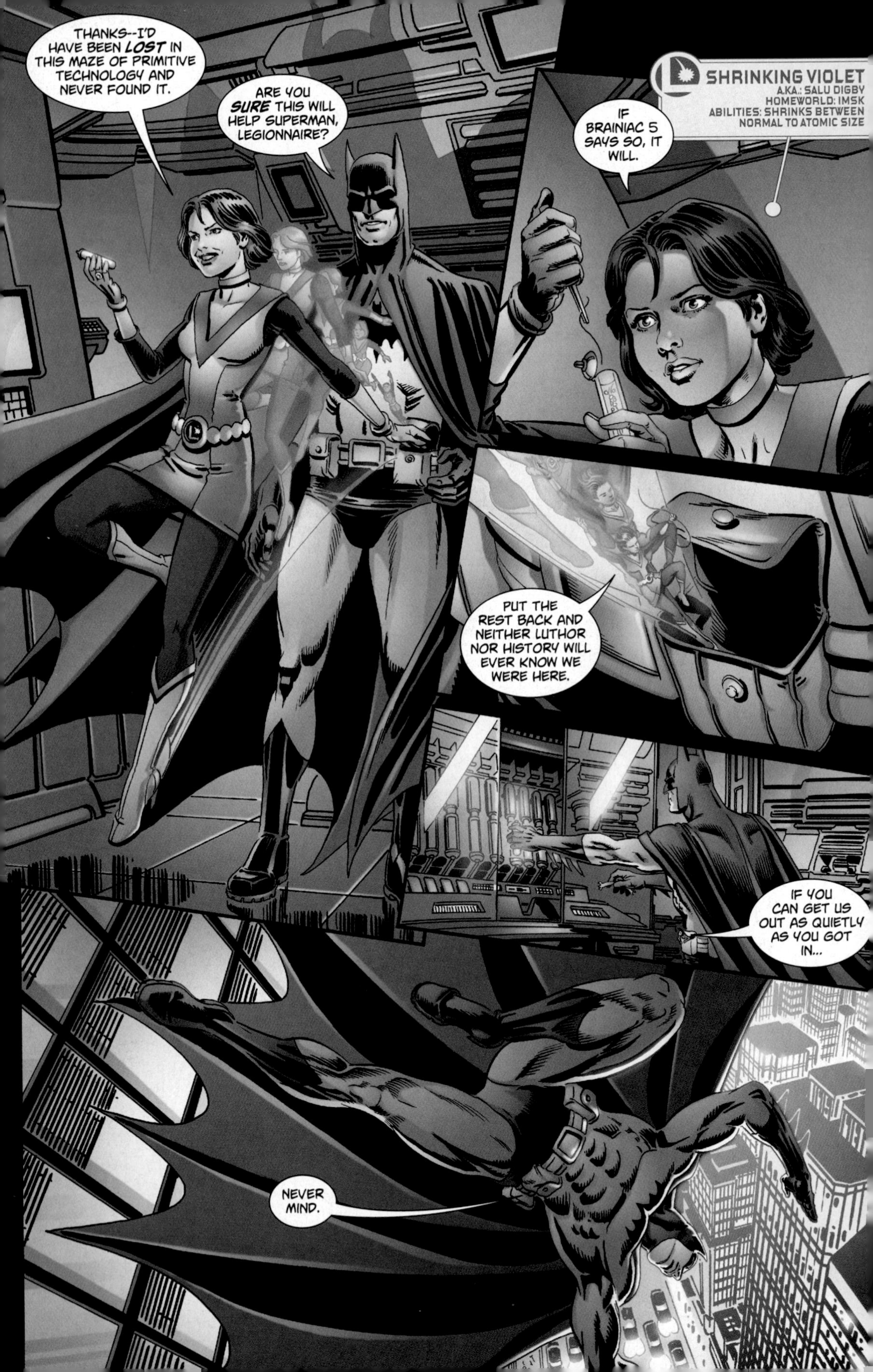
THANKS--I'D HAVE BEEN LOST IN THIS MAZE OF PRIMITIVE TECHNOLOGY AND NEVER FOUND IT.
ARE YOU SURE THIS WILL HELP SUPERMAN, LEGIONNAIRE?
SHRINKING VIOLET
A.KA.: SALU DIGBY
HOMEWORLD: IMSK
ABILITIES: SHRINKS BETWEEN NORMAL TO ATOMIC SIZE
IF BRAINIAC 5 SAYS SO, IT WILL.
PUT THE REST BACK AND NEITHER LUTHOR NOR HISTORY WILL EVER KNOW WE WERE HERE.
IF YOU CAN GET US OUT AS QUIETLY AS YOU GOT IN...
NEVER MIND.

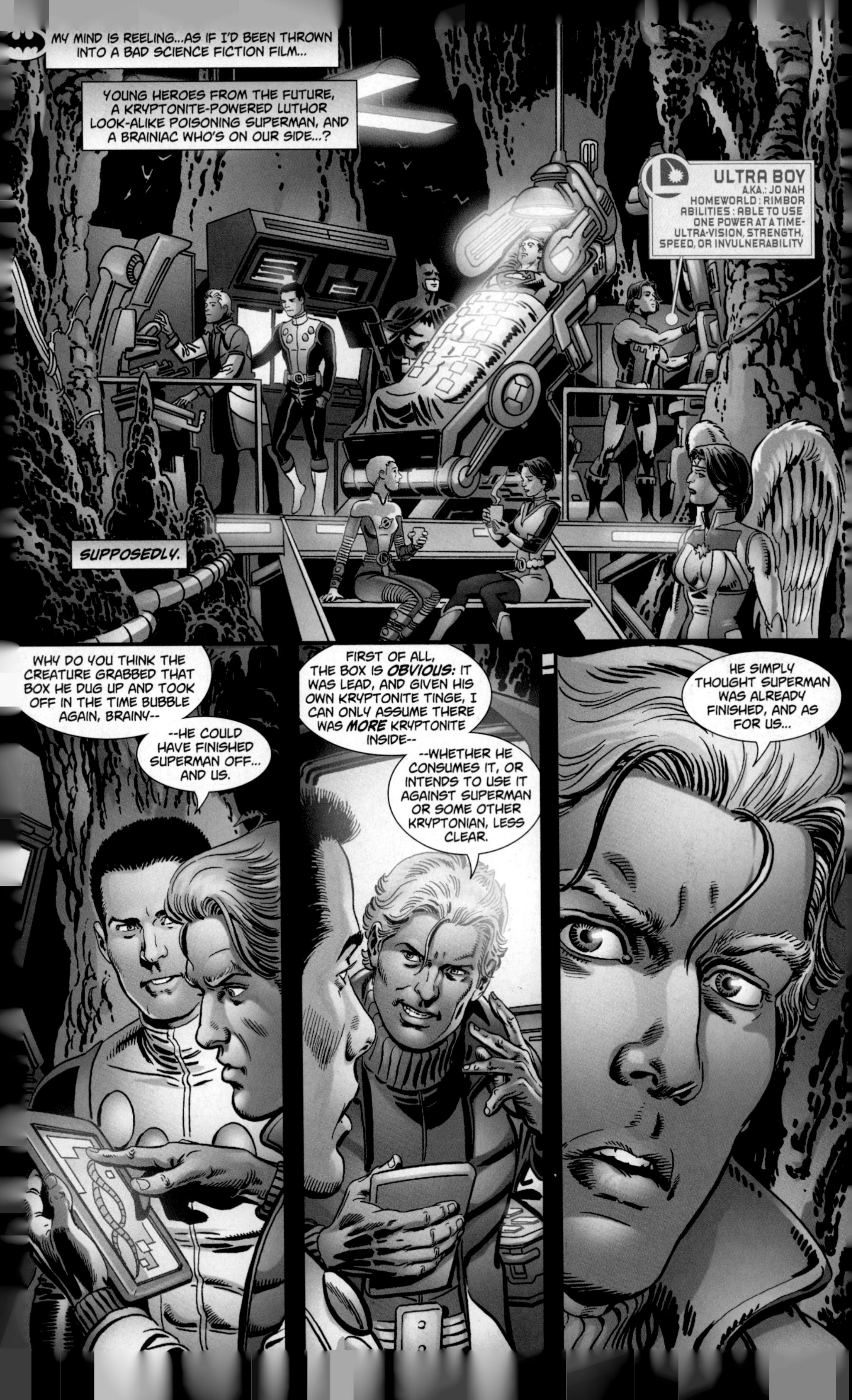

MY MIND IS REELING...AS IF I'D BEEN THROWN INTO A BAD SCIENCE FICTION FILM...
YOUNG HEROES FROM THE FUTURE, A KRYPTONITE-POWERED LUTHOR LOOK-ALIKE POISONING SUPERMAN, AND A BRAINIAC WHO'S ON OUR SIDE...?
ULTRA BOY
A.KA.: JO NAH
HOMEWORLD : RIMBOR
ABILITIES : ABLE TO USE ONE POWER AT A TIME-ULTRA-VISION, STRENGTH, SPEED, OR INVULNERABILITY
SUPPOSEDLY.
WHY DO YOU THINK THE CREATURE GRABBED THAT BOX HE DUG UP AND TOOK OFF IN THE TIME BUBBLE AGAIN, BRAINY--
--HE COULD HAVE FINISHED SUPERMAN OFF... AND US.
FIRST OF ALL, THE BOX IS OBVIOUS: IT WAS LEAD, AND GIVEN HIS OWN KRYPTONITE TINGE, I CAN ONLY ASSUME THERE WAS MORE KRYPTONITE INSIDE--
--WHETHER HE CONSUMES IT, OR INTENDS TO USE IT AGAINST SUPERMAN OR SOME OTHER KRYPTONIAN, LESS CLEAR.
HE SIMPLY THOUGHT SUPERMAN WAS ALREADY FINISHED, AND AS FOR US...

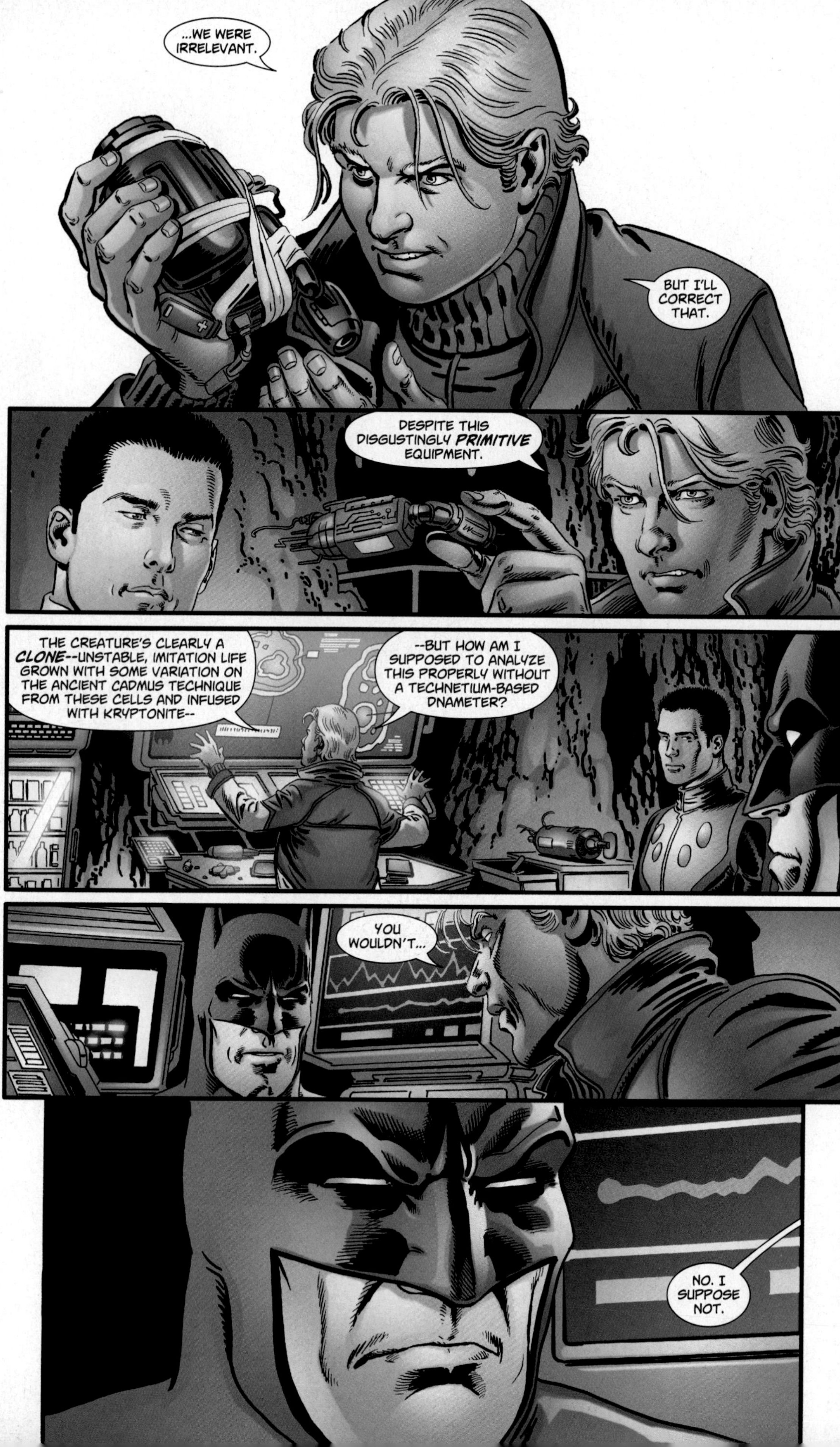
...WE WERE IRRELEVANT.
BUT I'LL CORRECT THAT.
DESPITE THIS DISGUSTINGLY PRIMITIVE EQUIPMENT.
THE CREATURE'S CLEARLY A CLONE--UNSTABLE, IMITATION LIFE GROWN WITH SOME VARIATION ON THE ANCIENT CADMUS TECHNIQUE FROM THESE CELLS AND INFUSED WITH KRYPTONITE--
--BUT HOW AM I SUPPOSED TO ANALYZE THIS PROPERLY WITHOUT A TECHNETIUM-BASED DNAMETER?
YOU WOULDN'T...
NO. I SUPPOSE NOT.

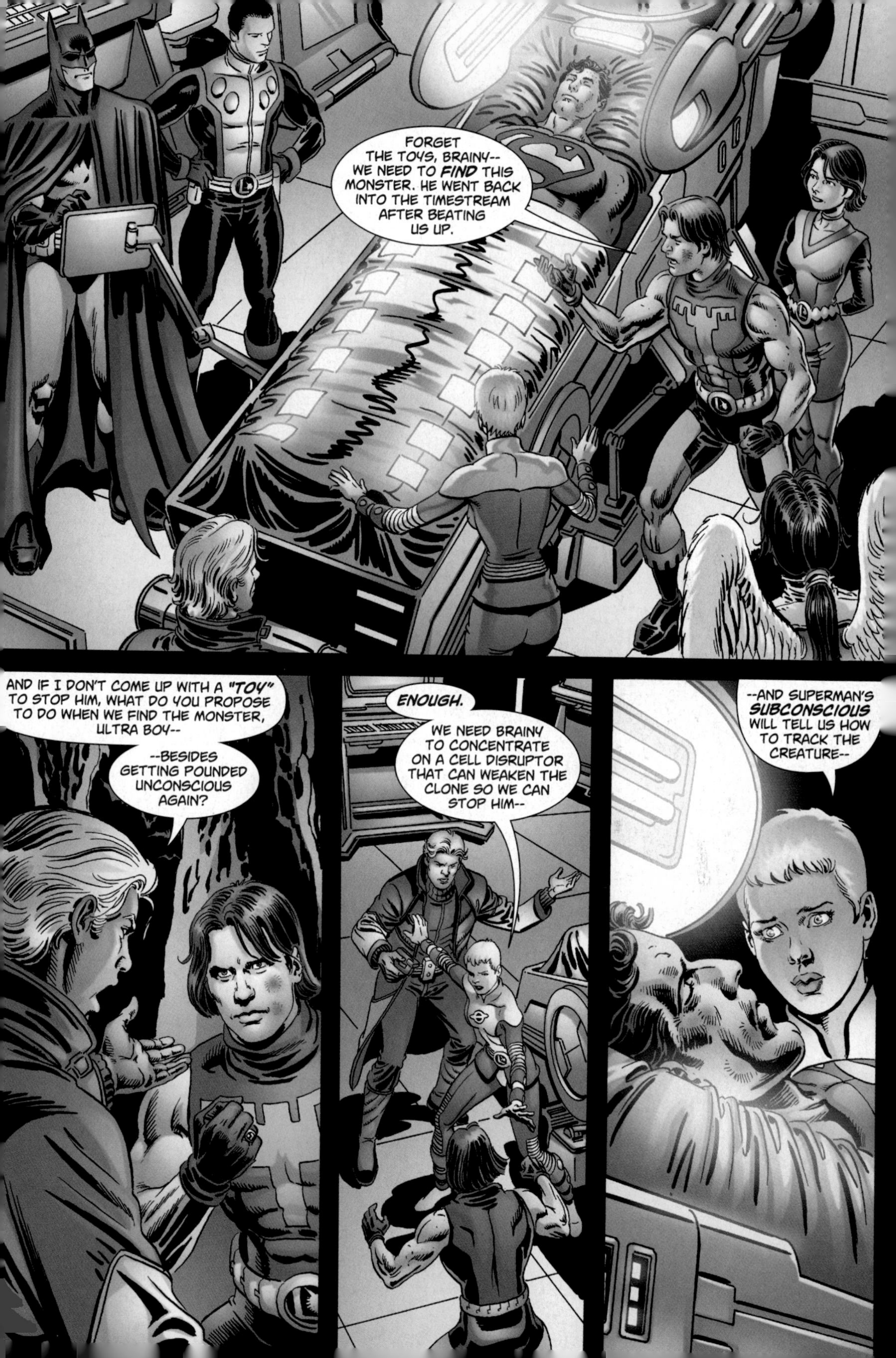
FORGET THE TOYS, BRAINY-- WE NEED TO FIND THIS MONSTER. HE WENT BACK INTO THE TIMESTREAM AFTER BEATING US UP.
AND IF I DON'T COME UP WITH A "TOY" TO STOP HIM, WHAT DO YOU PROPOSE TO DO WHEN WE FIND THE MONSTER, ULTRA BOY--
--BESIDES GETTING POUNDED UNCONSCIOUS AGAIN?
ENOUGH.
WE NEED BRAINY TO CONCENTRATE ON A CELL DISRUPTOR THAT CAN WEAKEN THE CLONE SO WE CAN STOP HIM--
--AND SUPERMAN'S SUBCONSCIOUS WILL TELL US HOW TO TRACK THE CREATURE--

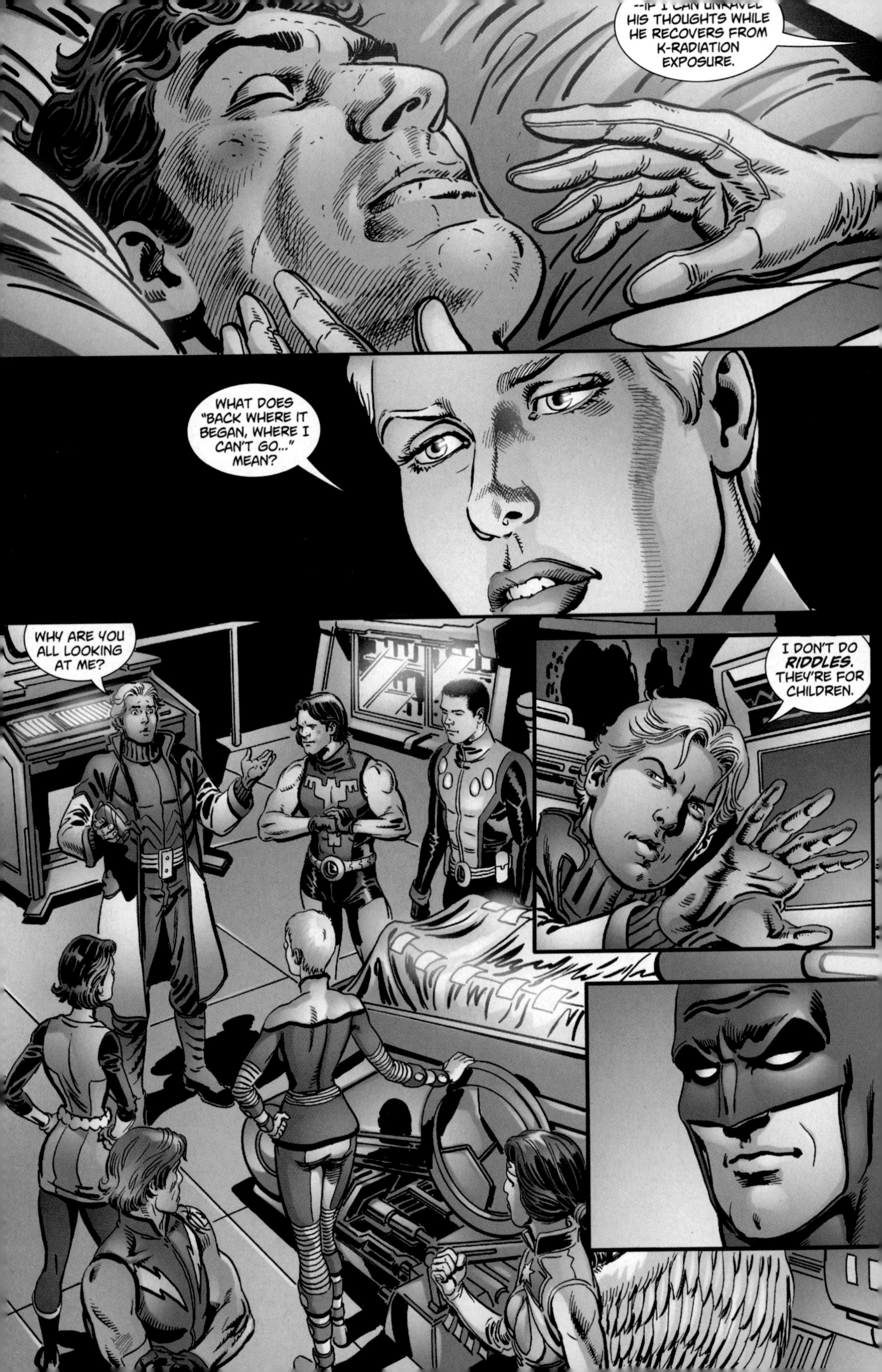
HIS THOUGHTS WHILE HE RECOVERS FROM K-RADIATION EXPOSURE.
WHAT DOES "BACK WHERE IT BEGAN, WHERE I CAN'T GO..." MEAN?
WHY ARE YOU ALL LOOKING AT ME?
I DON'T DO **RIDDLES.** THEY'RE FOR CHILDREN.

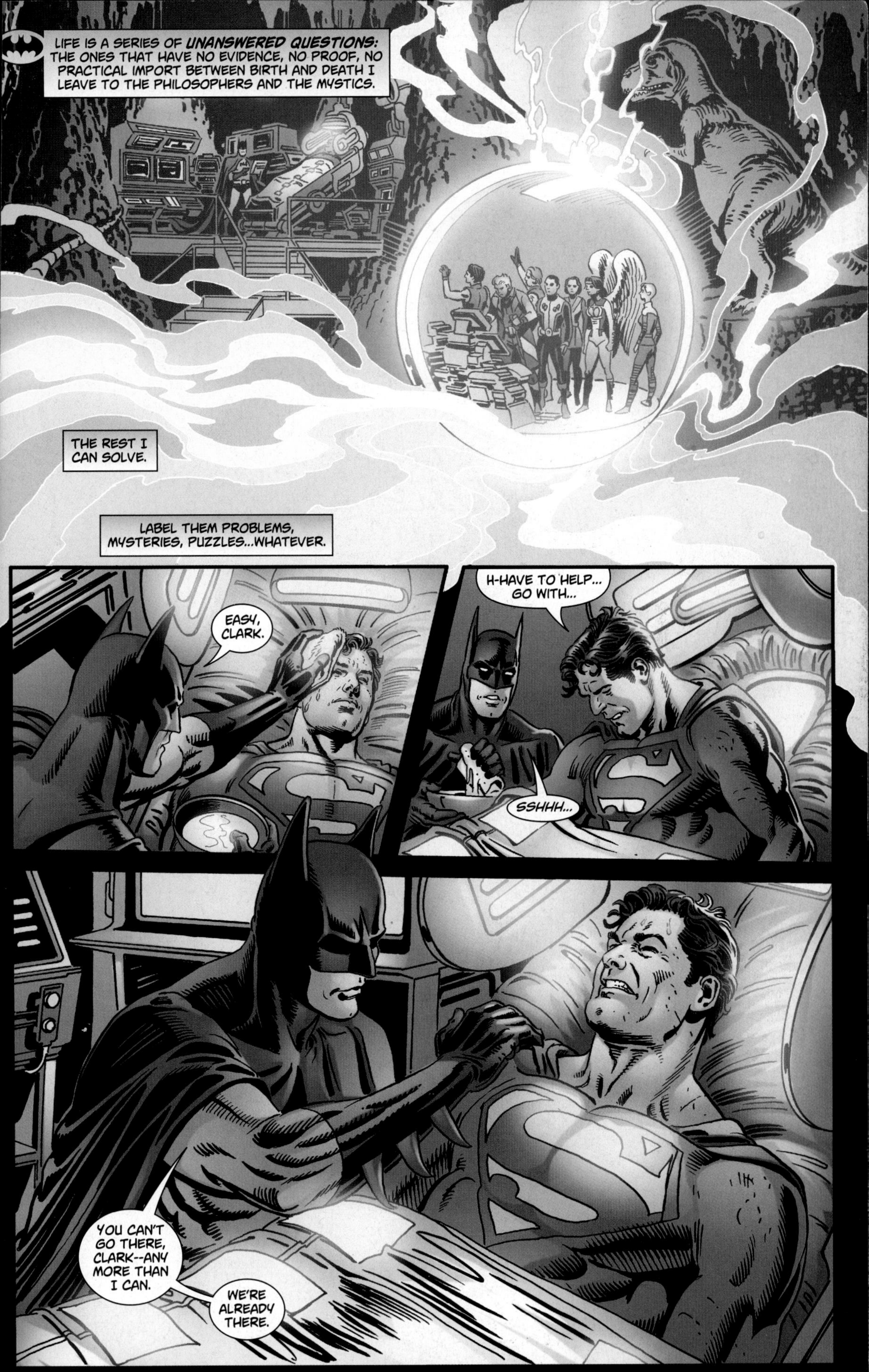
LIFE IS A SERIES OF UNANSWERED QUESTIONS: THE ONES THAT HAVE NO EVIDENCE, NO PROOF, NO PRACTICAL IMPORT BETWEEN BIRTH AND DEATH I LEAVE TO THE PHILOSOPHERS AND THE MYSTICS.
THE REST I CAN SOLVE.
LABEL THEM PROBLEMS, MYSTERIES, PUZZLES...WHATEVER.
EASY, CLARK.
H-HAVE TO HELP... GO WITH...
SSHHH...
YOU CAN'T GO THERE, CLARK--ANY MORE THAN I CAN.
WE'RE ALREADY THERE.

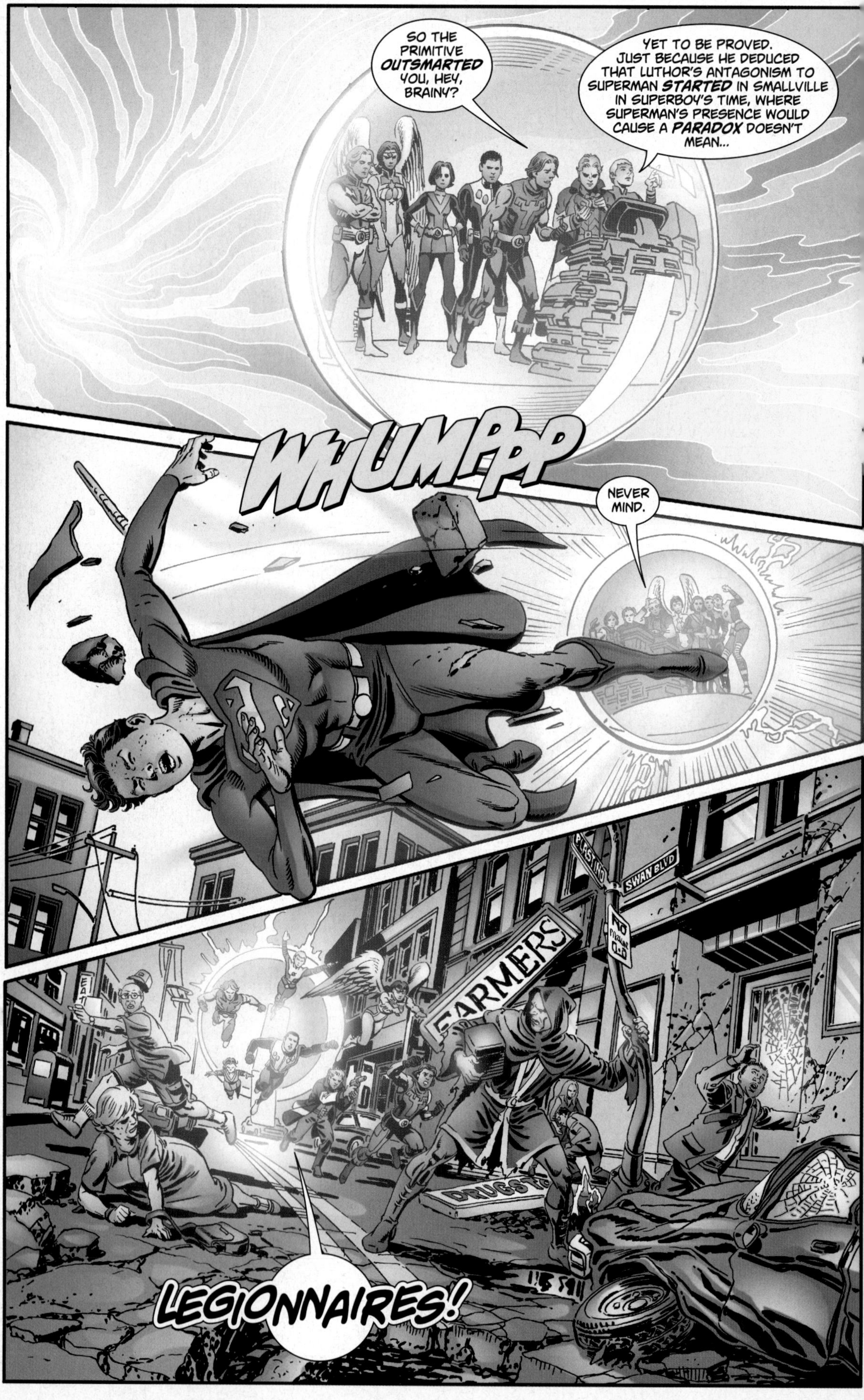
SO THE PRIMITIVE OUTSMARTED YOU, HEY, BRAINY?
YET TO BE PROVED. JUST BECAUSE HE DEDUCED THAT LUTHOR'S ANTAGONISM TO SUPERMAN STARTED IN SMALLVILLE IN SUPERBOY'S TIME, WHERE SUPERMAN'S PRESENCE WOULD CAUSE A PARADOX DOESN'T MEAN...
WHUMPPP
NEVER MIND.
SWAN BLVD
NO
FARMERS
DRUGS
LEGIONNAIRES!

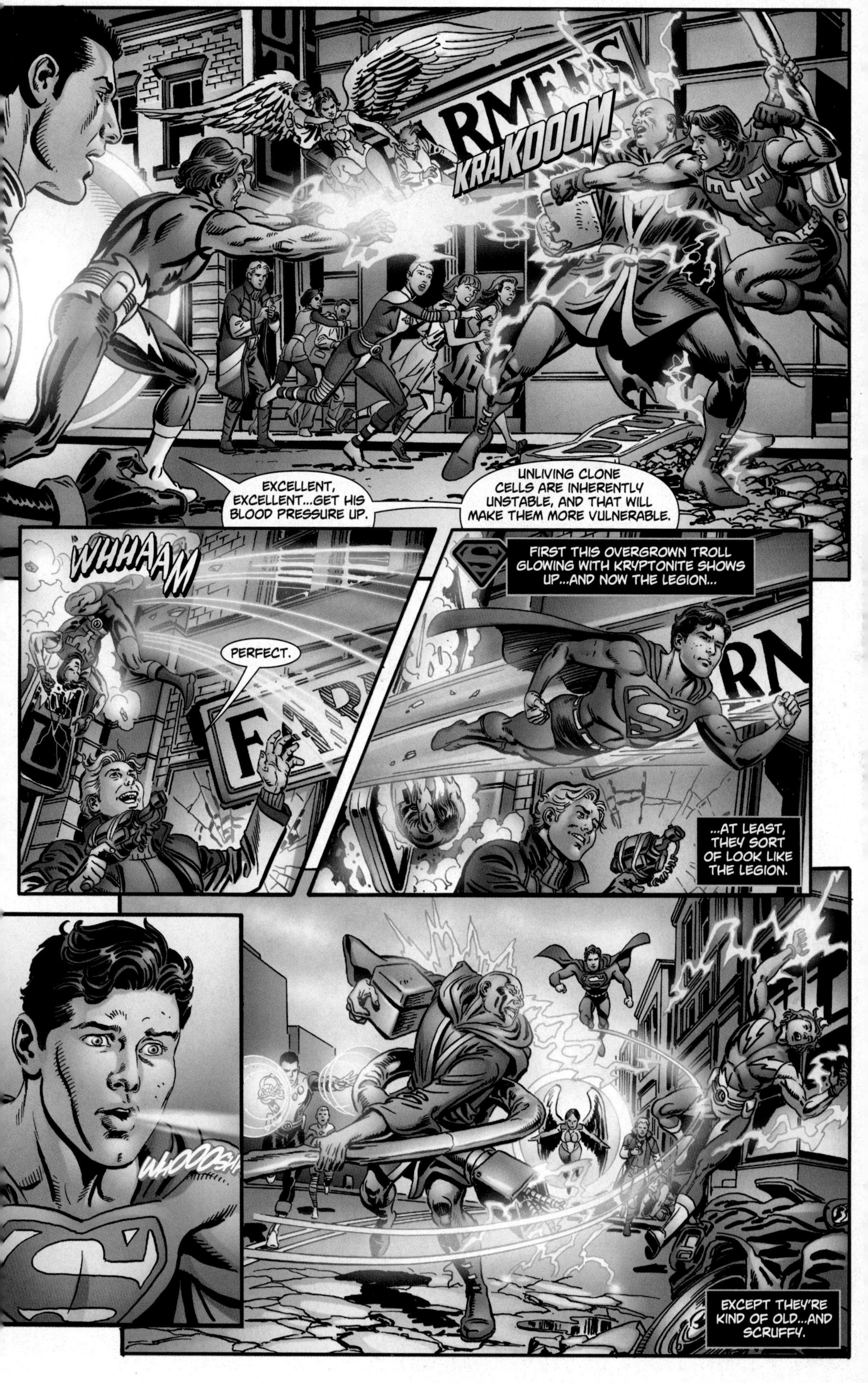

KRAKOOOM
EXCELLENT, EXCELLENT...GET HIS BLOOD PRESSURE UP.
UNLIVING CLONE CELLS ARE INHERENTLY UNSTABLE, AND THAT WILL MAKE THEM MORE VULNERABLE.
WHHAAM
PERFECT.
FIRST THIS OVERGROWN TROLL GLOWING WITH KRYPTONITE SHOWS UP...AND NOW THE LEGION...
...AT LEAST, THEY SORT OF LOOK LIKE THE LEGION.
WHOOOSH
EXCEPT THEY'RE KIND OF OLD...AND SCRUFFY.

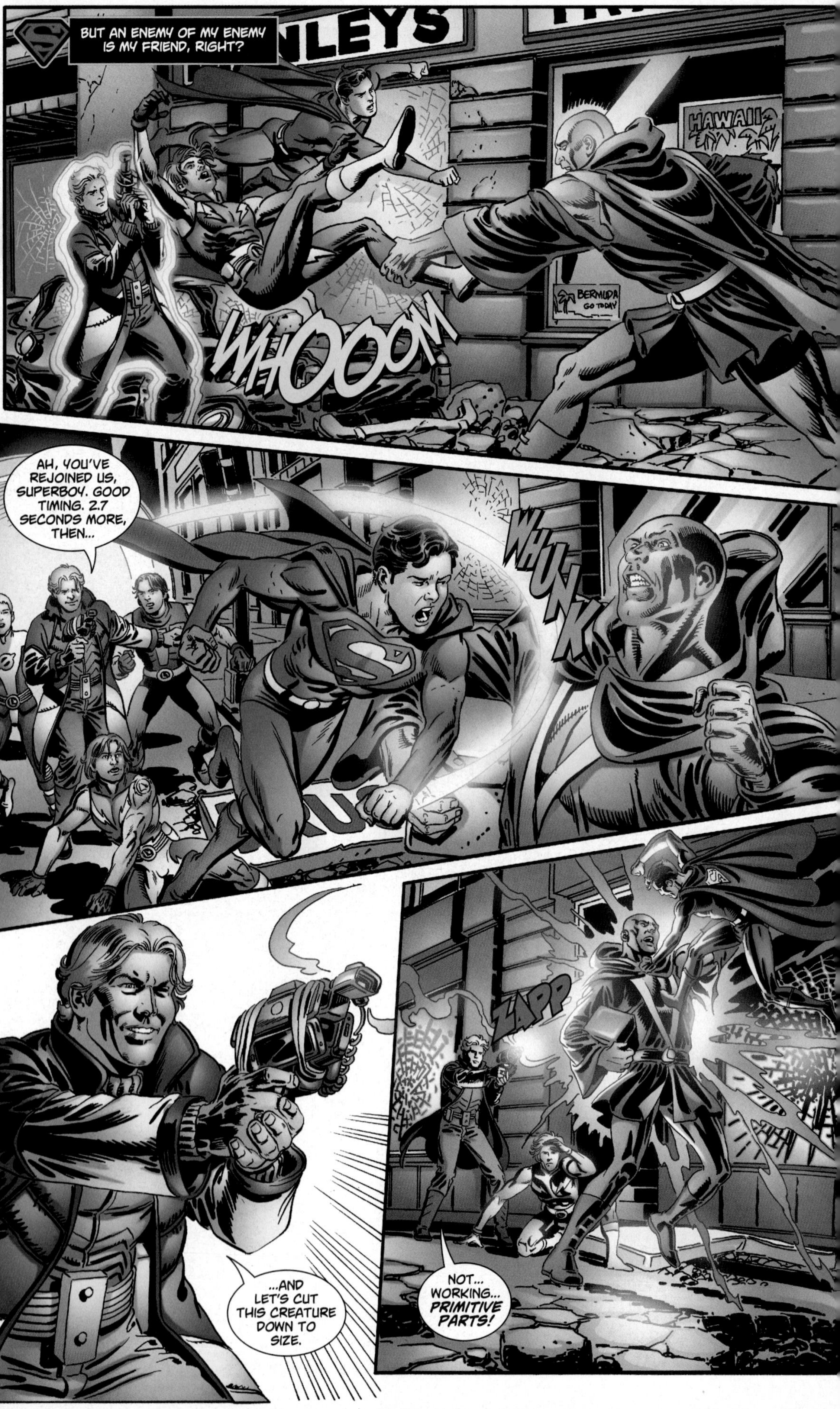

BUT AN ENEMY OF MY ENEMY IS MY FRIEND, RIGHT?
NLEYS
HAWAII
BERMUDA GO TODAY
WHOOOM
AH, YOU'VE REJOINED US, SUPERBOY. GOOD TIMING. 2.7 SECONDS MORE, THEN...
WHUNK
...AND LET'S CUT THIS CREATURE DOWN TO SIZE.
ZAPP
NOT... WORKING... PRIMITIVE PARTS!

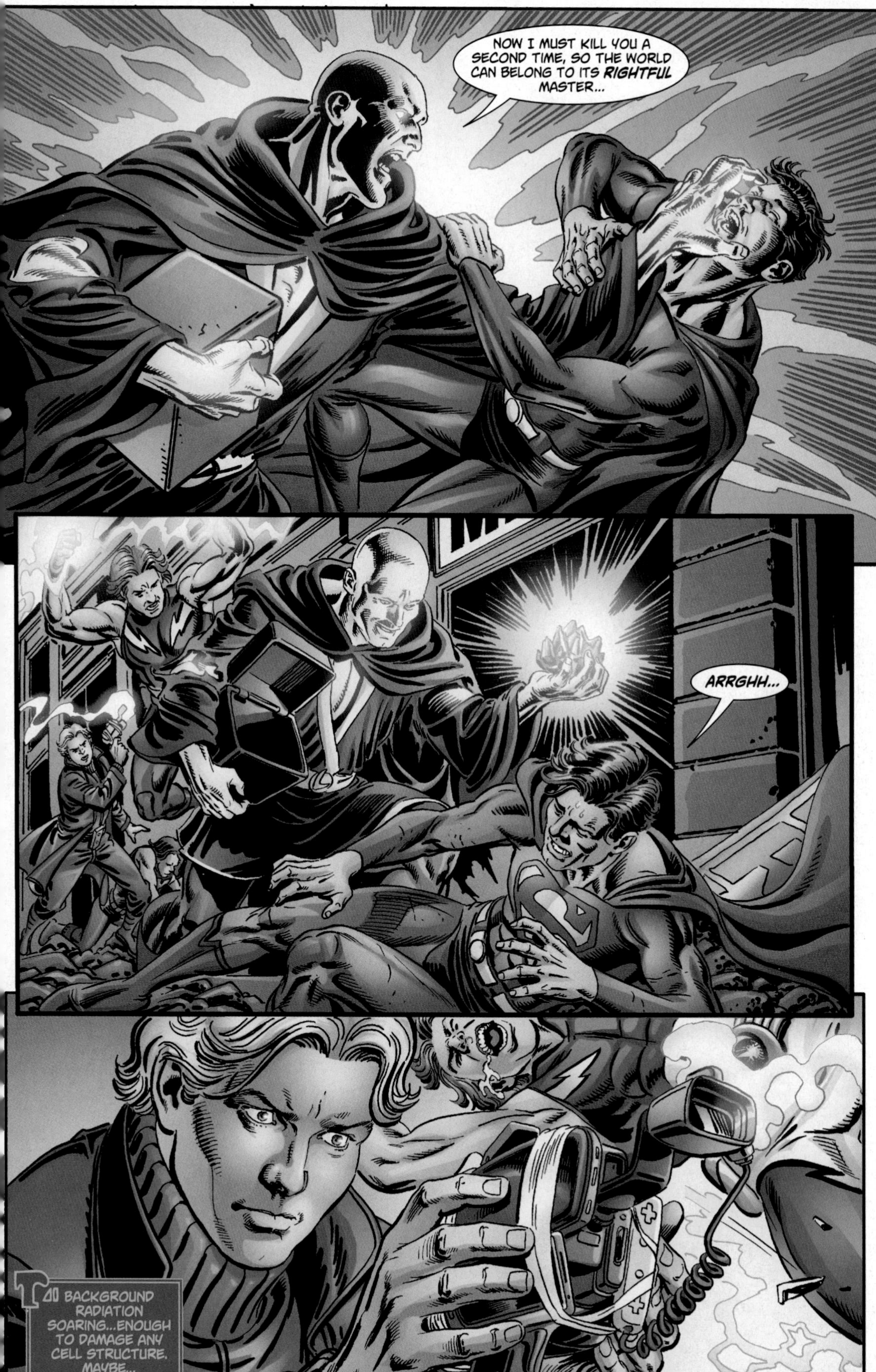
NOW I MUST KILL YOU A SECOND TIME, SO THE WORLD CAN BELONG TO ITS RIGHTFUL MASTER...
ARRGHH...
BACKGROUND RADIATION SOARING...ENOUGH TO DAMAGE ANY CELL STRUCTURE. MAYBE...

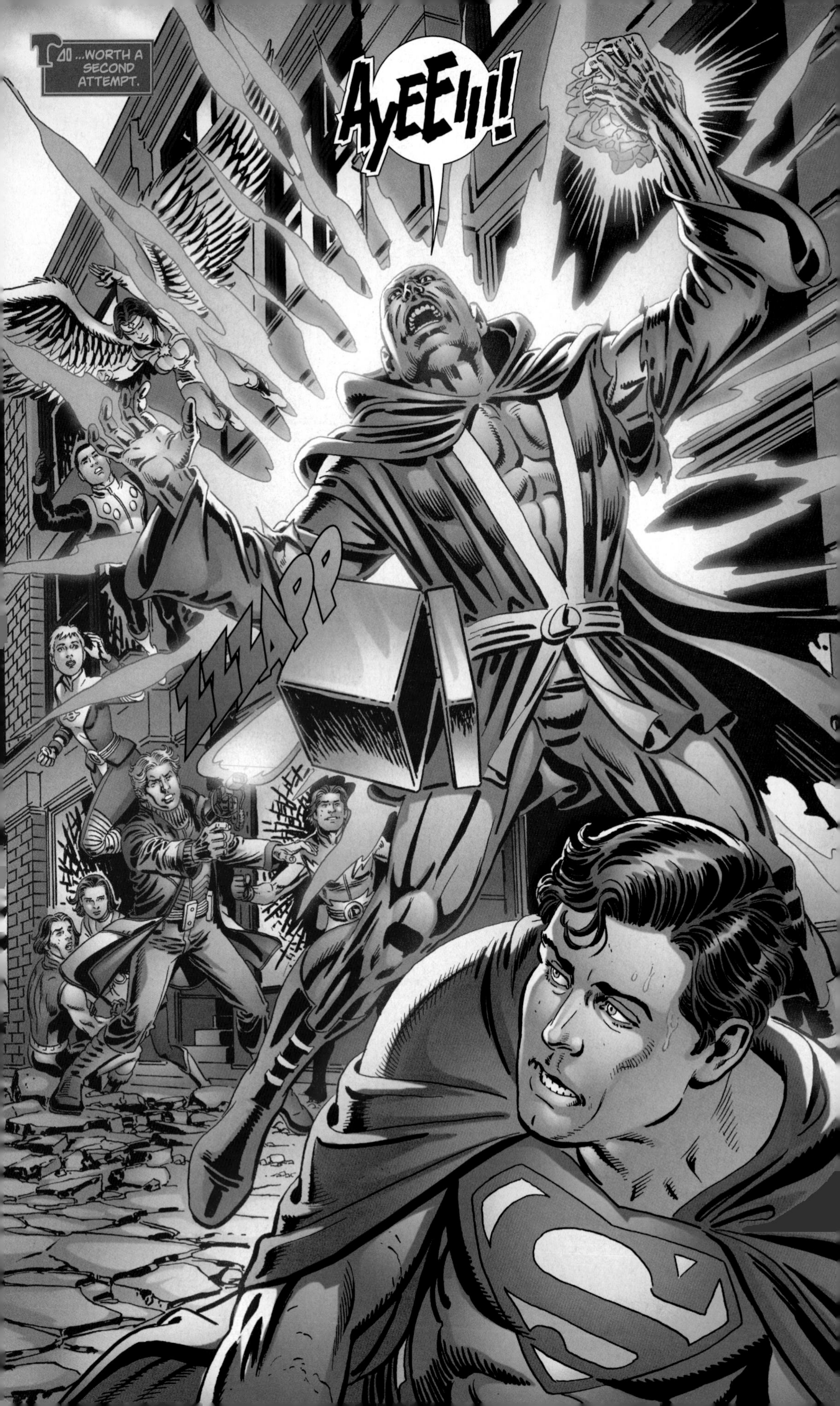
...WORTH A SECOND ATTEMPT.
AYEEII!
ZZZAPP

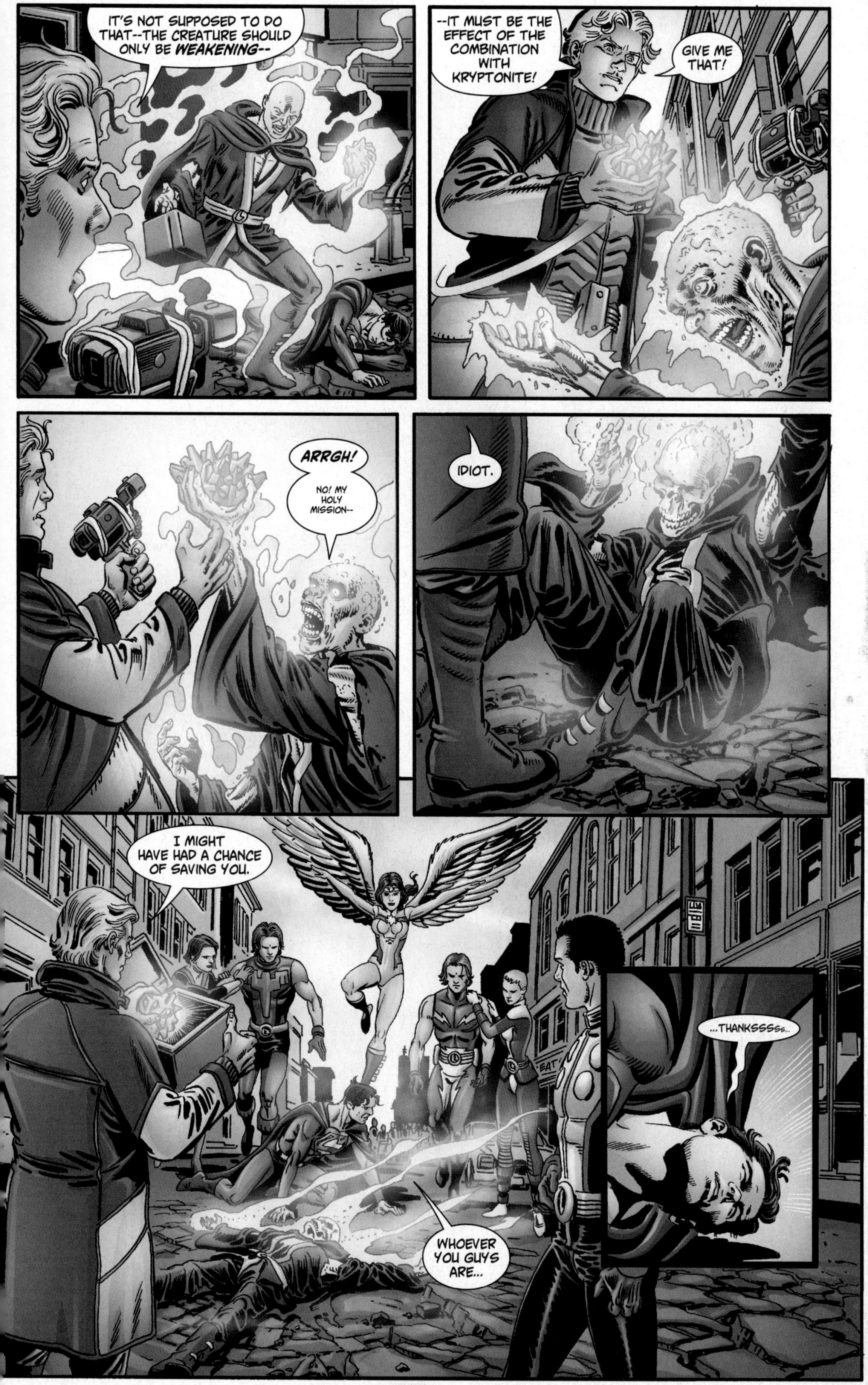
IT'S NOT SUPPOSED TO DO THAT--THE CREATURE SHOULD ONLY BE WEAKENING--
--IT MUST BE THE EFFECT OF THE COMBINATION WITH KRYPTONITE!
GIVE ME THAT!
ARRGH!
NO! MY HOLY MISSION--
IDIOT.
I MIGHT HAVE HAD A CHANCE OF SAVING YOU.
WHOEVER YOU GUYS ARE...
...THANKSSSSs...

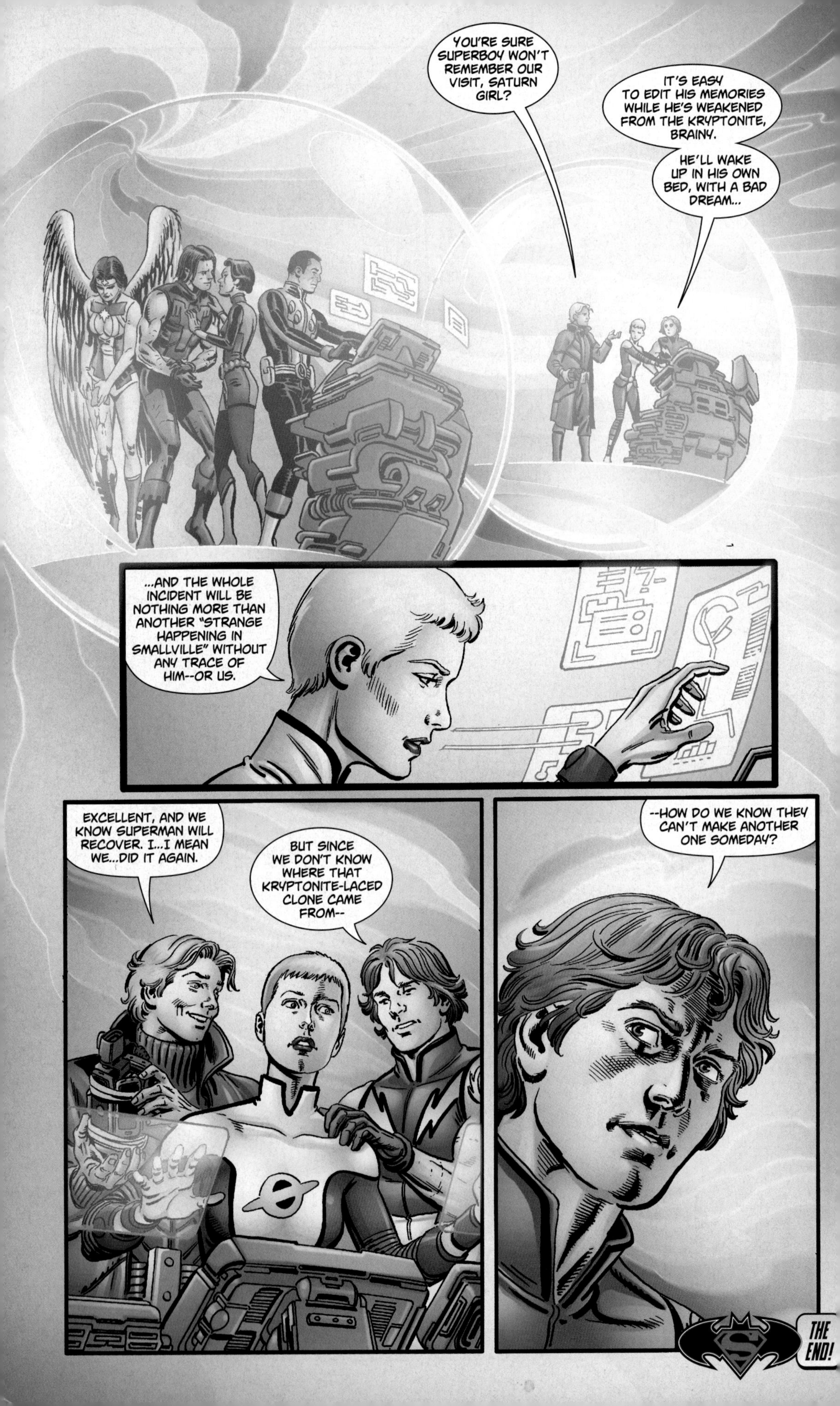
YOU'RE SURE SUPERBOY WON'T REMEMBER OUR VISIT, SATURN GIRL?
IT'S EASY TO EDIT HIS MEMORIES WHILE HE'S WEAKENED FROM THE KRYPTONITE, BRAINY.
HE'LL WAKE UP IN HIS OWN BED, WITH A BAD DREAM...
...AND THE WHOLE INCIDENT WILL BE NOTHING MORE THAN ANOTHER "STRANGE HAPPENING IN SMALLVILLE" WITHOUT ANY TRACE OF HIM--OR US.
EXCELLENT, AND WE KNOW SUPERMAN WILL RECOVER. I...I MEAN WE...DID IT AGAIN.
BUT SINCE WE DON'T KNOW WHERE THAT KRYPTONITE-LACED CLONE CAME FROM--
--HOW DO WE KNOW THEY CAN'T MAKE ANOTHER ONE SOMEDAY?
THE END!

THE FUTURISTIC ADVENTURES OF BATMAN CONTINUE IN
BATMAN BEYOND: HUSH BEYOND!

Adam Beechen
Writer

Ryan Benjamin
Penciller

John Stanisci
Inker

David Baron
Colorist

Travis Lanham
Letterer

Dustin Nguyen
Cover

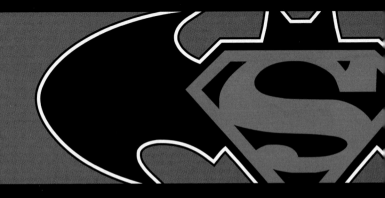

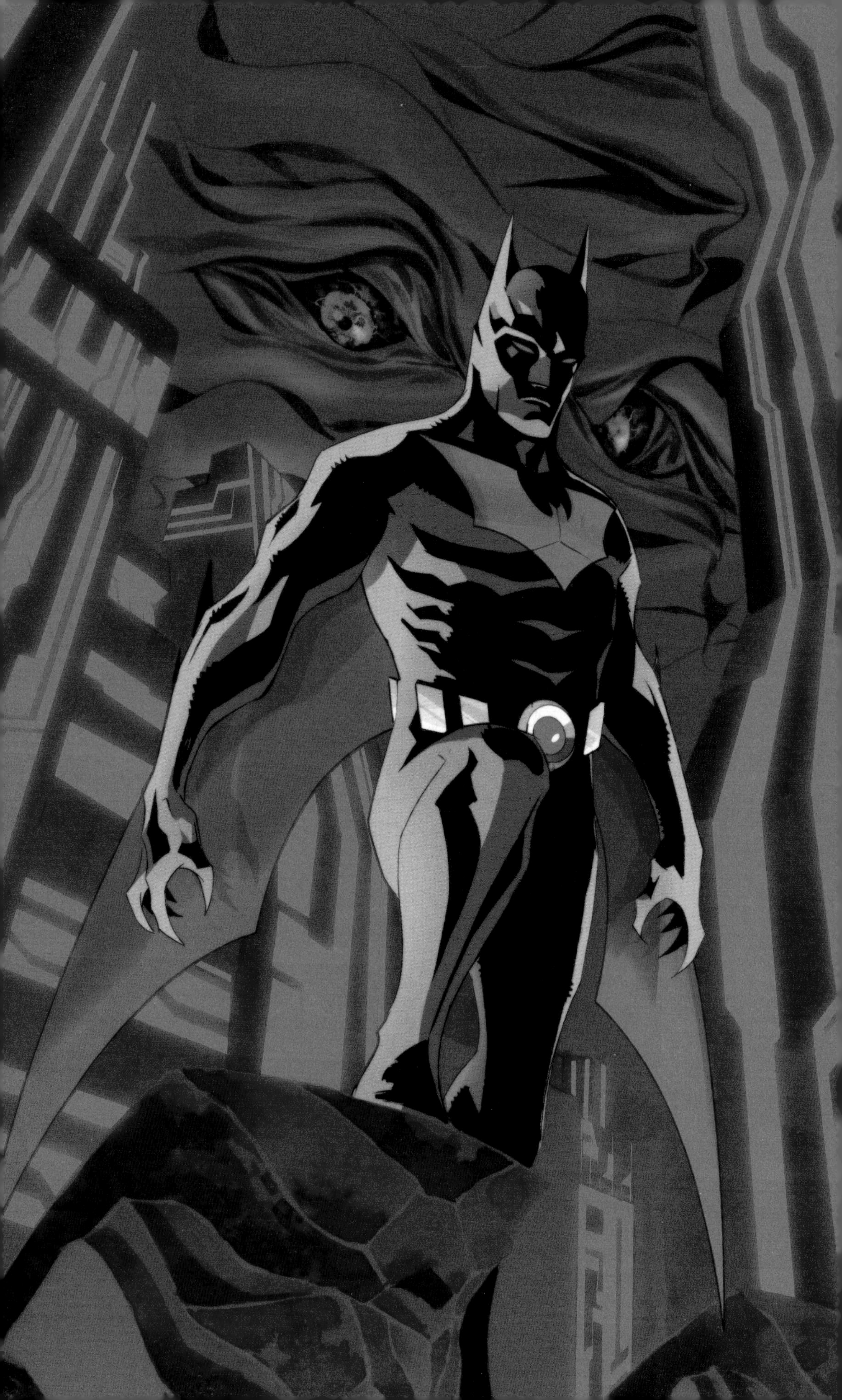

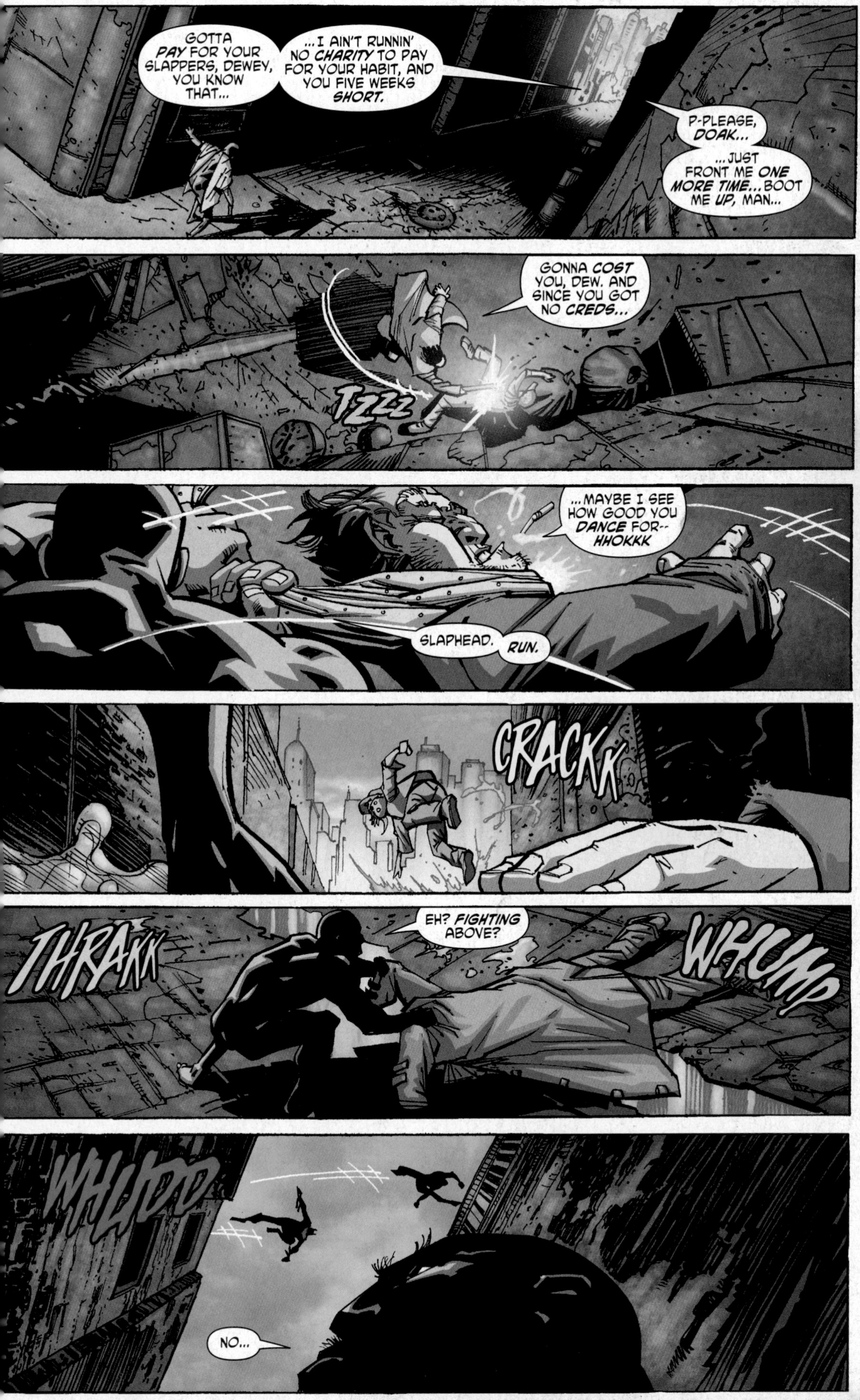
GOTTA PAY FOR YOUR SLAPPERS, DEWEY, YOU KNOW THAT...
...I AIN'T RUNNIN' NO CHARITY TO PAY FOR YOUR HABIT, AND YOU FIVE WEEKS SHORT.
P-PLEASE, DOAK...
...JUST FRONT ME ONE MORE TIME... BOOT ME UP, MAN...
GONNA COST YOU, DEW. AND SINCE YOU GOT NO CREDS...
TZZZ
...MAYBE I SEE HOW GOOD YOU DANCE FOR--HHOKKK
SLAPHEAD.
RUN.
CRACKK
THRAKK
EH? FIGHTING ABOVE?
WHUMP
WHUDD
NO...

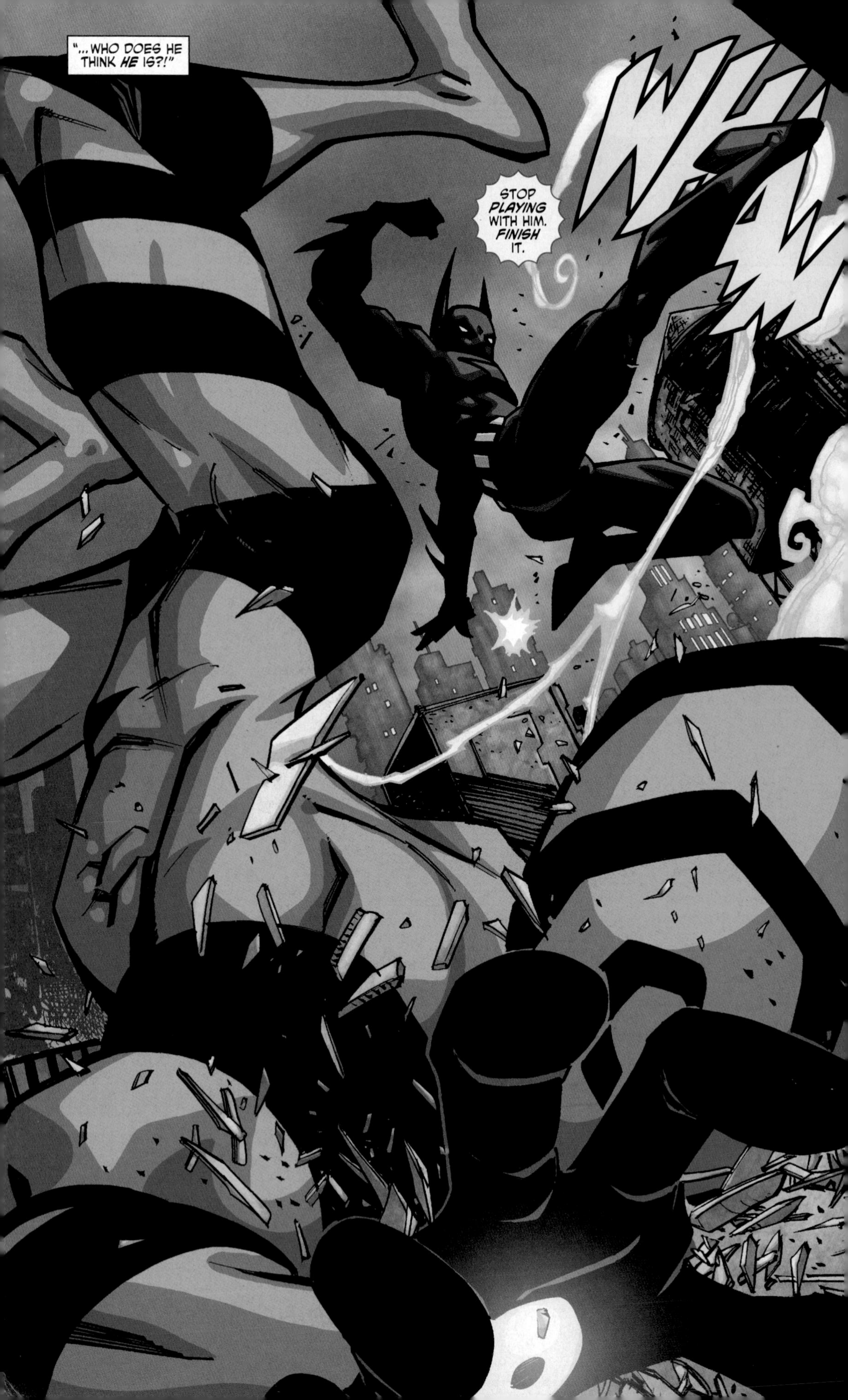
"...WHO DOES HE THINK HE IS?!"
STOP PLAYING WITH HIM. FINISH IT.

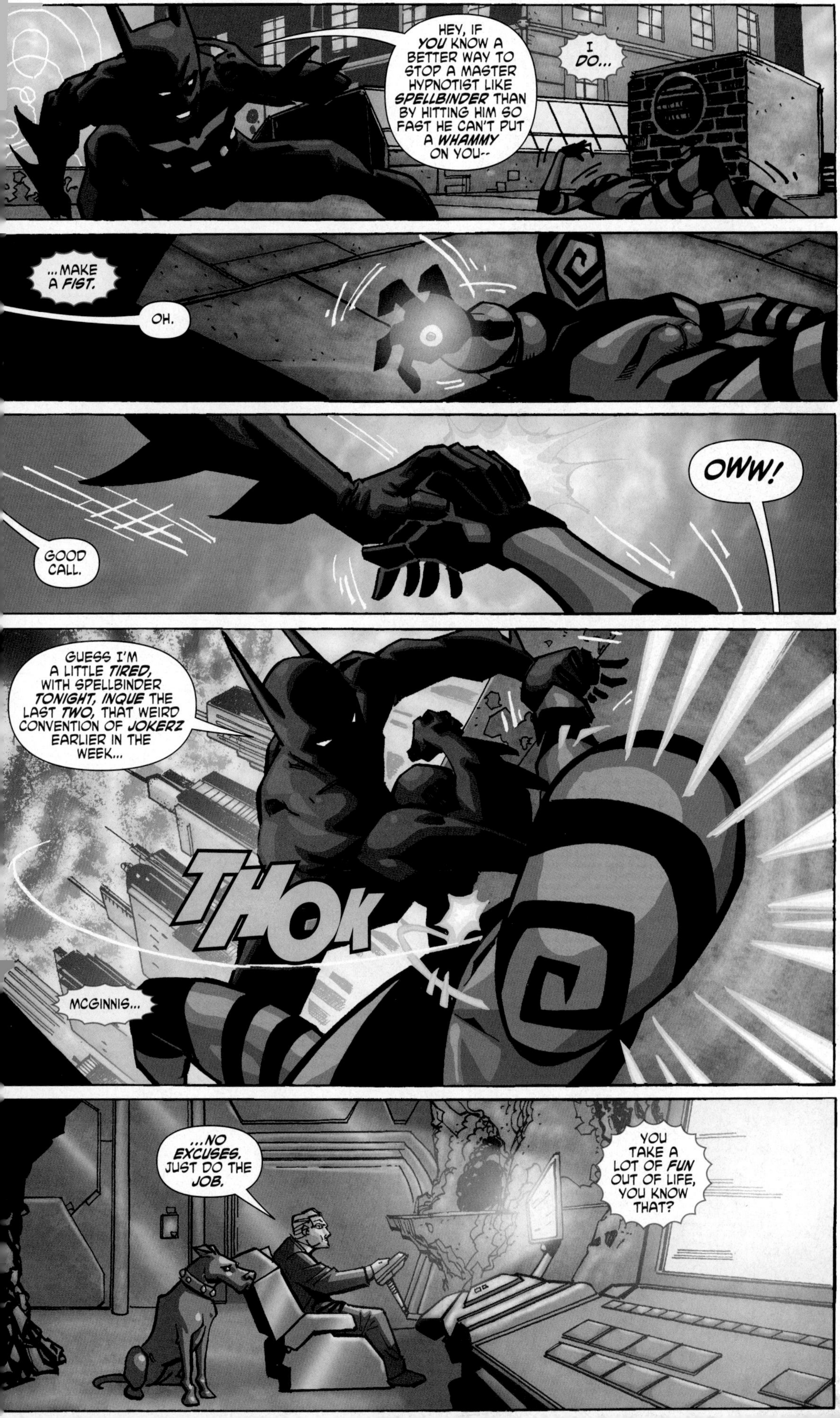
HEY, IF YOU KNOW A BETTER WAY TO STOP A MASTER HYPNOTIST LIKE SPELLBINDER THAN BY HITTING HIM SO FAST HE CAN'T PUT A WHAMMY ON YOU--
I DO...
...MAKE A FIST.
OH.
OWW!
GOOD CALL.
GUESS I'M A LITTLE TIRED, WITH SPELLBINDER TONIGHT, INQUE THE LAST TWO, THAT WEIRD CONVENTION OF JOKERZ EARLIER IN THE WEEK...
THOK
MCGINNIS...
...NO EXCUSES. JUST DO THE JOB.
YOU TAKE A LOT OF FUN OUT OF LIFE, YOU KNOW THAT?

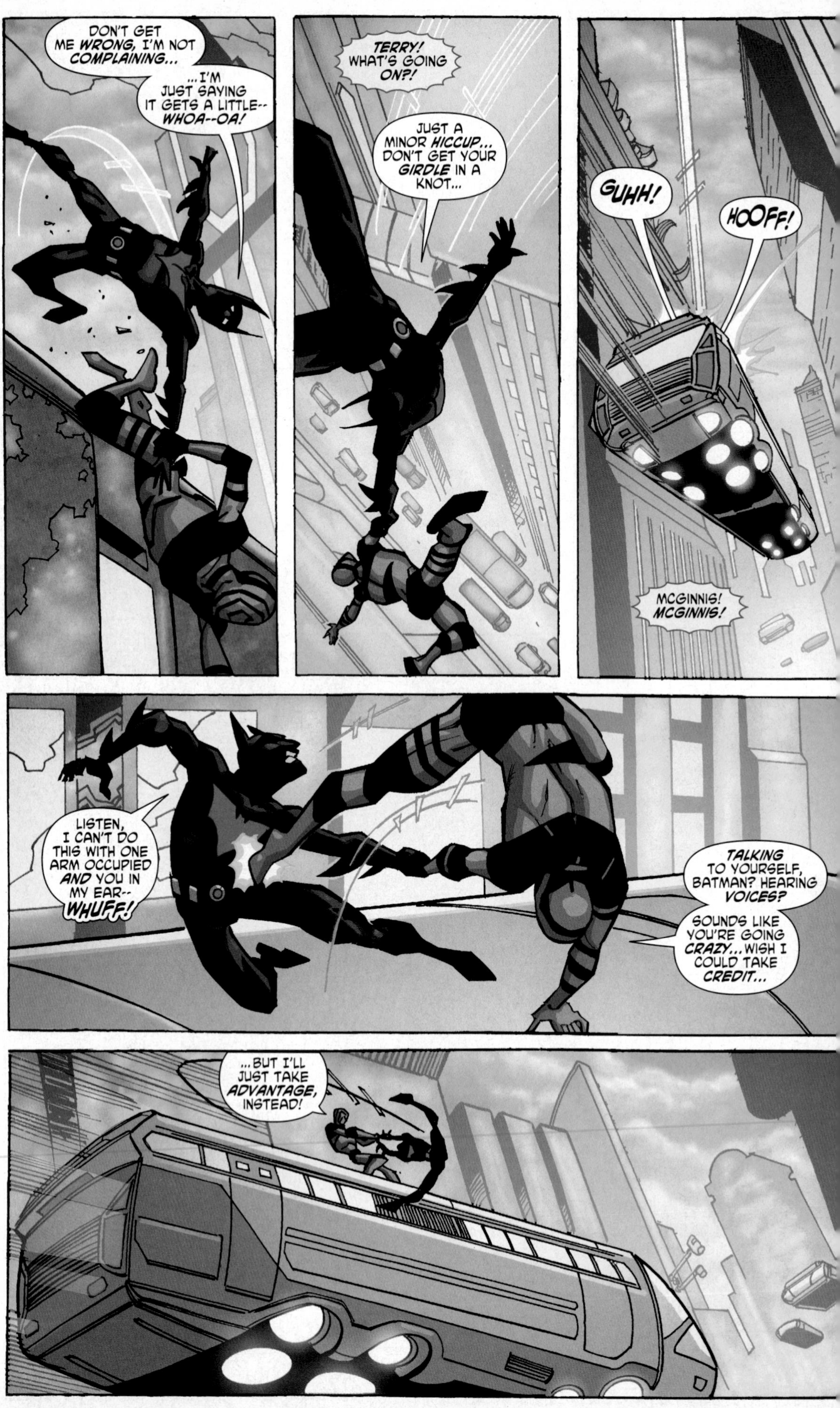

DON'T GET ME WRONG, I'M NOT COMPLAINING...
...I'M JUST SAYING IT GETS A LITTLE-- WHOA--OA!
TERRY! WHAT'S GOING ON?!
JUST A MINOR HICCUP... DON'T GET YOUR GIRDLE IN A KNOT...
GUHH!
HOOFF!
MCGINNIS! MCGINNIS!
LISTEN, I CAN'T DO THIS WITH ONE ARM OCCUPIED AND YOU IN MY EAR-- WHUFF!
TALKING TO YOURSELF, BATMAN? HEARING VOICES?
SOUNDS LIKE YOU'RE GOING CRAZY... WISH I COULD TAKE CREDIT...
...BUT I'LL JUST TAKE ADVANTAGE, INSTEAD!

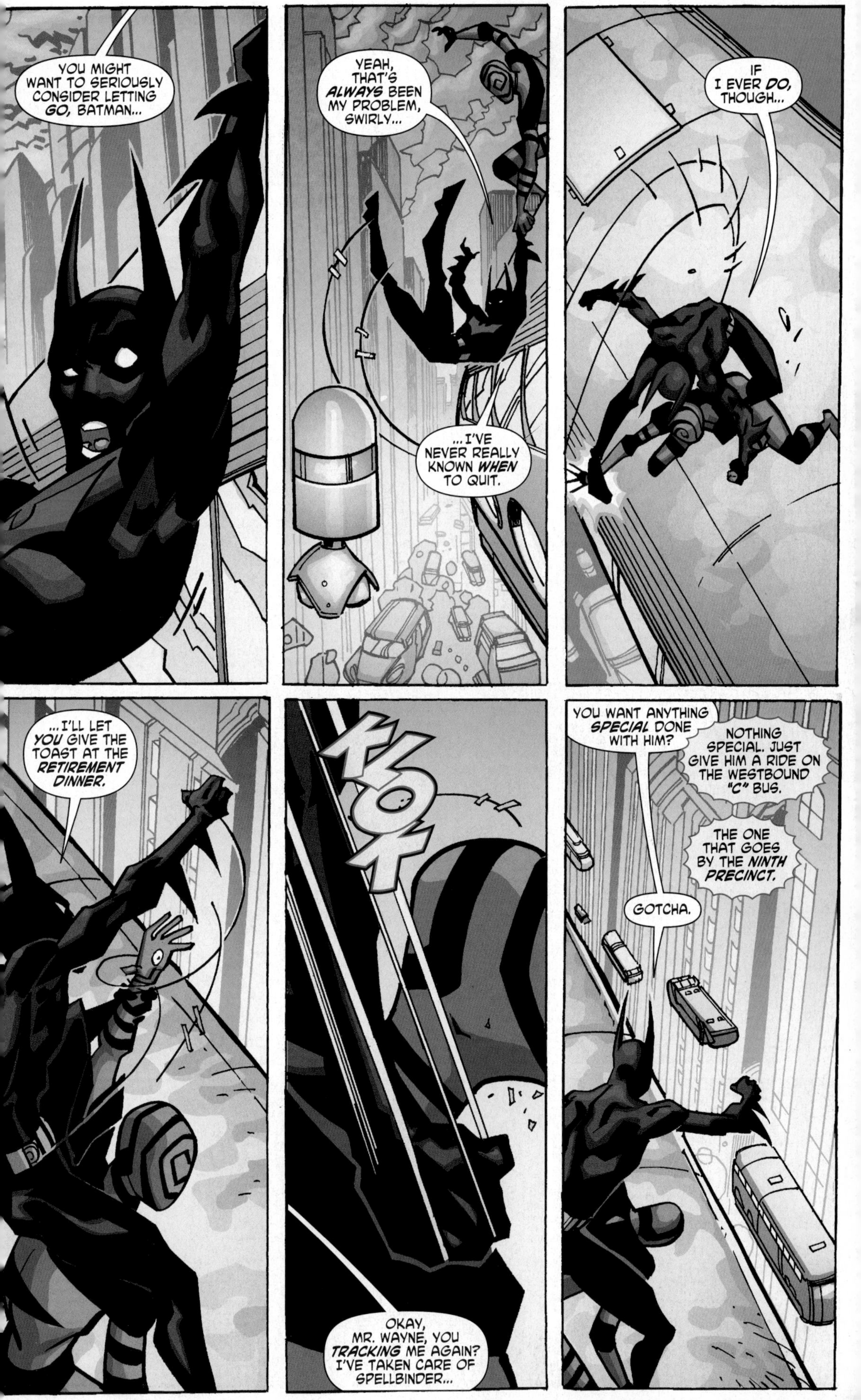
YOU MIGHT WANT TO SERIOUSLY CONSIDER LETTING GO, BATMAN...
YEAH, THAT'S ALWAYS BEEN MY PROBLEM, SWIRLY...
...I'VE NEVER REALLY KNOWN WHEN TO QUIT.
IF I EVER DO, THOUGH...
...I'LL LET YOU GIVE THE TOAST AT THE RETIREMENT DINNER.
KLOK
OKAY, MR. WAYNE, YOU TRACKING ME AGAIN? I'VE TAKEN CARE OF SPELLBINDER...
YOU WANT ANYTHING SPECIAL DONE WITH HIM?
NOTHING SPECIAL. JUST GIVE HIM A RIDE ON THE WESTBOUND "C" BUS.
THE ONE THAT GOES BY THE NINTH PRECINCT.
GOTCHA.

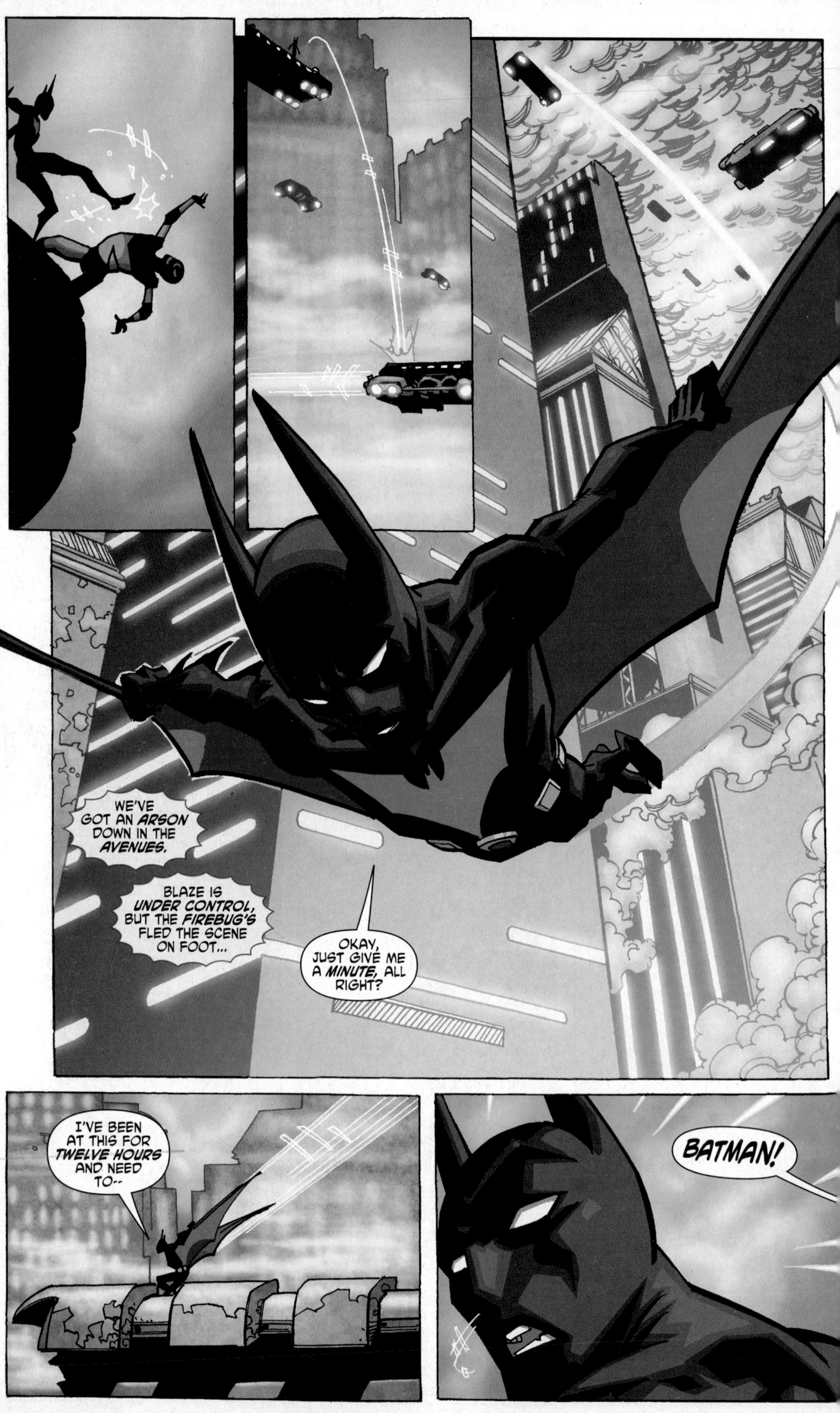

WE'VE GOT AN ARSON DOWN IN THE AVENUES.
BLAZE IS UNDER CONTROL, BUT THE FIREBUG'S FLED THE SCENE ON FOOT...
OKAY, JUST GIVE ME A MINUTE, ALL RIGHT?
I'VE BEEN AT THIS FOR TWELVE HOURS AND NEED TO--
BATMAN!